PATERNOSTER BIBLICAL MONOGRAPHS

The Physically Disabled in Ancient Israel According to the Old Testament and Ancient Near Eastern Sources

Series Editors

PATERNOSTER BIBLICAL MONOGRAPHS

The Physically Disabled in Ancient Israel According to the Old Testament and Ancient Near Eastern Sources

Michael D. Fiorello

First published 2014 by Paternoster

Paternoster is an imprint of Authentic Media
52 Presley Way, Crownhill, Milton Keynes, Bucks, MK8 0ES, UK

www.authenticmedia.co.uk
Authentic Media is a division of Koorong UK, a company limited by guarantee

09 08 07 06 05 04 03   8 7 6 5 4 3 2 1

British Library Cataloguing in Publication Data
A catalogue record for this book is available from the British Library

ISBN 978–1–84227–848–2

Typeset by Michael Fiorello
Printed and bound in Great Britain
for Paternoster

PATERNOSTER BIBLICAL MONOGRAPHS

Series Preface

One of the major objectives of Paternoster is to serve biblical scholarship by providing a channel for the publication of theses and other monographs of high quality at affordable prices. Paternoster stands within the broad evangelical tradition of Christianity. Our authors would describe themselves as Christians who recognise the authority of the Bible, maintain the centrality of the gospel message and assent to the classical credal statements of Christian belief. There is diversity within this constituency; advances in scholarship are possible only if there is freedom for frank debate on controversial issues and for the publication of new and sometimes provocative proposals. What is offered in this series is the best of writing by committed Christians who are concerned to develop well-founded biblical scholarship in a spirit of loyalty to the historic faith.

This work is dedicated to both my Lord Jesus Christ and to Robin, his incredible gift to me

Table of Contents

Acknowledgements

First, I thank my Lord Jesus Christ for making me what I am and for his constant love and provision. I am very grateful to my wife Robin who is God's gift of inestimable value to me. You are amazing and I do not know what I would do without you. Special thanks are also due to my incredible children Sarah and Daniel who pitched in and did so much to make this possible. Margaret Hoeckele also deserves thanks for encouraging me to press on. Thanks are due to Dr. Richard Averbeck who shepherded me through this project. It is amazing what you do. Thanks to Dr. Daniel C. Timmer for his prayer, friendship, encouragement, suggestions, reading, and so much more. Thanks are also due to Tony Rossodivita, Dr. Igou Hodges, Adrienne Williams, Tim Burton, and the entire Columbia International University Library staff for aiding me in acquiring needed rare books. Your exceptional service in getting me obscure references is greatly appreciated. Thanks are also due to Debbie Lineberger at Lutheran Seminary. Special thanks are due to Dr. Jim Roché for believing in me and to Warden Michael McCall for your friendship and encouragement.

Abbreviations

AB	Anchor Bible
BDB	Brown, F., S.R. Driver, and C.A. Briggs, *A Hebrew And English Lexicon of the Old Testament.* Oxford: Clarendon, 1906.
CAD	A.L. Oppenheim, et al., editors. *The Assyrian Dictionary of the Oriental Institute of the University of Chicago.* Chicago: The Oriental Institute, *1956-*.
NIDOTTE	*New International Dictionary of Old Testament Theology and Exegesis.* Edited by W.A. VanGemeren. 5 vols. Grand Rapids: Zondervan, 1997.

Chapter 1

Introduction

The need for this study

Language referring to the physically disabled is not unique to Old Testament literature. Other cultures discuss issues related to disabled persons as well. Literature from throughout the ancient Near East indicates that disabled people were not uncommon. The question at hand concerns how the disabled were regarded and treated.

In addition to its literal use of disability language in the Torah and historical books, the prophetic books of the Hebrew Bible frequently use this terminology metaphorically to describe moral or spiritual conditions. A primary purpose of this study is to explore the connection between disability language and the prophetic critique of Israel's relationship with God. Biblical prophetic literature utilizes the language of dysfunctional human faculties to censure Israel's faith and unfaithfulness. Biblical prophets used this vocabulary to analyze Israel's spiritual condition during and after the divided monarchies, stressing the precedence of one's internal disposition of heart over external actions. Faith must precede or operate in concert with, religious activity. Participation in religious ritual was not merely a matter of form and content but required the involvement of the heart.

Evangelicals have focused on the moral or ethical obligations the church has to care for those who cannot provide for themselves.[1] Little has been written discussing the theological implications of this motif as it is imbedded in Scripture. I will also examine the theological implications of the biblical use of disability motifs as opposed to non-disabled motifs.[2] Further, the stereotypical belief that the disabled were the poor and outcasts of society[3] has also been

---

1 Millard J. Erickson, *How Shall They Be Saved? The Destiny of Those Who Do Not Hear of Jesus* (Grand Rapids: Baker, 1996). Also, Gene Newman and Joni Eareckson Tada, *All God's Children: Ministry with Disabled Persons* (rev. ed.; Grand Rapids: Zondervan, 1993).

2 Motifs such as seeing, hearing, walking, and vision versus spiritual visions.

3 Hector Avalos, "Blindness," in *Eerdmans Dictionary of the Bible* (ed. David Noel Freedman; Grand Rapids, Mich.: Eerdmans, 2000), 193; Jonathan Tubb, "Two Examples of Disability in the Levant," in *Madness, Disability and Social Exclusion: The Archaeology and Anthropology of "Difference* (ed. Jane Hubert; London: Routledge, 2000), 84f; Richard Jones, "Lame, Lameness," in *Anchor Bible Dictionary* (ed. David Noel Freedman; New York: Doubleday, 1992), 4:136; Johannes Renger, "Kranke, Krüppel, Debile – eine Randgruppe im Alten Orient?" in

called into question. In this regard, the archaeological record has prompted some to reexamine long held presumptions.

This examination of ancient texts related to disabilities is an attempt to understand community responses to disabled persons among the peoples of the ancient Near East. By examining the law collections, societal conventions, and religious obligations toward individuals who were physically disabled we acquire an understanding of the world a disabled person would enter. In addition, I intend to demonstrate that the Bible assumes that there would be physically disabled persons in the community of faith and that they were to be cared for and accorded dignity (Exod 4:11; Lev 19:14-15). It will also be demonstrated that the Bible utilizes the language of human faculty and disability not etiologically to explain divine judgment, but in relation to expressions of wholeness/holiness. The link between holiness and life can be seen in matters related to physical imperfections.[4] The human body itself was the ordained scheme expressing completeness established at creation. Consequently, physical perfection of both worship leader (Lev 21:17-23) and offerings (Lev 1:3, 10; 3:1, 6; 4:3, 23, 28, 32; 5:15, 18; 6:6; 9:2-3; 14:10; 22:19-21, 25; 23:12, 18; Num 6:14; 19:2; 28:3, 9, 11, 19, 31; 29:2, 8, 13, 20, 23, 26, 29, 32, 36; Deut 15:21; 17:1) is essential inasmuch as holiness is characterized by completeness. Further, the terms associated with physical impairment came to be used as metaphors for rejecting God (Isa 6:10; 30:20-21; 32:1-7; 35:4-10; 42:16-25; Hos 4:6; Ezek 5:6; 20:13, 16; Jer 5:21-31; 6:10-21; 12: 2; 17:23; Zech 7:11-14). Prophetic models indicate that healing of the physically impaired, opening the eyes and ears of understanding, and a reversal of the consequences of the fall would be initiated in the Eschaton (Isa 32:1-7; 35:4-10; 42:6-7, 16-19; 43:7-8; Jer 31:8).

General description of the topic

This work examines concepts of physical disabilities in the Old Testament and its ancient Near Eastern context and the use of these concepts metaphorically. To accomplish this task, a differentiation must be made between literal and figurative disability.

Disability is seen in ancient literature as both a category of living experience and as a literary motif. This is especially evident in biblical literature. In the literal sense, the various terms used for the disabled symbolized physical imperfections. The literal use of terms expressing various disabilities in narratives gives way to a metaphorical use of these terms in later prophetic

---

Außenseiter und Randgruppen: Beiträge zu einer Sozialgeschichte des Alten Orients, Xenia: Konstanzer Althistorische Vorträge und Forschungen, heft 32 (ed., Volkert Haas; Konstanz: Universitätsverlag, 1992), 113-26; Jan Heller, "David und die Krüppel," *Communio Viatorum* 8 (1965): 251-258.

4 Joe M. Sprinkle, "The Rationale of the Laws of Clean and Unclean in the Old Testament," *Journal of the Evangelical Theological Society* 43 (2000): 650.

literature. In both uses the language may appear to evaluate disability negatively, suggesting that it was the result of divine edict for some moral defect (known or unknown) or a willful organ operating according to its predilection.[5]

How a given ancient culture defined disability is important to understanding the physical condition.[6] It is impossible, however, to arrive at a clear sense of how cultures in the ancient Near East comprehended disability. In ancient literature disability is simply described rather than defined. As best as can be determined, disability was not thought about in terms that separated a disabled condition from disease or illness. Consequently, any attempt at an ancient definition of disability is, at best, incomplete. It is easier to explain the ancient definition of illness and disease and then to extrapolate from this an understanding coherent with the text's historical and ideological situation of disability. Van der Toorn notes that illness generally "comprises all deviations from an ideal of individual fulfillment, the physiognomy of which is to a large extent culturally determined."[7] Disability, then, is a category defined by society. The ancients knew how the body normally should function and from this were able to deduce what was abnormal. Arthur Kleinman provides for us a working definition of illness in contrast with that of disease that, for our purposes, we shall adopt. Kleinman notes that *disease* refers to a malfunctioning of biological and/or psychological processes, while the term *illness* refers to the psycho-social experience and meaning of perceived disease.[8] For the purposes of this study, a physical disability will be defined as a permanent illness resulting in a partial or complete loss of one's capacity for mobility, hearing, seeing, or speech.

The focus on the diagnosis of illness in relation to disability is warranted in light of ancient man's quest to understand and treat physical anomalies. Symptom patterns lending to diagnosis were prevalent in antiquity.[9] The fact that to treat an illness an evil spirit could be bought off or a ritual could be performed and misbehaving organs could be placated with medicine suggests that ancient Near Eastern peoples often attributed bodily problems to unseen

---

5 Joann Scurlock and Burton R. Andersen, *Diagnosis in Assyrian and Babylonian Medicine: Ancient Sources, Translations, and Modern Medical Analysis* (Chicago: University of Chicago, 2005), 11, 116-154. Scurlock and Andersen do not argue that illness was viewed in the ancient Near East as the result of divine action alone. Indeed, malevolent spirits are causers of disease, but organs with an independent mind can malfunction on their own as well.

6 Hector Avalos, *Illness and Healthcare in the Ancient Near East: The Role of the Temple in Greece, Mesopotamia, and Israel* (Atlanta: Scholars Press, 1995), 27.

7 Karel van der Toorn, *Sin and Sanction in Israel and Mesopotamia: A Comparative Study* (Assen: Van Gorcum, 1986), 67.

8 Arthur Kleinman, *Patients and Healers in the Context of Culture* (Berkeley Calif.: University of California Press, 1980), 72.

9 Scurlock and Andersen, *Diagnosis in Assyrian and Babylonian Medicine*, 11.

forces (much like modern medicine attributes maladies to unseen bacteria resulting in better and preventative sanitary practices).[10] Similarly, the Bible also does not provide precise definitions for the impairments it alludes to. It appears to have been universally accepted that one understood the difference between a normatively functioning physical condition in contrast with one which was not. For example, a blind person would be one who lacks the ability to find their way.[11] One's physical abilities may become compromised through a variety of pathological conditions such as trauma, congenital defect, metabolic, nutritional, or degenerative disease. Mesopotamian medical tradition attributes both traumatic and non-traumatic disabilities to the "hand" of a (sometimes obscure) god.[12] In recent scholarship it was common to infer from the accessible medical information that a disability resulting from a disease was attributed to an implacable spirit or renegade organ of the body. Although recent scholars like Scurlock and Andersen downplay the frequency with which an etiological diagnosis would have been arrived at, they nevertheless affirm that the medical tradition was predisposed toward supernaturalistic causations to explain illnesses.[13]

Physical disabilities would have been the result of birth defects, deformity inflicted on an individual by means of an accident, the natural deterioration of the body, wounds obtained in battle in the course of military service, inadequate hygiene, deficient nutrition,[14] or poor standards of cleanliness during food preparation or at the meal table.[15] Causes of blindness throughout the ancient Near East include congenital defect and physical trauma. It was common for prisoners of war to be mutilated so as to discourage further armed

---

[10] Scurlock and Andersen, *Diagnosis in Assyrian and Babylonian Medicine*, 11-12. According to Scurlock and Andersen, organs with a mind to malfunction came to be viewed, not as inanimate matter but as a lower order of spirit.

[11] Lawrence H. Schiffman, "Exclusion from the Sanctuary and the City of the Sanctuary in the Temple Scroll," *Hebrew Annual Review* 9 (1985): 310. Schiffman notes that the tannā'im interpret Lev 21:19 more broadly so as to include those who had only one eye and those suffering from eye ailments and deformities.

[12] If he was wounded on his head and consequently his eyes are *erēpu*'d (darkened), "hand" of Ningirsu (Tablet 3.75). If he has was wounded on his head and consequently, his hearing is low (and) his ears [...], "hand" of a murderous god; it is serious; he will die (Tablet 3.80). If he has a viselike headache and his ears do not hear, the "hand" of his god has been imposed on him; he will die (Tablet 4.4). See René Labat, *Traité Akkadien de Diagnostics et Pronostics Médicaux. I: Transcription et Traduction*, Collection de travaux de l'académie internationale d'histoire des sciences No.7 (Paris: Académie internationale d'histoire de sciences, 1951), 27, 33.

[13] Scurlock and Andersen, *Diagnosis in Assyrian and Babylonian Medicine*, 429-30.

[14] R. Ellison, "Some Thoughts on the Diet of Mesopotamia from c. 3000-600 B.C.E.," *Iraq* 45 (1983): 146-150.

[15] Edward Neufeld, "Hygiene Conditions in Ancient Israel (Iron Age)," *Biblical Archaeologist* 34 (1971): 52-56.

resistance (Judg 1:4-7; 16:21; 2 Kgs 25:7; Jer 39:7; 52:11).[16] Blinding a prisoner was equal to castration, so that to be blind was to be impotent.[17]

A number of persons with a visual disability or serious visual impairments are mentioned in the Bible: Isaac (Gen 27:1), Jacob (Gen 48:10), Balaam (Num 24:3), Shimshon (Judg 16:12), Eli (1 Sam 3:2), Achiya (1 Kgs 14:4), and Zedekiah (2 Kgs 25:7; Jer 52:11). Jacob, after wrestling with the angelic being beside the Jabbok *wadi*, walked with a limp (Gen 32:32) and Mephibosheth was injured as a child so that he was lame in both feet (2 Sam 4:4; 9:13). A lame priest could not serve in the Temple (Lev 21:18). Along these lines, a speech impediment is referred to as "lameness of the tongue" (Mic 4:6; Zeph 3:19). All animal offerings brought to the Temple were to be free from physical disfigurement of any kind (Lev 22:20-21; Mal 1:4).

In Israel, those who suffered from physical disabilities were not granted preferential status or treatment but were treated equally as fully enfranchised members of the community of faith. The reason for this may be because God allows some to be complete and some to be disabled. Therefore, to dodge God's call because of a physical weakness as Moses attempted to do (Exod 4:11) or to mock or injure one disabled were equally reprehensible (Lev 19:14). Priests who were physically impaired, however, were ineligible for sanctuary service. Nevertheless they were fully vested as priests who could still engage in worship as a member of the community of faith (Lev 21:16-24). In contrast, those members of the community who contract a disease of one sort or another were to be treated specially, being put in isolation from the population until the disease was healed. At that time the communicant would be fully vested again to return to the community and participate in the cult. Even though disability is less serious than disease, it shows up as a fatal issue in the metaphors of the prophetic literature.

Once the literal sense of disability has been explored, this study will identify patterns of theological belief/rejection of God expressed metaphorically via the terminology of disability as prerequisites for approaching God in the cult and/or obedience to his Word with genuine faith. The metaphorical use of disability language is a partial description of moral imperfection. As mentioned previously, faith is not the ritualistic exercise of the cult but a sincere and genuine acceptance of Yahweh and his Word. Hence, disability motifs found in the Bible's prophetic literature are intended as a polemic against superficial faith and moral complacency among members of the community of Israel. These motifs reach their full bloom in the prophetic descriptions of Israel

---

16 Victor H. Matthews and Don C. Benjamin, *Social World of Ancient Israel: 1250-587 BCE* (Peabody, Mass.: Hendrickson, 1993), 103. See also plate LVI in Leonard W. King, *Bronze Reliefs from the Gates of Shalmaneser, King of Assyria B.C. 860-825* (London: The Trustees, 1915), 31.

17 Matthews and Benjamin, *Social World of Ancient Israel*, 103. Matthews and Benjamin note that there was a legal and symbolic equivalence between the eyes and the testicles. See Middle Assyrian Code (MAL 8).

herself as blind and deaf to the Word of God. In the metaphorical sense, these terms were used by Israel's prophets as labels to deal with spiritual weakness or imperfection. The question to be answered is when, why, and how these terms came to be used in this way.

As this study concerns the plight of the disabled in the ancient world, it follows that ancient texts from Mesopotamia, Egypt, Anatolia, and the Levantine civilizations will be examined in contrast and comparison with biblical texts for an understanding of the conditions faced by those who were physically challenged and the prevailing attitudes of their cultures toward them. Specifically, this study will probe the linguistic, sociological, religious and theological issues associated with being physically disabled in the ancient Near East.

The study will suggest answers to certain questions such as: What were the prevailing social conditions and religious attitudes disabled persons faced throughout the ancient Near East? What types of difference and similarity did the Hebrew and ancient Near Eastern concepts of disability show toward one another? Were there medical procedures known and used in ancient Israel that were introduced by them or borrowed from other cultures? Are the Hebrew Scriptures positive, negative or ambivalent regarding the blind and lame, and why? Can neighboring cultures shed light on Israel's cultural attitude toward the blind and lame? To what extent did magic and ritual impact medical therapy practiced in and around Israel?[18] Were the early Israelites contemptuous, empathetic, or indifferent toward the blind and lame? At times God gives the sighted visions of the unseen (2 Kgs 6:8-23). Does this imply that the sighted are themselves disabled and how does this limitation impact the issue of the disabled?

Religion and its relationship to disabilities

"Religion is a system(s) of belief(s) and ritual through which people relate to and express their experience of God(s), the sacred or divine dimensions of life, and their understanding of the meaning of life."[19] Religion is, and will continue to be, a major force influencing society's understanding of the meaning of disability and the shaping of its concept of community. Religion can either affirm or challenge the prevailing attitudes of society.[20] Since religious and social identities are intertwined, people with disabilities are directly impacted by religious traditions. Contact between religion and the disabled has raised questions about the meaning of life, the nature of suffering, the role of divine

18 Robert D. Biggs, "Medicine in Ancient Mesopotamia," *History of Science* 8 (1969): 94-105.

19 Bill Gaventa and Christopher Newell, "Religion," in *Encyclopedia of Disabilities* (Thousand Oaks, Calif.: Sage, 2005), 1374-75.

20 Gaventa and Newell, "Religion," 1374-75.

purpose and justice, difference and community.[21] History has demonstrated that religion has, at times, supported the handicapped as a core aspect of the mission of the church. At other periods in history, however, the handicapped have been dehumanized or shunned, being viewed either as objects of pity or as under divine judgment for sin.[22]

Because few religious leaders live with a disability, little has been done to thoroughly examine the relationship between religion and the disabled. There has simply been a lack of interest among theologians toward understanding how biblical writers dealt with disabilities, prompting discomfiture among the disabled. This, however, is not due to a conscious or orchestrated attempt to predisposition against disabled persons, but largely due to the fact that representations of disabled persons in ancient societies were rare, giving interpreters little information to work with.[23] Even today, while the disabled enjoy more legal protections and rights, making the world more accessible to them than ever before, they are still misinterpreted, stereotyped, or simply overlooked.

Recently, however, a reexamination of biblical and other ancient texts related to disabilities has begun to change this and the issue now is being given more deserved attention.[24] On the comparative level, scholars are seeking to understand the source of disability and the implications of this for the disabled, and the role and purpose of both the affected person and the community.[25]

Limitations of this Study

This project is limited to an analysis of language denoting disabilities in the Bible and in ancient Near Eastern literary parallels. Focus will exclusively be on the plight of the disabled in the ancient world on account of the restricted attention previously given to the topic by those employing social-scientific methods. This project will also analyze the theological implications of the disability motifs found throughout the Bible. The analysis of disability language in this work does not include that of disease. Although a physical disability may result from disease, those afflicted and suffering as a result of disease will not be discussed in this study.

---

21 Gaventa and Christopher Newell, "Religion," 1374-75.

22 Gaventa and Christopher Newell, "Religion," 1374-75.

23 Tubb, "Two Examples of Disability in the Levant," 81.

24 Anthony Ceresko, "The Identity of 'the Blind and the Lame' (*'iwwēr ūpissēah*) in 2 Samuel 5:8b," *Catholic Biblical Quarterly* 63 (2001): 23-30; Thomas Hentrich, "The 'Lame' in Lev 21, 17-23 and 2 Sam 5, 6-8," *Annual of the Japanese Biblical Institute* 29 (2003); Saul Olyan, "Anyone Blind or Lame Shall Not Enter the House: On the Interpretation of Second Samuel 5:8," *Catholic Biblical Quarterly* 60 (1998): 218-27; Shmuel Vargon, "The Blind and the Lame," *Vetus Testamentum* 46 (1996): 498-514.

25 Gaventa and Newell, "Religion," 1376.

Research Methodology

This study will attempt to clarify any misunderstanding that might exist as to the perspective of the Old Testament toward the plight of the disabled. It will also explore the biblical warrants for the community of faith in its ongoing compassionate ministry toward the disabled in the face of pressure from advocates of euthanasia or abortion as legitimate means for resolving the social problems resulting from the demands of the physically disabled.[26]

The basic plan of this study is to perform an analysis of relevant ancient Near Eastern literature so as to identify the ideological foundations for the treatment of the disabled followed by an exegetical-historical and theological analysis of biblical texts. This analysis will be worked out through the utilization of social-scientific[27] and comparative methodologies.[28]

From a comparative perspective, this study will analyze attitudes toward, and treatment of, the disabled in the ancient Near East in comparison and contrast with biblical data that illumine our general understanding of the Bible's attitude and prescribed treatment of the disabled in ancient Israel. Parallels in representative ANE law collections and other literature will also be examined in an attempt to identify and describe typological features between ancient Near Eastern texts and their biblical counterparts, so as to establish points of incongruity and correspondence between the two sets from which conclusions may be drawn. Ancient Near Eastern texts that will be examined include: *The Enki and Ninmah Myth* lines 58-82; The *Šumma Izbu Omen Series* Tablet II, lines 19-20, Tablet III, line 58, Tablet III, line 85, Tablets VI; *The Šumma Ālu Series*; A *Šumma Text*, lines 28-29, 36-37; *Nabopolassar's Royal Autobiography*; *Code of Hammurabi* §§ 148, 196-99, 204, 206, 215-226; *Azatiwada Inscription* (*KAI* 26 *AI* 11-13); The Reforms of *Uru-inimgina*; The

---

26 Peter Singer, *Rethinking Life and Death: The Collapse of Our Traditional Ethics* (New York: St. Martin's Griffin, 1996).

27 P.L. Berger, *The Sacred Canopy: Elements of a Sociological Theory of Religion* (Garden City, N.Y.: Doubleday, 1973).

28 Shemaryahu Talmon, "The 'Comparative Method' in Biblical Interpretation–Principles and Problems," in *Congress Volume: Göttingen, 1977* (ed. J.A. Emerton; Vetus Testamentum Supplements 29; Leiden: Brill, 1978). Richard E. Averbeck, "Sumer, the Bible, and Comparative Methodology: Historiography and Temple Building," in *Mesopotamia and the Bible* (ed. Mark W. Chavalas and K. Lawson Younger, Jr.; Grand Rapids: Baker, 2002), 88-125. William W. Hallo, "Biblical History in Its Near Eastern Setting: The Contextual Approach," in *Scripture in Context: Essays on the Comparative Method* (ed. Carl D. Evans, Williams W. Hallo, and John B. White; Pittsburgh Theological Monograph Series 34. Pittsburgh: Pickwick, 1980), 1-26. Idem, "Compare and Contrast: The Contextual Approach to Biblical Literature," in *The Bible in Light of Cuneiform Literature: Scripture in Context III*, Ancient Near Eastern Texts and Studies 8 (ed., William W. Hallo, Bruce W. Jones, and Gerald L. Mattingly; Lewiston, N.Y.: Edwin Mellen, 1990). John H. Walton, *Ancient Israelite Literature in Its Cultural Context* (Grand Rapids: Zondervan, 1989).

Panamuwa Inscription; *Ur-Nammu* Laws 18-22; *Hittite Laws* Tablet 1:7-8, 11; *Middle Assyrian Laws* A8; *The Instruction of Amenemope* 4:1-5, 20:20-21:6, 24:8-12; *Kirta Epic,* Tablet I col. 2 lines 45-47; *Tale of Aqhat* Tablet I, col. 5, lines 4-8, Tablet III, col.1, lines 19-25; *Hurrian Myth Cycle* Tablet 2, line 36; Hittite treaty between Muršili II and Duppi-Tešub of Amurru; *Lipit-Ishtar* 34-38; documents related to the priests of *Enlil*; and *Sennacherib's Monumental Inscriptions.* Because rulers were expected to administer justice to the disadvantaged, possible connections between the concept of the king as the one who establishes a just and righteous society and the Servant figure in Isaiah will also be considered.[29]

Given the serious criticisms of historical critical methodology made by Whybray and others,[30] biblical texts will be treated as aggregate whole, presenting a consistent theology. Primary Old Testament texts to be examined will include: law collections (Exod 3:1-4; 4:11; 23:8, 19; 34:26; Lev 1:3, 10; 3:1, 6; 4:3, 23, 28, 32; 5:15, 18; 6:6; 9:2-3; 14:10; 18; 19; 20; 21:17-23; 22:19-22, 25; 23:12, 18; Deut 14:21; 15:21; 17:1; 23:1; 27:20-23), historical texts (2 Sam 4:4; 9:6-13; 2 Kgs 6:8-23), wisdom literature (Job 29:15; Ps 46:8), and prophetic texts (Isa 6:10; 29:9-24; 30:20-21; 32:1-7; 35:4-10; 42:6-7, 42:16-25; 43:7-8; 56:10; 59:10; Jer 5:21-31; 6:10-21; 17:23; 31:8; Ezek 5:6; 12:2; 20:13, 16; Hos 4:6; Mic 4:6-7; 7:16; Zeph 1:12-17; 3:19; Zech 7:11-14; 11:17; Mal 1:8, 13).

In the process of comparative inquiry, a synchronic analysis[31] of related biblical terms will be performed along with a diachronic examination[32] of the literary terms the Bible uses for the disabled and their related transformation from a literal to a metaphorical label. Literary analysis of related texts will include an analysis of each text's historical and cultural background and an evaluation of lexical and semantical meanings, syntactical relations, structure, and rhetorical devices and larger literary contexts used so as to provide an

---

[29] Moshe Weinfeld, *Social Justice in Ancient Israel and in the Ancient Near East* (Minneapolis: Fortress, 1995), 20f, 57f. See also Avraham Gileadi, *The Literary Message of Isaiah* (New York: Hebraeus Press, 1994), 119f.

[30] R.N. Whybray, *The Making of the Pentateuch: A Methodological Study* (JSOTS 53; Sheffield: Sheffield Academic Press, 1987), 129-31; Idem, *An Introduction to the Pentateuch* (Grand Rapids: Eerdmans, 1995); T.D. Alexander, *From Paradise to the Promised Land* (Grand Rapids: Baker, 2002), 1-61.

[31] For an understanding of synchronic see Tremper Longman, "Literary Approaches to Old Testament Study," in *The Face of Old Testament Studies: A Survey of Contemporary Approaches* (ed. David W. Baker and Bill T. Arnold; Grand Rapids: Baker, 1999), 97-115; Kevin Vanhoozer, "Language, Literature, Hermeneutics and Biblical Theology: What's Theological About a Theological Dictionary?" in *A Guide to Old Testament Theology and Exegesis: The Introductory Articles from the New International Dictionary of Old Testament Theology and Exegesis* (ed. Willem A. VanGemeren, Grand Rapids: Zondervan, 1999), 11-47.

[32] Peter Cotterell and Max Turner, *Linguistics and Biblical Interpretation* (Downers Grove, Ill.: InterVarsity, 1989), 25, 131, 175.

adequate contextual foundation from which the text may be given its full voice. This study will consider the genre of a text and its context in biblical literature.[33] An inter-textual examination and analysis will be done of the words, theological themes and social concepts in the Old Testament that are associated with the physical impairment in order to identify their meaning and contribution to the attitudes and approaches taken toward the disabled in biblical times.

While a great deal of work has been done employing a social-scientific methodology to address issues related to class structures,[34] there is still much work to do toward defining a biblical understanding of the concern and care of the disabled. Rather than examining the social factors which influence the form and content of the Old Testament texts, this study will attempt to identify the theological basis for Israel's values and beliefs through observed regularities and explanatory generalizations rather than merely pursuing ideographic aims.[35] Hence, this study does not intend to engage in reductionism, relativism, positivism, determinism, or to anachronistically transfer modern sociological paradigms to that of ancient Israel.[36] Further, sociological methodology also, at times fails to take into consideration the distinct world views of a modern western culture in contrast with an ancient eastern culture. It is hoped that the principle of analogy will be employed through comparative methodology through examining biblical and other ancient texts to identify their influence on social attitudes toward the disabled, while respecting differentiations between modern and ancient world-views.

The Contribution of this Study

The church is called to walk by faith and not by sight. What will become evident in this study is that faith is analogous to having physical senses while, in contrast, being disabled is analogous to walking without sight. What emerges is not only an image of Yahweh that affirms his role as the One who determines the "fate" of the people and of individuals but also a picture of what functional faith, or lack thereof, implies in terms of one's consanguinity with Yahweh.

Further, this study will correct the enduring misconception about the ancient Near East that disease or physical disability was commonly believed to be a

---

[33] For a discussion of the importance of genre see Vanhoozer, "Language, Literature, Hermeneutics and Biblical Theology," 34-37.

[34] Representative of this are: Avalos, *Illness and Healthcare in the Ancient Near East*; J. David Pleins, *The Social Visions of the Hebrew Bible: A Theological Introduction* (Louisville: Westminster John Knox, 2001).

[35] Matthews and Benjamin, *Social World of Ancient Israel*, xiii-xxiii; Jack Sasson, "On Choosing Models for Recreating Israelite Pre-Monarchic History," *Journal for the Study of the Old Testament* 21 (1988): 8.

[36] Gary A. Herion, "The Impact of Modern and Social Science Assumptions on the Reconstructions of Israelite History," *Journal for the Study of the Old Testament* 34 (1986): 1-33.

sign of divine censure.[37] Hentrich argues that a divine punitive cause was a prevalent belief throughout the ancient Near East, including Israel (Deut 28:15).[38] Indeed, it is commonly suggested that the Bible affirms that a physical disability was a sign of some impurity and a consequent divine displeasure (Deut 28:15, 28-29). In fact, the disciples of Jesus, when seeing a blind man on the side of the road asked, "Rabbi, who sinned, this man or his parents that he should be born blind" (John 9:2). It is my intention to clarify the issues related to the rationale behind biblical proscriptions linked to handicapped persons that may have led to this assumption.

In addition, there is a lot of confusion today regarding the role of faith in healing,[39] government efforts to assure equality of opportunity, full participation, independent living, and economic self-sufficiency for disabled persons (Americans with Disabilities Act), and pending legislation related to the disabled. It is hoped that this study will resolve some of that confusion. This thesis intends to describe theological patterns that may arise from a study of the use of disability motifs in the Bible. An analysis of this motif could provide a building block for further study in an area of research which has been largely neglected.

What is Metaphor?

Metaphor is not intended to be understood as substituting one term for another, but shall be defined as "a figure of speech whereby we speak about one thing in terms which are seen to be suggestive of another."[40] A metaphor is established semantically rather than syntactically when it is recognized that one thing is

---

37 Henri-Jocques Stiker, *A History of Disability* (trans. by William Sayers; Ann Arbor, Mich.: University of Michigan Press, 1999), 27; see e.g., J.V. Kinnier Wilson, "Medicine in the Land and Times of the Old Testament," in *Studies in the Period of David and Solomon and Other Essays: Papers Read at the International Symposium in Tokyo, Japan, 1979* (ed., T. Ishida; Winona Lake: Eisenbrauns, 1982), 349 n. 37, who bases this on the presumption that *qāt DN* means disease or punishment.

38 Hentrich, "The 'Lame' in Lev 21, 17-23 and 2 Sam 5, 6-8," 5-6. Although he sees this as a distinguishing factor between ancient Near Eastern literature and the Bible, Hentrich nevertheless makes the assumption that illness was consequential to breaking Yahweh's law. It was easier in Israel because there was only one God and one reason for affliction but he conjectures that the cause and effect relationship was still the same. He notes, however, that Israel had the benefit of knowing the reason for the punishment (breaching the covenant) and who was responsible for the punishment (since there was only one God). In other ancient cultures, which god and the reason for the punishment was unknown.

39 Henry H. Knight III, "God's Faithfulness and God's Freedom: A Comparison of Contemporary Theologies of Healing," *Journal of Pentecostal Theology* 1 (1993): 65-89; Jacques P.J. Theron, "Toward a Practical Theological Theory for the Healing Ministry in Pentecostal Churches," *Journal of Pentecostal Theology* 7 (1999):49-64.

40 Janet Martin Soskice, *Metaphor and Religious Language* (London: Oxford University, 1987), 15.

being spoken of in terms suggestive of another, and possesses limited elasticity.[41] Contra Ricoeur,[42] metaphors do not redescribe something but serve to introduce or disclose something new.[43] Soskice distinguishes "on the one hand, between meaning and reference of an utterance, and on the other, between the sense and denotation of a term."[44] Rather than picking out a second subject or another referent, the metaphorical vehicle describes "the referent picked out by the whole of the utterance."[45]

Some suggest that the process of representing disabilities with metaphorical language creates a break between experiential disability and the portrayal of it as a metaphor.[46] However, "metaphor, as a figure of speech, is a form of language use."[47] Non-intrinsic meanings are encoded into prophetic literature.[48] Rather than being a mental event or process of imagination whereby one thing is substituted for another (metonymy), metaphor must primarily be understood as a figure of speech.[49] Using metaphor enables one to say or write about things which cannot be spoken or written about in any other way.[50]

An examination of prophetic literature and the metaphorical use of physical disability language shows that such language is used in situations immediate to them as well as projecting eschatologically to the anticipated event. A parallel exists between the eschatological and the immediate in that there is a concern for the social ideal. Eschatologically, biblical prophets described the utopia that is to come, while lamenting the failure of Israel in attaining the reachable utopian situation promised to them by God if they would only keep the

---

41 Soskice, *Metaphor and Religious Language*, 23.

42 Paul Ricoeur, *The Rule of Metaphor* (London: Routledge, 1978), 216-21. Ricoeur argued that metaphor is characterized by a duality of reference (a split reference) and that discourse points to an extralinguistic reality which is its referent. The sense is what the proposition states; the reference is that *about which* the sense is stated. He asserts that referent is opened by sense so that primary reference is suspended. The literary work is second level denotation by means of the suspension of the first level reference. Metaphor is addressed in terms of this suspension of reference. The metaphor captures its sense in the ruins of the literal sense and achieves its reference in its literal reference. Literal and metaphorical sense are both distinguished and articulated in an interpretation. The second-level reference *is* the metaphorical reference and is set free by the suspension of the first level reference.

43 Soskice, *Metaphor and Religious Language*, 88.

44 Soskice, *Metaphor and Religious Language*, 53.

45 Soskice, *Metaphor and Religious Language*, 53.

46 Rosemarie Garland Thomson, *Extraordinary Bodies* (New York: Columbia University Press, 1996), 12, 15.

47 Soskice, *Metaphor and Religious Language*, 16.

48 Rebecca Raphael, "Images of Disability in Hebrew Prophetic Literature" (paper presented at the annual meeting of the 2003 American Academy of Religion, Atlanta, November 23, 2003), 4.

49 Soskice, *Metaphor and Religious Language*, 16.

50 Soskice, *Metaphor and Religious Language*, 24.

covenant (Deut 26-28).[51] Metaphor expresses ontological tension, speaking of "it is" and "it is not," at the same time.[52] Literal and metaphorical sense give rise to literal and metaphorical reference and these are paralleled by literal and metaphorical truth.[53] It is in this ontological tension that biblical prophets make use of disability language, depicting transcendent reality, capturing conceptual possibilities of the metaphysical rather than proving it.[54] Soskice writes,

> Metaphors are by nature revisable, abridged, and inexact in their attempt to define or describe characteristics of the inexhaustible vastness of transcendent deity. Metaphor does not breach God's transcendence but allows members of a linguistic community to express in annotated form, aspects of His divine actuality for human consideration. Although metaphors posit claims in abstract and qualified terms the uncaused Causer of all things, they nevertheless retain their referential value in that reference is established through communal lexicon and communal interest within a particular communal tradition.[55]

The metaphorical use of disabled language in biblical prophetic literature voices the perceived spiritual condition of the community of faith. What is less understood is that the literal use of the language in the Pentateuch and historical books also addresses the community's spiritual condition. These laws and narratives effectually determine the substance of Israel's spiritual condition and by doing so define for them a national identity intended to differentiate them from the nations around them.

The function of these metaphors in Israel's prophetic literature is to challenge Israel's national character in relation to the covenant that not only put them in relationship with a holy God but also circumscribed holy conduct that was to distinguish Israel as people in a unique relationship with this holy God. Israel's spiritual imperception comes to the fore in prophetic literature. Sight, or the lack thereof, was used in prophetic metaphor for faith and faithfulness, or the lack thereof. The metaphorical use of terms related to physical disabilities to refer to faith and faithfulness is understood typologically as correspondence and escalation rather than as allegorical extensions.[56] These correspondences are worked out in the Old Testament patterns of trusting in God for deliverance

---

[51] Benjamin Uffenheimer, "From Prophetic to Apocalyptic Eschatology," in *Eschatology in the Bible and in Jewish and Christian Tradition* (ed., Henning Graf Reventlow; Journal for the Study of the Old Testament Supplement Series 243; Sheffield: Sheffield Academic Press, 1997), 200.

[52] Soskice, *Metaphor and Religious Language*, 88.

[53] Soskice, *Metaphor and Religious Language*, 88.

[54] Soskice, *Metaphor and Religious Language*, 150.

[55] Soskice, *Metaphor and Religious Language*, 150-51.

[56] Earl Ellis, "Foreword," in *Typos: The Typological Interpretation of the Old Testament in the New* (ed. L. Goppelt; Grand Rapids: Eerdmans, 1982), x.

from national destruction.[57] Just as physical completeness is symbolic of Yahweh's nature, Israel's lack of belief and obedience, to which the prophets opined, is largely an actualization of physical incapacitation rendering her equally incomplete. Faith is, therefore, an essential component of the covenant relationship between Yahweh and his people.

Finally, though extremely useful in discourse about humans and God alike, Soskice reminds us that metaphors are by nature revisable, abridged, and inexact in their attempt to define or describe characteristics of the inexhaustible vastness of transcendent deity. Metaphor does not breach God's transcendence but allows members of a linguistic community to express in annotated form aspects of his divine actuality for human consideration. Although metaphors posit claims in abstract and qualified terms about the uncaused Causer of all things, they nevertheless retain their referential value in that reference is established through communal lexicon and communal interest within a particular communal tradition.[58]

---

57 The spiritual impairments in Isaiah do not allude to ignorance but have broader implications. Geoffrey W. Grogan, *Isaiah* (EBC; Grand Rapids: Zondervan, 1998), 6:222-23. Grogan represents those who identify the "symbolic relationship" existing between our imperfect (physical and spiritual) earthly condition and the perfected condition to come in the Escaton. Edward J. Young, *The Book of Isaiah* (NICOT; Grand Rapids: Eerdmans, 1969), 2:314. Young contends that the people choose to be blind. Gileadi, *The Literary Message of Isaiah,* 49-52. Gileadi argues that Israel's blindness is the result of a treaty malediction.

58 Soskice, *Metaphor and Religious Language*, 150-51.

Chapter 2

The History of Research on this Topic

A Review of Precedent Literature

A review of the precedent literature indicates that scholarly biblical studies in this area are lacking. Published materials focus on the moral and ethical obligation the community of faith has to care for the disabled, or medical and legal issues pertaining to the disabled, or the educative challenges concomitant with the rehabilitation of the disabled. To my knowledge, there has not been a study which ties the broad panorama of biblical revelation together so as to show the larger picture, nor has there been a study which draws theological implications from the texts. This overview of precedent literature includes a variety of works covering a broad range of literature related to disabilities and related issues. Most critical for this study are those sources which recognize illness and disabilities in psycho-social terms with respect to identity and functionality.[1]

As for ancient Near Eastern studies, until the early twentieth century, little research was done on the subject of illness and healthcare in early antiquity in the ancient Near East. On the European continent, prior to World War II, Erich Eberling published several articles on the medical texts from the Assyrian cities of Assur and Nineveh.[2] Further studies of medical traditions in the ancient Near East were stimulated by Bruno Meissner and George Contenau both of whom reviewed medicine in ancient Babylon.[3] About the same time, Reginald Thompson also published his work on the tablets of the library of Assurbanipal.[4]

After World War II, both in Europe and the United States, the examination of ancient medical traditions continued, so that at present a number of works which deal with medical traditions throughout the entire ancient Near East have

---

1 The term psycho-social relates to the interrelation of social factors and individual thought and behavior. In other words, attitudes toward illness and disabilities are culturally determined.

2 Erich Eberling, *Keilschrifttexte aus Assur religiösen Inhalts* (Leipzig: Biblio-Verlag, 1915-19).

3 Bruno Meissner *Babylonien und Assyrien* (vol. 2; Heidelberg: C. Winter, 1923), 283-323; George Contenau, *La médicine en Assyrie et en Bablonie* (Paris: Maloine, 1938).

4 Reginald C. Thompson, *Assyrian Medical Texts from the Originals in the British Museum* (London: Milford, 1923).

been published.[5] Some works discuss the linguistic aspects of disability.[6] Other scholars have specifically examined the treatment of the disabled in the ancient world.[7] For example, Mesopotamian medicine has been examined by Robert Biggs, Martin Stol and René Labat,[8] with Biggs claiming that it is incorrect to assume that in Mesopotamia, illness was attributed to evil sources or divine displeasure as has generally been done.[9] Both magic as a curative method and therapeutic medicine developed early and were independent of each other.[10] In addition, there is textual evidence that pharmaceuticals were also used as part of the process of healing.[11] There is very little information as to Physician's training, level of technical knowledge, or relation to social tradition, though it is certain that they were considered craftsmen and not members of the clergy.[12]

Albrecht Goetze has examined the Hittite practice of magic and religion, and provides an important evaluation of their concept of purity.[13] Oliver Gurney likewise discusses the matter of purity in the Hittite culture.[14] From the *Šumma*

---

5 Avalos, *Illness and Healthcare in the Ancient Near East*; Idem, "Medicine," in *The Oxford Encyclopedia of Archaeology in the Ancient Near East* (ed. Eric M. Meyers; New York: Oxford University Press 1997), 3:450-59; Klaus Seybold and U.B. Mueller, *Sickness and Healing* (trans. by D.W. Stott; Nashville: Abingdon, 1978); E.H. Ackerknect, *A Short History of Medicine* (Baltimore: Johns Hopkins, 1982); Simon Byl, "Molière et la médecine antique," *Études Classiques* 63 (1995): 55-66; Paavov Castrén, ed. *Ancient and Popular Healing* (symposium on ancient medicine; Finnish Institute at Athens, Athens, 1986, Helsinki 1989); Ludwig Edelstein, *Ancient Medicine* (ed. Owsei and C. Lilian Temkin; Baltimore: Johns Hopkins University Press, 1987); A. Finet, "Les médecins ua royaume de Mari," *Annuaire de l'Institut de Philologie et d'Histoire Orientales et Slaves* 14 (1954): 122-44; Huldrych M. Koelbing, *Arzt und Patient in der antiken Welt* (Zurich: Artemis, 1977); Labat, *Traité Akkadien de Diagnostics et Pronostics Médicaux I*; Charles Lichtenthaeler, *Geschicte der Medizin* (Band 1; Cologne: Ergänzungsband, 1988); Donald Wiseman, "Medicine in the Old Testament World," in *Medicine and the Bible* (Carlisle, U.K.: Paternoster, 1986).

6 B. Adamson, "An Assessment of Some Akkadian Medical Terms," *Revue d'Assyriologie* 87 (1993): 153-59.

7 Gaventa and Newell, "Religion," in *Encyclopedia of Disabilities*; Stiker, *A History of Disability*; Gary L. Albrecht, Katherine D. Seelman, and Michael Bury, eds., *Handbook of Disability Studies* (Thousand Oaks, Calif.: Sage, 2003).

8 Biggs, "Medicine in Ancient Mesopotamia," 94-105; Martin Stol, "Old Babylonian Ophthalmology," in *Reflets des Deux Fleuves: Volume de Mélanges offerts à André Finet,* Akkadic Supplementum 6 (eds., Marc Lebeau and Philippe Talon; Leuven: Peeters, 1989), 163-66; René Labat, "A propos de la chirurgie babylonienne,"*Journal Asiatique* 242 (1954): 207-18.

9 Biggs, "Medicine in Ancient Mesopotamia," 95-96.

10 Biggs, "Medicine in Ancient Mesopotamia," 96.

11 Biggs, "Medicine in Ancient Mesopotamia," 97.

12 Biggs, "Medicine in Ancient Mesopotamia," 97-98.

13 Albrecht Goetze, *Kleinasien: Kulturgeschichte des alten Orients* (2nd ed.; Munich: C. H. Beck, 1957).

14 Oliver R. Gurney, *The Hittites* (2nd ed.; Baltimore: Penguin Books, 1961).

izbu Series it is known that the Hittites examined human and animal birth anomalies for the purpose of predicting the future.[15] Generally, Henry Sigerist did a good job of describing the medical traditions known in the ancient world, but it should be noted that in his work on Babylonian medicine he did not properly distinguish or describe the function of magic and ritual working in cooperation with the medical arts.[16] Others have published materials which clarify and distinguish the function and relationship of magic and medicine in healing.[17] Others have examined the broader issue of medical practices in Anatolia.[18] H.G. Güterbock explains that the Hittites did not have a medical tradition of their own but were dependent on the Babylonian medical tradition.[19]

Egyptian medicine is presented in the Ebers papyrus, and in hieroglyphs on tomb walls alongside mummified remains.[20] Egyptians placed a great amount of faith for their health in deities such as Heket, Hathor, Imhotep, Isis, and Sekhmet (goddess of disease).[21] A medical tradition may have begun early in Egypt,[22] and medical examinations were simple, direct, and sought to determine if treatment would be beneficial to the patient.[23] Treatment included incantations, drugs, and physical procedures.[24] Sanitary conditions in antiquity were also examined. In Egypt, like other areas of the ancient Near East, the

---

15 Gary Beckman, *Hittite Birth Rituals* (Studien zu den Boğazköy-Texten 29; Wiesbaden: Harrassowitz, 1983).

16 Henry E. Sigerist, *A History of Medicine Volume I: Primitive and Archaic Medicine* (New York: Oxford University Press, 1955).

17 Erica Reiner, "Medicine in Ancient Mesopotamia," *Journal of the International College of Surgeons* 41 (1964): 544-550; A. Leo Oppenheim "Mesopotamian Medicine," in *Ancient Mesopotamia: Portrait of a Dead Civilization* (Chicago: University of Chicago, 1964).

18 Franz Köcher, *Keilschrifturkunden aus Boghazköy*, Vol. 37 (Berlin: Academie Verlag, 1953).

19 H.G. Güterbock, "Hittite Medicine," *Bulletin of the History of Medicine* 36 (1962): 109-113. Güterbock notes that physicians from Babylon and Egypt were part of the Hittite court.

20 J. Worth Estes, *Medical Skills of Ancient Egypt* (Canton, Mass.: Watson, 1989); Ange-Pierre Leca, *La médecine égyptienne au temps de Pharaons* (Paris: Roger Dacosta, 1971); Gustave LeFebvre, *Essai sur la médecine Égyptienne de l'époque pharaonique* (Paris: Presses Universitaires de France, 1956). Paul Ghalioungui, *The House of Life, Per Ankh: Magic and Medical Science in Ancient Egypt* (Amsterdam: B.M. Israël, 1973); Paul Ghalioungui and Zeinab El-Dawakhly, *Health and Healing in Ancient Egypt* (Cairo: Dar Al-Maaref, 1965).

21 Hector Avalos, "Medicine," in *The Oxford Encyclopedia of Archaeology in the Near East* (ed. Eric M. Meyers; New York: Oxford, 1996), 3:452.

22 Avalos, "Medicine," 3:452.

23 Avalos, "Medicine," 3:452.

24 Avalos, "Medicine," 3:452.

improper disposal of trash and human waste was such that public health suffered as a result.[25]

Within the Jewish culture, a number of sources provide good summaries of medical traditions in ancient Israel.[26] Hector Avalos has examined medicine specifically in Israelite tradition and concluded that in Israel, like other ancient cultures, a combination of cultic and healing remedies were available to the sufferer.[27]

Ancient Greece and Rome were somewhat ambivalent toward disabilities. On the one hand, the early Roman attitude was that children born with physical impairments were considered to have been born to parents who had displeased the gods and as such they "embodied the wrath of God and should be killed."[28] Ancient Athens allowed deformed children to be parents and to be supported by the government.[29] Throughout most of the Greco-Roman world, however, the impoverished would have been socially marginalized, excluded, and deprived of many of the necessities their condition required for life.[30]

In light of the attitudes of some ancient cultures toward the disabled, it comes as no surprise that the same ambivalence is projected on the Bible in light of such Scriptures as Deuteronomy 28:15, 28-29 which some scholars

---

25 Avalos, "Medicine," 3:454.

26 Samuel Vaisrub, "Medicine," *Encyclopedia Judaica* (Jerusalem: Keter, 1971), 11:1177-1211; J.Z. Baruch, "The Social Position of the Physician in Ancient Israel," *Janus* 51 (1964): 161-68; Idem. "The Relation between Sin and Disease in the Old Testament," *Janus* 51 (1964): 295-302; Eli Davis, "Aspects of Medicine in the Hebrew Bible," *Koroth* 9 (1985): 265-68; Harry Friendenwald, *The Jews and Medicine* (Baltimore: Johns Hopkins University Press, 1994); Kinnier Wilson, "Medicine in the Land and Times of the Old Testament," in *Studies in the Period of David and Solomon and Other Essays: Papers Read at the International Symposium in Tokyo, Japan, 1979*; Neufeld, "Hygiene Conditions in Ancient Israel (Iron Age)," 41-66; Maurice Nicolas, *La Médecine dans la Bible* (Paris: Librairie le François, 1977); Julius Preuss, *Biblical and Talmudic Medicine* (trans. by Fred Rosner; Brooklyn, N.Y.: Hebrew Publishing Co., 1977); Johann Gottlieb Peter Trusen, *Die Sitten, Gebräuche und Krankheiten der alten Hebräer: Nach der heiligen Schrift historisch und Kritisch dargestellt* (Breslau: Verlag von Wilh. Gottl. Korn., 1853); Wilhelm Ebstein, *Die Medizin im Alten Testament* (München: Werner Fritsch, 1965).

27 Hector Avalos, "Ancient Medicine: In Case of Emergency, Contact Your Local Prophet," *Bible Review* 11 (1995): 27.

28 David L. Braddock and Susan L. Parish, "An Institutional History of Disability," in *Handbook of Disability Studies* (ed. Gary L. Albrecht, Katherine D. Seelman, and Michael Bury; Thousand Oaks, Calif.: Sage, 2003), 12; Stiker, *A History of Disability*, 40; Robert Garland, *The Eye of the Beholder: Deformity and Disability in the Graeco-Roman World* (Ithaca, N.Y.: Cornell University Press, 1995), 35. Garland cites the *Constitution of Athens* (49.4). Later, Garland notes that this attitude toward the deformed was tempered.

29 Garland, *The Eye of the Beholder*, 35. Garland cites the *Constitution of Athens* (49.4).

30 Garland, *The Eye of the Beholder*, 28f.

view as hostile to the disabled.[31] Yet Leviticus 19:14 is an attempt to legislate protection for disabled individuals.

An Anthropological/Historical Approach to Ancient Health Care

Beyond the summaries of medical traditions in various ancient Near Eastern cultures, there are two distinct analytical approaches to the issue of health care. There is, first, a theological approach which is apologetic and diagnostic in nature. Second, there is an anthropological/historical approach which seeks to apply medical anthropology to the text to ascertain the sociological implications of the disabled within the rubric of health care.

Historically, disability, when depicted literarily, has been represented as a debilitating phenomenon in need of medical intervention and correction. A trend in recent disabilities studies has been to refocus the discussion toward a social-functional model. This model distinguishes between a biological condition (impairment) and disability (functional limitations within one's social environment). This approach characterizes disabilities studies in terms of categories of social identity.[32] Disability is frequently a metaphor for social downfall in extra-biblical literature.[33] This approach views literary references of disabilities as designating more than cognitive and physical conditions derived from normative ideas of mental ability and physiological function.[34] It denotes "social, political, and mythological coordinates that define disabled people as excessive to traditional social circuits of interaction and as the *objects*

---

31 Carole R. Fontaine, "Disabilities and Illness in the Bible: A Feminist Perspective," in *A Feminist Companion to the Hebrew Bible in the New Testament* (Feminist Companion to the Bible Series 10; ed. Athalya Brenner; Sheffield: Sheffield Academic Press, 1996), 286-300; Thomson, *Extraordinary Bodies,* 65; Hentrich, "The "Lame" in Lev 21, 17-23 and 2 Sam 5, 6-8," 6.

32 David, T. Mitchell and Sharon L. Snyder, eds. "Disability Studies and the Double Bind of Representation," in *The Body and Physical Difference: Discourses of Disability* (Ann Arbor: University of Michigan Press, 1997); Jeremy Schipper, *Disabilities Studies and the Bible: Figuring Mephibosheth in the David Story* (Edinburgh: T & T Clark, 2006); Idem, "Reconsidering the Imagery of Disability in 2 Samuel 5:8b," *Catholic Biblical Quarterly* 67 (2005): 422-34; Thomson, *Extraordinary Bodies;* Stiker, *A History of Disability;* Lennard Davis, ed., *The Disability Studies Reader* (London: Routledge, 1997); Rebecca Raphael, "Things Too Wonderful: A Disabled Reading of Job," in *Perspectives in Religious Studies* 38 (2004): 399-424.

33 David T. Mitchell and Sharon L. Snyder, *Narrative Prosthesis: Disability and the Dependencies of Discourse* (Ann Arbor: University of Michigan Press, 2001), 47-48; Carole Fontaine, "'Be Men, O Philistines!' Iconographic Representations and Reflections on Female Gender as Disability in the Ancient World," in *This Abled Body: Rethinking Disabilities in Biblical Studies* (ed. Hector Avalos, Sarah J. Melcher, and Jeremy Schipper; Atlanta: Society of Biblical Literature, 2007), 71.

34 Mitchell and Snyder, "Disability Studies and the Double Bind of Representation," 1.

of institutionalized discourses."[35] It argues that using language to isolate the disabled into categories is as pejorative, discriminatory and socially subordinating as one would be if using similar categorical terminology to isolate gender, sexual orientation, or racial groups.[36] Mitchell and Snyder argue that in literary contexts, disabilities are represented as malignant, inherently dependent, and often parasitic.[37] The latest contribution in this area of disabilities studies analyzes various biblical texts to determine how "social, literary, and institutional discourses produce and represent a conception of disability."[38] This work, like those before it, also looks at disabilities in terms of conceptual categories and seeks to recast those categories and to deconstruct the walls of human distinction.[39]

Recent studies have described what today is commonly considered normalcy and how this impacts the way society looks at disabled persons and culturally distinct persons.[40] It is generally argued that the concept of normalcy impacts upon concepts of the ideal, making physical differences ideological differences.[41] This, in turn, produces hegemony in cultural production over the aberrant.[42] Establishing a concept of normalcy drives toward ideological differences and contributes to a configuration of an ideology of the ideal or Utopian society.[43] Judith Abrams provides a definition and theory of disability from a Judaic perspective:

> Judaism defines disabilities as the inability to hear and speak, the inability to learn because of mental illness, mental disability, or immaturity and, to a lesser extent, the inability to see, and physical disabilities . . . The basic theory of disabilities

---

35 Thomson, *Extraordinary Bodies,* 6; Mitchell and Snyder, "Disability Studies and the Double Bind of Representation," 3; David T. Mitchell, "Narrative Prosthesis and the Materiality of Metaphor," in *Disability Studies: Enabling the Humanities* (ed. Sharon Snyder, Brenda Jo Breuggemann, and Rosemarie Garland Thomson; New York: Modern Language Association, 2002), 15f.

36 Mitchell, and Snyder, *Narrative Prosthesis: Disability and the Dependencies of Discourse*, 2.

37 Mitchell and Snyder, "Disability Studies and the Double Bind of Representation," 3.

38 Hector Avalos, Sarah J. Melcher, and Jeremy Schipper, eds., *This Abled Body: Rethinking Disabilities in Biblical Studies* (Atlanta: Society of Biblical Literature, 2007). The various scholars contributing to this volume employ liberationist, literary, and post-scripturalist approaches in their essays. According to the introduction (4) the book's purpose is to rescue the biblical text from itself and to repudiate its negative attitude toward the disabled (even to the extent of their disuse), and to recontextualize it toward positive modern applications.

39 Avalos, Melcher, and Schipper, *This Abled Body*, 3-5.

40 Lennard Davis, "Constructing Normalcy," in *The Disability Studies Reader* (London: Routledge, 1997), 9f.

41 Davis, "Constructing Normalcy," 12ff.

42 Davis, "Constructing Normalcy," 26.

43 Davis, "Constructing Normalcy," 26.

> depends, in the main, on an individual's ability to receive knowledge, communicate verbally, and act upon his intentions.[44]

She asserts that physical wholeness and blemishlessness metaphorically testify to a person's utter, moral wholeness.[45] Consequently, and erroneously, a physical blemish attests to physical or moral imperfection.[46] This is attested in Hebrew prophetic literature where Israel is sometimes characterized as a person with a disability.[47] The implication, she notes, is that "moral disability is equated with physical disability."[48] She writes,

> In the idealized environment of the Temple, death, decay, disorder, and disease could be banished so that a static, perfect environment of blemishlessness was achieved. However, the human body is itself not static, and the basic processes of human life involve disease, decay, and ultimately death.[49]

Abrams asserts elsewhere that attitudes toward illness (and disabilities) are culturally determined. According to Abrams, ancient Near Eastern society as a whole saw "a link between the body and soul, between society's need for order and the good health that results when that order is fostered."[50] As noted earlier, disease and illness are distinct taxonomies of physical abnormalities. Abrams not only does not make this differentiation but also makes the assumption that Israel associated physical disorders of every classification with immorality in religious ideation.

It seems, though, that an approach that associates moral and physical perfection is not only highly speculative in nature and cannot result in a positive perspective on Hebrew biblical literature, but will drive one's conclusions regarding the nature of ancient man's attitude toward the physically disabled. As we begin to analyze further evidence regarding the social, legal, and religious attitudes toward the disabled and examine possible rationales for these attitudes, it will become clear that Abrams' theory is untenable.

Modern assumptions employed in social scientific methodology include positivism, reductionism, relativism, and determinism.[51] These assumptions are evident in many sociological treatments of the Old Testament. Projecting a

---

44 Judith Z. Abrams, "Judaism and Disabilities," in *Encyclopedia of Medicine in the Bible and the Talmud* (Northvale, 1993), 1696.

45 Abrams, "Judaism and Disabilities," 1701.

46 Abrams, "Judaism and Disabilities," 1701.

47 Judith Z. Abrams, *Judaism and Disability: Portrayals in Ancient Texts from the Tanach through the Bavli* (Washington, D.C.: Gallaudet University Press, 1998), 76.

48 Abrams, *Judaism and Disability*, 76.

49 Abrams, *Judaism and Disability*, 104.

50 Abrams, *Judaism and Disability*, 104. She cites Plato to corroborate her claim (ca. 427-347 B.C.E.).

51 Herion, "The Impact of Modern and Social Science Assumptions on the Reconstructions of Israelite History," 4.

modern social organization backward onto biblical society appears to be normative and quite predetermined and, shall we say, compulsory assumption.[52] Finding parallels between the formal, organizational, and institutional structures of ancient life and modern society are universal and prerequisite for sociological analysis. A further complication results when the interdisciplinary activity between social scientific approaches and history become imbalanced resulting in these assumptions interfering with and limiting the historian who seeks to reconstruct the past.[53] While historiography has become subject to criticism, social scientific models and theories have not.[54]

A Medical/Apologetic Approach to Ancient Health Care

Methodologically different from that of the Anthropological/Historical approach but still applying sociological methodology is that of the Medical/Apologetic approach. Rather than eliminate sociology from the realm of biblical studies, these approaches employ sociology sensitively, taking care to avoid allowing the social sciences to dominate historical reconstructions by rigorously maintaining a balanced cross-disciplinary application of sociology and biblical studies.[55] Such methodologies are aware of the differences between advanced and primitive types of societies and between Eastern and Western cultures, utilize cultural anthropology to identify contemporary analogous cultures unaltered by modern industrialism that are stable, agricultural, communal, and respect the wisdom of age.[56] Within the framework of the anthropological/historical approach are scholars who analyze the text as part of a larger, more holistic perspective, preserving the interdependence of texts rather than allowing modern sociological theories to encroach upon the text and premeditate (consciously or unconsciously) conclusions. From an anthropological perspective, Edward Tylor[57] and James Frazer[58] both used anthropology in their work but do not fall prey to sociological assumptions although their methodological framework was flawed.[59]

Modern medical analysis of illnesses concludes that many which resulted in a permanent disability were caused by unsanitary conditions. Works such as those by JoAnn Scurlock and Burton Andersen deserve notice here. They

---

52 Herion, "The Impact of Modern and Social Science Assumptions," 4.

53 Herion, "The Impact of Modern and Social Science Assumptions," 4.

54 Herion, "The Impact of Modern and Social Science Assumptions," 6-7.

55 Herion, "The Impact of Modern and Social Science Assumptions," 23-24.

56 Matthews and Benjamin, *Social World of Ancient Israel: 1250-587*, xii-xx.

57 Edward B. Tylor, *Primitive Culture: Researches into the Development of Mythology, Philosophy, Religion, Language, Art and Custom* (2 vols.; New York: Putman, 1920).

58 James G. Frazer, *The Golden Bough* (12 vols.; 3rd ed.; London: Macmillan, 1911-18).

59 Tylor and Frazer both applied an evolutionary method to their studies of primitive societies. Their conclusions have led to the persistent myth that, like man, religious belief evolved.

examine Assyrian and Babylonian diagnostic texts and apply modern medical knowledge so as to correlate ancient symptoms with modern determinations.[60] Their contribution is generally in the area of ancient diagnosis and prognosis and their intention is to recover ancient medical texts. John Wilkinson also stresses diagnosis in his work. He looks specifically at matters such as the definition of health as presented in the Bible and the diagnostics which would have either been epidemically or systemically known to the people of the ancient world of the Bible.[61]

Purity and its Relationship to Disabilities

A number of works have been published regarding the concept of purity. A proper understanding of this concept in Israel and the greater ancient Near East is essential to this study in that there is a general understanding that the posture of the Old Testament toward the disabled is that they, along with other minority groups, were under God's judgment and consequently to be ostracized from the community.[62]

Within the area of understanding the concepts of purity and impurity, two distinct lines of argumentation have emerged. Both lines connect moral purity with physical purity in some way. However, while one seeks to understand this connection as connoting a negative assessment of disabled persons, the other understands the connection between body and sacral sanction as having an anthropological explanation that does not connote anything about the moral quality of the disabled person.

In the broad scope of the subject of purity, specifically in relation to Israel, a number of persons have examined the interrelationship between impurity and sin.[63] A brief summary of the various positions in Judaism with reference to the

---

60 Scurlock and Andersen, *Diagnosis in Assyrian and Babylonian Medicine.*

61 John Wilkinson, *The Bible and Healing: A Medical and Theological Commentary* (Grand Rapids: Eerdmans, 1998).

62 Paul Kalluveettil, "The Marginalizing Dialectics of the Bible," *Bible Bhashyam* 11 (1985): 204; Thomas Hentrich, "Masculinity and Disability in the Bible," in *This Abled Body: Rethinking Disabilities in Biblical Studies* (ed. Hector Avalos, Sarah J. Melcher, and Jeremy Schipper; Atlanta: Society of Biblical Literature, 2007), 75-76.

63 Eli Davis, "Purity and Impurity," *Encyclopedia Judaica* (Jerusalem: Keter, 1971), 13:1405-14; Mary Douglas, *Purity and Danger: An Analysis of Concepts of Pollution and Taboo* (London: Routledge, 1966); Idem, *Leviticus as Literature* (London: Oxford University Press, 2001); Jacob Neusner, *The Idea of Purity in Ancient Judaism* (Leiden: E.J. Brill, 1973); Tikva Frymer-Kensky, "Pollution, Purification, and Purgation in Biblical Israel," in *The Word of the Lord Shall Go Forth: Essays in Honor of David Noel Freedman* (ed. C.L. Meyer and M O'Conner; Winona Lake, Ind.: Eisenbrauns, 1983), 399-414; Jonathan Klawans, *Impurity and Sin in Ancient Judaism* (Oxford, England: Oxford University Press, 2000); John Gammie, *Holiness in Israel: Overtures in Biblical Theology* (Minneapolis: Fortress, 1989); David P. Wright, "The Spectrum of Priestly Impurity," in *Priesthood and Cult in Ancient Israel* (ed. G.A. Anderson and S.M. Olyan; Sheffield: Sheffield Academic

connection between impurity and sin is necessary at this point. Most scholars identify a duality of both purpose and result in the concepts of purity and impurity. Jacob Neusner, for example, emphasizes the cultic and metaphorical duality of purity and impurity.[64] Tikva Frymer-Kensky, on the other hand, compartmentalizes ritual impurity, arguing that while some forms of impurity can be removed by ritual prescription, the person who intentionally committed certain deeds "would suffer catastrophic retribution."[65] Jonathan Klawans likewise argues that, in contradistinction with ritual impurity (which is not sinful), moral impurity is dangerous and results in severe punishment. Sin, he argues, is not *like* impurity but *produces* impurity, having its own distinct, defiling force.[66] The implication, he argues, is that there are two distinct and juxtaposed concepts of defilement at work in the literature of ancient Israel that, as far as the Hebrew Bible is concerned, are not interrelated.[67] David P. Wright's work searches for a rationale for priestly impurity laws that takes into account these classifications.[68]

Other scholars look for anthropological explanation for the concepts of purity and impurity. John Gammie, for example, examines genre as a deciding factor in identifying variations in the concept of holiness. Examining the priestly concept of holiness he asserts that "holiness demands separation."[69] Separation, he further asserts, is evident from creation (the classification of air, water, and earth were was established by separation), to the tabernacle (which served as a counterpart to creation) and its cult, which were set apart by the presence of Yahweh, to the observation of the legal codes which by nature were, in themselves, effects of separation.[70] The main issue, then, is separation, not morality. The protection and continuance of the fundamental distinction between the sacred and the profane in the Israelite classificatory system was for Israel a categorical imperative generated by the understanding that Yahweh's presence was within the community of Israel (Deut 12:5, 11; Lev 11:44, 45; 19:2; 20:7, 26:7, 11, 26). In order for this presence to continue Israel's people must remain pure. Since God is holy, his people must, of necessity, be holy too. In some cases, holiness involved maintaining those things that kept Israel separate from other nations. The observation of Yahweh's commandments

---

Press, 1991), 150-82; Wilfried Paschen, *Rein und Unrein; Untersuchung zur biblischen Wortgeschichte*, Studien zum Alten und Neuen Testament 12 (München: Kösel-Verlag, 1970).

64 Neusner, *The Idea of Purity in Ancient Judaism*, 108.

65 Frymer-Kensky, "Pollution, Purification, and Purgation in Biblical Israel," 399.

66 Klawans, *Impurity and Sin in Ancient Judaism*, 11.

67 Klawans, *Impurity and Sin in Ancient Judaism*, 38.

68 Wright, "The Spectrum of Priestly Impurity," 151. According to Wright, there are two main categories of impurities: tolerated and prohibited.

69 Gammie, *Holiness in Israel*, 9-70. Gammie advances Douglas' anthropological approach.

70 Gammie, *Holiness in Israel*, 9-70.

generates holiness. When Israel placed her confidence in Yahweh and thus explicitly obeyed his commands, she was pure. Faith and purity are connected. When Israel lost confidence in Yahweh and his word and turned to other gods for solutions to problems she intentionally blinded herself. This validates the metaphorical use of disability language by the prophets.

It has been suggested by some that the physically disabled were considered unclean in that their affliction is linked to divine punitive causations. Hence, the disabled were religious and social outcasts. A few scholars have undertaken to write regarding the connection of the concept of purity/impurity as it related to physical disability.[71] Hans-Joachim Kraus makes the argument that there exists in the Old Testament an unbreakable causal connection between guilt and sickness (Pss 32:1-4; 38:3-11; 39:8, 11). "In the sickness, guilt is made manifest as the cause of ruin and as the target of God's wrath."[72] A man's illness would prompt his enemies to eagerly make a case that the affected one has been abandoned by God and enduring his well-deserved divine punishment.[73] Restitution accompanies acts of atonement but if restitution is denied, the sick could be perceived by their enemies as separated from God and deserving of condemnation.[74] These enemies are human (Pss 9:19; 10:18; 12:8; 56:1; 76:10) but possess eerie, demonic attributes.[75] Their acts are intended to cause separation between God and the poor.[76] The victim can do nothing but cast himself upon Yahweh alone for mercy (Pss 3:7; 4:1; 7:1, 6; 10:12; 22:10, 19; 35:3) who puts to shame the enemies (Pss 6:10; 7:16; 9:3, 6).

As one might guess, these interpretive connections have generated a variety of reactions. Some offer pragmatically-oriented corrective measures that seek to provide dignity to those living with disability and ministry for this sometimes excluded group.[77] Others are less conciliatory and more combative. Of particular note is Nancy Eiesland, who writes,

---

[71] Christian Klopfenstein, *La Bible et la Santé* (Paris: La Pensée Universelle, 1978); Nancy Eiesland, *The Disabled God: Toward a Liberation Theology of Disability* (New York: Abingdon, 1994); Sarah J. Melcher, "Visualizing the Perfect Cult: The Priestly Rationale for Exclusion," in *Human Disability and the Service of God: Reassessing Religious Practice* (ed. Nancy Eiesland and Don Saliers; New York: Abingdon, 1998), 55-71; Yehezkel Kaufmann, *The Religion of Israel* (Chicago: The University of Chicago Press, 1960).

[72] Hans-Joachim Kraus, *Theology of the Psalms* (Minneapolis: Augsburg, 1986, 132.

[73] Kraus, *Theology of the Psalms*, 132.

[74] Kraus, *Theology of the Psalms*, 132.

[75] Kraus, *Theology of the Psalms*, 133.

[76] Kraus, *Theology of the Psalms*, 133.

[77] Newman, and Tada, *All God's Children: Ministry with Disabled Persons*; John M. Hull, *In the Beginning There Was Darkness: A Blind Person's Conversations with the Bible* (Harrisburg, Pa.: Trinity Press International, 2002); Michael Dick, *Born in Heaven, Made on Earth* (Winona Lake, Ind.: Eisenbrauns, 1999).

> The Christian interpretation of disability has run the gamut from symbolizing sin to representing an occasion for supererogation. The persistent thread within the Christian tradition has been that disability denotes an unusual relationship with God and that the person with disabilities is either divinely blessed or damned: the defiling evildoer or the spiritual superhero.[78]

According to Eiesland, these representations are rooted in the Old Testament. She notes that Leviticus 21:17-23 conflates moral impurity with physical disability and in the process provides a warrant for barring the disabled from ecclesiastical auspex.[79] The exclusion of the disabled from ecclesiastical duties and the warranting of such on the basis cited cannot be disputed.[80] However, the interpretation of Leviticus 21:17-23, as conflating immorality and disability, is in dispute. This text's interpretation as asserting perfect physical condition as a representation of Yahweh's wholeness provides a legitimate warrant for proscribing one with a disability from officiating as a priest. Nevertheless, a disabled priest enjoyed other prerogatives and privileges of the priestly class.

Contra Douglas, Eiesland argues that anthropological interpretations suggest that "physical disability is a travesty of the divine image and an inherent desecration of all things holy."[81] She writes,

> Theological interpretations of the meaning of perfection have historically included physical flawlessness as well as absolute freedom. Both understandings necessarily exclude the lived realities of people with disabilities (as well as most other humans). According to such standards, people with disabilities lack perfection and embody un-wholeness.[82]

She proffers liberation theology as a solution to pervasive discrimination and exclusionary ecclesiastical policies, presenting the risen Christ as the disabled God and an affirmation of both those with disabled bodies and their right to full participation in the community of faith.[83]

It is Mary Douglas who is credited with providing the best rationale for the rise of taboos and the formation of the concept of purity.[84] Previously, concepts of purity and defilement were considered primitive, inspiring fear for the

---

78 Eiesland, *The Disabled God*, 70.

79 Eiesland, *The Disabled God*, 71.

80 The Old Testament is even more exclusive: only Levites; only the family of Aaron; only Zadokites may serve. Physical disability is only a part of a much larger exclusivity for the cult.

81 Eiesland, *The Disabled God*, 72.

82 Eiesland, *The Disabled God*, 72.

83 Eiesland, *The Disabled God*, 87.

84 Douglas, *Purity and Danger*; Idem, "Sacred Contagion," in *Reading Leviticus: Responses to Mary Douglas* (ed. John F.A. Sawyer; Journal for the Study of the Old Testament Supplemental Series 227; Sheffield: Sheffield Academic Press, 1996); Idem, *Leviticus as Literature* (London: Oxford University Press, 2001).

purpose of maintaining order and compliance.[85] Douglas' three main points are: purity is normal and wholeness; purity is not derived from objective, physical reality but from the cultural understanding which reflect larger social concerns; and that the body is the locus where purity concerns are manifest. Her groundbreaking work demonstrated through an anthropological approach that ancient concepts of defilement are structured and therefore comparative to modern concepts and are not to be understood as something primitive as they previously had been.[86] She points out that although every culture's concept of defilement is systematic in nature,[87] the categories for each culture are not the same.[88] In addition, she notes that the systematic concepts of impurity can be interpreted symbolically and that they function socially to control behavior.[89]

Douglas notes that purity specifically concerns ritual status.[90] In Leviticus, purity is a dominant theological idea. As such it is explained in Leviticus by its symbolic contrast with bodily imperfection and broken boundaries.[91] Contagions must be understood in the context of holiness.[92] Sacred contagion fixes blame on offenders, defines the identity of individuals in the community of faith, and is derived from those laws which specify the kind of society Yahweh chose for his people to live in.[93]

What we find in Leviticus is the dissociation of uncleanness from sin. The effect of this is to defuse arbitrary accusations, calm prophetic attack, and deflect sectarian denunciation.[94] As a result,

> It supports at a practical level the doctrine of the perfect unity and singleness of God by tendering into God's hands, through the work of his priests, all claims of magic spells to harm and to cure. Any claims not coming from an authenticated source are invalidated.[95]

In addition, she notes that the concept of purity in the Old Testament is based on theological reasoning. Its intent was to maintain the divinely placed barriers established between various classes and species (divine and human, and human and animal). Admixtures between classes or species of creation are a reversal of God's created order.[96] She points out that although the root meaning of

---

85 Douglas, *Purity and Danger*, 1-2.
86 Douglas, *Purity and Danger*, 8-50.
87 Douglas, *Purity and Danger*, 35, 40.
88 Douglas, *Purity and Danger*, 37-40. With respect to ancient Israel, she argues that the categories correspond between the body and creation.
89 Douglas, *Purity and Danger*, 3, 4.
90 Douglas, "Sacred Contagion," 89.
91 Douglas, "Sacred Contagion," 89.
92 Douglas, "Sacred Contagion," 90.
93 Douglas, "Sacred Contagion," 93.
94 Douglas, "Sacred Contagion," 98-99.
95 Douglas, "Sacred Contagion," 99.
96 Douglas, *Purity and Danger*, 53.

holiness is separation (reflecting Yahweh's total otherness), the concept of holiness is not limited to this one particular. This is seen in those statutes which maintain the distinction between categories of creation. It is evident in those statutes related to sexual purity and dietary laws (Exod 23:19; 34:26; Lev 18; 20; Deut 14:21; 27:20-23). Douglas writes,

> Holiness requires that individuals shall conform to the class to which they belong. And holiness requires that different classes of things shall not be confused . . . Holiness means keeping distinct the categories of creation. It therefore involves correct definition, discrimination, and order.[97]

The concept of holiness is illustrated in separation, order, goodness and moral justice. According to Douglas, the concept of holiness is founded on the idea of wholeness and completeness.[98] She writes,

> Much of Leviticus is taken up with stating the physical perfection that is required of things presented in the temple and of persons approaching it. The animals offered in sacrifice must be without blemish, women must be purified after childbirth, and lepers should be separated and ritually cleansed before being allowed to approach once they are cured.[99]

The concept of purity intersects with disabilities studies on several levels. As this study progresses, the distinctions and similarities between ancient Israel and other contemporary cultures appertaining to the disabled will shed light on how a state of ritual purity was secured and maintained in their various cultures and the implications for those living with disability regarding contact with the divine.

---

97 Douglas, *Purity and Danger*, 53.
98 Douglas, *Purity and Danger*, 49ff.
99 Douglas, *Purity and Danger*, 55.

Chapter 3

Ancient Near Eastern Literature

Religious Customs

The Creation of Disabilities

The following Sumerian myth text is a creation story.[1] It provides a mythical etiology for the existence of the physically impaired.[2] As such it gives us hints into the religious attitude of this culture. The gods created man to do their physical labor for them (lines 1-11). After man's creation Enki is praised for having planned and directed mankind's creation.[3] In the second episode of the myth it is during a feast celebrating man's creation that Ninmah creates a number of disabled persons and challenged Enki to solve their problems which he does successfully, not by eliminating the disability but by devising ways the physically disabled can adjust to society, be productive, and sustain themselves.[4] Following is a portion of the myth Enki and Ninmah:

> Ninmah took in her hand clay from the top of the Abzu;[5]
> She fashioned from it the first man: one (who) could not bend his stiffened(?) hands to reach out (for anything).
> Enki–upon seeing the first man (who) could not bend his stiffened(?) hands to reach out (for anything),
> Decreed its fate: he made him stand in attention at the head of the king.
> Second–she fashioned from it one 'deprived of light,' a blind(?) man.[6]
> Enki–upon seeing the one 'deprived of light,' the blind(?) man,
> Decreed its fate: he allotted to it the musical art,
> And seated it (as) chief-[musician] in a place of honor, before the king.
> Third–[she fashioned from it one la]me as to [both feet],[7] crippled of feet.

---

1 Kenton Sparks, *Ancient Texts for the Study of the Hebrew Bible: A Guide to the Background Literature* (Peabody, Mass.: Hedrickson, 2005), 309.

2 Sparks, *Ancient Texts for the Study of the Hebrew Bible*, 309.

3 Jacob Klein, "Enki and Ninmah," in *The Context of Scripture: Canonical Compositions from the Biblical World* (ed. William W. Hallo and K. Lawson Younger; New York: E.J. Brill, 1997), I:516.

4 Klein, "Enki and Ninmah," I:518.

5 Klein, "Enki and Ninmah," I:617, fn.10; 517, fn.17. This is identified as the subterranean sweet water ocean, a cosmic location beneath the earth in days of yore.

6 Klein, "Enki and Ninmah," I:518, fn.30. This term, literally means "a seeing man" which may be a euphemism for blindness.

> Enki–[upon seeing] the one lame as to both feet, crippled of feet,
> He taught(?) it the work of [the metal-caster] and silver-smith, his .....
> Fourth–she fashioned from it a man discharging semen.[8]
> Enki–upon seeing the man discharging semen,
> Bathed him in water (blessed) with incantation, and removed Death from his body.
> Fifth–she fashioned from it a woman who could not give birth.
> Enki–upon seeing the woman who could not give birth,
> Decreed her fate, he assigned her to do work in the Woman's Quarter.
> Sixth–she fashioned from it a man, in whose body neither male organ nor female organ was placed.[9]
> Enki–upon seeing the man in whose body neither male organ nor female organ was placed,
> He called him: "Nippurean(?)-the-courtier,"
> And decreed him his fate to stand in attendance before the king.
> Ninmah threw the pinch of clay in her hand on the ground, and a great silence fell.
> The great lord, Enki, said to Ninmah:
> "I have decreed the fate of those whom you have fashioned, and given them (their daily) bread.
> Now come, let me fashion (one) for you: and do you decree the fate of that newborn!" (*Enki and Ninmah Myth* lines 58-82).[10]

The text shows that the gods are assigned responsibility for creating disabled persons. The ill created by Ninmah is mitigated by Enki, the all wise god, who takes these paralytic, blind, lame, incontinent, infertile, and asexual creations and makes places for them in the life and the economy of creation. In so doing a viewpoint of the disabled as useful rather than freakish is formed. They are not looked upon as societal outcasts but integrated into society. This supports not only the theory put forth by Hartmut Waetzoldt that the disabled were not marginalized but integrated into ancient Mesopotamian society[11] but also provides insight into ancient man's attitude toward the physically disabled. They may not have been considered unclean beings as some suggest.

---

7 Klein, "Enki and Ninmah," I:518, fn.33. This is restoring [ĞÌR-MIN H]UM, literally meaning "two feet broken."

8 Klein, "Enki and Ninmah," I:518, fn.35. A man leaking urine.

9 Klein, "Enki and Ninmah," I:518, fn.38. This refers to a eunuch.

10 Klein, "Enki and Ninmah," I:518.

11 Hartmut Waetzoldt, Der Umgang mit Behinderten in Mesopotamien," in *Behinderung als Pädagogische und politische Herousforderung: Historische und Systematische Aspekte* (Schriftenrihe zum Bayerischen Schulmuseum Ishenhousen 14; ed. Max Liedtke; Bad Heilbrunn: Verlag Julius Klinkhardt, 1996), 77-91. Waetzoldt's assertion is supported by textual evidence indicating that prominent families had no compunction against giving children personal names reflecting their particular disability. He suggests that in Mesopotamia, disabilities were not considered a punishment but a result of the whims of a god.

Prophecy and Disability

Considerable interest in acquiring divine knowledge was common throughout the ancient Near East.[12] According to Martti Nissinen, prophecy "is human transmission of allegedly divine messages."[13] Nissinen notes that in order to understand the meaning of the term "prophet" in the ancient Near East, one must subordinate all other features of the prophetic message (such as predictive possibilities) to the communicative aspect.[14] He was the gods' mouthpiece.[15] The belief was that the prophet could either make the future known or inquire as to divine approval for a planned activity.[16] Inquiry into the mind of the gods was made through various channels including dreams, oracular inquiry, ecstatic prophetic declaration, or by priestly incubation.[17] It is likely that diviners or prophets were consulted by most persons on every level of ancient society regarding the outcome of plans, business ventures, or military campaigns.[18] Preferred divination techniques included extispicy,[19] astrology, augury,[20] kleromancy,[21] and oneiromancy,[22] but literary prophecies, possibly produced for propaganda purposes, are also extant.[23] These techniques form a vivid

---

12 Harry A. Hoffner Jr., "Ancient Views of Prophecy and Fulfillment: Mesopotamia and Asia Minor," *Journal of the Evangelical Theological Society* 30 (1987): 257.

13 Martti Nissinen, *Prophets and Prophecy in the Ancient Near East* (Atlanta: Society of Biblical Literature, 2003), 1.

14 Nissinen, *Prophets and Prophecy*, 1-2. According to Nissinen, "the prophetic process of transmission consists of the divine sender of the message, the message itself, the human transmitter of the message, and the recipient(s) of the message. These four components should be transparent in any written source to be identified as a specimen of prophecy."

15 David L. Petersen, "Defining Prophecy and Prophetic Literature," in *Prophecy in Its Ancient Near Eastern Context* (ed. Martti Nissinen; Atlanta: Society of Biblical Literature, 2000), 33, 39-41. Petersen defines a prophet typologically, asserting that he has an intense experience of the deity, speaks or writes in a distinctive way, acts in a particular social setting, possesses distinctive personal qualities, acts as an intermediary, and brings a distinctive message.

16 Nissinen, *Prophets and Prophecy*, 1.

17 Nissinen, *Prophets and Prophecy*, 1, 6. Although dreamers and visionaries ought not be lumped in with "prophets," the line between them is difficult to draw. See also Gary Beckman, "Plague Prayers of Muršili II," in *The Context of Scripture* (ed. William W. Hallo and K. Lawson Younger; New York: E.J. Brill, 1997), 1:159, sec. A, lines 41-44. At the time, King Muršili was seeking information regarding the cause of the plague among the Hittites. See also John Currid, *Ancient Egypt and the Old Testament* (Grand Rapids: Baker, 1997), 42.

18 Hoffner, "Ancient Views of Prophecy and Fulfillment," 258.

19 The examination of sacrificial sheep entrails.

20 The examination of the movements and behavior of birds.

21 The casting of lots. Possibly the Urim and Thummin in Israel.

22 The interpretation of symbolic elements in dreams. It was believed that dreams were direct divine verbal communication. This is perhaps demonstrated with Jacob, Joseph, Daniel, and others in the Old Testament.

23 Hoffner, "Ancient Views of Prophecy and Fulfillment," 258-62, 263-64.

contrast with ancient Israel which rejected divination as a means of knowing the mind of God (Lev 19:26; Deut 18:10). John Currid notes,

> Numerous biblical references (e.g., Deut 18:9-11) indicate that the Canaanites engaged in soothsaying, divination, sorcery, witchcraft, and necromancy (communication with the dead) as part of their worship. Moreover, they ritually beat and cut themselves during worship (see 1 Kings 18:28; cf. Lev 19:28). All of these were magical acts intended to discover what decisions the divinities might have made concerning particular situations.[24]

In the ancient Near East, prophecy was equivalent to divine knowledge. Describing Mesopotamian divination, Oppenheim writes,

> Basically, divination represents a technique of communication with the supernatural forces that are supposed to shape the history of the individual as well as that of the group. It presupposes the belief that these powers are able and, at times, willing to communicate their intentions . . . and that if evil is predicted or threatened, it can be averted through appropriate means.[25]

There exists a collection of 120 tablets containing a terrestrial omen corpus known as the *Šumma Ālu* series (*CT* 38-41) formed to interpret a variety of unusual events that were believed to be omen laden.[26] These omens were intended for the average man rather than the royal courts as other omen texts were known to be.[27] These omen texts are referred to as the SA.GIG. The SA.GIG contains medical omens. The meaning of the term SA.GIG is uncertain but probably means "symptoms."[28] It was found in Mesopotamian (Akkadian) Medical Incantations (*Enūma ana bīt martsi āšipu illaku*). This is a diagnostic handbook more than a compendium of medical omens. These medical omens were incorporated into the *Šumma Ālu*. Below are selected lines from this omen series:

> 65 If there are many lame men in a city, [ ].
> 66 If there are many lame women in a city, that will be a good city to go in
> 75 If there are many blind persons in a city, sorrow is over the city
> 78 If there are many wasting away/crippled in a city, sorrow is over the city
> 83 If there are many crippled in a city, [the city] will be destroyed

---

24 Currid, *Ancient Egypt and the Old Testament*, 42.

25 A. Leo Oppenheim, *Ancient Mesopotamia* (Chicago: University of Chicago, 1964), 207.

26 Sparks, *Ancient Texts for the Study of the Hebrew Bible*, 221.

27 Sparks, *Ancient Texts for the Study of the Hebrew Bible*, 221.

28 J.V. Kinnier Wilson, "Two Medical Texts from Nimrud," *Iraq* 18 (1956): 140. Wilson recognized that "symptoms" is a useful, albeit inaccurate meaning of SA.GIG.

84 If there are many abnormal in a city, sorrow is over [the city] go into (*Šumma Ālu* Tablet I, lines 65-66, 75, 78, 83-84).[29]

Although the above text shows that the presence of disabled persons in the city was considered portentous in character, it does not show that infanticide of disabled children was practiced. To the contrary, like the Enki Myth, Hartmut Waetzoldt suggests that this text implies that the disabled were integrated into society, were gainfully employed, and generally lived productive lives in the communities in which they lived.[30] Johannes Renger likewise argues that in ancient Mesopotamia, disabled persons have been found working in temples, on ration lists of institutional households, and holding regular jobs suggesting they were put to work in the temple to relieve the family's burden for their care and did not experience any social disadvantage.[31] Waetzoldt bases his claim on the observation that words expressing disability were used as personal names.[32] He notes that the above text is not the only incidence of disability terminology used for proper names. He points to the broad use of terms referring to disabilities used in other ancient Near Eastern texts for proper names.[33] This suggests to him that the disabled were not isolated from society but were well integrated. For example, there is the Sumerian term *Ba.za* in texts from Ebla[34] and Ur[35] which refers to a disability and used as a proper name. In the Ebla text *Ba.za* refers to what is believed to be what today would be termed a minor disability and is used in its context as a personal name.[36] In several texts the same term (in Akkadian) is *hummuru*[37]which is also attested to as a personal

---

[29] Volkert Haas, "Soziale Randgruppen und Außenseiter altorientalischer Gesellschaften in Alten Orient," in *Außenseiter und Randgruppen: Beiträge zu einer Sozialgeschichte des Alten Orients* (ed. Volkert Haas; Xenia: Konstanzer Althistorische Vorträge und Forschungen, Heft 32; Konstanz: Universitätsverlag, 1992), 38f.

[30] Waetzoldt, "Der Umgang mit Behinderten in Mesopotamien," 80-91.

[31] Renger, "Kranke, Krüppel, Debile – eine Randgruppe im Alten Orient?" 113-26.

[32] Waetzoldt, "Der Umgang mit Behinderten in Mesopotamien," 77f.

[33] Waetzoldt, "Der Umgang mit Behinderten in Mesopotamien," 77. Waetzoldt cites the *Šumma Izbu* omen series, tablet I, line 87ff and tablet II, lines 11ff as evidence for this.

[34] Amalia Catagnoti, "Les nains à Ebla," in *Nouvelles Assyriologiques Brèves et Utilitaires* 31 (1989): 20-21. She notes that there are three attestations in the Ebla texts used as the personal name for dwarfs. A number of individuals show up with this term as a proper name. At one point *Ba.za* may refer to a dwarf who served as a palace jester. See also Waetzoldt, "Der Umgang mit Behinderten in Mesopotamien," 79.

[35] Mary I. Hussey, "Sumerian Tablets in the Harvard Semitic Museum, Part II," in *Harvard Semitic Series* 4 (Cambridge: Harvard Press, 1915), 26. See also Waetzoldt, "Der Umgang mit Behinderten in Mesopotamien," 79.

[36] Waetzoldt, "Der Umgang mit Behinderten in Mesopotamien," 81.

[37] *CAD* 6:235. From Old Babylonian meaning shrunken, shriveled, crippled, or couchant.

name.[38] Waetzoldt also notes that in a Babylonian text, a loan was made to someone named *Passalum*.[39] For a loan to have been made, one would have to be found credit-worthy.[40] In addition, Waetzoldt cites the prophecy texts from Mari which make use of the term *sukkuku*.[41] Piotr Steinkeller notes that in the inscription on the Seal of Aman-Eshtar the same word is used to refer to the personal name of a deaf woman who was maidservant to the high priestess of the gods *Enlil* and *Aman Eštar*.[42] Olivier Rouault notes also that in the inscription the term *sukkuku* is also found in the Mari texts used as the personal name of one who received material for the work being performed and did business in the community.[43]

Although no decisive evidence can be put forth to contradict Waetzoldt's and Renger's claims, there are other possible explanations. It is possible that these terms may have been personalized for mere identification purposes as the people would have been quite familiar with the infirmity but communication would require that a particular person be identified. *Sukukuum* is possibly used for a nickname (*ARM* 18 55 i 13 and 14). These names may, in fact, be a means of depersonalizing an individual as perhaps with the word *hummuru*, a crippled slave who was a leather-worker (*YOS* 7 114:7). It should be noted that several of these terms are also used for deities. It is possible, then, that parents to which a child has been born with a birth defect might give that child a name similar to a deity with that name as a dedication to that deity with the hope of future healing. Too little information is available to make conclusive statements on the matter. Omen texts present only a limited expression of life for the disabled.

Another oracle text mentions disabled persons in the context of negative outcomes for the city in which these persons reside. The *Šumma Izbu* series is

---

38 T. Clay, "Documents from the Temple Archives of Nippur," in *The Babylonian Expedition of the University of Pennsylvania,* 15 (Philadelphia: University of Pennsylvania Press, 1906), 178:16, 200 II 26. Waetzoldt, "Der Umgang mit Behinderten in Mesopotamien," 82.

39 *CAD* 12:327-28. From the word *pessû*, meaning crippled or deformed.

40 Emile Szlechter, *Tablettes juridiques et administratives de la III*[e] *Dynastie d'Ur et de la I*[re] *Dynastie de Babylone,* Conservées au Musée de l'Université de Manchester et à Cambridge, au Musée Fitzwilliam, à l'Institut d'Etudes Orientales et à l'Institut d'Egyptologie (Paris: Publications de l'Institut de droit romain de l'Université de Paris, 1963), I:20 b 4. See also Waetzoldt, "Der Umgang mit Behinderten in Mesopotamien," 81.

41 *CAD* 15: 362-63. The term *sukkuku* is an adjective normally translated as "deaf" or "obtuse."

42 Piotr Steinkeller, "Comments on the Seal of Aman-Eshtar," in *Nouvelles Assyriologiques Brèves et Utilitaires*, no. 9 (Paris: F. Joannès, 1993), 7-8. The high priestess was the daughter of the king. See also Waetzoldt, "Der Umgang mit Behinderten in Mesopotamien," 85.

43 See *ARM* 55 i 13-14 in Olivier Rouault, *Mukannišum: L'administration et l'économie palatiales à Mari*, Archives royales de Mari, 18 (Paris: Geuthner, 1977), 74-75. See also Waetzoldt, "Der Umgang mit Behinderten in Mesopotamien," 84.

believed to have originated in Mesopotamia but was widely disseminated throughout the ancient Near East as is evident from copies found at Ugarit, Boğazköy (Hittite), Babylon, and Aššur.[44] These omens were written on twenty-four tablets containing over 2,000 omens.[45] The importance of these omen texts is seen by the number of copies of the text in a variety of languages.[46] *Izbu* is the technical term for "a malformed new born human or animal."[47] These divinations seek to tell the future through the interpretation of defective births by both animals and humans.[48] They date to the 7th century B.C. They point to the circumstances of an unusual birth and then its implications. These omens speak to both public and private issues. The *Šumma Izbu* series reads in part,

> If a woman gives birth, and (the child) has (a knob of) flesh like a turban on top of his head, and the base (of the flesh) is constricted and falls in folds, its right eye is contorted, its right hand and foot are crippled, and it has teeth[49] – an enemy will confiscate the land of Akkad and desecrate its shrines; the weapons of the king will be idle.
> If a woman gives birth, and (the child) has two heads[50] – there will be a fierce attack against the land and the king will give up his throne (The *Šumma Izbu* Series, Tablet II, lines 19-20).[51]
> If a woman gives birth, and (the child) has six toes on its right foot – (the child) is endowed with worrying (The *Šumma Izbu* Series, Tablet III, line 58).[52]
> If a woman gives birth, and the right foot (of the child) is withered[53]– that house will not prosper (The *Šumma Izbu* Series, Tablet III, line 85).[54]

---

44 Dennis Pardee, "Ugaritic Birth Omens," in *The Context of Scripture: Canonical Compositions from the Biblical World* (ed. William W. Hallo and K. Lawson Younger; New York: E.J. Brill, 1997), I:287.

45 Erle Leichty, *The Omen Series Šumma Izbu* (TCS 4; Locust Valley, N.Y.: Augustin, 1970), 2.

46 Leichty, *The Omen Series Šumma Izbu*, 7.

47 *CAD* 7:317-18. *Izbu* can be compared to the Hebrew word עָזַב which means "to forsake." After extispicy, breaches in patterns were the most important form of divination in Mesopotamia.

48 Beckman, *Hittite Birth Rituals,* 12-13.

49 Scurlock and Andersen, *Diagnosis in Assyrian and Babylonian Medicine*, 394. Scurlock and Andersen identify this birth defect as neurofibromatosis, suggesting that trunk tremors often accompany the skin lesions described in this text. These skin lesions are frequently caused by the papilloma virus.

50 Scurlock and Andersen, *Diagnosis in Assyrian and Babylonian Medicine*, 398-99. Scurlock and Anderson address this characterization of a birth defect under the category of conjoined twins.

51 Leichty, *The Omen Series Šumma Izbu*, 47.

52 Leichty, *The Omen Series Šumma Izbu*, 60.

Specific birth defects are identified and an omen is made on the basis of these defects.[55] Omens were a form of divination.[56] "Virtually every natural occurrence which was out of the ordinary was considered ominous."[57] Many of these omens were added to make the series all inclusive and thus are subject to a metaphorical interpretation.[58] The first four tablets deal with human births. Many of these omens contain fanciful descriptions of women giving birth to animals, humans with animal body parts, or other objects not human. The majority of these omens were developed on the basis of observable birth anomalies.[59] The remaining twenty tablets deal with animal births. There would have been a greater percentage of anomalies in births in ancient times than in many societies today as conceptions for women in the ancient Near East would have been more frequent.[60] Erle Leichty writes,

> When an abnormal birth occurred, the series was consulted and the pertinent omens were selected and excerpted, and a report was prepared. Then an appropriate ritual was performed in order to expiate the evil effects of the bad omen.[61]

Hallo points out that most omens

> Portend a rather undesirable outcome for the client, but such outcomes could be averted by priestly intercession with the deity, whose intent the omen had divined. The contrast with biblical prophecy could not be greater; there an immutable divine dispensation, but free will on humanity's part to avoid divine displeasure, here a wholly capricious pantheon, largely indifferent to human behavior, and to be appeased rather by elaborate and costly cultic performance.[62]

It is uncertain as to why these conditions resulted in either a good or bad omen. Haas notes that there does not appear to be any discernible rationale for the positive or negative attitude of some categories. It is possible that an inventory was kept over the years where certain birth anomalies were associated with events that followed after the pattern of the liver casts that marked certain

---

53 Scurlock and Andersen, *Diagnosis in Assyrian and Babylonian Medicine*, 403. Scurlock and Andersen suggest this is a description of a birth defect known as phocomelia.

54 Leichty, *The Omen Series Šumma Izbu*, 63.

55 Leichty, *The Omen Series Šumma Izbu*, 31-72.

56 Sparks, *Ancient Texts for the Study of the Hebrew Bible,* 216.

57 Leichty, *The Omen Series Šumma Izbu*, 7.

58 Leichty, *The Omen Series Šumma Izbu*, 19-20.

59 Leichty, *The Omen Series Šumma Izbu*, 20.

60 Leichty, *The Omen Series Šumma Izbu*, 20. The lack of birth control, high infant mortality, and the lack of medicine and prenatal controls which result in higher proportions of miscarriage are cited by Leichty as reasons for this claim.

61 Leichty, *The Omen Series Šumma Izbu*, 7.

62 Hallo, "Compare and Contrast: The Contextual Approach to Biblical Literature," 13.

events.[63] Some disabilities are viewed positively and some vocations are viewed negatively.[64] It is obvious that the more serious the disability, the worse the omen appears to be. It is also apparent that occasionally a situation of multiple disabled persons (the lame and deaf) in a city receives a positive omen while negative omens result from an overabundance of industrious and productive persons (salesmen and artists) being in the city. The *Šumma Izbu* series, tablet I, lines 56-66 reads,

> If a woman gives birth to a crippled boy[65]–the house of the man will suffer.
> If a woman gives birth to a crippled girl–the house of the man will be scattered; ditto (i.e., will suffer).
> If a woman gives birth to a male form[66]–good news will arrive in the land.
> If a woman gives birth to a female form–that house will get ahead; he (i.e., the father) will have good luck.
> If a woman gives birth to a blind child–the land will be disturbed; the house of the man will not prosper.
> If a woman gives birth to . . . .[67]–that city will experience destruction outside (?).
> If a woman gives birth to a cripple (lit. contorted one)–the land will be disturbed; the house of the man will be scattered.
> If a woman gives birth to a deaf child[68]–that house will prosper outside (of its city).
> If a woman gives birth to a . . . .[69]–that house will be brought to want through . . . .; that city will be laid waste.

---

63 Numerous liver models were discovered at Hazor, Megiddo, Ebla, and Ugarit.

64 Haas, "Soziale Randgruppen und Außenseiter altorientalischer Gesellschaften in Alten Orient," 43.

65 Scurlock and Andersen, *Diagnosis in Assyrian and Babylonian Medicine*, 406. Scurlock and Andersen reconstruct the first phrase of this and the next omen to read, "if a woman gives birth to a powerless (child) . . ." They suggest the powerlessness of the child indicates brain injury.

66 Scurlock and Andersen, *Diagnosis in Assyrian and Babylonian Medicine*, 391. Scurlock and Andersen reconstruct the first phrase of this and the next omen to read, "if a woman gives birth to a male/female creature . . ." They identify this as undeveloped fetal tissue. The *Šumma Izbu* contains numerous descriptions of abnormal births including a head (I 36), a hand (I 26, 37, 38), a foot (I 39), the likeness of a tortoise (I 17-18, 80), a gecko (I 77, 78), a goat horn (I 41, 42-43), matted hair (I 40, 46), clay (I 33-34, 45), snake (I 16, 79; IV 55), scepter (I 79), and a membrane of flesh full of blood (I 28, 29, 31-32, 35).

67 Scurlock and Andersen, *Diagnosis in Assyrian and Babylonian Medicine*, 406. Scurlock and Andersen reconstruct the first phrase of this and the next omen as "if a woman gives birth to an immobilized (child) . . ." They identify the immobility diagnose this immobility as resulting from brain damage or malfunction perhaps resulting from intrauterine infection or trauma.

68 Scurlock and Andersen, *Diagnosis in Assyrian and Babylonian Medicine*, 395. Scurlock and Andersen identify this as congenital deafness.

> If a woman gives birth to a . . . .[70]–its (the child's) father will die, and (there will be) dissension (among) his (the father's) children.
> If a woman gives birth to a . . . .–the owner of the house will bring . . . . tribute (The *Šumma Izbu* Series, Tablet I, lines 56-66).[71]

It is not only the oracle texts that show concern about the disabled. These oracles were widely disseminated throughout the ancient Near East and would have been consulted regularly. This may explain why in Babylonia it was considered a disaster for any household if a deformed child was born to it.[72] It is interesting to note that the attitude toward the disabled in this text would contrast significantly with the Enki Myth which shows that the Sumerians were more favorably inclined toward those with disabilities in that the Enki Myth envisions the disabled as productive members of society while the *Šumma Izbu* saw them as auguring ill for the household and community into which the disabled were born.

In Mesopotamia, prophets were those who habitually received and relayed divine messages.[73] Their low status in Mesopotamian society may suggest West Semitic origins rather than Babylonian or Assyrian.[74] It was the prophets' responsibility to discern what has angered the gods and to know what ritual procedure to follow in order to appease the gods. The concern for the issues related to the temple that might anger their god is recognized in a Hittite oracle (*KUB* 5.7) which reads,

OBVERSE

> We asked the temple officials and they said, "two deficient people came into the temple." Bird omina unfavorable.
> If it is only this, ditto. Bird omina, unfavorable. We asked them again and they said, "mutilated people walked about the temple." Bird omina, unfavorable. If it is only this, ditto. The first bird omen was favorable, but afterward it was unfavorable.
> Since deficient and mutilated people walked about (the temple), the Hittite Old Woman will perform a rite for the god in the manner to which she is accustomed.

---

69 Scurlock and Andersen, *Diagnosis in Assyrian and Babylonian Medicine*, 393. Scrulock and Andersen reconstruct this line as, "If a woman gives birth to a warty (child) . . ." They identify these skin lesions as a form of neurofibromatosis.

70 Scurlock and Andersen, *Diagnosis in Assyrian and Babylonian Medicine*, 404. Scurlock and Andersen reconstruct the reading of this and the next omen to read, "if a woman gives birth to a male/female (child with) short (limbs) . . ." They identify this as achondroplasia, or what is commonly referred to as a type of dwarfism.

71 Leichty, *The Omen Series Šumma Izbu*, 36f.

72 Marten Stol, *Epilepsy in Babylonia* (Cuneiform Monographs 2; Groningen: Styx, 1993), 146.

73 Hoffner, "Ancient Views of Prophecy and Fulfillment," 262.

74 Oppenheim, *Ancient Mesopotamia*, 221.

Bird omina, favorable (Hittite Omen Text Investigating the Anger of the Gods, lines 28-29, 36-37).[75]

The above text gives a clue as to the religious attitude toward the disabled. Their presence in the temple angered that temple's god. The Hittites believed that most evils were caused by divine displeasure.[76] It was important, then, to pay attention to omens in order to deal with offenses that could bring trouble from the gods. Divination was developed as a means of communicating with the gods so as to ascertain precisely why the gods were angry and to "bargain about required restitution."[77] Among the possible offences identified was that the temple precincts had been trespassed by *invalids* and *mutilated people.*[78] This indicates that the presence of such persons in the sacred precincts was considered a bad omen.[79] Another oracle (*KUB* 5.4 + *KUB* 18:53 and *KUB* 5.3 + *KUB* 18:52) is concerned with keeping the king healthy during the long Anatolian winter by discovering ahead of time any problems the gods may foresee and by discovering the correct method to rectify these concerns.[80]

Conclusions

Ancient Near Eastern prophetic literature also provides hints of the attitude of ancient people toward the disabled. The *Šumma Ālu* shows that the presence of disabled persons was considered a harbinger of ill. However, there is no hint that step were taken to rid the city of such negative births. This text implies that the disabled were integrated into society, were gainfully employed, and generally lived productive lives in the communities in which they lived. They were not isolated from society but were well integrated into it. This is reinforced by the fact that texts from Ebla, Ur, and Mari contain words connoting a disability were used for the proper names of individuals.

The *Šumma Izbu* series, however, does refer to disabled persons in negative terms, identifying specific birth defects as omen. However, there does not appear to be any discernible rationale for the positive or negative attitude of some birth categories. Some disabilities are viewed positively while some vocations are viewed negatively.

---

75 Albrecht Goetze, "Investigating the Anger of the Gods," in *Ancient Near Eastern Texts Relating to the Old Testament* (ed. James B. Pritchard; Princeton N.J.: Princeton University Press, 1969), 497.

76 Gary Beckman, "Excerpts from an Oracle Report," in *The Context of Scripture: Canonical Compositions from the Biblical World* (ed. William W. Hallo and K. Lawson Younger; New York: E.J. Brill, 1997), I:204.

77 Beckman, "Excerpts from an Oracle Report," I.204.

78 Sparks, *Ancient Texts for the Study of the Hebrew Bible*, 233.

79 Beckman, "Excerpts from an Oracle Report," in *Context of Scripture*, I:204-05.

80 Richard H. Beal, "Assuring the Safety of the King During the Winter," in *The Context of Scripture: Canonical Compositions from the Biblical World* (ed. William W. Hallo and K. Lawson Younger; New York: E.J. Brill, 1997), I:207-11.

Attitude toward the disabled in the *Šumma Izbu* series contrasts significantly with the Enki Myth which shows that the Sumerians were more favorably inclined toward the disabled. The Hittite oracle (*KUB* 5.7) also casts the disabled in a negative light, indicating that their presence in the temple had angered that temple's god. Conclusions regarding the conflicting and contradictory nature of these omen texts are difficult to draw. Preliminarily, though, the *Šumma Ālu* may indicate normal condition while the *Šumma Izbu* series may depict abnormal circumstances from which negative connotations are drawn by prophets. It could be that a moderate level of any one category is acceptable but too much may be construed as an omen of divine disfavor.

The material above may suggest more of a fear of the supernatural than a disdain for physically impaired persons. The existence of the disabled is explained as being the creation of the gods. There is evidence that they were incorporated into society and religious community rather than being expelled. Although there is the suggestion in medical omen texts and prophetic oracles that too many disabled persons in a city could result in a bad outcome, there is nothing to suggest they were disabled because of divine disfavor. In addition, there was nothing that suggests that ritually, the disabled were immutably impure. While no one could be ordained a priest who was physically disabled, the texts examined do not propose that it was due to divine sanction on them.

Legal Obligations

Defining and Identifying the Source of Justice in the Ancient Near East

An understanding of the world in which a disabled person lived begins with an examination of ancient legal collections. Could a disabled person expect justice or were they denied the rights of the average citizen? For that matter, could anyone expect justice? Did the disabled have rights? Were the disabled integrated into society or did they live on the fringes of society? Did the law allow the disabled to be financially independent or were they dependent on the charity of others? What, if anything, can be known about the quality of life the law would allow for a disabled person? An examination of ancient legal codes reveals the definition and the source of justice and suggests that for at least some of the questions posed above an affirmative answer can be given.

A just society was the concern of all ancient Near Eastern societies. It was (among other things) the obligation of rulers to wield their authority for the purpose of executing justice on behalf of the disadvantaged within their domain (see, for example, *Nabopolassar's royal autobiography*; *Aqhat* tablet I, col. 5, lines 4-8; *Law of Hammurabi* rev. XXV 7-13; 2 Sam 12:1-15; 14:1-24; 15:3-4;

23:3b-4; 1 Kgs 3:16-28; Ps 72:1-4).[81] Ancient Near Eastern kings held life in the balance.

Although numerous legal collections were known to have existed, nowhere in the ancient Near East was there a thoroughly worked out system of justice.[82] In the ancient Near East legal observance was not moral. Nor could it be suggested that the goal of justice was an egalitarian state or even democratic government. The underlying principle of justice appears to have been a reason of self-preservation, what was prosecutable in criminal proceedings, or what constitutes a reasonable monetary compensation. The two words most associated with justice were *kittu* and *mêšaru* (from *ešēru*). *Kittu* evokes something firm, unmovable, and solid,[83] like that in conformity with the law. *Mêšaru* can mean to make sure justice is done.[84] Bottéro and Van de Mieroop note that it can indicate a state of being or an activity, depending on its context.[85] As a state of being it reflects good order, but as an activity it suggests one's destiny. "It renders or attributes to each being and to each man that which comes to him by nature or by his place in society."[86] In this culture, one's destiny was what he deserved, i.e. justice. Only the king could undo this. Thus, *mêšaru*, in this context, was an exercise in equity by the king par excellence, indicating an act of grace[87] A related word often translated justice is *ešēru*.[88] This word, however, communicates the idea of a demonstration of justice, administrative orderliness conducive to productivity, or of maintaining the status quo.[89] This term also contributes to the sense that, contrary to modern belief, justice was an ongoing concern in the ancient world.[90] It seems, then, that the Mesopotamian concept of a just society was not derived from "rigid and mind-numbing legalism" but from a tendency or impulse that "confers

---

81 Weinfeld, *Social Justice in Ancient Israel and in the Ancient Near East*, 20f, 57f. See also Gileadi, *The Literary Message of Isaiah*, 119f.

82 Jean Bottéro and Marc Van de Mieroop, *Mesopotamia: Writing, Reasoning, and the Gods* (Chicago: University of Chicago Press, 1987), 179.

83 *kittu* means truth, justice, or correct procedure in all things contrary to falsehood (*CAD* 8:468-72).

84 *mīšaru* in Old Babylonian means to provide redress as a legislative act in order to remedy certain economic malfunctions (*CAD* 10 II:116-19). When *kittu* and *mīšaru* are used in tandem they mean "to protect justice, to provide the weak with legal protection" (*CAD* 8:470).

85 Bottéro and Van de Mieroop, *Mesopotamia: Writing, Reasoning, and the Gods*, 182.

86 Bottéro and Van de Mieroop, *Mesopotamia: Writing, Reasoning, and the Gods*, 182.

87 Bottéro and Van de Mieroop, *Mesopotamia: Writing, Reasoning, and the Gods*, 182.

88 *CAD* 4:352-63.

89 *CAD* 4:361.

90 "When Marduk gave me orders to provide justice for the people of the country;" "If this ruler has sound judgment and is able to provide justice for his country;" "May our lord grant us justice, the runaway evildoers should not prevail over us;" "Why is it that you do not have justice done to me when I come to you?" "look into his case and have justice done to him" (*CAD* 4:361).

upon it its obligatory strength."[91] Justice in the courts meant equity of plaintiff against a defendant at the bench, but this did not necessarily translate to equity in everyday life.

The social bias evident in ancient Eastern codes is believed to have resulted from the divine entrustment of the legal protection of the oppressed and disadvantaged to the king.[92] Evidence of this is found in the prevailing attitudes regarding the source of justice and the obligations of rulers to perform the will of the gods by ensuring a just society. For example, according to the Reforms of Uru-inimgina the ruler made a compact with his god to protect orphans and widows.[93] The royal inscription of *Azatiwata* (*KAI* #26 *AI* 11-13) dating from the late 8th to early 7th century B.C. also contains a theologically oriented statement of divine appointment to bring prosperity and to remove evils from the land.[94] Although *Azatiwata* only acted as regent and not king of the Danuna people, he wielded much power.[95] He also saw his appointment, commission, and success as being from the hand of his god, Tarhunza.[96] The *Panamuwa Inscription* (*KAI* # 215; *SSI* 2.76-86) dating from the 8th century, memorializes the just deeds of Panamuwa II upon his ascending the throne.[97] The first part of this inscription describes how the gods protected Panamuwa from difficulty. He was a much loved ruler.[98] Nabopolassar (626-605 B.C.) was the founder of the Neo-Babylonian Empire who destroyed the Assyrian capitol of Nineveh. During the Neo-Babylonian Period, scribes began to keep systematic and precise records of historical events.[99] Nabopolassar begins his text with an assertion of divine authorization and elevation to the throne, as other monarchs in the ancient Near East do. Later in the text he describes his life-long study of

---

91 Bottéro and Van de Mieroop, *Mesopotamia: Writing, Reasoning, and the Gods*, 182.

92 Hans Jochen Boecker, *Law and the Administration of Justice in the Old Testament and Ancient Near East* (Minneapolis: Augsburg, 1980), 54.

93 William W. Hallo, "Reforms of Uru-inimgina," in *The Context of Scripture: Monumental Inscriptions from the Biblical World* (ed. William W. Hallo and K. Lawson Younger; New York: E.J. Brill, 1997), II:408.

94 J.D. Hawkins, "Azatiwata," in *The Context of Scripture: Monumental Inscriptions from the Biblical World* (ed. William W. Hallo and K. Lawson Younger; New York: E.J. Brill, 1997), II:125. *Azatawata Inscription*, lines 1-13.

95 Hawkins, "Azatiwata," II:125, nf. 15.

96 Hawkins, "Azatiwata," II:125, fn. 10. Azatiwata calls himself "the Sun-blessed man, Tarhunsa's servant." Hawkins notes that Tarhunsa is the usual name of the Hittite-Luwian Storm-God, equated in the bilingual with the Phoenician, Ba'al.

97 K. Lawson Younger, "The Panamuwa Inscription," in *The Context of Scripture: Monumental Inscriptions from the Biblical World* (ed. William W. Hallo and K. Lawson Younger; New York: E.J. Brill, 1997), II:158-60; Josef Tropper, *Die Inschriften von Zincirli* (Münster, Westfalen: Ugarit-Verlag, 1993), 98-131. The *Panamuwa Inscription*, lines 6b-8.

98 Sparks, *Ancient Texts for the Study of the Hebrew Bible*, 470.

99 Albert K. Grayson, *Assyrian and Babylonian Chronicles*, Texts from Cuneiform Sources 5 (Locust Valley, N.Y.: Augustin, 1975), 87.

the gods' teaching, in particular to an understanding of justice and equity. It is this preoccupation which caused him to be elevated over the nation.[100] Weinfeld notes that justice would often take the form of prisoner releases, repatriated exiles, returned property, rebuilt temples, and tax relief.[101]

The obligation to administer justice was hallowed, being conferred upon the ruler by the gods. Justice, then, was a theological matter in that the king was placed on the throne by his god to represent the god and to carry out the god's will. Walton writes,

> These law collections are intended to testify to the gods how successful the king has been at establishing and maintaining justice in his kingdom. As such, the laws are designed to reflect the wisest and fairest decisions the king could imagine.[102]

It is clear, then, that a just society included a degree of protection of those who would be among the least represented class of that society, the underprivileged. Although disabled persons are not explicitly mentioned in these texts, neither are they explicitly excluded from the cause of justice. Nevertheless, the very nature of their life circumstances places them among those who would be particularly vulnerable and dependent on others for economic and physical security. The lack of an explicit mention of disabled persons in the texts cited above may simply be due to the fact that they are part of the prologue to a larger text, or it may imply that the disabled were considered a subcategory of the underprivileged, or that they are accepted among the general population and under the same obligations as them.

Justice and the Disabled

Justice for the disadvantaged was a divine mandate for a ruler. The question is whether or not physically disabled persons were placed within the category of the disadvantaged or were a category unto themselves. The following texts indicate that the codification of protections for victims of injuries that would result in permanent disabilities, albeit to a limited degree, were provided for by the ruler in the name of justice.

The *laws of Ur-Nammu* date from the late third/early second millennium. These laws come from Sumer and are the earliest law codes in existence. They are so named because they were written under the auspices of their patron.[103] When Ur-Nammu took the throne it was with the intent of bringing justice by

---

[100] Paul-Alain Beaulieu, "Nabopolassar's Restoration of Imgu-Enlil, the Inner Defensive Walls of Babylon," in *The Context of Scripture: Monumental Inscriptions from the Biblical World* (ed. William W. Hallo and K. Lawson Younger; New York: E.J. Brill, 1997), II:307. *Royal Autobiography of Nabopolassar*, i.1, 9-11.

[101] Weinfeld, *Social Justice in Ancient Israel and in the Ancient Near East*, 61.

[102] John H. Walton, Victor H. Matthews, and Mark W. Chavalas, *The IVP Bible Background Commentary: Old Testament* (Downers Grove, Ill.: InterVarsity, 2000), 24.

[103] Dale Patrick, *Old Testament Law* (Atlanta: John Knox Press, 1985), 29.

ending abuse and corruption, liberating the oppressed, standardizing weights and measures, opening transportation and trade, and establishing equality.[104]

King Shulgi (2094-2047 B.C.), son of Ur-Nammu, continued the tradition by introducing administrative and organizational reforms into the bureaucracy.[105] The laws of Ur-Nammu themselves deal primarily with family issues, bodily injury, slavery, false witness, and property. Temporary injuries that would heal and injuries that resulted in a permanent disfigurement are also addressed. Compensation for both permanent and temporary injuries came through the payment of a fine:

> If [a man] cuts off the foot of [another man with ...],
> he shall weigh and deliver 10 shekels of silver.
> If a man shatters the ... bone of another man with a club,
> he shall weigh and deliver 60 shekels of silver.
> If a man cuts off the nose of another man with ...,
> he shall weigh and deliver 40 shekels of silver.
> If [a man] cuts off [the ... of another man] with
> [..., he shall] weight and deliver [x shekels of silver].
> If [a man knocks out another man's] tooth with [...],
> he shall weigh and deliver 2 shekels of silver. (*Laws of Ur-Namma* 18-22).[106]

In the *Code of Hammurabi* (ca. 1750 B.C., Babylon), the moral authority for establishing justice is again divinely ordained. In the beginning of the second millennium, Hammurabi represents himself as being chosen by the gods to the kingship.[107] The prologue to the code stresses Hammurabi's role as ruler, guardian and protector of the weak and powerless, and care-giver for the cultic needs of the patron deities of the many cities in Hammurabi's realm.[108] The prologue of the *Code of Hammurabi* reads,

> At that time, the gods Anu and Enlil, for the enhancement of the well-being of the people, named me by my name: Hammurabi, the pious prince, who venerates the gods, to make justice prevail in the land, to abolish the wicked and the evil, to prevent the strong from oppressing the weak, to rise like the sun-god Shamash over all humankind, to illuminate the land (*Hammurabi Laws,* prologue, i.27-49).[109]

---

[104] Martha Roth, "The Laws of Ur-Namma (Ur-Nammu)," in *The Context of Scripture: Monumental Inscriptions from the Biblical World* (ed. William W. Hallo and K. Lawson Younger; New York: E.J. Brill, 1997), II:409, prologue, lines 1-180.

[105] Martha Roth, *Law Collections from Mesopotamia and Asia Minor* (Hittite laws translated by Harry A. Hoffner Jr.; Atlanta: Scholars, 1997), 13-14. This collection of statutes considers the free-born class of persons and his family.

[106] Roth, "The Laws of Ur-Namma," in *The Context of Scripture*, II:410.

[107] Roth, *Law Collections from Mesopotamia and Asia Minor*, 71.

[108] Roth, *Law Collections from Mesopotamia and Asia Minor*, 71.

[109] Roth, *Law Collections from Mesopotamia and Asia Minor*, 76-77.

Not only does this indicate that the king is divinely called to kingship, but also that he is deputized to administer a righteousness that is dispensed from the gods.

In ancient Near Eastern law a theological element can be discerned. Justice was a concern of the gods and the duty of their appointed rulers was to establish it among the people. The Mesopotamian sense of justice appears vague. Some attributed this to the fact that a completely worked out system of laws did not exist at that time.[110] It is true that none of the law collections from the ancient Near East are comprehensive or exhaustive. However, given the many other legal texts extant, it is clear that they had a sense of justice.[111] The legal system as it is revealed in the law collections is incomplete, although they may reflect royal intervention into the legal practices of the time.[112] The Mesopotamians had a strong sense of social obligation and justice.[113]

It is uncertain whether the following laws were codified because the king was rightly just, judges had a tendency to behave badly, or because they fell under the rubric of divinely oriented justice. It is reasonable to conclude that if not for all these reasons, then certainly the third. Law five of the Hammurabi Code reads,

> If a judge renders a judgment, gives a verdict, or deposits a sealed opinion, after which he reverses his judgment, they shall charge and convict that judge of having reversed the judgment which he rendered and he shall give twelve-fold the claim of that judgment; moreover, they shall unseat him from his judgeship in the assembly, and he shall never again sit in judgment with the judges (*Hammurabi Laws,* §5).[114]

The Code of Hammurabi provides the most far-reaching and exhaustive means of obtaining justice in the ancient world. The abstraction of justice in the Hammurabi's code makes provisions for the long-term care of married women who become incurably ill and are not able to care for the home or provide offspring. Although the husband of a chronically ill woman (one who contracts *la̓bum*) may marry another woman, he cannot divorce his ill wife or remove her from the home and he must support her for the rest of her life.[115] The infected woman may opt out of this arrangement and return to her father's house but

---

[110] Bottéro and Van de Mieroop, *Mesopotamia: Writing, Reasoning, and the Gods*, 179.

[111] Roth, *Law Collections from Mesopotamia and Asia Minor*, 4-5.

[112] Bottéro and Van de Mieroop, *Mesopotamia: Writing, Reasoning, and the Gods*, 180.

[113] Bottéro and Van de Mieroop, *Mesopotamia: Writing, Reasoning, and the Gods*, 182.

[114] Roth, *Law Collections from Mesopotamia and Asia Minor*, 82. Law 5 parallels Exodus 23:6-8, Leviticus 19:15, and Deuteronomy 16:19. It is an aspect of social justice that all judgments should be rendered fair.

[115] Scurlock and Andersen, *Diagnosis in Assyrian and Babylonian Medicine*, 18. Scurlock and Andersen suggest that this law may have been prompted by husbands who may have wanted to quarantine their infected wives so as to avoid the spread of their disease.

that is her choice to make. Evidently, the home was the central place for the care of the chronically ill. Law one hundred and forty-eight reads,

> If a man marries a woman, and later *lȧbum*[116]-disease seizes her and he decides to marry another woman, he may marry; he will not divorce his wife whom *lȧbum*-disease seized; she shall reside in quarters he constructs and he shall continue to support her as long as she lives (*Hammurabi Laws,* §148).[117]

The Code of Hammurabi also supplies protections by way of *Lex Talion*[118] or compensation to redress the matter of injuries sustained. The basis for legal formulation in the Code of Hammurabi is *lex talion* which was considered a legal advancement in that it limited and thereby reduced retributive behavior so that there was some equivalence rather than unrestricted revenge. The form of requital the injured could expect depended on their social status. Interestingly, serious injury or dismemberment in itself was not considered heinous. Nevertheless, the code demonstrates that injuries, permanent or otherwise, were not a part of the normal course of life but an intrusion in it. Therefore, it was not ignored. Justice called for restitution for the injury. Below are several examples of mandated reparations:

> §196-200- If an *awīlu* should blind the eye of another *awīlu*, they shall blind his eye. If he should break the bone of another *awīlu*, they shall break his bone. If he should blind he eye of a commoner or break the bone of a commoner, he shall weigh and deliver 60 shekels of silver. If he should blind the eye of an *awīlu*'s slave or break the bone of an *awīlu*'s slave, he shall weigh and deliver one-half of his value (in silver). If an *awīlu* should knock out the tooth of another *awīlu* of his own rank, they shall knock out his tooth.
> § 205: If an *awīlu*'s slave should strike the cheek of a member of the *awīlu*-class, they shall cut off his ear.
> §206: If a *awīlu* should strike another *awīlu* during a brawl and inflict upon him a wound, that *awīlu* shall swear "I did not strike intentionally," and he shall satisfy the physician (i.e., pay his fees).[119]

In §§196 and 198 the term *huppudu* (blind) is used.[120] Shalom Paul notes that law §§196-205 contain a series of laws where *talion* is required. *Talion* allowed

---

[116] Scurlock and Andersen, *Diagnosis in Assyrian and Babylonian Medicine*, 233. Scurlock and Andersen reconstruct this word to read *li'bu* a serious and infection skin disease, possibly leprosy.

[117] Roth, *Law Collections from Mesopotamia and Asia Minor*, 109.

[118] Shalom M. Paul, *Studies in the Book of the Covenant in the Light of Cuneiform and Biblical Law* (Leiden: Brill, 1970), 74. Raymond Westbrook, *Studies in Biblical and Cuneiform Law* (Cahiers de la Revue Biblique 26; Paris: J. Gabalda et Cie, Éditeurs, 1988), 39-41. *Talion* is defined as requiring a loss in kind to that which has been sustained to the extent and degree that it is possible (Exod 21:24-25; Lev 24:18-20; Deut 19:21). It is the law of equal retribution.

[119] Roth, *Law Collections from Mesopotamia and Asia Minor*, 121-22.

for an indemnification to serve as a substitute for a literal *talion* allowing the offender to compensate the victim who has sustained an injury.[121] The next law (§206) contains an provision whereby the offending party can swear that the injury was not intentionally inflicted. Paul points out that the distinguishing feature between laws §§196-205 where *talion* is prescribed and §206 where *talion* is not prescribed is intent.[122] Paul concludes that application of *talion* is directly related to whether injuries were intentionally inflicted or not.[123]

The Code of Hammurabi also contains laws that regulate the fair compensation of physicians for their services,

> §215: If a physician performs major surgery with a bronze lancet upon an *awīlu* and thus heals the *awīlu*, or opens an *awīlu*'s temple with a bronze lancet and thus heals the *awīlu*'s eye, he shall take 10 shekels of silver (as his fee).
> §216: If he (the patient) is a member of the commoner-class, he shall take 5 shekels of silver (as his fee).
> §217: If he (the patient) is an *awīlu*'s slave, the slave's master shall give the physician 2 shekels of silver.[124]

According to René Labat, these laws are based on the crude understanding of disease. One became ill either through his own fault for having committed sin, or as the victim of an evil spirit or god.[125] The word for physician is *asûm*.[126] The word for operation is *summam kabtam* (to make a deep incision).[127] The word *nakkaptum* is not an operation of the eye but one performed around the area of the eye.[128] Stol specifies further that *nakkaptum* refers to the temple rather than to the eye-socket.[129]

---

[120] *CAD* 6:240. There is uncertainty as to the extent of the injury. It may indicate anything from a simple eye injury to blinding.

[121] Paul, *Studies in the Book of the Covenant in the Light of Cuneiform and Biblical Law*, 67.

[122] Paul, *Studies in the Book of the Covenant in the Light of Cuneiform and Biblical Law*, 68. According to Paul, *talion* is applied to cases where injury is inflicted on another with malice aforethought and the intent to do harm and not in cases where harm is caused to another accidentally.

[123] Paul, *Studies in the Book of the Covenant in the Light of Cuneiform and Biblical Law*, 68.

[124] Roth, *Law Collections from Mesopotamia and Asia Minor*, 123.

[125] Labat, *Traité Akkadien de Diagnostics et Pronostics Médicaux I*, xxiii, line 1f.

[126] *CAD* 1b:344-47. This term refers to one who practices medicine. Its use in the Code of Hammurabi supports the fact that a medical tradition existed at this time and that illnesses were treated not merely as being caused by supernatural beings.

[127] *CAD* 1b:346, 5.

[128] Labat, "A propos de la chirurgie babylonienne," 211.

[129] Stol, "Old Babylonian Ophthalmology," 163.

Babylonian exorcists and physicians were known to observe the patient's pulse beating in the temple as a standard part of the diagnostic process.[130] A symptom called *mušarqidu* (standing up) of the vein was a serious condition related to eye disease.[131] Stol points out that the passage does not mean to prick (*takāpu*) but to hit (*mahāxum*) indicating that this text refers to the procedure of incising the temple to allow blood-letting.[132] Although Oppenheim and Reiner suggest that CH §§215-220 is concerned with scaring as a result of surgery,[133] the evidence suggests that a procedure involving a deep incision being made for blood-letting in a person's temple to relieve symptoms of distress is more likely.

The next series of laws in the Code of Hammurabi, however, address injury inflicted either intentionally or as a result of incompetence. In such cases malpractice cases, *talion* would be required:

> §218: If a physician performs major surgery with a bronze lancet upon an *awīlu* and thus causes the *awīlu*'s death, or opens an *awīlu*'s temple with a bronze lancet and thus blinds the *awīlu*'s eye, they shall cut off his hand.
>
> §219: If a physician performs major surgery with a bronze lancet upon a slave of a commoner and thus causes the slave's death, he shall replace the slave with a slave of comparable value.
>
> §220: If he opens his (the commoner's slave's) temple with a bronze lancet and thus blinds his eye, he shall weigh and deliver silver equal to half his value.
>
> §221: If a physician should set an *awīlu*'s broken bone or heal an injured muscle, the patient[134] shall give the physician 5 shekels of silver.
>
> §222: If he (the patient) is a member of the commoner-class, he shall give 3 shekels of silver.

---

[130] Stol, "Old Babylonian Ophthalmology," 163. Stol notes that even when the veins in the temple are not explicitly mentioned, texts simply speak of "the temple" when speaking of its pulsing. See also Labat, *Traité Akkadien de Diagnostics et Pronostics Médicaux I*, 40, lines 11-29; Idem, "A propos de la chirurgie babylonienne," 211.

[131] Stol, "Old Babylonian Ophthalmology," 164. See *BAM* 1 3 i 1-19 and par. 480 i 1-12; 3 iii 15, 20-27; *STT* 1 105 rev. 16, 18. The association between the veins in the temple and eye disease was not new in Babylonian medical tradition. Egyptians believed that blood was fed to the eye through four veins in the temple and that causes of eye disease were to be found there. For a fuller discussion of this see Monika Helbling, *Der altägyptische Augenkranke, sein Arzt und seine Götter,* Zürcher Medizingeschichtliche Abhandlungen, Neue Reihe 141 (Zurich: Juris, 1980).

[132] Stol, "Old Babylonian Ophthalmology," 164. See also *STT* 1 89:155f., ([s]a sag.k[i . . .*ša*] *na-šu-u* ina kin.tur zabar sìg-*m*[*a*]). Two Sumerograms used here are gír.zal (knife) and gi.dù.a (hitting).

[133] Oppenheim, *Ancient Mesopotamia*, 27-33; Reiner, "Medicine in Ancient Mesopotamia," 547f.

[134] Literally, "the owner of the injury."

§223: If he (the patient) is an *awīlu*'s slave, the slave's master shall give the physician 2 shekels of silver.
§224: If a veterinarian[135] performs major surgery upon an ox or a donkey and thus heals it, the owner of the ox or of the donkey shall give the physician as his fee one-sixth (of a shekel, i.e., 30 barleycorns) of silver.
§225: If he performs major surgery upon an ox or a donkey and thus causes its death, he shall give one-quarter(?) of its value to the owner of the ox or donkey.[136]

Laws 196-200 appear to identify injuries caused intentionally which are therefore subject to *talion*. §§196-99 contains the chapter on battery and assault. No general rule is established for addressing personal molestations.[137] Within this section is a list of tariffs for surgical care:

If a man has destroyed the eye of a member of the aristocracy . . .
If a man has destroyed the eye of a commoner . . .
If a man has destroyed the eye of a slave . . .

The only protection any one of the three social classes could expect for a personal injury was a tariff of one form or another.[138] The upper class citizens (aristocrats) could expect a *talion* to be applied while the other two classes received monetary compensation for their loss. For a Commoner the tariff was one *mina* (about 500 grams – still a large sum). The tariff for damaging a slave, however, would be half his value.[139] §215-17 contains a similar structure:

If a physician has operated successfully on the eye of a member of the aristocracy . . .
If a physician has operated successfully on the eye of a commoner . . .
If a physician has operated successfully on the eye of a slave . . .

---

[135] Veterinarian is derived from the phrase *asû alpim ulu imērim* which literally means a physician of an ox or donkey.
[136] Roth, *Law Collections from Mesopotamia and Asia Minor*, 123-24.
[137] G.R. Driver and John C. Miles, *The Babylonian Laws: Legal Commentary*, vol. 1 (Oxford: Clarendon, 1935), 406f.
[138] Driver and Miles, *The Babylonian Laws*, 407. This sort of compensatory status for permanent injury is common in Hittite and Assyrian Laws as well. See Hittite Laws 3-18 (Roth, *Law Collections from Mesopotamia and Asia Minor*, 217-20); Middle Assyrian Laws A 7-8 (Roth, *Law Collections from Mesopotamia and Asia Minor*, 156-57).
[139] Bottéro and Van de Mieroop, *Mesopotamia: Writing, Reasoning, and the Gods*, 176. Bottéro and Van de Mieroop suggest that the Code of Hammurabi cannot be considered an organized law code in that it does not address matters such as justice or criminal law, the codification of the social hierarchy or political obligations, administration, and fiscal policy. Those matters which were addressed were only done so in a cursory fashion. Rather, the "Code" is more to be viewed as containing verdicts of justice based on the best wisdom available at the time (see p.161f).

Just as in §196-99, each of these there is a recurring condition within the same framework of variations applied to various social classes.[140] A successful physician could charge set fees. If a cure was not effected, no penalty was assessed against the physician.[141] Although Finkelstein argues that this was not intended to be taken literally,[142] it appears that the penalty was intended to prevent a malpracticing surgeon from the future practice of his craft.[143] However, §218-20 stipulates that if a physician causes an aristocrat or a commoner to loose an eye or unintentionally die, he was subject to a mutilation of the hand (in this case the instrument of mutilation) for the satisfaction of the patient. In the case that the patient is a slave and he dies or is damaged, the physician restores a slave to the master or pays half the price of the slave to his owner respectively.[144]

§196 indicates that a ransom system operated in which one mina was paid for an injury which resulted in the loss of an eye. Westbrook points out that a ransom system also operated in Israel (*lex talionis*) in which monetary compensation serves as a substitute for the literal *talion* (Exod 21:18-19, 29-30; 1 Kgs 20:39).[145] He notes that a ransom rather than revenge was an advance in jurisprudence and was extended, in some cases, even to murder.[146]

The *Hittite Laws* date from the Old Kingdom to the end of the New Kingdom (17th to the 12th century).[147] These laws are therefore later than the Sumerian law collections of Ur-Nammu and Lipit-Ishtar, the Akkadian laws of Eshnunna, and the Code Hammurabi from Babylon but earlier than (or sometimes contemporary with) Hebrew law.[148] In this legal tradition there are about 200 casuistic laws arranged topically. The revisions of laws through the Old to Late Hittite Kingdom follow a pattern. Corporal punishments were replaced with lesser penalties (fines) and a general reduction of fines is also

---

140 Bottéro and Van de Mieroop, *Mesopotamia: Writing, Reasoning, and the Gods*, 176.

141 Driver and Miles, *The Babylonian Laws*, 417.

142 J.J. Finkelstein *The Ox That Gored* (Philadelphia: American Philosophical Society 1981), 20-25.

143 Driver and Miles, *The Babylonian Laws*, 413.

144 Driver and Miles, *The Babylonian Laws*, 418.

145 Westbrook, *Studies in Biblical and Cuneiform Law*, 45, 47-55. Westbrook builds on Cassuto's view (Umberto Cassuto, *A Commentary on the Book of Exodus* [trans. by Israel Abrahams; Jerusalem: Magnes, 1967], 276-77). He argues that one could seek revenge for a loss but that a judgment could be commuted to a pecuniary penalty.

146 Westbrook, *Studies in Biblical and Cuneiform Law*, 47-55. Middle Assyrian law Tablet B, law 2 reads: "If one among the brothers who have not divided (the inheritance) took a life, they shall give him up to the next-of-kin; if he chooses, the next-of-kin may put him to death, or if he chooses, he may be willing to settle [and] take his share." See also James B. Pritchard, ed., *Ancient Near Eastern Texts relating to the Old Testament* (3rd ed.; Princeton: Princeton University Press, 1969), 185.

147 Roth, *Law Collections from Mesopotamia and Asia Minor*, 214; Sparks, *Ancient Texts for the Study of the Hebrew Bible*, 426.

148 Roth, *Law Collections from Mesopotamia and Asia Minor*, 214.

evident (sometimes as a result of abolishing the palace's share of the fine or to the king's forfeiture of his share of the fine).[149] Revisions also indicate a greater specificity of infractions.[150] These laws are formulated as casuistic rather than apodictic injunction.[151] There are provisions for the compensation for injuries suffered to free person as well as for slaves:

> ¶7- If anyone blinds a free person or knocks out his tooth, they used to pay 40 shekels of silver. But now he shall pay 20 shekels of silver. He shall look to his house for it.
>
> > ¶V (= late version of ¶7) If anyone blinds a free man in a quarrel, he shall pay 40 shekels of silver. If it is an accident, he shall pay 20 shekels of silver.
>
> ¶8- If anyone blinds a male or female slave or knocks out his tooth, he shall pay 10 shekels of silver. He shall look to his house for it.
>
> > ¶VI (= late version of ¶8) If anyone blinds a male slave in a quarrel, he shall pay 20 shekels of silver. If it is an accident, he shall pay 10 shekels of silver.
> >
> > ¶VII (= late version of ¶¶7-8) If anyone knocks out a free man's tooth – if he knocks out 2 or 3 teeth – he shall pay 12 shekels of silver. If the injured party is a slave, his assailant shall pay 6 shekels of silver.[152]

11-12 read as follows,

> ¶11- If anyone breaks a free person's arm or leg, he shall pay 20 shekels of silver. He shall look to his house for it.
>
> > ¶X (= late version of ¶11) If anyone breaks a free man's arm or leg, if the injured man is permanently handicapped(?), he shall pay him 20 shekels of silver. If he is not permanently handicapped(?), he shall pay him 10 shekels of silver.
>
> ¶12- If anyone breaks a male or female slave's arm or leg, he shall pay 10 shekels of silver. He shall look to his house for it.
>
> > ¶XI (= late version of ¶12) If anyone breaks a slave's arm or leg, if he is permanently disabled (?), he shall pay him 10 shekels of silver. If he is not permanently disabled (?), he shall pay him 5 shekels of silver.[153]

These laws make class distinctions and, in their revisions, also make distinctions between permanent and temporary handicapping. It is reasonable to conclude that injuries to slaves would be compensated for because they, like domestic animals, were essential to economic stability. The rationale for compensation to free persons may have more to do with their social status than with a concern for their loss of status, ability to accumulate wealth, or long-term care and rehabilitation.

---

[149] Roth, *Law Collections from Mesopotamia and Asia Minor*, 214.
[150] Roth, *Law Collections from Mesopotamia and Asia Minor*, 214-15.
[151] Roth, *Law Collections from Mesopotamia and Asia Minor*, 216.
[152] Roth, *Law Collections from Mesopotamia and Asia Minor*, 218.
[153] Roth, *Law Collections from Mesopotamia and Asia Minor*, 219.

Middle Assyrian laws (ca. 1076 B.C., Assur) also address matters pertaining to human dismemberment. These laws appear to overlap one another.[154] In most of these laws women are figured as victims.[155] These laws pertain to persons of the free-born and slave classes.[156] As in the legal collections the *talion* is usually employed for reparation of personal injuries.[157] Here is an example from Assyrian law:

> If a woman should crush a man's testicle during a quarrel, they shall cut off one of her fingers. And even if the physician should bandage it, but the second testicle then becomes infected (?) along with it and becomes ..., or if she should crush the second testicle during the quarrel – they shall gouge out both her ...s (*Middle Assyrian law,* A8).

Conclusions

Ancient law collections indicate that a justice was the concern of all ancient Near Eastern societies and rulers were obligated to wield their authority for the purpose of executing justice on behalf of the disadvantaged (*Nabopolassar's royal autobiography*; *Aqhat* tablet I, col. 5, lines 4-8; *Law of Hammurabi* rev. XXV 7-13; The Reforms of Uru-inimgina; the royal inscription of *Azatiwata*; the *Panamuwa Inscription*; 2 Sam 12:1-15; 14:1-24; 15:3-4; 23:3b-4; 1 Kgs 3:16-28; Ps 72:1-4). The king was divinely entrusted with the legal protection of the oppressed and disadvantaged. It is clear from ancient law collections that a just society included a degree of protection of those who would be among the least represented class of society, the underprivileged. The lack of an explicit mention of disabled persons in these texts may simply be due to the fact that they are part of the prologue to a larger text, or it may imply that the disabled were considered a subcategory of the underprivileged, or that they are accepted among the general population and under the same obligations as them. This ambiguity remains to be clarified.

Each of the law collections examined above refer to persons who are disabled intentionally, either permanently or temporarily. These codes address injuries sustained through assault and battery or inflicted on a patient by a physician either intentionally or as a result of malpractice. The earliest law collections from Sumer (The *Laws of Ur-Nammu*) suggest that the physically disabled were compensated for their injuries by the one who inflicted the injury. The *Code of Hammurabi,* which provides the most far-reaching and exhaustive means of obtaining justice in the ancient world, also supplies protection and compensation for sustained injuries. Like the Sumerian and Mesopotamian law collections, *Hittite Laws* and *Middle Assyrian Laws* make

[154] Roth, *Law Collections from Mesopotamia and Asia Minor*, 153.
[155] Roth, *Law Collections from Mesopotamia and Asia Minor*, 153.
[156] Roth, *Law Collections from Mesopotamia and Asia Minor*, 154.
[157] Westbrook, *Studies in Biblical and Cuneiform Law*, 45.

distinctions between permanent and temporary handicapping, providing compensation appropriate to each case. Although recompense for injuries depended on one's social status, the codes demonstrate that injuries, permanent or otherwise, were not considered a part of the normal course of life and were therefore not ignored.

The law codes of the ancient Near East sought to secure social order. They were not intended to communicate the value and dignity of life. There is nothing in the legal codes examined which suggests that disabled persons were integrated into their respective societies with their status being secured and protected by legal rights or that they were spurned by society and denied rights. This suggests that ancient governments were neutral as to their status. This also suggests that the disabled may have enjoyed equal protection under the law. One might note the multiple cases where the disability is caused by another. There are no references to congenital conditions in early legal documents. This suggests either infanticide or that they were disregarded. However, if infanticide was practiced, this would likely have been codified as well.

Certainly, the legal codes of the day would have impacted the treatment of disabled persons in one way or another. With that in mind, we turn our attention to the social structure of the ancient world for understanding the circumstance one with disabilities would face in everyday life.

The Relationship of Physical Disabilities to the Priesthood

There is broad representation of priestly physical perfection throughout the ancient Near East. The priests (*nišakku* or *pašīšu*) of Enlil had a requirement of physical perfection like that of Hebrew priests (Lev 21:16-23).[158] In this priestly document, the father, Enmeduranki, was taught oil and liver divination and the holding of a cedar-rod by Šamaš and Adad (lines 7-9).[159] In lines 22b-27, he is faithfully passing on this knowledge to his son.[160] Line 11 mentions only three cities, implying that "only the priests of these cities are really competent to use these kinds of divination."[161] The document reads, in part,

> 19. The learned savant, who guards the secrets of the great gods 20-21. will bind his son whom he loves with an oath before Šamaš and Adad by tablet and stylus and 22. will instruct him. When a diviner, 23. an expert in oil, of abiding descent, offspring of Enmeduranki, king of Sippar, 24. who set up the pure bowl and held

---

[158] Wilfred G. Lambert, "Enmeduranki and Related Matters," *Journal of Cuneiform Studies* 21 (1967): 127. Lamberts notes that this tradition parallels, to some degree, the Mishnaic tractate *Aboth* in which Moses passes on the oral tradition he received on Sinai to Joshua.

[159] Lambert, "Enmeduranki and Related Matters," 127.

[160] Lambert, "Enmeduranki and Related Matters," 127.

[161] Lambert, "Enmeduranki and Related Matters," 127. Lambert notes that these three cities were exempt from taxation (*BWL* 110 ff.). And Nabopolassar used the labor of the people of these cities while in the rebuilding of the temple of Babylon.

> the cedar-(rod), 25. a benediction priest of the king, a long-haired priest of Šamaš, 26. as fashioned by Ninhursagga, 27. begotten by *nišakku*-priest of pure descent: 28. if he is without blemish in body and limbs 29. he may approach the presence of Šamaš and Adad where liver inspection and oracle (take place).[162]

As lines 28-29 shows, the *bārû* (diviner) must be physically perfect[163] in his appearance and limbs if he is to enter the presence of the gods.[164] The text indicates that physical integrity was the concern of not only the biblical Levitical priesthood. Concerning the consecration of priests, *nišakku* and *pašíšu* reads,

> I 11f.) From the (hair) part of his head to his fingertips (respectively, toe tips) you shall inspect him.
> I 13f.) When your body is so pure it is as a statue of gold.
> I 15f.) And the fear of god and humility in your body is present.
> I 17f.) So there he will enter the Temple of Enlil and Ninlil.
> I 19f.) Ekur, the great mountain, there a *liqûtu* (an adopter) shall not enter, so that the temple will not be destroyed.
> I 21f.) When an *liqûtu* arrives, he will not descend from the priests.
> I 23f.) An initiate who is of the profession of the temple can enter but he cannot speak.
> I 25f.) This one can . . . but (who) cannot speak, thus will be stuck in a pit.
> I 27f.) When the *liqûtu* of different gods arrive, he will not be examined.
> I 29f.) One who is blood-stained, who is a thief, or a robber is caught.
> I 31f.) A convict, who has been in the stocks or lashed.
> I 33f.) ... with a wrecked eye ...
> I 35.) ...
> I 37f.) Who complains of a kidney stone ...
> I 39f.) ...
> I 41f.) He who is afflicted with a mole/birthmark, with an irregular face, this one [...].
> I 43f.) He may not enter the temple of Enlil and Ninlil, the temple is denied him (Lines 11-43).[165]

---

[162] Lambert, "Enmeduranki and Related Matters," 132.

[163] *CAD* 17, part 3:220-26. The word used here is *šuklulu*. Conceptually, it carries the main idea of Levitical laws concerning priestly qualifications for service.

[164] Van der Toorn, *Sin and Sanction in Israel and Mesopotamia*, 29; Lambert, "Enmeduranki and Related Matters," 127. Van der Toorn notes that a variety of defects similar to those cataloged in Leviticus 21 are enumerated in Babylonian texts. Deformities which disqualify a priest from the place of divine judgment included *naqtu ēnā* (crossed-eyes), *heppu šinnā* (chipped teeth), *ša ubāni nagpi* (bruised fingers), *saharšubbê* (leprosy), and *pilpilānu* (homosexuality or transvestitism) would all stigmatize a candidate for ordination.

[165] Rykle Borger, "Die Weihe Eines Enlil-Priesters," *Bibliotheca Orientalis* 30 (1973): 172.

This text deals with the consecration of priests to the temple of Enlil and Ninlil, and indicates that certain physical imperfections such as a face disfigured with mutilated eyes, irregular features, or branding were sufficient grounds for disqualifying one from the priesthood.[166]

The concern for the body of a priest in Leviticus 21 parallels texts dealing with the consecration of the priests of Enlil.[167] Although he offers no grounds for his assertion, Grünwaldt claims that these proscriptions are based on the tradition that priests must be morally pure in order to perform their duties and that disease and impurity are associated with sin and death.[168] However, in the Levitical system a priest, although having a blemished body, may enter the sanctuary precincts where the priestly portion was brought and partake of it there.[169] One unsanctified as a priest could neither enter the area nor eat the portion. The only distinction noticed is that a physically defective priest was permanently prohibited from entering the veil to officiate as a priest (Lev 21:16-23).[170] It is unlikely, therefore, that morality is associated with defect either with the priests of Enlil or the priests of Yahweh.

Conclusions

There is broad representation of priestly physical perfection throughout the ancient Near East. The priests of Enlil had a requirement of physical perfection like that of Hebrew priests (Lev 21:16-23). These texts deal with the consecration of priests to the temple of Enlil and Ninlil, and indicate that physical imperfections such as facial disfigurement such as mutilated eyes, irregular features, or branding were sufficient grounds for disqualifying one from the priesthood. Evidence indicates that there was sensitivity to the supernatural with respect to negative and positive circumstances of life in every society of the ancient world.

Social Attitudes

The Disabled in Wisdom Literature

In an effort to understand the nature of the community and the social construct within which the disabled lived it is necessary to examine a broad range of literature for clues regarding social attitudes toward the disabled. These

---

166 Borger, "Die Weihe Eines Enlil-Priesters," 164.

167 Klaus Grünwaldt, *Das Heiligkeitsgesetz Leviticus 17-26: Ursprüngliche Gestalt, Tradition und Theologie* (Beihefte der Zeitschrift für die alttestamentliche Wissenschaft 271; Berlin: De Gruyter, 1999), 268-69; Van der Toorn, *Sin and Sanction in Israel and Mesopotamia*, 29-30.

168 Grünwaldt, *Das Heiligkeitsgesetz Leviticus 17-26*, 69, 269.

169 Jacob Milgrom, *Studies in Levitical Terminology* (Berkeley: University of California, 1970, 40.

170 Milgrom, *Studies in Levitical Terminology*, 40.

attitudes toward the disabled in the ancient world are expressly in the wisdom literature, as for example in the *Instruction of Amenemope* (c. 1300-600 B.C.).[171]

The book's worth is in "its quality of inwardness."[172] The teaching this book contains is on the practice of personal morality in society. Like other literature of its time, the *Instruction of Amenemope* deals with the subject of the ideal man, but it is distinct from other texts in that it redefines the ideal man by shifting the focus from action and success to contemplation and endurance.[173] The ideal man was he who controlled himself especially in the time of *Amenemope*. Clearly, in Egyptian wisdom literature, the disadvantaged included the disabled,

> You will find my words a storehouse for life,
> your being will prosper upon earth.
> Beware of robbing a wretch,
> of attacking a cripple (4:1-5).[174]

And further on it reads,

> Do not laugh at a blind man,
> nor tease a dwarf
> nor cause hardship for the lame.
> Don't tease a man who is in the hand of god,
> nor be angry with him for his failings.
> Man is clay and straw,
> the god is his builder (24:8-12).[175]

Although the *Instruction of Amenemope* makes broad use of similes and metaphors, it is most probable that the passages cited above depict the ideal man. According to Plumley, the message of this text is that morality matters and the source of true morality is religion.[176] He sees this as having a parallel

---

[171] J.M. Plumley, "The Teaching of Amenemope," in *Documents from Old Testament Times* (ed. D. Winton Thomas; London: Nelson, 1958), 173; Miriam Lichtheim, "The Instruction of Amenemope," in *The Context of Scripture: Canonical Compositions from the Biblical World* (ed. William W. Hallo and K. Lawson Younger; New York: E.J. Brill, 1997), I:116; Idem, *Ancient Egyptian Literature, vol. II: The New Kingdom* (Berkeley: University of California Press, 1976), 146. There is some question regarding the dating of this text in this book. Lichtheim suggests its date should be assigned to the Ramesside period.

[172] Miram Lichtheim, *Ancient Egyptian Literature, vol. II: The New Kingdom* (Berkeley: University of California Press, 1976), 146.

[173] Lichtheim, *Ancient Egyptian Literature*, II.146. The ideal man is modest, self-controlled, kind toward people, and humble before his God.

[174] Lichtheim, "The Instruction of Amenemope," in *Context of Scripture*, I:117.

[175] Lichtheim, "The Instruction of Amenemope," I:121.

[176] Plumley, "The Teaching of Amenemope," 173.

with Leviticus 19:14 and Deuteronomy 27:18.[177] Grünwaldt also sees a parallel. He writes,

> Die Verbote, Taube zu verfluchen und Blinden ein Hindernis in den Weg zu legen (V.14a), haben darin ihre Gemeinsamkeit, daß es jeweils um den Schutz für Wehrlose geht. Der Taube kann den Fluch nicht erwidern, der Blinde das Hindernis nicht aus dem Weg räumen. Ein Schutzgebot für den Blinden steht im Fluchdekalog (Dtn 27,18), dessen Alter aber umstritten ist. Eine entfernte Parallele zu Lev 19,14 ist in der Weisheit des *Amenemope* zu finden.[178]

Grünwaldt goes on to discuss this parallel by noting that both Leviticus and *Amenemope* touch on the religious rationale for anti-discrimination laws. "A handicapped person is in the hand of God, this handicap returns on God without reflection on why he is handicapped."[179] Since, however, the *Instruction of Amenemope* is wisdom literature, it would make more sense to view it as falling under the category of ethical conduct which was also encouraged by Hebrew wisdom literature (especially Job and Proverbs).

Pictured on the wall of the tomb of Paatenemheb from Saqqara, dating from the reign of Amenhotep IV (1352-1336 B.C.), is a group of four musicians led by a blind harpist.[180] Above their heads is an incomplete copy of a funerary hymn from the tomb of Intef in which the phrase "make holiday" appears.[181] It is known that in ancient Egypt funerary banquets were held in cemeteries on feast days.[182] The phrase "make holiday" had multiple meanings being employed in daily life and used with reference to death and the afterlife.[183] The scene described above suggests that the blind were utilized in such ceremonies to either offer laments at burial ceremonies or to raise the spirits of celebrants at funerary banquets.

Disability in Ugaritic Epic Literature and Hurrian Literature

In Ugaritic epic literature there is limited information relating to the matter of physical perfection but even this little bit does not indicate that physical imperfection was socially stigmatizing. For example, the *Kirta* Epic (*CTA* 14-16; *KTU* 1.14) describes a king who suffered in a way paralleling Job.[184] The

---

[177] Plumley, "The Teaching of Amenemope," 173.
[178] Grünwaldt, *Das Heiligkeitsgesetz Leviticus 17-26*, 235.
[179] Grünwaldt, *Das Heiligkeitsgesetz Leviticus 17-26*, 235.
[180] Miram Lichtheim, *Ancient Egyptian Literature, vol. I: The Old And Middle Kingdoms* (Berkeley: University of California Press, 1973-80), 195.
[181] Lichtheim, *Ancient Egyptian Literature*, I:194-95.
[182] Lichtheim, *Ancient Egyptian Literature*, I;195.
[183] Lichtheim, *Ancient Egyptian Literature*, I.195. At funerary banquets the various meanings of this phrase blended together.
[184] Michael David Coogan, *Stories from Ancient Canaan* (Philadelphia: Westminster Press, 1978), 52. The description of his suffering is found in the second and third tablet.

theme of the story is the survival of Kirta's dynasty after the loss of his wife and family as a result of divorce, disease, and warfare.[185] As the story unfolds, Kirta is approached by El in a dream who assures him a new wife and heir (tablet I, col. 1, line 26- col. 3, line 153). Kirta organizes his army and begins a campaign to seize the daughter of King Pabil of Udum for his wife (tablet 1, col. 3, line 154 to the end of the tablet). Along the way he makes a vow with Asherah to give her riches if she would grant him success in his campaign (tablet I, col. 4, lines 198-204). Kirta is successful and is blessed by El with a new family as promised (tablet 2, col. 2, line 1- col. 3, line 25). In the process he neglects the vow made to Asherah (tablet 2, col. 3, lines 25-29?). This sets up the debilitating disease that befalls Kirta (tablet 2, col 4, line 14 to the end of the tablet).[186] While still ill, Kirta's son Yassib seeks to usurp Kirta, charging Kirta with neglecting the duties as king by not bringing justice to his people (tablet 3 col. 6, lines 25-53):

> Listen, noble Kirta,
> listen closely and tend [(your) ear:
> When raiders] led (raids),
> and creditors [detain (debtors)],
> You let your hands fall slack:
> you do not judge the widow's case,
> you do not make a decision regarding the oppressed.
> Illness has become as it were (your) bedfellow,
> sickness (your) constant companion in bed.
> So descend from your kingship, I will reign,
> from your dominion, I, yes I, will sit (on your throne) (*Kirta* Tablet III, col. 6, lines 33-39).[187]

Again, it must be pointed out, an illness is being described rather than a physical disability. In this case, however, Asherah decreed a terminal illness, and it would have been terminal were it not for the intercession of El at the council of the gods. The disease, in the meantime, was disabling. It precluded Kirta from performing his duties as king. Nevertheless, while ill unto death, Kirta remained on the throne.

Earlier in the epic, the army is mustered to confront a military danger. A line from the epic indicates that disabled received some kind of attention in order to cope with life. *Kirta* is ordered by his father *Ilu* to muster the military to have it at his disposal (*Kirta* tablet 1 col. 2 lines 85-87)[188] and to allow no exceptions

---

[185] Coogan, *Stories from Ancient Canaan*, 52.
[186] Coogan, *Stories from Ancient Canaan*, 53.
[187] Dennis Pardee, "The Kirta Epic," in *The Context of Scripture: Canonical Compositions from the Biblical World* (ed. William W. Hallo and K. Lawson Younger; New York: E.J. Brill, 1997), I:342.
[188] Pardee, "The Kirta Epic," I:334.

for military service. *Kirta* complies with the call, mustering the army.[189] This muster was to have no exceptions. The blind, who had guides to lead them would need to find their own way around in times of military need, for the guides would have been mustered into the military. The following text describes the departure of these conscripts for military service:

> The only (son) shut up his house, the widow hired someone (to go). *The invalid took up his bed, the blind man groped his way along.* The newly-wed conducted (his bride), entrusted his wife to someone else, his beloved to someone unrelated (*Kirta*, tablet 1 col. 2, lines 92-103, *italics added*).[190]

Pardee notes the dispute regarding the meaning of *mzl ymzl.*[191] Some suggest it means that the blind man hires an able-bodied person to go in his place while others suggest it means the invalid and blind are actually conscripted into the army. The latter suggestion seems untenable. All able-bodied persons would be inducted anyway, and by its nature an army requires a level of physical skill that the disabled could not provide. Whichever interpretation one takes, the point is still that there were disabled in Ugarit and these do not appear to have been ostracized from society. The italicized lines above suggest that some form of assistance for the lame and guides for the visually impaired was utilized suggesting that these disabled were not ostracized. The text does not specify if these services were sponsored by the government, volunteers, able-bodied family members, or others. The context, though, implies that these guides would normally have been exempt from military service. Whatever the situation, the text does show, at least, that the government approved of their task of guiding the blind. In addition, this implies that the physically disabled were not ostracized from mainstream society.

The *Hurrian Myth Cycle* depicts the conflict between the gods Kumarbi (a netherworld deity) and Tessub (a storm god). Kumarbi attempts to supplant Tessub as king of the gods. Kumarbi tries, unsuccessfully, to seduce Ullikummi (one of the creatures brought forth from this conflict) for the task of supplanting Tessub. Ullikummi is portrayed as blind and deaf and so not able to respond to the seduction. Nothing derogatory toward the disabled Ullikummi is implied in the song. The song reads, in part,

> Sauska kept on singing and put on herself a seashell and a pebble (as adornment). A great wave (?) <arose> out of the sea. The great wave (?) said to Sauska, "For whose benefit are you singing? For whose benefit are you filling your mouth with wind? The man (meaning Ullikummi) is deaf; he can[not] hear. He is blind in his eyes; he cannot see. He has not compassion. So go away, Sauska, and find your

---

[189] *Kirta* tablet I, col. 4, lines 154-193.
[190] Pardee, "The Kirta Epic," I:334.
[191] Pardee, "The Kirta Epic," I:334, n.23.

> brother before he (Ullikummi) becomes really valiant, before the skull of his head becomes really terrifying (*The Song of Ullikummi*, Tablet 2, line 36).[192]

In this text, Ullikummi is cast in a positive light in that he could not be seduced by Sauska because he was visually and hearing impaired.

Conclusions

An examination of ancient Near Eastern wisdom literature indicates provides several important clues as to social attitudes in the ancient world toward the disabled. The *Instruction of Amenemope* presents the ideal man in ancient Egyptian society, focusing on true morality and ethical conduct. Paintings on the wall of the tomb of Paatenemheb at Saqqara show a group of musicians led by a blind harpist, suggesting that the blind participated in funerary banquets.

Ugaritic epic literature does not contain much information concerning human physicality but even this does not suggest that physical imperfection was socially stigmatizing. In the *Kirta* epic, *Kirta* become debilitated to the extent that he cannot perform his royal duties. While ill, *Kirta* remained on the throne, suggesting his debilitation did not automatically trigger his removal from the throne. Prior to this, *Kirta* was required to muster his army for battle to confront a military danger. This conscription was such that it allowed for no exceptions so that even those who aided the lame and the blind were summoned. It is uncertain whether these aides were hired, provided, or family. The point is that the disabled were not ostracized from Ugarit society. The text also implies that these guides would normally have been exempt from military service. Nevertheless, it appears that services of some sort were available providing assistance to the lame and guides for the visually impaired.

The *Hurrian Myth Cycle* too contains an episode involving a disabled person. This episode depicts the seduction of Ullikummi who is blind and deaf. Hence, he does not respond to the seduction. Nothing derogatory toward Ullikummi is implied in the song. Ullikummi is cast in a positive light in that he could not be seduced. It is evident from Egyptian wisdom literature, Hittite treaties, and Ugaritic epic literature that a physical defect was not socially stigmatizing. To the contrary, Egyptian wisdom literature affirms the morals of the ideal man as being respectful toward those with physical disabilities.

The Medical Tradition in the Ancient Near East

The medical arts are known to have been practiced in the ancient Near East since the third millennium B.C. Some of the earliest medical texts known to exist include over half the original 3,000 entries in the diagnostic/prognostic handbook and over 900 tablets or tablet fragments containing instructions for

---

[192] Harry A. Hoffner, "The Kumarbi Cycle: Song of Ullikimmi," in *Hittite Myths* (Atlanta: Scholars Press, 1990), 54.

the preparation of treatments.[193] A therapeutic manual from Sumer (2112-2004 B.C.) is believed to be the oldest medical text extant. This manual continues a long medical tradition that may date as early as the mid-fourth millennium B.C.[194] Medical texts dating from the Old Babylonian period (1894-1595 B.C.) include descriptions of signs and symptoms, diagnoses, and instructions for the preparation and administration of medication.[195] By the Middle Assyrian and Middle Babylonian periods (1430-1050 B.C.) medical knowledge increased to the point where a separate diagnostic and prognostic handbook was prepared.[196] It was at this same time, according to Scurlock and Andersen, that labors were divided between two separate healing experts; the *āšipu*, for whom the handbook was intended, and the *asû* "who seemed to have played the role of a pharmacist."[197] It appears that medical services were readily available to all in need of them.[198]

Although the medical tradition in the ancient Near East was not as primitive as Herodotus claimed,[199] many of its practices were based on superstitious beliefs.[200] In early studies of ancient Near Eastern texts, it was believed that diseases were contracted as a result of offending one or more of the multiple gods or demons believed to exist.[201] "For the ancient Mesopotamians, 'sins' included crimes, moral offenses, errors and omissions in ritual performance, and unintentional breaking of taboos."[202] As to the significance of this on permanent physical disabilities, very little has been uncovered.

Modern research, however, has discredited the belief that in the ancient Near East, *all* illnesses were considered the result of witchcraft, demonic activity, or divine displeasure.[203] The *āšipu* was always open to the possibility that a

---

193 Scurlock and Andersen, *Diagnosis in Assyrian and Babylonian Medicine*, 1. This manual contains instructions for the treatment of patients, they do not contain diagnosis. It originally may have contained descriptions and diagnosis and these may have been lost.

194 Scurlock and Andersen, *Diagnosis in Assyrian and Babylonian Medicine*, 2.

195 Scurlock and Andersen, *Diagnosis in Assyrian and Babylonian Medicine*, 6.

196 Scurlock and Andersen, *Diagnosis in Assyrian and Babylonian Medicine*, 6.

197 Scurlock and Andersen, *Diagnosis in Assyrian and Babylonian Medicine*, 6-7.

198 Karen Rhea Nemet-Nejat, *Daily Life in Ancient Mesopotamia* (Westport, Conn.: Greenwood, 1998), 77.

199 Herodotus, *The History* (translated by David Grene; Chicago: University of Chicago Press, 1988), I.197 and II.84; H.W.F. Saggs, *The Greatness That Was Babylon: A Sketch of the Ancient Civilization of the Tigris-Euphrates Valley* (New York: New American Library, 1962), 460. Herodotus describes numerous medical procedures and their availability to patients living in ancient Mesopotamia.

200 Nemet-Nejat, *Daily Life in Ancient Mesopotamia*, 77.

201 Nemet-Nejat, *Daily Life in Ancient Mesopotamia*, 78.

202 Nemet-Nejat, *Daily Life in Ancient Mesopotamia*, 77-78.

203 Oppenheim, *Ancient Mesopotamia*, 289-305; Reiner, "Medicine in Ancient Mesopotamia," 545f.

patient's symptoms were due to an invisible external force.[204] Karel van der Toorn points out that a prolonged disease could be viewed as a sign of divine admonition, but was more generally believed to simply be according to the will of the gods.[205] He notes that in "many apodoses of the diagnostic vade-mecum interpret the observable symptoms as signs of the 'hand' of a god, named or unnamed."[206] The word *qātu* means "hand."[207] When used with a deity's personal name it is often automatically believed to contain maleficent implications. It was believed to express a calamity in the form of a specific illness. The phrase *qāt Ištar* (hand of Ishtar), for example, formed the name of an illness inflicted by the hand of a god provoked by an act of sin by the afflicted one.[208] Often the calamity is punishment inflicted on the sufferer. There is no doubt as to the fact that *qāt* DN establishes a relationship between the observed symptom and supernatural involvement.[209] Van der Toorn, however, has convincingly argued that *qātu* (plus that which signifies a deity's name) does not automatically indicate sin on the part of the afflicted but is merely meant to "localize the source of the signs rather than to give a definite answer concerning the nature and cause of the disease."[210] This is not to say, however, that there was no involvement by the gods. Hector Avalos likewise points out that it was generally understood that not all adverse conditions (especially illnesses) were punitive in nature. Avalos notes the belief among Mesopotamians that, "most illnesses were divine instruments or messages of which punishment was one, though not the only, sub-category or motive."[211] Magic is frequently identified as the source of illness in Mesopotamian literature.[212] Knowing the sender of the illness was key to its successful treatment.[213]

---

[204] Scurlock and Andersen, *Diagnosis in Assyrian and Babylonian Medicine*, 11. Scurlock and Andersen point out that the *āšipu* would almost certainly have realized that it was a possibility that the patient's body was malfunctioning on its own and that this would not have conflicted with their belief in malevolent spirits as causers of disease. Consequently, diagnoses and treatment of a disease would have been based on analysis of prior observation rather that supernatural tendencies.

[205] Van der Toorn, *Sin and Sanction in Israel and Mesopotamia*, 72-80.

[206] Van der Toorn, *Sin and Sanction*, 78.

[207] *CAD* 13:183-98.

[208] *CAD* 13:186.

[209] Van der Toorn, *Sin and Sanction*, 79.

[210] Van der Toorn, *Sin and Sanction*, 78. He refers to the use of *qātu* (DN) in *KTS* 24 which indicates that illness was not always prompted by the patient's behavior.

[211] Avalos, *Illness and Healthcare in the Ancient Near East*, 134. Avalos notes that sometimes the illness was an instrument or message intended to motivate the patient to an action that promoted the interest of the god(s).

[212] Jean Bottéro, "Magie A," in *Reallexikon Der Assyriologie und Vorderasiatischen Archäologie* (ed. P. Calmeyer, J.N. Postgate, W. Röllig, E. von Schuler, W. von Soden, M. Stol, and G. Wilhelm; Berlin: Walter De Gruyter, 1990), 7:200-34.

[213] Avalos, *Illness and Healthcare in the Ancient Near East,* 135.

It appears that both magic and medical arts were practiced as exorcist (*āšipu*) and physician (*asû*) worked together to cure the sufferer,[214] but the two functioned independently of one another. According to Scurlock and Andersen, *āšipu*s formed part of the temple staff, occasionally performing purification rites in connection with calendric celebrations in addition to their medical duties.[215] The *āšipu*s practiced magical duties that would include exorcising demons from haunted houses.[216] Apart from this, though, he engaged in medical duties and the *āšipu* was considered to be a craftsmen.[217] Scurlock and Andersen assert that

> this means that he was responsible for dealing with the spirit or malfunctioning body part whose irritation or malevolent activities were producing the observed symptoms. He was, his 'magical' duties excluded, a close equivalent to a modern 'physician.'

The *āšipu* were careful observers of clinical symptoms. In fact, Scurlock and Andersen remark that "Mesopotamian medicine was remarkable for its foundation in prior observations . . ." and that an *āšipu* "could not approach a medical problem without bringing to it a bit of preconceived theory."[218] It is noted that some medical texts also show that neurological testing was being done.[219] Along with detailed and organized diagnosis, prognosis, and therapeutic treatment information, ancient medical texts contain case histories, and "demonstrate a knowledge of organ pathology that could only have been gained from direct examination, that is, during surgical procedure or in the course of an autopsy."[220]

The *āšipu* was an intellectual, "well versed in the scribal arts, Sumerian, the classics of literature, and a wide variety of 'magical' rituals in addition to the forty tablets of the diagnostic/prognostic handbook and innumerable therapeutic texts."[221] However, observed realities took precedence over causal factors.[222] Scurlock and Anderson note that, "he seems frequently to have been unhappy with the attribution of specific problems to *any* of the spirits or demonic forces known to him," preferring instead to occasionally make

---

[214] Biggs, "Medicine in Ancient Mesopotamia," 95-96; Scurlock and Andersen, *Diagnosis in Assyrian and Babylonian Medicine*, 8-9.

[215] Scurlock and Andersen, *Diagnosis in Assyrian and Babylonian Medicine*, 8.

[216] Scurlock and Andersen, *Diagnosis in Assyrian and Babylonian Medicine*, 8.

[217] Scurlock and Andersen, *Diagnosis in Assyrian and Babylonian Medicine*, 8; Biggs, "Medicine in Ancient Mesopotamia," 98.

[218] Scurlock and Andersen, *Diagnosis in Assyrian and Babylonian Medicine*, 429.

[219] Scurlock and Andersen, *Diagnosis in Assyrian and Babylonian Medicine*, 9.

[220] Scurlock and Andersen, *Diagnosis in Assyrian and Babylonian Medicine*, 10.

[221] Scurlock and Andersen, *Diagnosis in Assyrian and Babylonian Medicine*, 429.

[222] Scurlock and Andersen, *Diagnosis in Assyrian and Babylonian Medicine*, 8, 429-30. According to Scurlock and Andersen the *āšipu* employed every sensory perception (except taste) in the process of making clinical observations.

associations with anatomic areas, or in case this failed, sets of connected symptoms or syndromes would be given a name that referred to some characteristic of the disease.[223]

Fines were levied on physicians for malpractice as seen in the code of Hammurabi (§§ 215-17). On the basis of the phrase "before the (surgeon's) stone knife and razor have reached you,"[224] contained in a Babylonian charm, some argue that before a surgical remedy would be attempted an exorcism would precede it.[225] This, however, may be similar to a prayer for healing in an attempt to avoid surgery altogether rather than suggesting a procedural note. For example, Benno Landsberger has examined several Babylonian incantations that entreat various deities for healing of eye disease (*AMT*, 12, No.1; *AMT*, 9, No.1, II, 26-28; *AMT*, 10, No.1, III, 10-12; *AMT*, 12, No. 1, IV 44-47).[226] These incantations directly speak to an attempt to avert surgery, or cure eye disease. His data suggests that these prayers rather than exorcism repeatedly asked for healing before the scalpel was used.

The underlying presumption of physical calamity was that it was an attack, and not just on the patient but on the entire household.[227] Appealing to the deity who sent the illness was key to restored health. Noting the importance of identifying the "sender/controller" of a disease, Avalos points out that appealing to a deity for the restoration of health required that the DN and the *qātu* which this DN signified be identified in each particular case.[228] The myriad of possible sender deities, however, made this process problematic, resulting in cumbersome and contradictory diagnosis and therapy.[229] A complex medical theology developed to address the multiple illnesses and multiple sending deities.[230] The following are some texts from the diagnostic/prognostic handbook known to have existed in ancient Mesopotamia.[231]

---

[223] Scurlock and Andersen, *Diagnosis in Assyrian and Babylonian Medicine*, 430. Scurlock and Andersen acknowledge that over time these characteristics would often evolve into a demonic force in their own right.

[224] *AMT*, 12, No. 1, IV 44-47, in Benno Landsberger, "Corrections to the Article 'An Old Babylonian Charm Against *Merhu*'," *Journal of Near Eastern Studies* 17 (1958): 58.

[225] Helmut Freydank, "Chirurgie im alten Mesopotamien?" *Das Altertum* 18 (1972): 134.

[226] Landsberger, "Corrections to the Article 'An Old Babylonian Charm Against *Merhu*'," 56-58.

[227] Avalos, *Illness and Healthcare in the Ancient Near East*, 172-82.

[228] Avalos, *Illness and Healthcare in the Ancient Near East*, 135-39.

[229] Avalos, *Illness and Healthcare in the Ancient Near East*, 135.

[230] Avalos, *Illness and Healthcare in the Ancient Near East*, 142.

[231] Scurlock and Andersen, *Diagnosis in Assyrian and Babylonian Medicine*, 429f.

> If he was wounded on his head and consequently his eyes are *erēpu*'d, "hand" of Ningirsu (*TDP* 26:75).[232]
> If he was wounded on his head and, consequently, his eyes are heavily clouded, "hand" of Ningirsu (*TDP* 26:75).[233]
> If he has was wounded on his head and consequently, his hearing is low (and) his ears [...], "hand" of a murderous god; it is serious; he will die (tablet 3.80).[234]
> If he has a viselike headache and his ears do not hear, the "hand" of his god has been imposed on him; he will die (tablet 4.4).[235]

The *āšipu* saw neurological conditions as stemming from divine or demonic causal agents. Scurlock and Andersen identify Ningirsu, one of the many warfare gods to which neurological trauma to the second cranial nerve was often attributed.[236]

The Medical Tradition in Ancient Israel

Many cultures in the ancient Near East developed a medical tradition to which individuals suffering from physical malfunctions may apply for relief and/or healing. A number of texts dealt with this chapter indicate that medical methods were brought to bear in attempts to heal some of the diseases that commonly resulted in permanent physical disability. Some suggest Israel did not support any type of medical tradition and that Israel's monotheism rules out such a tradition and thus deprives members of the community of medical services that, although crude, would prevent permanent physical disabilities and the social stigmas associated with them.[237]

Are the roots of medicine located in ancient Near Eastern paganism? Israel preserved almost no ancient medical literature. However, in light of the fact that the purpose of the Scriptures is "theological rather than medical," it is not surprising to find only those health related details that are relevant to the issue at hand in any given text.[238] There are sufficient grounds to affirm that Israel did indeed have a medical tradition of its own. Exodus 21:19b directs the party that injures another party to pay the physician's fees if that injured party ultimately becomes well (וְנִקָּה הַמַּכֶּה רַק שִׁבְתּוֹ יִתֵּן וְרַפֹּא יְרַפֵּא). The term

[232] Scurlock and Andersen, *Diagnosis in Assyrian and Babylonian Medicine*, 186.
[233] Scurlock and Andersen, *Diagnosis in Assyrian and Babylonian Medicine*, 471.
[234] Labat, *Traité Akkadien de Diagnostics et Pronostics Médicaux I*, 27.
[235] Labat, *Traité Akkadien de Diagnostics et Pronostics Médicaux I*, 33.
[236] Scurlock and Andersen, *Diagnosis in Assyrian and Babylonian Medicine*, 470.
[237] Seybold and Mueller, *Sickness and Healing;* Carroll Stuhlmueller, "Sickness and Disease: An Old Testament Perspective," *Bible Today* 27 (1989): 5f. Stuhlmueller argues that Israel did not even possess proper words in its language for lungs, stomach, or nervous system where Egyptian medical knowledge was far more advanced.
[238] D.H. Trapnell, "Health, Disease and Healing," in *New Bible Dictionary* (2nd ed.; ed. I. Howard Marshall, A.R. Millard, J.I. Packer, and D.J. Wiseman; Downers Grove, Ill.: InterVarsity Press, 1996), 448.

physician (רפא) is used (Exod 15:26; Jer 8:22) to describe a person who would have functioned like modern physicians do.[239]

The Scriptures also contain a host of medical terminology including various distinctive types of skin spots (סַפַּחַת, Lev 13:2; 14:56; מִסְפַּחַת, Lev 13:6-8; יַלֶּפֶת, Lev 21:20) and scurvy (גָּרָב, Lev 21:20), fever (Deut 28:22), inflamation (Deut 28:22), hemorrhaging and bloody discharges (Lev 15:2f; 12:7), itchy skin rashes (Lev 13:30-37; 14:54), madness (Deut 28:28), menstruation (Lev 12:2, 5; 15:33; 18:19; 20:18), prolapsed rectum (2 Chron 21:15; 18-19), leprosy (צָרַעַת, Lev 13:1-46) plague (נֶגַע, Lev 13-14; 26:21), tumors and warts (1 Sam 5:6, 9; Lev 22:22), speechlessness (Exod 4:11), boils (Lev 13:18-24), burns (Lev 13:24, 28), deafness (Lev 19:14), consumption (Lev 26:16) and dysentery (2 Chron 21:15, 18-19). All this indicates a familiarity with physical diseases and disabilities to the degree lexical distinctions could be made between them. In addition, a primitive form of bone setting is mentioned (Ezek 30:21).[240]

Carroll Stuhlmueller also asserts that medicine and miracles in the prophetic tradition are exemplified in the healing of Hezekiah (Isa 38:6-8) and in Jeremiah's rhetorical question regarding the fact that in spite of the availability of remedies and physicians sickness persisted for lack of their utilization (Jer 8:22).[241] He also cites Isaiah 35:4-6 as evincing a reversal of this neglected segment of society with their impending inclusion in a future messianic kingdom.[242] He sees Isaiah 53:3-5 as the sum total of Old Testament theology of sickness and disease.[243] Avalos, however, has convincingly shown that biblical and archaeological evidence contradicts this negative assessment.[244] He notes that the term *shalom* "encompasses a physical state associated with the fulfillment of covenant stipulations."[245] In non-Hebrew cultures, the healing

[239] Trapnell, "Health, Disease and Healing," 452. Unlike pagan religions, there was no confusion between the offices of priest and physician.

[240] Trapnell, "Health, Disease and Healing," 452.

[241] Stuhlmueller, "Sickness and Disease: An Old Testament Perspective," 6.

[242] Stuhlmueller, "Sickness and Disease: An Old Testament Perspective," 9.

[243] Stuhlmueller, "Sickness and Disease: An Old Testament Perspective," 9.

[244] Avalos, "Ancient Medicine: In Case of Emergency, Contact Your Local Prophet," 27-35, 48. Avalos cites herbal remedies as in the case of Rachel and Leah's belief that mandrakes could reverse infertility (Gen 30:14ff), Jeremiah's derisive comment about Balsam (balm) as an ineffective cure for Israel's maladies (Jer 46:11) as examples of this. See also Alan Kam-Yua Chan and Thomas B. Song/Michael L. Brown, "רפא," in *New International Dictionary of Old Testament Theology and Exegesis* (ed. Willem A. VanGemeren; Grand Rapids: Zondervan, 1997), 3:1162-73. In addition, a flask found at Qumran contained a potion used for healing (See Joseph Patrich, "Hideouts in the Judean Wilderness," *Biblical Archaeological Review* 5 [1989]: 32-42). If Stuhlmueller is correct, Qumran would be the last place one would expect to find this.

[245] Avalos, "Ancient Medicine," 28.

process frequently involved an exorcist and a physician which were two distinct functions frequently working together.[246]

Within the framework of Yahwism, the most accessible and cheapest means of healing were prayer and consulting a *nebi* (2 Kgs 4:32-34; 5:15-17).[247] The רפאים (healers) were known to exist throughout the ancient world. In Israel, the *ropheim* served positive functions of physical healing.[248] Yahweh declares himself as Israel's Healer (Exod 15:26) and in this light the term has covenantal connotations as health was associated with divine blessing in consequence to Israel's obedience (i.e., Exod 15:26; 23:25-26; Deut 7:12-15).[249] Further, when Asa sought out the *ropheim* to heal his feet (2 Chron 16:12f), the broader context indicates that his action must be understood in light of his fervent admonitions to the people to trust the Lord (14:4-7, 8-15; 15:1-15) and his own failure to do so at a critical juncture (16:1-9). Consequently, he was afflicted with this disease and yet still did not trust the Lord but rather consulted *ropheim* from Egypt who were magical, idolatrous practitioners.[250] Evidence, therefore, supports the fact that Israel did not reject all healing practices, only those practices which were not associated with the cult of Yahweh.[251]

Conclusions

It appears that medical services were readily available to all in need of them. Fines were levied on physicians for malpractice (Code of Hammurabi §§ 215-17). Deities were invoked in the process of healing or attempted healing, but this was not the only convention available to one afflicted. Especially in ancient Babylon, medical practices were also readily available and extensive enough to have been known to later historians such as Herodotus.

In the ancient Near East, medical arts are known to have been practiced since the third millennium B.C. Therapeutic manuals from Sumer (2112-2004 B.C.) and medical texts from the Old Babylonian period (1894-1595 B.C.) helped physicians to identify symptoms, diagnose infirmities and provided instructions for the preparation and administration of medication. Medical knowledge continued to develop to the point that by the Middle Assyrian and Middle Babylonian periods (1430-1050 B.C.) a handbook for diagnosis and prognosis was available. Experts associated with the medical arts were the

[246] Biggs, "Medicine in Ancient Mesopotamia," 94-105.

[247] Avalos, "Ancient Medicine," 28.

[248] Chan and Song/Brown, "רפא," 3:1168.

[249] Chan and Song/Brown, "רפא," 3:1168. It is generally believed that Exod 15:26 is more a polemic against rival deities than against physicians as Stuhlmueller supposes. The *ropheim* in non-Hebrew cultures were not religiously neutral but were aligned with pagan gods.

[250] Chan and Song/Brown, "רפא," 3:1169. 2 Chronicles 16:12 cannot be seen as a condemnation of medical practitioners generally, but as a rebuke to those who rely on sinful, human support rather than to trust in the Lord.

[251] Avalos, "Ancient Medicine," 28.

āšipu and the *asû*. The *āšipu*, who was considered an intellectual and a craftsman, carefully observed clinical symptoms, often approaching a medical problem with a bit of preconceived theory. Evidence shows that he not only performed neurological testing on his subjects but also may have performed surgical procedures or autopsies because he also had an advanced knowledge of organ pathology.

Medical tradition in the ancient Near East was not as primitive although many practices were based on superstitious beliefs. However, modern research has discredited the belief that in the ancient Near East, *all* illnesses were considered the result of witchcraft, demonic activity, or divine displeasure. There is nothing that suggests that sin on the part of the afflicted was automatically believed to be the cause of physical suffering. Both magic and medical observation worked together to find a cure but the two functioned independently of one another.

Although some scholars suggest that Israel did not support any type of medical tradition and that Israel's monotheism rules out such a tradition, there is ample evidence that Israel did have a medical tradition. This misunderstanding may be a result of the fact that the purpose Scripture is theological rather than medical; it is not surprising to find only those health related details that are relevant in any given text. The term physician (רֹפֵא) is used (Exod 15:26; Jer 8:22) to describe a person who would have functioned like modern physicians do. There is also host of medical terminology describing a variety of known physical issues. All this indicates Israel's familiarity with physical diseases and disabilities to the degree that lexical distinctions could be made between them.

Chapter 4

The Old Testament and Disabilities

The Literal Use of Disability Language in the Old Testament

Legal Protections Related to the Disabled

The giver of biblical law codes constantly looks back at the narratives contained in the Torah (Exod 20:2; 22:21; 23:9, 15; 29:46; 34:18; Lev 11:45; 18:3; 19:34, 36; 22:33; 23:43; 25:38, 42, 55; 26:13, 45; Num 8:17; 9:1; 15:41; Deut 5:6, 15; 6:12, 21; 10:19; 13:5, 10; 15:15; 16:1, 3, 6, 12; 24:18, 22) while at the same time looking forward to the entry into Canaan, which is the fulfillment of a previous divine promise to Abraham (Exod 20:12; 23:10, 23, 26, 29, 30, 31, 33; 33:1; 34:12, 15, 21; Lev 14:34; 18:13, 28; 19:29, 34; 20:2, 22, 24; 22:24; 23:10, 22, 39; 25:2-7, 18-19, 23, 38; 26:1-6, 18-38; Num 15:2, 18; 35:10, 29-34; 36:2; Deut 4:14, 40; 5:16, 31, 33; 6:1, 18, 23; 7:13; 8:1, 6-10; 11:8-32; 12:1, 10, 29; 29:1-29; 30:16). In shaping the law, the Exodus event is pivotal in formulating the legal codes by which Israel's society was to be designated as distinctly the people of God. The presence of Yahweh in the midst of Israel was also a motivational foundation for the formation of biblical legal codes (Lev 26:3-13; Deut 12:1-5). Consequently, purity was a concern. Through obedience to the covenant, Israel's existence would be a sign of his presence.

Israelite casuistic law is based on the apodictic laws contained in the covenant code.[1] Apodictic law established that which was normative in Israelite society. A unique element to Israelite legal formation is the fact that it contains cultic law.[2] Another prominent formal element in Israelite law is the use of the motive clause appended to the laws justifying the observance of that law.[3] Consequently, Israelite law "represents an absolute standard of behavior prescribed by God, 'You will behave in this way because I am holy and you are to be holy as well,' thus placing demands on the people."[4]

In contrast with other ancient Near Eastern societies, justice in Israel, as defined in the Old Testament, was grounded on the two-dimensional affiliation

---

1 Walton, *Ancient Israelite Literature in its Cultural Context*, 81; Sparks, *Ancient Texts for the Study of the Hebrew Bible*, 417.

2 Walton, *Ancient Israelite Literature in its Cultural Context*, 76.

3 Rifat Sonsino, *Motive Clauses in Hebrew Law* (Chico, Calif.: Scholars, 1980), 61.

4 Walton, *Ancient Israelite Literature in its Cultural Context*, 92.

of Yahweh as Israel's God and Israel as Yahweh's people as reflected in the Covenant.[5] Covenant loyalty demanded that Israel "build a just society with fraternal spirit among its members."[6] Justice affected all members of the community in that all were to show fidelity to each member of the community.[7] Israel's conduct was to reflect her Redeemer's, respecting life, renouncing moral and ritual impurity, beneficent actions, etc. The legal prescriptions contained in the Torah find their root in the very nature of God.[8] It is because he is holy, righteous, and full of compassion and mercy that Israel was to conduct herself with these same attributes. Through Israel's compliance to the laws of the covenant, Yahweh was sanctified. Compliance, though, can only generate a symbolic observance of holiness.[9] As J. Barton Payne notes, ". . . the believer is committed to God and to his laws, not just in certain externalities of conduct, but from his innermost spirit. God's love for men becomes his own standard of guidance, first in love toward God, then toward fellow men . . ."[10] Reverence for Yahweh's name demanded more than conformity and acquiescence. Through the socially oriented ordinances contained in Leviticus 19, the people of God were induced to practice that holiness in and among themselves.[11] Biblical law emphasizes religious law, has an apodictic basis for its case law, has morality as a goal, is more prescriptive than descriptive, and is based on adherence to covenant.[12] This is evident in the following texts which address the treatment of the physically disabled in the midst of the community of faith who were to be treated impartially, be protected, and have equal access to justice.

Consideration Toward the Disabled: Leviticus 19:13-14

Chapter 19 is significant because it elaborates on laws already given in the book of Leviticus and makes unambiguous the meaning of righteousness.[13] More specifically, we discover what is at the core of Israelite society, its spiritual heart. Thus we have Israel's spiritual identity defined. Their spiritual rank was not merely imprinted by the law which defined it but was typified in the way they cared for other members of the community, responded to those

---

5 Matthew Vellanickal, "Just Society: Biblical Perspective," *Bible Bhashyam* 8 (1982): 81.

6 Vellanickal, "Just Society: Biblical Perspective," 82.

7 Vellanickal, "Just Society: Biblical Perspective," 86.

8 Norman H. Snaith, *The Distinctive Ideas of the Old Testament* (New York: Schocken, 1964), 53.

9 J. Barton Payne, *Leviticus* (The Biblical Expositor 1; ed. C.F.H. Henry; London: Pickering & Inglis, 1960), 141.

10 Payne, *Leviticus*, 141.

11 Payne, *Leviticus*, 141.

12 Walton, *Ancient Israelite Literature in Its Cultural Context*, 91.

13 Mary Douglas, *Leviticus as Literature* (London: Oxford University Press, 2001), 239.

outside the community, separated themselves from moral and ritual impurity, and worshiped the One who dwelt in the midst of the community.

The statutes in Leviticus 19 are grouped together "according to a loose association of ideas more than according to any logical arrangement, they are linked together by the common purpose."[14] This purpose is clearly expressed in verse 2, "you shall be holy" (קְדֹשִׁים תִּהְיוּ). "This chapter opens with a command to Israel to be holy and then specifies how holiness is to be achieved."[15] By so doing, it conceives of holiness as positive ethical standards that illustrate God's nature and not merely a matter of divinely imposed restrictions.[16] Everything holy must act and be treated as holy. "Everything identified as holy is subject to rules involving special care and caution."[17] Obviously, this applies to the entire nation. It is the moral implication of holiness which drives the regulation of conduct outside the tabernacle.[18] The concepts of holiness and purity were, in fact, meant to be the distinguishing factors between Israel and other nations.[19]

The prohibitions in verses 11-18 focus on the theme of neighborliness by describing what a bad neighbor is. While the focus on verses 11-12 is on the treatment of an equal, verses 13-14 focuses on the one who exploits and oppresses the weak.[20] The five prohibitions in this unit focus on the theme of exploiting the helpless.[21] Each command in this section is based on the prohibition against oppression (עשׁק) in verse 13a.[22] This first prohibitive addresses the exploitation of one's neighbor. It simply reads, "you shall not oppress your neighbor or rob him" (לֹא־תַעֲשֹׁק אֶת־רֵעֲךָ וְלֹא תִגְזֹל). It links this with the prohibition against keeping a hired man's wages overnight in verse 13b (לֹא־תָלִין פְּעֻלַּת שָׂכִיר אִתְּךָ עַד־בֹּקֶר) and the ban against harming the physically disabled in v. 14 "you shall not curse a deaf man or put a stumbling block in front of a blind man" (לֹא־תְקַלֵּל חֵרֵשׁ וְלִפְנֵי עִוֵּר לֹא תִתֵּן מִכְשֹׁל). As Allen Ross

---

14 C.F. Keil, and Franz Delitzsch, *The Pentateuch,* Biblical Commentary on the Old Testament; Grand Rapids: Eerdmans, n.d.), 2:418.

15 Jacob Milgrom, *Leviticus 17-22* (The Anchor Bible 3A; New York: Doubleday, 2000), 1596.

16 Milgrom, *Leviticus 17-22*, 1715.

17 David A. Dorsey, *The Literary Structure of the Old Testament* (Grand Rapids: Baker, 1999), 79.

18 Richard E. Averbeck, "The Theology of Leviticus," in *NIDOTTE* (ed. Willem A. VanGemeren; Grand Rapids: Zondervan, 1997), 4:907. Averbeck points out that Leviticus contains regulations that are "often specific and detailed, being tied to the very fabric of personal and communal life in ancient Israel."

19 Averbeck, "The Theology of Leviticus," 4:915.

20 Gordon J. Wenham, *The Book of Leviticus* (New International Commentary on the Old Testament; Grand Rapids: Eerdmans, 1979), 267; Milgrom, *Leviticus 17-22,* 1641.

21 Milgrom, *Leviticus 17-22*, 1641.

22 Hartley, *Leviticus*, 315.

notes, "the deaf man cannot hear a curse; the blind man cannot see a stumbling block. But God can hear and see."[23]

The inclusion of disabled persons in this section along with other categories of socially weak persons may imply that they were generally included in that category and that other biblical texts concerning the weak should not exclude the disabled.[24] Norman Snaith, however, treats these prohibitions as figurative statements meaning to not take advantage of people who do not know what is happening.[25] Similarly, Milgrom contends that the words חֵרֵשׁ and עִוֵּר stand for all helpless people.[26] He argues that to "curse" (קלל) the deaf, or to put a "stumbling block " (מִכְשֹׁל) before the blind is metaphorical language for taking advantage of the helpless and deliberately misdirecting them or deliberately giving them unsuitable advice.[27] Israel's mandate instead, he argues, is basically to defend the poor.[28] Indeed there are warnings against cursing one's parents (Exod 21:17), or God and rulers he places over the people (Exod 22:28), but קלל means to consider something a trifle or worthless and therefore deserving of mockery. It would be more cogent to argue that the intention of each prohibitive in Leviticus 19:13-14 is to allow those who are dependent on others (economically or for physical assistance) access to that which is vital to life and the dignity thereof. If this is the case, it is more than defending the disadvantaged but of being a benefit to them by not denying them what they need to survive. This is consistent with the meaning of the word אָהֵב (love) in verse 18 which, as already mentioned, serves as the anchor for the commands set forth in Leviticus 19.

The word קָלַל in the *piel* stem commonly means to curse (Lev 19:14).[29] The Hebrew use of קלל parallels its Akkadian cognate *qullulu* meaning to diminish, discredit, or ridicule.[30] It is the antonym of the *piel* stem of כבד (to honor), inferring that something is considered a trifle or worthless and therefore deserving of mockery. It applies to one's acting with contempt toward another.[31] Leviticus 19:15 contains a chiastic structure:

---

23 Allen P. Ross, *Holiness to the Lord: A Guide to the Exposition of the Book of Leviticus* (Grand Rapids: Baker, 2002), 361.

24 Milgrom, *Leviticus 17-22*, 1640-42.

25 Norman H. Snaith, *Leviticus and Numbers* (London: Oliphants, 1977), 361. See also Ross, *Holiness to the Lord*, 361.

26 Milgrom, *Leviticus 17-22*, 1640-41.

27 Milgrom, *Leviticus 17-22*, 1641.

28 Milgrom, *Leviticus 17-22*, 1642.

29 Robert P. Gordon, "קלל," in *NIDOTTE* (ed. Willem A. VanGemeren; Grand Rapids: Zondervan, 1997), 3:927.

30 Gordon, "קלל," 3:927.

31 Gordon, "קלל," 3:927.

לֹא־תַעֲשׂוּ עָוֶל בַּמִּשְׁפָּט a

b לֹא־תִשָּׂא פְנֵי־דָל

b' וְלֹא תֶהְדַּר פְּנֵי גָדוֹל

a' בְּצֶדֶק תִּשְׁפֹּט עֲמִיתֶךָ

a You shall not do injustice in judgment

b You shall not be partial to the poor

b' Nor honor the great

a' In righteousness you are to judge your neighbor

The inclusion of the poor and the wealthy within just judgment suggests that the special interests of either category of persons was under the authority of the courts and the outcome of their cases were to be determined by the merits of their particular cases, not their status.[32]

The verb "do" is plural (תַעֲשׂוּ) indicating that it applied to the entire community of faith. The word "injustice" (עָוֶל) is the exact opposite of "justice" (מִשְׁפָּט) and refers to the skewing of judicial rectitude.[33] Theologically, it is a vice that has no part in God's character (Deut 32:4; Job 34:10) and expresses opposition to God (Job 18:21; Jer 2:5; Zeph 3:5).[34]

Justice can be perverted not only by taking a bribe but also by lifting up the poor (לֹא־תִשָּׂא פְנֵי־דָל) or deferring to the great (לֹא תֶהְדַּר פְּנֵי גָדוֹל). The mandate to resist the inclination to favor the poor echoes Exodus 23:3. The two phrases, תִשָּׂא פְנֵי and תֶהְדַּר פְּנֵי, form a merism commanding that no preferential treatment be shown to anyone.[35] דָל (poor) in combination with גָדוֹל (great) is unique in Scripture, functioning rhetorically for assonance.[36] This reinforces the concept of justice as a universal right. The phrase עֲמִיתֶךָ brings all members of the community of Israel into close relation. Each member of the community is a neighbor. A judge must adjudicate his neighbors justly (בְּצֶדֶק תִּשְׁפֹּט עֲמִיתֶךָ). Attempts to portray aliens, widows, and orphans as needing protection because they lack "a social network" are questionable.[37] Contra Sneed, Exodus 23 provides for the exercise of impartiality toward all citizens and ought not be viewed as a vestige of some premonarchal voice of the oppressed contained in altruistic sentiment. Torah provides access to justice to every segment of society (Deut 10:18; 16:11, 14; 24:17-21; 26:12-13; 27:19; Ps 146:9) and hears the cries of the disenfranchised when they are oppressed (Exod 22:20-24). It

[32] Milgrom, *Leviticus 17-22*, 1642.

[33] David W. Baker, "עול," in *NIDOTTE* (ed. Willem A. VanGemeren; Grand Rapids: Zondervan, 1997), 3:343.

[34] Baker, "עול," 3:342-43.

[35] Milgrom, *Leviticus 17-22*, 1643.

[36] Jonathan Magonet, "The Structure and Meaning of Leviticus 19," *Hebrew Annual Review* 7 (1983): 158.

[37] Mark Sneed, "Israelite Concern for the Alien, Orphan, and Widow: Altruism or Ideology?" *Zeitschrift für die Alttestamentliche Wissenschaft* 111 (1999): 500.

can be concluded, then, that it was the norm in Israelite society to protect them.[38]

When preferential treatment was shown to one member of the community over another member, the result was that the sanctity of every member of the community of faith was diminished. The whole nation was to be a kingdom of priests–a holy nation (Exod 19:6). Hence, all who belong to Yahweh are to be accorded fair treatment (Lev 19:15). Passing judgment based on external appearance is discriminatory, compromises the purity of the community, and shows disrespect to the Lord.[39] The mandate for blind justice aligns with the emphasis on the holiness of the name of Yahweh found throughout Leviticus 19.

Verse 16 highlights the concern for impartial and fair judgment (v. 15) by focusing on the witness. Witnesses were to be equally impartial and fair, "showing no favoritism either to the rich or the poor (see Exod 23:1-3, 6-8; Deut 16:19-20; 19:15-21; 27:25)."[40] Slander (רָכִיל) was a form of false witness.[41] It could not only ruin a person's reputation but could also put a person's life at risk.[42] These were things the community was supposed to safeguard against (16b).[43] The prohibition against murder (לא תַעֲמֹד עַל־דַּם רֵעֶךָ) in verse 16a makes the translation "slander" for the word רכיל preferred.[44]

Verse 17 warns against hatred (לֹא־תִשְׂנָא). Reproof (תוכחה)[45] was acceptable, but hatred to the point that sin would be incurred (וְלֹא־תִשָּׂא עָלָיו חֵטְא) was not. 19:18 opens by defining what is in mind when the concern for sin is expressed in verse 17. A member of the community must not avenge (לֹא־תִקֹּם), nor keep a grudge (וְלֹא־תִטֹּר) on anyone or anyone's descendent (אֶת־בְּנֵי עַמֶּךָ).[46] On the contrary, one must have genuine concern for one's neighbor.

Structurally, verse 18 is the climax of the chapter. At the center of the concern for a pure community is a summons for the practice of love. The command to love one's neighbor like oneself consists of three simple words

---

38 This is evidenced by the apodictic formula used in Exodus 22. Similarly, Levites had no inheritance to sustain them and could be associated with widows, orphans, and aliens as disenfranchised members of the community. Nevertheless, provision was made for their continuance (Exod 14:29).

39 Dorsey, *The Literary Structure of the Old Testament*, 79.

40 Ross, *Holiness to the Lord*, 361.

41 Robert H. O'Connell, "רָכִיל," in *NIDOTTE* (ed. Willem A. VanGemeren; Grand Rapids: Zondervan, 1997), 3:1115. O'Connell notes that "given the possibility of bloodshed described in the context and the syntagm of *rgl* + *b*-, the preposition *b*-here may be adversative (against).

42 Ross, *Holiness to the Lord*, 361.

43 Hartley, *Leviticus*, 316.

44 O'Connell, "רָכִיל," in *NIDOTTE,* 3:1115.

45 The legitimacy of a rebuke is stressed when the *hiphil* infinitive follows the *hiphil* imperfect (הוֹכֵחַ תּוֹכִיחַ) as seen here.

46 Keith N. Schoville, "נטר," in *NIDOTTE* (ed. Willem A. VanGemeren; Grand Rapids: Zondervan, 1997), 3:98.

(וְאָהַבְתָּ לְרֵעֲךָ כָּמוֹךָ). Understanding these words is key to understanding how one is to relate to every other member of the community of faith. In this context the word אהב does not express romantic interpersonal feelings between two individuals but functionality for the benefit of others in the community. Usually אָהֵב takes an object when intending to express interpersonal relationships (Gen 24:67; 25:28; 29:18, 30; 34:3; 37:3, 4; Deut 4:37; 7:8; Judg 16:4; 1 Sam 1:5; 18:1, 3, 16, 20, 28; 20:17; 2 Sam 12:24; 13:1; 1 Kgs 3:3; 10:9; 11:1; 2 Chr 9:8; 11:21; 26:10; Esth 2:17; Pss 45:7; 91:14; 109:17; Jer 2:25; 31:3; Hos 9:1; 11:1; Mal 1:2). In Leviticus 19, אָהַבְתָּ is intransitive and followed by an indirect object introduced with the prepositional particle לְ. This is a limited construction occurring in only three other places (Lev 19:34; 1 Kgs 5:1; 2 Chron 19:2). Malamat suggests that this particular construction in contexts outside of Leviticus 19:18 does not suggest a call to "love" as we would use the term, but to "help" or "to be beneficial to."[47] Hence, the meaning of אָהֵב in Leviticus 19:18 also suggests rendering assistance to others within the community. In other words, rather than expressing mere emotion, feeling, or attitude, it addresses certain behavioral patterns in actual practice.[48]

In calling the covenantal community to ethical relationships, Leviticus 19 is calling the community to functional purity beyond and distinct from moral or ritual purity. Functional purity is horizontal, being reflected in interactive community custodianship and justness. What legitimates this call to holiness in action? It is the fact that the same One who prohibits murder and adultery is the One who brought Israel out of Egypt and into existence as a covenantal community. Purity is essential for the community of faith and love is essential to purity. In Leviticus 19 purity is defined in terms of personal, relational realities expressed in actions of love (19:18) in response to God's own holiness. To own a faith in which deeds or displays of love and mercy are absent is to not own genuine faith. It is, instead, a faith that is devoid of purity and not grounded in the person of Yahweh. The community of faith is a holy community and therefore, all must act and be treated in a loving manner.

An obligation exists between the members of the community of faith to exercise custodial responsibility for one another. Hans-Peter Mathys writes, "Der Taube kann sich gegen einen Fluch nicht wehren, da er ihn nicht hört, ein Blinder ist auf die Führung durch Sehende angewiesen."[49] Walter Kornfeld concurs, noting that there is a religious foundation to this precept founded in "die Gottesfurcht," which is fulfilled in the "Ordnung in Israel."[50] The

[47] Abraham Malamat, "'Love Your Neighbor as Yourself': What It Really Means," *Biblical Archaeology Review* 7 (1990): 51.

[48] P.J.J.S. Els, "אָהֵב," in *NIDOTTE* (ed. Willem A. VanGemeren; Grand Rapids: Zondervan, 1997), 1:290.

[49] Hans-Peter Mathys, *Liebe deinen Nächsten wie dich selbst: Untersuchungen zum alttestamentlichen Gebot der Nächstenliebe (Lev 19, 18)* (Orbis biblicus et orientalis 71; Göttingen: Vandenhoeck & Ruprecht, 1986), 60.

[50] Walter Kornfeld, *Das Buch Leviticus* (Düsseldorf: Patmos Verlag, 1972), 125.

prohibition against "playing on a person's disability was designed to prevent them from being exploited or ridiculed and the abuser from taking profit or from acting spitefully."[51] A unique factor in ancient Israelite law is its concern for disabled members of the population. This deference is connected with one's religious responsibility of functioning holiness.

Laws protecting disabled people are conspicuously absent from other ancient Near Eastern legal codes. Indeed, there are provisions for compensating those who are injured (LH §§196-99) and renders both incentives and punishments to physicians who attempt healing with successful or unsuccessful results, respectively (LH §§215-23).[52] The Bible, however, goes far beyond prescribing healing procedures and restitution for injury to the non-monetary, ethical protection of a class.[53] With these protections, a new and powerful social value of the worth of an individual was formed that did not merely protect an investment but limited the power of one man over another.[54]

Leviticus 19 presents positive moral precepts, emphasizing the call to holiness–God's holiness. In the Hebrew Bible holiness is assigned to God alone and he is its unique source.[55] The basis for ritual purity within the community was Yahweh's personal holiness.[56] Milgrom notes that "holiness is the extension of his nature; it is the agency of his will."[57] Holiness basically means to be set apart for God and applies only to certain spaces, persons, and times.[58]

The oft repeated declarative, "I am the Lord your God" (11:44, 45; 18:2, 4, 5, 6, 21, 30; 19:2, 3, 4, 10, 12, 14, 16, 18, 25, 28, 30, 31, 32, 34, 36, 37; 20:7, 8, 24, 26; 21:8, 12, 15, 23; 22:2, 3, 8, 9, 16, 30, 31, 32, 33; 23:22, 43; 24:22; 25:17, 38, 55; 26:1, 2, 13, 44, 45) and the association of the word קדוש (11:44, 45; 19:2; 20:3, 7, 26; 21:6, 7, 8; 22:2, 32; 23:20; 27:9, 14, 21, 23, 28, 30, 32) with that name refers to the personal character of God. It is reasonable to suggest that the primary interest in the laws given is the person of God. And, as Hartley notes, "holiness is the quintessential quality of Yahweh."[59]

Leviticus 19 goes further than simply asserting the holy nature of Yahweh, it moves to show exactly what the practice of holiness looks like (devout

---

51 Hartley, *Leviticus*, 315. Hartley points out that as Leviticus 19:3 asserts, the one who fears God could not act with cruelty but with a high regard for human life and compassion toward the disadvantaged.

52 Milgrom, *Leviticus 17-22*, 1641.

53 Milgrom, *Leviticus 17-22*, 1641.

54 Walter C. Kaiser, *Exodus* (Expositor's Bible Commentary 2; Grand Rapids: Zondervan, 1991), 434.

55 Jacob Milgrom, "The Changing Concept of Holiness in the Pentateuchal Codes with Emphasis on Leviticus 19," in *Reading Leviticus: Responses to Mary Douglas* (ed. John F.A. Sawyer; Journal for the Study of the Old Testament Supplemental Series 227; Sheffield: Sheffield Academic Press, 1996), 65.

56 Paschen, *Rein und Unrein*, 63-64.

57 Milgrom, "The Changing Concept of Holiness in the Pentateuchal Codes," 65.

58 Milgrom, "The Changing Concept of Holiness in the Pentateuchal Codes," 67.

59 Hartley, *Leviticus*, 312.

worship, honesty, justice, charity, and love).[60] In entering into covenant with Yahweh, "Israel was admitted to God's covenant and thus it was sanctified," being "admitted to his holy sphere of life."[61] The derived holiness of the community was meant to be disclosed within the community by its separation from sin and all that defiles.[62] This holiness was to be lived out naturally and "the means by which they are to do this is love."[63]

The new section of laws evident in Leviticus 19 signals a shift from a concern for ritual purity to a concern for behavioral holiness. Emphasis is put on a theocentric, functional holiness within the covenantal community. Milgrom notes that each of the units within this chapter fall under the heading of individual holiness (קְדֹשִׁים תִּהְיוּ) making each of these ordinances "Israel's mandatory commandments for achieving holiness," taking holiness outside of the sphere of the sanctuary and putting it "within reach of every Israelite provided that he or she heeds the cultic prohibitions and fulfills the ethical requirements specified in this chapter.[64] In Leviticus 19 law centers around the idea of holiness rather than simply listing the categorical imperatives intended to be a formulation of the conditions for membership in the community of faith.[65] The holiness stressed in Leviticus 19 is a functional holiness generated by the presence of God and sustained through ritual holiness.

The second motif within this chapter is that of love. The holiness and love motifs are conjoined throughout chapter 19. Effectively, the laws in chapter 19 broaden the concerns about holiness to every level of relationship. Wenham makes mention of the frequent relational terms used in Leviticus 19 suggesting the nature of one's relationship with Yahweh and with others was more organic than contractual, compelling one to love those to whom one is organically related.[66] Averbeck takes this one step further,

> Holiness in Israel was to have its effect in all walks of life and for everyone who lived there, not just one's family and Israelite neighbors but even strangers and

---

[60] Ross, *Holiness to the Lord*, 352.

[61] Theodorus C. Vriezen, "The Nature of the Knowledge of God," in *The Flowering of Old Testament Theology* (Sources for Biblical and Theological Study, vol.1; ed. Ben C. Ollenburger, Elmer A. Martens, and Gerhard F. Hasel; Winona Lake: Eisenbrauns, 1992), 96.

[62] Hartley, *Leviticus*, 312.

[63] Ross, *Holiness to the Lord*, 351.

[64] Milgrom, *Leviticus 17-22*, 1598.

[65] Moshe Weinfeld, "The Decalogue: Its Significance, Uniqueness, and Place in Israel's Tradition," in *Religion and Law: Biblical, Jewish, and Islamic Perspectives* (ed. E. Firmage, J. Welch and B. Weiss; Winona Lake, Ind.: Eisenbrauns, 1990), 15, 18.

[66] Wenham, *The Book of Leviticus*, 267. The terms include: sons, your people, your brothers, your friends, your neighbor, and your associates (עֲמִיתֶךָ; רֵעֶךָ; עַמֶּיךָ; אָחִיךָ; בְּנֵי עַמֶּךָ) are frequently used in Leviticus 19.

> aliens in the land (vv. 33-34). The presence of the holy Lord in their midst demanded a kind of lifestyle that set this nation apart from other nations.[67]

This mandate to love one's neighbor (Lev 19:18) is situated in the middle of a chapter addressing communal holiness. This climactic adjurative supplanting hate with love is one of several literary devices employed to unify the chapter, serving to concretize the concept of holiness.[68] The implication is that communal holiness is defined as love communicated in displays of integrity and guardianship for one's neighbor (his extended family). Examples of this expressed in such things as the concern over favoritism go to the very heart of the concern for holiness stressed in Leviticus and concretize the concept of love as well. To practice favoritism is to have a divided heart. Favoritism is counter-love and, therefore, counter-holiness.

The covenantal community is to show love precisely because *it is* a holy community; it is not a matter of showing love in order to *become* holy. Fellowship with fellow believers is at the heart of Israel's covenant relationship with Yahweh.[69] It was in this relationship that the prescribed protections were forged and within the community that it was meant to be practiced. Prescription and practice, both, were critical relational components.

Purity was so vital to the community because it was the primary barometer of the community's relationship with Yahweh. It was the vitality of this relationship that was imbedded in the Holiness Code. The community's conduct toward both God and others displayed the community's spiritual condition. Their condition was intended to be the outward expression of their unique covenant status. Consequently, life was to be protected from both physical harm and an impugned honor. Dignity and safety were guaranteed to all members of the community (Lev 19:13-14).

On this basis, the disabled appear to have been treated with respect. Leviticus 19:14 suggests that, along with other subgroups within the community, they were weak and therefore accorded special concern. Abusing or taking advantage of the disabled was prohibited. Perhaps this is because Yahweh treated his covenant people in a manner which did not exploit or abuse them when they were most vulnerable. Since it was his nature to act this way, so it was to be his people's nature as well.

Protecting the Disabled: Deuteronomy 27:16-26

In Deuteronomy, the call to covenant relationship with Yahweh develops beyond the point of redemption and stipulation to the involvement of the heart.

---

67 Averbeck, "The Theology of Leviticus," in *NIDOTTE* 4:921.

68 Wenham, *The Book of Leviticus*, 264.

69 Eugene H. Merrill, "A Theology of the Pentateuch," in *A Biblical Theology of the Old Testament* (ed. Roy B. Zuck, Eugene H. Merrill, and Darrell L. Bock; Chicago: Moody 1991), 57.

The mistakes that Israel would make are anticipated. The covenant was not mere form but a vibrant and dynamic link between Yahweh and his people, and thus holiness and an unfeigned and ardent love for Yahweh were demanded. For the disabled, this meant that like aliens and other disadvantaged minority class people groups in Israel, they would enjoy peace, provision, and promise equally with all members of the community. Israel's holy identity was exhibited not only in maintaining purity but also in the treatment of her people.

There are eight curses in this pericope which shed light on the issue concerning this study. Four curses relate to social sins and four to sexual sins.[70] According to Cairns, "curse" has authoritative overtones being "used with God, ruler, or sovereign assembly as subject, to isolate and distance the guilty party and consign them unprotected to the realm of the malign."[71] The term ארר is more definitive in its use than קללה (curse) which is also found in the immediate context of 27:13.

In verse 16 (cursed is he who dishonors his father or mother), the word מַקְלֶה communicates the contemptuous treatment of one by another as here where the word is in the *hiphil* stem and means to cause to experience humiliation (rather than mere disrespect). The malediction in Deuteronomy 27:16 corresponds to the positive statement in Exodus 20:12 where the command is to honor (כַּבֵּד)[72] one's parents. In Exodus 21:17 and Leviticus 20:9, the penalty of death is directed toward those who curse their parents. Raymond Brown suggests that the act referred to here constitutes "a total and fierce rejection of parental authority."[73] The act of despising one's parents was a capital offence (Deut 21:18-21). Even if parents could not bring themselves to prosecute the issue, the act of dishonoring one's parents brought with it the automatic curse of God.[74]

The next three curses "have in common the fundamental imperative of respect and care for the life of the other."[75] Verse 17 (cursed is he who moves his neighbor's boundary mark) addresses moving or removing property landmarks.[76] Elizabeth Bellefontaine argues that the removal of the landmark

---

[70] Duane L. Christensen, *Deuteronomy 21:10-34:12* (Word Biblical Commentary 6B; Dallas: Word, 2002), 660.

[71] Ian Cairns, *Word and Presence: A Commentary on the Book of Deuteronomy* (Grand Rapids: Eerdmans, 1992), 236.

[72] This is a *piel* imperative, expressing the intensive degree to which honor was to be conferred.

[73] Raymond Brown, *The Message of Deuteronomy: Not by Bread Alone* (Downers Grove, Ill.: Inter-Varsity, 1993), 266.

[74] Peter C. Craigie, *The Book of Deuteronomy* (The New International Commentary on the Old Testament; Grand Rapids: Eerdmans, 1976), 332.

[75] J.G. McConville, *Deuteronomy* (Apollos Old Testament Commentary 5; Downers Grove, Ill.: InterVarsity, 2002), 393.

[76] The only other legislation addressing property rights is Deut 19:14.

"meant violating Yahweh's proprietorship."[77] It was a sin against God because God is the actual owner of the land and merely assigned it to the tribes under Joshua.[78]

Verse 18 (cursed is he who misleads a blind *person* on the road) indirectly parallels Leviticus 19:14. The concern about misleading a blind man as he is traveling (מַשְׁגֶּה עִוֵּר בַּדָּרֶךְ) is often translated broadly to include any misinformation, bad advice, or abetting sinners and criminals who are "blinded by their desires."[79] Leviticus 19:14 carries an additional prohibitive concerning the visually impaired that is similar in function and force to Deuteronomy 27:18.[80] "To mislead a blind man would be to fail to lead him on a safe – and unobstructed – path and to deliberately direct him along an unsafe – perhaps obstructed – way."[81] Deuteronomy 27:18 appears to expand the interpretation of Leviticus 19:14 so as to include all mean acts toward one who could not witness against a defendant in court.[82]

In verse 19 (cursed is he who distorts the justice due an alien, orphan, and widow) the focus is on those who are socioeconomically vulnerable and powerless (aliens, orphans, widows). These were safeguards against the perversion of justice against these vulnerable social groups as well.[83] "The exodus experience controls the treatment of all foreigners who assimilate to the community of Israel."[84] While not all differences are removed by these laws, they provided justice and for the right of the alien to enjoy the produce of God's land.[85] The mandate in verses 18-19 is to preserve justice for the most vulnerable.

Verse 24 parallels Exodus 20:13 thematically. However, different verbs are employed in the process. The curse formula in Exodus 20:13 commands, "do not kill" (לֹא תִּרְצָח) utilizing the common term for killing (רָצַח). According to Bellefontaine, Deuteronomy 27:24 sharpens the command in Exodus 20:13, specifying the action as premeditated.[86] Verse 25 prohibits taking a bribe to kill a person with which there is no grudge (לֹקֵחַ שֹׁחַד לְהַכּוֹת נֶפֶשׁ דָּם נָקִי). This law goes beyond vengeance to address the hired assassin.[87] While the admonition

---

77 Elizabeth Bellefontaine, "The Curses on Deuteronomy 27," in *A Song of Power and the Power of Song* (ed. Duane L. Christensen; Sources for Biblical and Theological Study 3; Winona Lake, Ind.; Eisenbrauns, 1993), 262.

78 Christensen, *Deuteronomy 21:10-34:12*, 662.

79 Jeffry. H. Tigay, *Deuteronomy* (JPS Torah Commentary; Philadelphia: Jewish Publication Society, 1996), 225.

80 Bellefontaine, "The Curses on Deuteronomy 27," 262.

81 Bellefontaine, "The Curses on Deuteronomy 27," 262.

82 Bellefontaine, "The Curses on Deuteronomy 27," 262.

83 Christensen, *Deuteronomy 21:10-34:12*, 662.

84 Gary J. Millar, *Now Choose Life: Theology and Ethics in Deuteronomy* (Grand Rapids: Eerdmans, 1998), 153.

85 Millar, *Now Choose Life*, 153.

86 Bellefontaine, "The Curses in Deuteronomy 27," 265.

87 Bellefontaine, "The Curses in Deuteronomy 27," 265.

against taking bribes is stated elsewhere (Exod 23:8; Deut 16:19), only here is there a curse attached to it. Bellefontaine correctly notes that the prohibition is not against murder, but the taking of a fee to commit murder.[88]

Verse 26 sums up the entire section, declaring that the law was of no effect if it was not upheld.[89] The verb קוּם used as it is here in a legal text implies "establishing," "making sure," or "binding."[90] Kalland further notes that the *hiphil* imperfect of קוּם, coupled with the infinitive of עָשָׂה (to do) may mean to persist in upholding the law or to continually uphold the law by following it.

The purpose of Deuteronomy was to explain the Torah to a new generation which was about to cross the Jordan and begin the conquest of the Promised Land and then elaborates on the social significance of the law to them.[91] Although Deuteronomy appears to restate the laws contained in Leviticus and Numbers, it does so uniquely by means of a homiletic style suggesting that rather than being indoctrinated with the legal code, Israel was being enjoined to take seriously their status as Yahweh's covenant people (4:35, 39; 6:4; 7:9; 10:17) and call to holiness (7:6; 26:19; 28:9), and to willfully submit to the law already put before them (9:7; chs. 28-30).[92]

By putting every generation in the place of that one generation at Sinai, historical qualities recede before the issue of faith.[93] Deuteronomy assembles diverse historical elements into one unifying theological imperative of purity, which God demands of his people.[94] The book reiterates material contained in other Pentateuchal books, rephrasing the material and dealing with it distinctively so as to articulate what life in Israel, organized under the authority of Yahweh, was supposed to be.[95]

Israel was to be just as covenantally oriented in private life as it was in public. Only in being so oriented publicly and privately could Israel truly correspond to a reverential estimation of Yahweh. Brueggemann asserts that covenant must be "intentionally enacted in a public way."[96] The curses in Deuteronomy 27:11-26 concern practices which would jeopardize the

---

88 Bellefontaine, "The Curses in Deuteronomy 27," 265.

89 Earl S. Kalland, *Deuteronomy* (Expositor's Bible Commentary 3; ed. Frank E. Gaebelein; Grand Rapids: Zondervan, 1991), 3:165.

90 Elmer A. Martens, "קוּם," in *NIDOTTE* (ed. Willem A. VanGemeren; Grand Rapids: Zondervan, 1997), 3:903.

91 Brevard S. Childs, *Introduction to the Old Testament as Scripture* (Philadelphia: Fortress, 1979), 211-12; Wilson G. Baroody and William F. Gentrup, "Exodus, Leviticus, Number, and Deuteronomy," in *A Complete Literary Guide to the Bible* (ed. Leland Ryken and Tremper Longman III; Grand Rapids: Zondervan, 1993), 127.

92 Gleason L. Archer Jr., *A Survey of Old Testament Introduction* (rev. ed.; Chicago: Moody Press, 1994), 272.

93 Childs, *Introduction to the Old Testament as Scripture*, 222.

94 Childs, *Introduction to the Old Testament as Scripture*, 223.

95 McConville, *Deuteronomy*, 19-20.

96 Walter Brueggemann, *Deuteronomy* (Abingdon Old Testament Commentaries; Nashville: Abingdon, 2001), 252.

community.[97] A series of conditional motive clauses in this section (vv. 15, 20, 45, 47, 58) indicate that curse and blessing were not arbitrary but conditioned either by Israel's obedience or disregard for a specific covenant stipulation.[98] The collection of socially-oriented laws in Deuteronomy 27 in the midst of a vituperate text projects a sense of urgency regarding compliance. In addition, they affirm that there was to be no hypocrisy in Israel. There was to be consistency between Israel's public bearing and its private bearing. Israel's world-view was to include the principle of concern and care for those classes of society that were traditionally left to fend for themselves. Their well-being was to be Israel's concern. Proper care of the disabled amounted to more than communal harmony or realizing an expected ethical decorum. With each act it was the effectuating of authentic faith.

The Priestly Qualifications and Disabilities: Leviticus 21:16-24 and Deuteronomy 23:2

Leviticus 21:16-24 contains the most extensive list of physical abnormalities in the Old Testament. In the Hebrew cult, in addition to satisfying conditions of lineage a priest had to be free from other factors that would threaten his priestly service such as poor health and physical defect.[99]

A heavy emphasis is placed on the matter of the priesthood in Leviticus as the medium through which access to God would be maintained.[100] The concept of the priesthood "accentuates the overall theme of God's holiness."[101] Priestly activity in the presence of Yahweh mandated that their behavior be regulated so as to remain both pure and set apart to perform their priestly role which included instruction as to the significance and means of holiness as well as actually maintaining holiness within the camp through the sacrificial system.[102]

Most of the words found in Leviticus 21 that are used to describe disqualifying disabilities are formed by the *qittēl* noun pattern, identified by a medial lengthening (doubling) of the second consonant and a *hireq* and *xere* vowel pattern.[103] These nouns signify the possession of a quality. It is possible that biblical writers saw these physical disabilities as a distinctive but normal aspect of a person's living experience.[104] The use of the *qittēl* for disability

---

[97] Brueggemann, *Deuteronomy*, 252.

[98] Merrill, "A Theology of the Pentateuch," 84.

[99] Erhard S. Gerstenberger, *Leviticus: A Commentary* (Louisville: John Knox, 1996), 316.

[100] Raymond B. Dillard, and Tremper Longman III, *An Introduction to the Old Testament* (Grand Rapids: Zondervan, 1994), 79.

[101] Dillard and Longman III, *An Introduction to the Old Testament*, 80.

[102] Dillard and Longman III, *An Introduction to the Old Testament*, 80.

[103] John Huehnergaard, "Historic Phonology and the Hebrew Piel," in *Linguistics and Biblical Hebrew* (ed. Walter Bodine; Winona Lake: Eisenbrauns, 1992), 220f.

[104] Joshua Fox, *Semitic Noun Patterns* (Winona Lake: Eisenbrauns, 2003), 5, 37, 39.

lexemes was a functional way of grouping together individuals possessing physical differences.

This list includes עִוֵּר (blindness) which appears 22 times in the Hebrew Bible in nominal or adjectival form and פִּסֵּחַ (lameness) which means an inability to walk normally.[105] It is the same term used to describe the defect in Meribbaal caused by his childhood accident. It is interesting that עִוֵּר and פִּסֵּחַ frequently appear in pairs.[106] This may underscore the severity of these afflictions and their impact on society. The term חָרֻם[107] (one with a disfigured face) is found in medical texts in the ancient Near East describing certain birth defects.[108] This may refer to a man with a split nose.[109] שָׂרוּעַ (one having a deformed limb) is exclusive to the book of Leviticus where it is used to describe a physical deformity.[110] This term may refer to a man with one limb shorter than the other,[111] or to one who has any malformed part of the body (such as an extra finger or possibly split ears).[112] Other defects include שֶׁבֶר יָד שֶׁבֶר רָגֶל אוֹ (a broken foot or broken hand), גִבֵּן (a hunchback),[113] and a דַק (a dwarf). דק literally means "small" or "thin."[114] The phrase תְּבַלֻּל בְּעֵינוֹ (one who has an eye defect) is also included in this list. The word תְּבַלֻּל is a rare deliberative term meaning a white spot in the eye that impairs one's vision.[115]

---

105 R.K. Harrison and Eugene H. Merrill, "פסח," in *NIDOTTE* (ed. Willem A. VanGemeren; Grand Rapids: Zondervan, 1997), 3:641. פִּסֵּחַ can only be construed as a condemnation of Israel's ambivalence toward Yahweh.

106 See the discussion of this phenomena *vis-à-vis* Deuteronomy 28:28-29.

107 *CAD* 6:89-90. The Akkadian word *harāmu* is a cognate.

108 Victor P. Hamilton, "חרם," in *NIDOTTE* (ed. Willem A. VanGemeren; Grand Rapids: Zondervan, 1997), 2:277.

109 Wenham, *The Book of Leviticus*, 289.

110 R.K. Harrison and Eugene, H. Merrill, "שרע," in *NIDOTTE* (ed. Willem A. VanGemeren; Grand Rapids: Zondervan, 1997), 3:1275. Here it is in the form of a *qal* passive participle (שָׂרוּעַ).

111 Wenham, *The Book of Leviticus*, 289.

112 Hartley, *Leviticus*, 350.

113 R.K. Harrison and Eugene, H. Merrill, "גִבֵּן," in *NIDOTTE* (ed. Willem A. VanGemeren; Grand Rapids: Zondervan, 1997), 1:805.

114 Francis Foulkes, "דַק," in *NIDOTTE* (ed. Willem A. VanGemeren; Grand Rapids: Zondervan, 1997), 1:981. This term is used in a number of biblical texts. For example, in Genesis 41:3-7, 23-24 it refers to the cows Pharaoh dreams of portending a famine. In Exodus 16:14 it describes the thin nature of the manna that fell in the wilderness. In Leviticus 13:30 it refers to thin hair as a symptom of skin disease and in Leviticus 16:12 it describes how fine incense is to be ground. In 1 Kings 19:11-12 it is used when Elijah ascends mount Horeb and discovers the presence of Yahweh in the "gentle whisper." And it is found in Isaiah 29:5 and 40:15 to describe how nations, which seem great and fearsome in man's sight, are insignificant and destined to be ground into powder before the Lord.

115 R.K. Harrison and Eugene H. Merrill, "תְּבַלֻּל," in *NIDOTTE* (ed. Willem A. VanGemeren; Grand Rapids: Zondervan, 1997), 4:273. In his commentary on Leviticus, Harrison indicates this as a cataract (R.K. Harrison, *Leviticus*, 211).

The nature of this affliction is unknown.[116] גָּרָב (eczema) is described as referring to "an inflamed or eruptive cutaneous condition, perhaps *Dermatitis epidemica*," a contagious and sometimes fatal disease.[117] Another possible identification of this disease is *Impetigo herpetiformis*, also a contagious and often fatal disease.[118] A cognate Akkadian term *gārāb* means scab.[119] יַלֶּפֶת (scabs) is believed to refer to "a febrile disease . . . marked by lassitude, malaise, an increased pulse rate, and occasionally collapse."[120] The reference to מְרוֹחַ אָשֶׁךְ (crushed testicles) is only found here. Its precise meaning is uncertain, though the word for "testicle" is attested in Akkadian.[121] It is possible that this refers to a eunuch (סָרִיס) although this term is a later development.[122] Thomas Hentrich suggests that the prohibition against one with crushed testicles was added later and that the issue seems irrelevant to one's functioning as a priest.[123] According to Jackie Naudé, however, the male sex organs were inviolable.[124] A defect or alteration in male reproductive organs may be due to a birth defect, deliberately inflicted for pagan religious ritual, or accidentally incurred. In any case, the priest would not be able to reproduce life or have life in him. Yahweh is God of life, and his priests were to worship him as such.[125] His priests represented life before the people in their intermediation and appearance. Consequently, having a defect in the reproductive organs permanently prohibit a priest from approaching the altar to officiate as a priest (Lev 21:16-23).[126] Miller identifies three integral factors related to participation in Israelite worship:

> Participation in Israelite worship was dependent upon obedience to the Torah and that within the laws there were various restrictions upon participation that depended upon purity and holiness and required various ritual acts of sacrifice and purification before appearing before the Lord in worship for fear that the presence of the impure and the unholy might profane the sanctuary. In addition, there were

---

[116] Harrison and Eugene H. Merrill, "תְּבַלֻּל".

[117] R.K. Harrison, "גרב," in *NIDOTTE* (ed. Willem A. VanGemeren; Grand Rapids: Zondervan, 1997), 1:890.

[118] Harrison, "גרב," 1:890.

[119] *SCAD* 5:46. *gārāb* could refer to leprosy.

[120] R.K. Harrison, "יַלֶּפֶת," in *NIDOTTE* (ed. Willem A. VanGemeren; Grand Rapids: Zondervan, 1997), 2:461.

[121] *CAD* 7:250-51. The Akkadian cognate *išku* to אֶשֶׁךְ also means testicle.

[122] Gordon H. Johnston, "סָרִיס," in *NIDOTTE* (ed. Willem A. VanGemeren; Grand Rapids: Zondervan, 1997), 3:288-95.

[123] Hentrich "Masculinity and Disability in the Bible," 83-86. Hentrich correctly notes that "circumcision is practically the only physical 'defect' that is not viewed as a blemish and is actually desired in Israelite men . . ."

[124] Jackie A. Naudé, "Sexual Ordinances," in *NIDOTTE* (ed. Willem A. VanGemeren; Grand Rapids: Zondervan, 1997), 4:1206.

[125] Milgrom, *Leviticus 17-22*, 1841.

[126] Milgrom, *Studies in Levitical Terminology*, 40.

> further restrictions on participation in the cultic assembly, such as genital impairment or birth by illicit union (presumably incest–Deut 23:1-2) or other forms of physical deformity, mutilation, or defect, such as blindness, lameness, broken limbs, itching disease, and the like (Lev 21:16-23; 2 Sam 5:8).[127]

Although a blemished priest may not officiate, he may still enter the sanctuary precincts. Verses 22-23 contain an epilogue explaining that although a Levite may not offer sacrifices, he is fully vested as a priest and entitled to the same provisions as other priests.[128] Milgrom deduces that if a priest may come into contact with the sacred food then he may also make contact with other sacred objects.[129] This strongly argues against the possibility that a physical defect which would bar a priest from officiating at the altar was due to the fact that a physical defect was equated with moral impurity. If it were so, the same defect that would bar the priest from altar officiating would likewise restrict him from the sacred precincts and from eating the holy priestly offerings (Lev 22:3-7).[130]

It is interesting that the term used in Leviticus 21 to refer to the priestly qualification and in chapter 22 to refer to the quality of animal sacrifices is מוּם whereas the term used in relation to animal sacrifices in Leviticus chapters 1-7 and 23:12, 18 is תָּמִים. Although this is possibly due to the specificity of the issues addressed in the different sections, it is more likely due to structural and theological considerations.

Presumably, an offering that is defective would be known to the offerer, the officiating priest, and Yahweh alone. Malachi 1:8-14 charges that the priests were making defective offerings stemming from their condescending contempt for the Lord. Although תָּמִים usually refers to the physical completeness of a sacrifice (Exod 12:5; Lev 1:3, 10; 3:1, 6; 4:3, 23, 28, 32; 5:15, 18, 25; 9:2, 3; 22:19, 21; 23:12; Ezek 43:22, 23; 45:18; 46:4, 13), it can also refer to flawlessness of character as well (Gen 6:9; 17:1; Deut 18:15; 2 Sam 22:24, 26, 31, 33; Pss 15:3; 18:24, 26, 31, 33; 101:2, 6; 119:80; Prov 11:5; 28:18; Ezek 28:15; Amos 5:10).

---

[127] Patrick Miller, *The Religion of Ancient Israel* (Louisville: Westminster/John Knox, 2000), 206-07.

[128] Milgrom, *Studies in Levitical Terminology*, 40. The holy offering could only be consumed inside the sacred precincts of the sanctuary where only ordained priests could enter (Lev 6:9, 19; 7:6; 10:13, 17; 24:9).

[129] Milgrom, *Studies in Levitical Terminology*, 41.

[130] David P. Wright, *The Disposal of Impurity: Elimination Rites in the Bible and in Hittite and Mesopotamian Literature* (Society of Biblical Literature Dissertation Series 101; Atlanta: Scholars Press, 1987), 233. Wright notes that מְקוֹם קָדֹשׁ refers to the Tabernacle court enclosure. The adjective מְקוֹם expresses the quality of this locale. In Leviticus 10:12-14 the term refers to the place where the holy offering was to be consumed by the priests. The rationale for eating the offering in the holy place is because these offerings were most holy (Lev 7:6; 10:12, 17; 24:9; Exod 29:33).

All the sacrifices prescribed in Leviticus were to be תָּמִים. This same prerequisite applied in Mesopotamia as well.[131] The Ugaritic cognate for תָּמִים is *tmm*. Although the noun and verbal usage of this word is not certain, its adjectival usage indicates "complete," or "come to an end" (*KTU* 1.23, 67).[132] In Hebrew the word תָּמִים means wholeness, completeness.[133]

In the Old Testament when תָּמִים conveys the meaning of that which is complete, blameless, just, honest, perfect, peaceful, etc., it expresses the concept of integrity, "conveying the meaning of that which is complete, blameless, just, honest, perfect, peaceful, etc.; hence an attribute or an attitude that reflects genuineness and reliability."[134] תָּמִים can also be used for the end of a speech (Job 31:40), a withered blossom (Isa 18:5), or an completed action (Josh 3:17). When used to express blamelessness as in Psalm 19:14, it conveys the idea of innocence.[135] In the context of cultic usage (Lev 1-7; 9:2), תָּמִים designates the unobjectionable condition of an offering animal (i.e., healthy, without defect, and free of any blemish). It also indicates an unclouded relationship between Yahweh and his righteous people (Gen 6:9; 17:1; Deut 18:13; Josh 24:14) as well as trust within all sincere human relationships (Judg 9:16; Amos 5:10).[136] To be תָּמִים also means to be pious (Ps 18:24) and is used to describe the way of Yahweh as perfect (2 Sam 22:31; Ps 18:31).[137] According to Mary Douglas, תָּמִים expresses the design of holiness.[138] "Holiness requires that individuals shall conform to the class to which they belong."[139] Transgressing these boundaries makes one unclean. A person must conform to the norms of moral and physical perfection (just as animals must conform to standards of their particular animal class) in order to be considered clean.[140]

The moral blemishes (מוּם) in chapters 20-22 are thematically linked with the physical blemishes (מוּם) in chapter 19.[141] Impurity is a perennial issue in Leviticus.[142] The topic is reiterated throughout the book. מוּם[143] (blemish,

---

[131] A. Falkenstein and W. von Soden, *Sumerische und akkadische Hymnen und Gebeten*, vol. 1 (Zurich: Artemis, 1953), 275. Although this text is poetic, it nonetheless describes the offering made as being pure.

[132] J.P.J. Olivier, "תמם," in *NIDOTTE* (ed. Willem A. VanGemeren; Grand Rapids: Zondervan, 1997), 4:306.

[133] Olivier, "תמם," 4:306.

[134] Olivier, "תמם," 4:306.

[135] Olivier, "תמם," 4:307.

[136] Olivier, "תמם," 4:307.

[137] Olivier, "תמם," 4:307.

[138] Douglas, *Purity and Danger*, 51-52.

[139] Douglas, *Purity and Danger*, 53.

[140] Douglas, *Purity and Danger*, 54.

[141] Jacob Milgrom, *Leviticus 23-27* (The Anchor Bible 3B; New York: Doubleday, 2001), 2106.

[142] Douglas, "Poetic Structure in Leviticus," 239.

defect), appears mostly in Leviticus 21-22, and 24 providing a thematic connection between these chapters. Douglas makes the argument that מוּם is implicit in the notion of injustice.[144] Regarding Leviticus 24:19-20 Douglas writes,

> So causing a blemish in a neighbor is doing him a damage according to the elementary principles of justice: taking away something that is his by right, leaving him with too little. Or by oppression, giving him a heavy load to bear . . . The interesting thing is that the neighbor who has suffered outrage in the case of the blasphemer is YHWH himself, and we soon see in ch. 26, that YHWH is included squarely in the law of talion with the rest of his creation.[145]

Douglas argues that the neighbor here is Yahweh himself. מוּם also implicitly provides the rational for, and is connected with, the inequitable acts described in Leviticus 19. Inflicting an injury on a person by depriving that person of their dignity (Lev 19) or property (Lev 25), is a מוּם that is just as unacceptable to Yahweh as any blemish before him in a priest (Lev 21) or a sacrifice (Lev 22).[146] Profanation of God's sanctuary, name, and of human dignity will be the basis for judgment of Israel as described in the prophets and forms the basis of the charge that Israel was disabled toward God.

The concepts of purity and impurity are based on theological reasoning. Its intent was to maintain the divinely placed barriers established between various classes and species (divine and human, and human and animal). Admixture between classes or species of creation is a reversal of God's created order.[147] Hence, animals which demonstrated characteristics which were outside of the natural order were considered unclean.[148] It can be concluded, then, that it is not so much the purity laws themselves that make Yahwism distinct from other religions but rather it is the lack of social demarcation that makes the biblical system of impurity distinct from other religious systems.[149] Other ancient Near Eastern cultures used pollution rules as instruments for keeping classes of the same population apart,[150] but in Israel all classes of people (aliens, poor,

---

[143] מוּם is central to the identifying qualifications of priests (21:17, 18, 21, 23), sacrifices (22:20, 21), those who may bring an offering (22:25) and the *talion* laws (24:19-20).

[144] Mary Douglas, "The Forbidden Animals of Leviticus," *Journal for the Study of the Old Testament* 59 (1993): 19-20.

[145] Douglas, "The Forbidden Animals of Leviticus," 20.

[146] Milgrom, *Leviticus 23-27*, 2106. Leviticus 10:1-7 and 24:10-23 form the only two narratives in the book. Both narratives deal with defilement. In chapter 10 Yahweh's sanctuary is defiled while in 19 it is Yahweh's name that is defiled. Consequently, Milgrom argues that Leviticus 24 counterbalances chapter 10 with chapter 19, which addresses respecting a person's dignity, being the fulcrum between them.

[147] Douglas, *Purity and Danger*, 53.

[148] Douglas, *Purity and Danger*, 54-57.

[149] Douglas, "Poetic Structure in Leviticus," 239.

[150] Douglas, "Poetic Structure in Leviticus," 240.

disabled) were included in the benefits of purification.[151] Impurity "is a statement about the nature of existence in a sacramental universe, a religious ontology."[152]

In ancient Israel, the priest "mediates between heaven and earth, between holy and profane. To survive in such a dangerous position, the priest had to be fit for the company of angels."[153] Abrams suggests that Leviticus 21:16-24 only mentions physical defects that are perceptible to the naked eye and does not include physical defects that would be imperceptible to the naked eye such as deafness, or mental defect, and this, perhaps, for the very fact that they are imperceptible.[154]

It is asserted by some that the Bible attributes physical imperfections to be the result of God's judgment on individuals for sin. Hence, only physically perfect offerings could be brought to the altar and physically perfect priests could officiate. Hans-Joachim Kraus, for example, makes the argument that there exists in the Old Testament an unbreakable causal connection between guilt and sickness (Ps 32:1-4; 38:3-11; 39:8, 11). "In the sickness, guilt is made manifest as the cause of ruin and as the target of God's wrath."[155] Grünwaldt also asserts that these proscriptions are based on the tradition that priests must be pure in order to perform their duties and that disease and impurity were associated with sin and death.[156] A rationale for priestly purity may be taken from Grünwaldt who notes that when the priest presents the cult sacrifices he is ". . . in direkten Kontakt mit der Gottheit kommen (21, 6.8.17; 22,15 u. ö.), ja sie kommen dem heiligen Gott selbst näher als irgend jemand sonst (21,23)."[157]

The exclusion of the disabled from ecclesiastical duties and the warranting of such on the basis cited cannot be disputed. However, the interpretation of Leviticus 21:17-23, as conflating immorality and disability, is in dispute. This text's proper interpretation asserting perfect physical condition as a representation of Yahweh's wholeness provides a legitimate warrant for its proscription against those with disabilities from officiating as a priest. One with disabilities was not ousted from the prerogatives and privileges of the priestly class although he could not perform priestly functions.

In Hebrew usage, clean and unclean is used to describe a state of being (status) or a condition.[158] "The desire for purity was so intense that a major social class, the priesthood, was entrusted with the task of determining and

---

[151] Douglas, "Poetic Structure in Leviticus," 240.
[152] Douglas, "Poetic Structure in Leviticus," 255.
[153] Abrams, *Judaism and Disability: Portrayals in Ancient Texts from the Tanach through the Bavli*, 23.
[154] Abrams, *Judaism and Disability*, 23.
[155] Kraus, *Theology of the Psalms*, 132.
[156] Grünwaldt, *Das Heiligkeitsgesetz Leviticus 17-26*, 69, 269.
[157] Grünwaldt, *Das Heiligkeitsgesetz Leviticus 17-26*, 393.
[158] Richard E. Averbeck, "Clean and Unclean," in *NIDOTTE* (ed. Willem A. VanGemeren; Grand Rapids: Zondervan, 1997), 4:477.

giving instruction about purity and impurity."[159] Douglas notes that although impurity concepts "normally maintain the accepted moral and social codes," and that these codes normally "separate categories of the same population," there is something unique in the Israelite impurity codes.[160] "Ritual impurity imposes God's order on his creation."[161] A person becomes unfit to approach the holy precincts when he comes into contact with something unclean or when a moral breach occurs (Lev 5:2, 5-6; 7:19-21). Both equally render a person in need of atonement.[162] Douglas writes,

> In so far as the Levitical rules for purity apply universally they are useless for internal disciplining. They maintain absolutely no social demarcation. It is true that only the priest can make atonement, and that the priest's dedication food must not be eaten by outsiders, but the book insists over and over again that the poor and the stranger are to be included in the requirements of the laws; no one is excluded from the benefits of purification.[163]

This is a reversal of her previous work that saw the function of these structures as being designed to influence societal conduct.[164] Douglas once held that on one level, the rules for purity were instrumental, working to influence one another's behavior.[165] On another level these rules were symbolic, expressing a general view of social order.[166] She now understands rules pertaining to defilement and dietary regulations in light of atonement and of justice, respectively.[167]

Fitness for the sacred precincts is also at the heart of the prohibition regarding priests who contracts leprosy. "The rule that prevents leper priests from ministering in the sanctuary targets a defined class."[168] Douglas further writes,

> Leprosy counts as a pollution, not as a maiming, for one could be purified from leprosy, but a maimed person was maimed for life. Thus a leper priest is excluded from both serving in the Temple and from eating holy food, but may resume both when purified. A maimed priest is excluded from serving in the Temple for life, but may eat holy food–unless he becomes temporarily polluted. The priests are

---

159 Tikva Frymer-Kensky, "Pollution, Purification, and Purgation in Biblical Israel," in *The Word of the Lord Shall Go Forth: Essays in Honor of David Noel Freedman* (ed. C.L. Meyer and M O'Conner; Winona Lake, Ind.: Eisenbrauns, 1983), 399.

160 Douglas, "The Forbidden Animals of Leviticus," 7.

161 Douglas, *Leviticus as Literature*, 151.

162 Douglas, *Leviticus as Literature*, 150-51.

163 Mary Douglas, "Atonement in Leviticus," *Jewish Studies Quarterly* 1, no. 2 (1993): 112-113.

164 Douglas, *Purity and Danger*, 3, 4.

165 Douglas, *Purity and Danger*, 3.

166 Douglas, *Purity and Danger*, 4.

167 Douglas, *Leviticus as Literature*, 109-33, 175, 216-17.

168 Douglas, "Sacred Contagion," 100-101.

> subject to the same laws of purity as the laity, but they face more severe penalties for breach.[169]

Offerings were not to be eaten by anyone in an unclean state. Leviticus 7:19-21 specifies that sacrificial meat can be rendered ritually impure and therefore inedible through contact with anything unclean (7:19a). In such cases it was to be burned rather than eaten. Only one who is in a state of cleanness was eligible to eat the meat (7:19b). Persons in an unclean state who partake of the meat offering suffer the consequence of being cut off from the congregation (נִכְרְתָה).[170] It does not matter whether the degree of impurity is significant or minor (Lev 7:20-21). A priest who is in the state of uncleanness must not partake of an offering (Lev 22:3).

It should be noted that it was not only a priest's physical form that was to be unblemished but his lineage as well. The priest was to avoid the taint of death (Lev 21:1-6) and to marry in a way that preserves the priestly lineage (Lev 21:7-9). Regulations regarding the high priest were even more restrictive (Lev 21:10-15).

A physical disability may disqualify a priest from officiating in the cult but he is still a priest in every respect and entitled to priestly emoluments. A defect in lineage, however, would render a priest ritually impure and therefore disqualify him from cultic officiation as well as priestly emoluments. "Thus a priest in a state of ritual impurity is more disabled than a priest who is blind."[171] Abrams suggests this is due to the fact that "nothing with the taint of death may be associated with the place of life in its purest form on earth: the Temple."[172] She writes,

> The priest must embody the best blood (i.e., not tainted by ritual impurity and of the best lineage) in a perfect vessel (i.e., a blemishless body) to withstand the lethal aura that surrounds the innermost parts of the Temple.[173]

The holiness of the Temple and the One who inhabited it were at issue.

A priest could be temporarily unfit to approach the altar for reasons of improper washing (Exod 30:20), drunkenness (Lev 10:9), or for being

---

[169] Douglas, "Sacred Contagion," 101.

[170] The *niphal* stem of the verb כרת as used in Leviticus 7 can either refer to the death penalty (*BDB,* 504) or to exclusion from the community by ostracization (Eugene Carpenter, "כרת," in *NIDOTTE* [ed. Willem A. VanGemeren; Grand Rapids: Zondervan, 1997], 2:729). It is more likely that the term indicates a kind of disenfranchisement from the covenant and excommunication from the community rather than suffering death (except in the cases of making child offerings to Molech [Lev 20:2] and Sabbath desecration [Exod 31:14]).

[171] Abrams, *Judaism and Disability*, 26. Here, however, the term "disabled" means "not-able." He could not eat the meat either, much less officiate.

[172] Abrams, *Judaism and Disability*, 26.

[173] Abrams, *Judaism and Disability*, 26.

improperly dressed (Exod 28:43).[174] To do such things would incur a penalty of death.[175] The rationale for such a harsh penalty appears to be the uncompromising and unconditional holiness of the sanctuary interior.[176] While the temporary disqualifying issue remains (until he is cleansed) the priest is considered a non-priest in regard to the sanctuary.[177] The blemished priest falls into a different category. He is not of a condition whereby he could defile or profane, yet he does not carry in his body the perfection requisite to officiate at the altar of the Lord.

As noted earlier, the criteria for an acceptable priest in Leviticus 21:16-24 parallels that of an acceptable animal sacrifice in Leviticus 22:21-24.[178] Hentrich notes,

> Whatever applies to the sacrifices, must also apply to the sanctifier. This would explain why certain human "blemishes" like deafness or muteness are absent from the list, because they were not easily detected in animals, and why one blemish, crushed testicles, was included in the priestly list.[179]

His rationale for differences in the list of blemishes for humans and animals is based on their obviousness.[180] He asserts that the priest's disabilities not only parallel those of animals but "are an arbitrary collection of disabilities in order to match the animal blemishes."[181] Hentrich does not appear to appreciate the fact that perfection in relation to the sacrifices expressed reverence toward God. If the offering was to mean anything in terms of communicating worship it must be perfect, but priestly perfection was an extension of holiness.[182]

Although the root meaning of holiness is separation (reflecting Yahweh's total otherness), the concept of holiness is not limited to this one particular. This is seen in those statutes which maintain the distinction between categories of creation. Order is also evident in those statutes related to sexual purity and dietary laws (Exod 23:19; 34:26; Lev 18; 20; Deut 14:21; 27:20-23). Holiness is exemplified in order rather than confusion (Lev 19). Douglas writes,

---

174 Milgrom, *Studies in Levitical Terminology*, 38-39.

175 A priest could die for not being properly dressed (Exod 28:43), for not washing before entering the tent of meeting (Exod 30:20-21), for deviating from Yahweh's prescribed from of ritual (Lev 10:2-3; 16:13; Num 18:1-3), for mourning for those who die as a result of deviating from prescribed rituals (Lev 10:6; Num 4:15, 19), or for being drunk (Lev 10:9).

176 Milgrom, *Studies in Levitical Terminology*, 39.

177 Milgrom, *Studies in Levitical Terminology*, 40.

178 Jacob Milgrom, *Leviticus 1-16* (The Anchor Bible 3; New York: Doubleday, 1991), 722.

179 Thomas Hentrich, "The 'Lame' in Lev 21, 17-23 and 2 Sam 5, 6-8," 15-16.

180 Hentrich, "The 'Lame' in Lev 21, 17-23 and 2 Sam 5, 6-8," 16.

181 Hentrich, "The 'Lame' in Lev 21, 17-23 and 2 Sam 5, 6-8," 15.

182 Douglas, *Purity and Danger*, 63-65.

> Holiness requires that individuals shall conform to the class to which they belong. And holiness requires that different classes of things shall not be confused . . . Holiness means keeping distinct the categories of creation. It therefore involves correct definition, discrimination, and order.[183]

The concept of holiness is illustrated in separation, order, goodness and moral justice. According to Douglas, the concept of holiness is founded on the idea of wholeness and completeness.[184] She writes,

> Much of Leviticus is taken up with stating the physical perfection that is required of things presented in the temple and of persons approaching it. The animals offered in sacrifice must be without blemish, women must be purified after childbirth, lepers should be separated and ritually cleansed before being allowed to approach once they are cured. All bodily discharges are defiling and disqualify from approach to the temple.[185]

The purity system arguably conveys in a symbolic way that Yahweh is the God of life (order) and is separated from that which has to do with death (disorder).[186] Corpses and carcasses rendered a person unclean because they obviously have to do with death.[187] Bodily discharges (blood for women, semen for men—blood and semen both being symbols of life) may represent a temporary loss of strength and life and movement towards death.[188] After ejaculation, men typically need some time to regenerate before being fully sexually functional again.[189] Decaying corpses too are reminders of sin and death.[190] Hence, purification rituals symbolized movement away from death towards life (Lev 17:11; 14:5, 50; Num 19:2, 17).[191]

---

183 Douglas, *Purity and Danger*, 53.

184 Douglas, *Purity and Danger*, 49ff.

185 Douglas, *Purity and Danger*, 55.

186 Sprinkle, "The Rationale of the Laws of Clean and Unclean in the Old Testament," 649.

187 Sprinkle, "The Rationale of the Laws of Clean and Unclean in the Old Testament," 649. Sprinkle notes that most (though not all) of the unclean animals are somehow associated with death, either being predators/scavengers (animals with paws rather than hoofs) or living in tomb-like caves (rock badgers). The pig in particular, in addition to being a scavenger, was associated with the worship of chthonic or underworld deities and/or demons among the Hittites, Egyptians, and Mesopotamians. The scale disease rendered a person unclean, because it made a person waste away like a corpse (cf. Num 12:12).

188 Sprinkle, "The Rationale of the Laws of Clean and Unclean in the Old Testament," 649.

189 Sprinkle, "The Rationale of the Laws of Clean and Unclean in the Old Testament," 649.

190 Sprinkle, "The Rationale of the Laws of Clean and Unclean in the Old Testament," 649.

191 Sprinkle, "The Rationale of the Laws of Clean and Unclean in the Old Testament," 649-50.

Even some food laws can be explained on this basis.[192] It is possible that Israel was not to cook a kid in its mother's milk (Exod 23:19; 34:26; Deut 14:21) because it was inappropriate to combine that which is a symbol of life (mother's milk) with the death of the kid the milk was meant to give life to, and this especially in the context of the festival of Tabernacles (so the context of Exod 23:19) celebrating the life-giving power of Yahweh.[193]

Yahweh is both a holy God and the God of life, and was to be worshiped as such. The pedagogic backdrop of Israel's divinely revealed law demonstrates a predisposition for the promotion of life and rejection of death.[194] Hence, activities related to dealings with death such as necromancy, spiritualism and ancestor veneration, would render a person unclean and so were forbidden (Lev 19:31; Isa 65:4). When boundaries between clean and unclean were violated, a purification ritual was required in order to re-consecrate the offender. Purification rituals "symbolize movement from death towards life and accordingly involved blood, the color red, and spring (literal "living") water, all of which are symbols of life (Lev 17:11; 14:5, 50; Num 19:2, 17, etc.)."[195] This emphasis on holiness and life continues to be seen in matters related to physical imperfections which represent a movement from life towards death, moving a person ritually away from God, who is to be associated with life.[196] The human body itself was the ordained scheme expressing completeness established at creation. Consequently, physical perfection of both worshiper (Lev 21:17-23) and offerings (Lev 1:3, 10; 3:1, 6; 4:3, 23, 28, 32; 5:15, 18; 6:6; 9:2-3; 14:10; 22:19-21, 25; 23:12, 18; Num 6:14; 19:2; 28:3, 9, 11, 19, 31; 29:2, 8, 13, 20, 23, 26, 29, 32, 36; Deut 15:21; 17:1) is essential inasmuch as holiness is exemplified by completeness. Consequently, physical impairment exemplifies a physical flaw, not a moral flaw. By extension, it can be affirmed that holiness means life. In biblical terms then, a holy man walks in the ways of Yahweh who defines a spiritual course for Israel to walk. Sight, mobility, etc., involves walking in what Yahweh prescribes as opposed to any other way.

Similarly, Wenham affirms that "the idea emerges clearly that holiness finds physical expression in wholeness and normality."[197] The author of Leviticus "is

---

192 Sprinkle, "The Rationale of the Laws of Clean and Unclean in the Old Testament," 650.

193 Sprinkle, "The Rationale of the Laws of Clean and Unclean in the Old Testament," 650.

194 Milgrom, *Leviticus 17-22*, 1841.

195 Sprinkle, "The Rationale of the Laws of Clean and Unclean in the Old Testament," 650.

196 Milgrom, *Leviticus 17-22*, 1836-39; Sprinkle, "The Rationale of the Laws of Clean and Unclean in the Old Testament," 650. Priests and animals with the same physical imperfections were ineligible for the sanctuary (Lev 21:17–21; 22:20–24). Physical imperfections, representing a movement from "life" towards "death," moved a person ritually away from God, who is to be associated with life.

197 Wenham, *The Book of Leviticus*, 292.

teaching the people of Israel to honour in their lives the order of creation, and by doing so to share in its work."[198] The body becomes both the paradigm and a measure of justice.[199] "Only the perfect body is fit to be consecrated, no animal with a blemish may be sacrificed, no priest with a blemished body shall approach the altar."[200] Douglas contends that Leviticus utilizes parallelism to correspond physical blemishes with blemishes of judgment.[201] Hartley writes,

> Physical wholeness corresponds to the holiness of his task. While such a person could not function as a priest, he maintained the prerogatives of a priest in regard to support and living quarters.[202]

Since priests represented the people in the presence of the Holy One of Israel, their physical condition was to display the perfections of God's creation.[203] In contrast to the temporary disallowance of the priest as an officiate in the cult due to being in an unclean condition, a physical disability would permanently prevent the priest from presiding in the cult.

The rational for these priestly restrictions is seen in the fact that Yahweh is both a holy God and the God of life, and was to be worshiped as such. The pedagogic backdrop of Israel's divinely revealed law demonstrates a predisposition for the promotion of life and rejection of death.[204] The demand for physical perfection is justified on the basis that bodily perfection was considered an extension of holiness.[205] "Holiness finds physical expression in wholeness and normality."[206]

The classification of holiness relates to the status of a priest distinguished for service in Yahweh's temple. The priest possessed the holy status of a holy person (Lev 8). His physical constitution and deportment related to his condition. A priest's condition would be affected upon coming into contact with something unclean but his status would not be changed by this. While a disabled priest maintained the physical status of holy, he was continually, but dint of his disability, in a ritual condition of unclean. Consequently, an abnormal physical condition would not hinder a priest from enjoying the benefits of being of the priestly class, provided he remains in a ritually clean condition, although he could not offer sacrifices himself. Levine points out that the defect may only be partial but it is still enough to remove the right of the

[198] Douglas, *Leviticus as Literature*, 45.
[199] Douglas, *Leviticus as Literature*, 45-46.
[200] Douglas, *Leviticus as Literature*, 46.
[201] Douglas, *Leviticus as Literature*, 46.
[202] Hartley, *Leviticus*, 351.
[203] Ross, *Holiness to the Lord*, 387.
[204] Milgrom, *Leviticus 17-22*, 1841.
[205] Douglas, *Purity and Danger*, 42, 51.
[206] Wenham, *The Book of Leviticus*, 292.

priest from officiating in the cult.[207] "God claimed the totality of their lives."[208] Accordingly, the spiritual leaders of Israel were expected to demonstrate holiness in every aspect of life (in both physical appearance and comportment). Ross asserts that the primary theological idea being communicated is that the priesthood was not an occupation but a life.[209]

A parallel between Leviticus 21:17-23 can be found in Ezekiel 44 where Israel, addressed as the house of rebellion, is accused of having "brought foreigners uncircumcised in heart and flesh into my sanctuary, desecrating my Temple" (Ezek 44:7-9).[210] Such an offence constitutes a breach in the covenant (Ezek 44:7).[211] Ezekiel's concern appears to be for protecting the sanctity of the holy precincts. With this in the background, he addresses the specific sins of the Levites in their straying far from Yahweh, serving the House of Israel before their idols, and leading Israel astray (Ezek 44:10-12). With the exception of the sons of Zadok (Ezek 44:15), their sinful behavior will result in their disqualification of the descendants of Levi from presiding at the altar of the sanctuary (Ezek 44:13). However, the moral defects of the Levites do not disqualify them from the priesthood. They are still priests charged with the care of the Temple precincts.

Deuteronomy 23:2 (Heb.) parallels the priestly qualifications specified in Leviticus 21. This text (vv. 1-3) addresses the matter of admission and exclusion into the assembly of Israel. Craigie asserts that the phrase קְהַל יְהוָה (the assembly of the Lord) refers to the nation of Israel as a whole.[212] The word assembly (קָהָל) refers to the formal gathering of the Lord's people as a community. Kalland adds that the phrase קְהַל יְהוָה refers more specifically to Israel's religious community.[213] While the theme of Deuteronomy 23 is the assembly (קָהָל) of the Lord, the usage of this term in verse 2 indicates that the expression is somewhat narrower in its intent than the whole nation of Israel.[214] This verb is also used in Deuteronomy 31:28-30 which specifically refers to the elder and officials assembled at Moses' bidding. The verb used throughout verses 2-4 (יָבֹא) suggests participation with the assembly rather than

[207] Baruch Levine, *Leviticus* (JPS Torah Commentary; Philadelphia: Jewish Publication Society, 1989), 145.

[208] Ross, *Holiness to the Lord*, 381.

[209] Ross, *Holiness to the Lord*, 381.

[210] Iain M. Duguid, *Ezekiel and the Leaders of Israel* (Supplements to Vetus Testamentum 56; Leiden: Brill, 1994), 76-78. Ezekiel may be referring to the practice of employing foreign Temple guards (2 Kgs 11:14-19). Duguid suggests that this would fit the context of Ezekiel well in that Israel is accused of poorly keeping charge of Yahweh's holy things by turning them over to others (Ezek 44:8).

[211] Duguid, *Ezekiel and the Leaders of Israel*, 77.

[212] Craigie, *The Book of Deuteronomy*, 296.

[213] Kalland, *Deuteronomy*, EBC 3:140.

[214] Craigie, *The Book of Deuteronomy*, 296.

introduction to it.[215] The indication is that this prohibition is not intended to eliminate any male from the assembly whose genitalia (שָׁפְכָה, penis) has been removed (כרות, cut off) for any reason. Isaiah 56:3-5 states, a eunuch is not cut off from the Lord's blessings. The condition for receiving this blessing, though, seems to be an avowed allegiance to Yahweh alone (Isa 56:3). This may imply that those with a self-inflicted emasculation (פְּצוּעַ־דַּכָּא, emasculated) for cultic reasons would be excluded.[216]

McConville argues that this is a polemic against ritual mutilation.[217] This would impact the issues in Leviticus 21 as possibly also being a polemic against self-mutilation practices known to have existed among other ancient Near Eastern cults. How does this affect those who have been mutilated by accident or birth defect? Merrill argues that this is a synecdoche representing all physical defects of ethnic or cultic identity.[218] Brueggemann asserts that verses one and two are related as it pertains to a holy people who sexually are both generative and chaste at the same time.[219] Craigie suggests that this text does not appear aimed at those who have suffered misfortune.[220] It is most probable that this text addresses the same issue for the common people of the congregation as Leviticus 21's proscription regarding the physical qualities required for those who officiate at the altar of Yahweh and for the same reasons.

David and the Disabled: 2 Samuel 5:6-8

Shortly after his coronation (5:5), David and his men march toward Jerusalem which was, at that time a Jebusite settlement.[221] David's intent is to capture the city from the Jebusites and to make it a centrally located headquarters of a unified nation.[222] Upon approaching the city, David finds the Jebusite city fortified and the Jebusites themselves feisty. 2 Samuel 5:6 reads:

וַיֵּ֨לֶךְ הַמֶּ֤לֶךְ וַֽאֲנָשָׁיו֙ יְר֣וּשָׁלִַ֔ם אֶל־הַיְבֻסִ֖י יוֹשֵׁ֣ב הָאָ֑רֶץ וַיֹּ֨אמֶר לְדָוִ֤ד לֵאמֹר֙
לֹֽא־תָב֣וֹא הֵ֔נָּה כִּ֣י אִם־הֱסִֽירְךָ֗ הַעִוְרִ֤ים וְהַפִּסְחִים֙ לֵאמֹ֔ר לֹֽא־יָב֥וֹא דָוִ֖ד הֵֽנָּה׃

---

215 Merrill, *Deuteronomy*, 307.

216 Adam C. Welch, *The Code of Deuteronomy: A New Theory of Its Origin* (London: James Clark, 1925), 200.

217 McConville, *Deuteronomy*, 348.

218 Merrill, *Deuteronomy*, 307.

219 Brueggemann, *Deuteronomy*, 227.

220 Craigie, *The Book of Deuteronomy*, 296-97.

221 Benjamin Mazar, "Jerusalem in the Biblical Period," in *Jerusalem Revealed: Archaeology in the Holy City 1968-1974* (ed. Yigal Yadin; Jerusalem: Israel Exploration Society, 1975), 4.

222 Ronald F. Youngblood, *1 & 2 Samuel* (Expositor's Bible Commentary 3; ed. Frank E. Gaebelein; Grand Rapids: Zondervan, 1991), 854.

> Now the king and his men went to Jerusalem against the Jebusites, the inhabitants of the land, and they said to David, “You shall not come in here for the blind and the lame will turn you away;” thinking “David cannot enter here.”

Verse 8 contains David’s reaction:

> וַיֹּ֨אמֶר דָּוִ֜ד בַּיּ֣וֹם הַה֗וּא כָּל־מַכֵּ֤ה יְבֻסִי֙ וְיִגַּ֣ע בַּצִּנּ֔וֹר וְאֶת־הַפִּסְחִים֙ וְאֶת־הַֽעִוְרִ֔ים
> (שְׂנֻאו) [שְׂנֻאֵ֖י] נֶ֣פֶשׁ דָּוִ֑ד עַל־כֵּן֙ יֹֽאמְר֔וּ עִוֵּ֣ר וּפִסֵּ֔חַ לֹ֥א יָב֖וֹא אֶל־הַבָּֽיִת׃
>
> Then David said on that day, “Anyone who strikes the Jebusites, he must reach the lame and blind, who are hated by David’s soul, through the water tunnel.” Therefore they say the blind and lame will not enter into the house.

David lays the strategy to take the city before his men. It is simple. Enter through the water tunnel and capture them. In the process of laying this out, the blind and lame are mentioned twice. First in reference to a group of people David’s soul “hates” (שְׂנֻאו), then in reference to their being banished from entering “the house” (הַבָּיִת).

A reference to the blind and lame is made three times in these five verses (v. 6; v. 8 [twice]). The Jebusite inhabitants respond to David’s instigation with a provocation of their own (v. 6). Many interpretations of the Jebusites’ comments have been offered. Some suggest that this indicates the Jebusite intention of holding out to the last man,[223] or a case of pre-battle taunting.[224] Others suggest it expresses confidence in the city’s impregnability.[225] Hertzberg proposes that this phrase is anecdotal, indicating that even the blind and lame would be able to repel David’s forces.[226] Still others argue that the phrase אִם־הֱסִירְךָ הַעִוְרִים וְהַפִּסְחִי (for the blind and lame will turn you away) cannot be taken in any other way than in its proper sense, asserting that the walls were “manned by cripples” as a sign of derision for David and his men.[227]

---

[223] Robert P. Gordon, *I and II Samuel: A Commentary* (Grand Rapids: Regency, 1986), 226; Peter R. Ackroyd, *The Second Book of Samuel: A Commentary* (The Cambridge Bible Commentary; Cambridge: University Press, 1979), 56.

[224] Ackroyd, *The Second Book of Samuel*, 56. Like that of the Rabshakeh at the walls of Jerusalem (2 Kgs 18:19-27).

[225] Walter Brueggemann, *First and Second Samuel* (Interpretation; Louisville: John Knox, 1990), 240; A. A. Anderson, *2 Samuel* (Word Bible Commentary 11; Dallas: Word, 1989), 82-83; Bruce C. Birch, *The Book of 2 Samuel*, in *The New Interpreter’s Bible* (ed. Leander E Kect, et al., Nahsville: Abingdon, 1994), 2:1236. Birch also notes that the brevity of the account suggests that the city, for all its security, was taken quickly and easily.

[226] Flavius Josephus, *Antiquities of the Jews*, VII 3:1 Translated by William Whiston. Grand Rapids: Baker, 1979.) Vol 2:423; Hans Wilhelm Hertzberg, *I and II Samuel* (The Old Testament Library; Philadelphia: Westminster, 1964), 269. Hertzberg asserts that it explains a proverbial expression known in Jerusalem and connected with David’s aversion to the blind and lame.

[227] Henry Preserved Smith, *The Books of Samuel* (International Critical Commentary; Edinburgh: T & T Clark, 1977), 287; Vargon, “The Blind and the Lame,” 498-514;

Josephus, in fact, claimed that disabled persons were placed on the wall to mock David and as a show of their confidence in the strength of their fortifications.[228] Gilbert Brunet suggests that, in light of an absence of precedent, the Jebusites would be so arrogant as to think that they would not need other, able-bodied soldiers to defend the city.[229] It is more likely, Brunet writes, that the phrase was intended either as an insult or was idiomatically expressing that they would hold out to the last man.[230] The indignity of the Jebusites' derisive comments distinguishes David as the alien and thus would literarily provide shock to the reader to whom the unity of David and Jerusalem was self-evident.[231]

Hans Stoebe notes the connection between verses 6 and 8, beginning with the explicit use of the word בוֹא (enter) both in verses 6 and 8. In verse 6, בוֹא is bound with הֱסִירְךָ (will turn you away), functioning in a prototypical sense to express antipathy for the crippled.[232] This contrasts with verse 8 which is not meant to point mockingly at those incapable of defending a city let alone themselves, but is intended to push aside the derision and direct his anger toward those who deserve it. When David and his men appear at the city gates, the Jebusites mock his pretensions of conquest. It is from these circumstances that the idiom finds explanation.[233] The fact is that the blind and lame were not needed to defend the city or to drive off the pretending conqueror.[234]

Although the use of the phrase "blind and lame" in verse 6 was intended to explain the idiomatic use of the phrase in verse 8, it has prejudiced our understanding of the phrase. The assumption is that David's abhorrence is directed toward those who are literally "blind and lame."[235] It is perhaps an irony that David attacked where it was least expected. The Jebusites were thus "blind" to the attack and being unable to respond quickly enough gave a somewhat "lame" defense for their city. David repudiates the insult of impenetrability versus impotence by pointing out the city's vulnerable points as

---

Heller, "David und die Krüppel," 251-258. Heller argues that the unclean nature of the disabled was precisely why they were chosen to defend the city. He also suggests that their disabilities may have a cultic causality behind them as well.

228 Josephus, *Antiquities*, VII 61. Josephus notes that this included one-eyed persons. Interestingly, the Semitic cognates for the word עִוֵּר can mean "one-eyed." See *BDB*, 734b.

229 Gilbert Brunet, "Les aveugles et boiteux jébusites," *Vetus Testamentum Supplements* 30 (1979): 68.

230 Brunet, "Les aveugles et boiteux jébusites," 68.

231 Fokkelman, *Narrative Art and Poetry in the Books of Samuel: Throne and City*, 160.

232 Hans Joachim Stoebe, *Das zweite Buch Samuelis* (Kommentar zum Alten Testament 8/2; Gütersloh: Gütersloher Verlagshaus, 1994), 165.

233 Stoebe, *Das zweite Buch Samuelis*, 162.

234 Stoebe, *Das zweite Buch Samuelis*, 165.

235 The Syriac and several Targum manuscripts make וַיֹּאמֶר a plural (וַיֹּאמְרוּ). This may be a means of attributing the quote to someone other than David. It is possible that the MT was corrupted at this point.

both the צִנּוֹר (water tunnel) and וְאֶת־הַפִּסְחִים וְאֶת־הַעִוְרִים (the lame and the blind). In essence, he hoists the Jebusites on their own petard by identifying the real weakness in the situation at the water pipe.[236]

Some assert that the phrase הַעִוְרִים וְהַפִּסְחִים (blind and lame) held in combination as it appears the MT as well as the LXX reading, suggests that the word "house" (הַבָּיִת) has sacral overtones.[237] They argue, on this basis, that verse 8 is an etiological interpolation for the exclusion of the blind and lame from the sanctuary.[238] Anderson argues, however, that it is unlikely that הַבָּיִת is referring to the Temple even though David is known to be the source of many of the cultic practices and regulations relating to the Temple (1 Chron 22-28).

Interestingly, Brunet refers to a text titled, The Soldiers' Oath. It contains a Hittite ritual in which a curse of blindness and deafness is called upon all who betray the oath of allegiance each soldier makes to the king and queen.[239] Cementing this oath, a blind woman and a deaf man were paraded before the troops. The text containing this oath scene reads:

> They lead before them a woman, a blind man
> and a deaf man and you say to them as follows:
> "Here (are) a woman, a blind man and a deaf man.
> Who takes part in evil against the king and queen,
> may the oath deities seize him and make (that) man (into) a woman.
> May they b[l]ind him like the blind man.
> May they d[ea]fen him like a deaf man.
> And may they utt[erly] destroy him, a mortal
> together with his wives, his sons, and his clan" (The Soldiers' Oath, §10).[240]

---

[236] The LXX inserts ἐν παραξιφίδι in place of בַּצִּנּוֹר as the MT reads.

[237] P. Kyle McCarter, *II Samuel* (Anchor Bible 9; New York: Doubleday, 1984), 136, 140.

[238] Smith, *The Books of Samuel*, 287-88; McCarter, *II Samuel*, 136, 140; Ackroyd, *The Second Book of Samuel*, 56; Avalos, *Illness and Healthcare in the Ancient Near East*, 319-20; Olyan, "Anyone Blind or Lame Shall Not Enter the House: On the Interpretation of Second Samuel 5:8," 218-27; Johannes P. Floss, *David und Jerusalem: Ziele und Folgen des Stadteroberungsberichts 2 Sam 5,6-9 literaturwissenschaftlich betrachtet* (Arbeiten zu Text und Sprache im Alten Testament, Band 30; Erzabtei St. Ottilien: EOS Verlag, 1987), 39-40.

[239] Brunet, "Les aveugles et boiteux jébusites," 68. See also Albrecht Goetze, "The Soldiers' Oath," in *Ancient Near Eastern Texts Related to the Old Testament* (ed. James B. Pritchard; Princeton, N.J.: Princeton University Press, 1969), 353-54.

[240] Billie Jean Collins, "The First Soldiers Oath," in *The Context of Scripture: Canonical Compositions from the Biblical World*, (eds., William W. Hallo and K. Lawson Younger; New York: E.J. Brill, 1997), I:166. See also Albrecht Goetze, "The Soldiers' Oath," 354. Yigael Yadin points to this ritual as the key to understanding this obscure passage (Yigael Yadin, *The Art of Warfare in Biblical Lands: In the Light of Archaeological Study* [London: Weidenfeld and Nicolson, 1963], 267-70). More recently, though, Yadin's assertion has been reexamined and

Brunet suggests that the Jebusites may have been performing this ritual on the battlements as proof of their commitment to hold out to the last man before moving in another direction. Brunet concludes that the Jebusites expected these handicapped defenders to magically protect the soldiers.[241] Edward Herbert notes that כִּי אִם rarely possess the force of strengthening כִּי as it does here in 2 Samuel 5:6.[242] Used in direct speech it refers to a past event so that the phrase means "surely," implying that defenders of inferior caliber had already been able to repulse David previously and would continue to do so.[243]

The suggestion that the temple is in focus in the word הַבָּיִת seems improbable in that the temple did not exist at the time of Jerusalem's fall and would not be envisioned for some time to come.[244] Going on the strength of the interpretation that the Jebusites were confident that their city could not be taken, others argue that the taunt was turned ironically against the Jebusites themselves (v. 8), "making 'the Jebusites' and 'the blind and lame' synonymous" as David turns them away from what will now be his house (i.e., palace).[245] In addition, viewing the combination of the two deformities here as etiological is derived from the appearance of this combination in Leviticus 21:18-20, Deuteronomy 15:21, and Malachi 1:8. This is a combination that would only be known to Israelites unless it had become idiomatic and broadly known.

Further, although Deuteronomy 23:1 may imply the exclusion of the physically handicapped from the Temple, no specific prohibition was known to have existed.[246] Note too that Eli serves in the temple even though he was going blind (1 Sam 1:9; 3:2-3; cf. 3:15). This suggests that at that time there was no prohibition in place. It must be noted that in 2 Samuel, even though the word "house" may at times refer to a temple (7:5, 6, 7, 13; 12:20), it mostly refers to David's palace which is the dominant use of the word (5:11; 7:1, 2;

---

discredited (see Norbert Oettinger, *Die Militärischen Eide der Hethiter* [Wiesbaden: Harrassowitz, 1976]). In order for such an oath to induce fear and therefore loyalty the threat of disability would need to be a distinct possibility of becoming reality, suggesting that physical disablement was both feared and considered a possible consequence of breaking an oath.

[241] Brunet, "Les aveugles et boiteux jébusites," 71. He claims to have derived this conclusion from Josephus' comments on the event. See also Gilbert Brunet, "David et le Sinnôr," *Vetus Testamentum Supplements* 30 (1979): 73-86.

[242] Edward Herbert, "2 Samuel 5:6: An Interpretative crux reconsidered in light of 4QSam[a]," *Vetus Testamentum* 44 (1994): 342f.

[243] Herbert, "2 Samuel 5:6: An Interpretative crux reconsidered in light of 4QSam[a]," 342f.

[244] Anderson, *2 Samuel*, 84.

[245] Robert D. Bergen, *1, 2 Samuel* (New American Commentary 7; Nashville: Broadman and Holman, 1996), 320; Anderson, *2 Samuel*, 82; Youngblood, *1 & 2 Samuel*, 856.

[246] Vargon, "The Blind and the Lame" 500. This rule was probably directed at those who intentionally emasculated themselves in dedication to a deity. The result is a permanent self-inflicted disability. See Kalland, *Deuteronomy*, 3:140.

11:2, 8; 15:16; 16:21; 19:6, 12, 13). Further, the house of the Lord is not the primary focus of the chapter. In addition, Leviticus 21:18 does not restrict disabled priests from entering the temple. In the immediate context, David works to fortify the area (v. 9) from the Millo outward suggesting that it is more plausible that הַבַּיִת refers to David's palace rather than the temple.[247]

2 Samuel 5:8 asserts that David hates the blind and lame,[248] and in the irony of the situation, he bans them from entering the house.[249] It does not seem likely that David's banishment of "the blind and the lame" from the house comment in verse 8, due to their being considered unclean as some suggest,[250] can be taken as literally referring to disabled people. To do so presupposes that the rationale behind the priestly injunctions in Leviticus 21 is on that basis. This has been proven not to be the case. It is not on the physically blind and lame that David's derision falls but on the Jebusites themselves.[251]

David is not pronouncing a "generic prejudice against invalids but introducing a reversal of fortunes."[252] Fokkelman writes,

> The people, not David, took to using the saying "lame and blind shall not enter the palace." In their experience it is connected with the capture of Jerusalem, long ago, when the famous king David had to verbally defend himself against the Jebusites and was abused by them with "lame and blind" who would be able to take him on. The context of 4:4 and ch. 9 shows that the line ought not indeed to be ascribed to David. The mutilated state of the house of Saul, illustrated in various ways in ch. 4, is not over, but the reader becomes conscious of it in ch. 9, when a crippled grandchild of Saul, brought in from somewhere far away, does obeisance to the king. David gives the lame a permanent place of honour in his palace.[253]

The motif of God's support and David's power continues from his showing kindness to Meribbaal and the taking of Jerusalem.[254]

---

[247] Vargon, "The Blind and the Lame" 499-500. See also, Anthony Ceresko, "The Identity of 'the Blind and the Lame' (*'iwwēr ūpisseāh*) in 2 Samuel 5:8b," *Catholic Biblical Quarterly* 63 (2001): 24, 30.

[248] Multiple Medieval manuscripts contain the Qere. The Qumran manuscript has שנאה rather than שְׂנֻאֵו as it reads in the MT ketib. The Qere reads this as a qal passive participle (שְׂנֻאֵי), but the Ketib reads this as a qal perfect (שָׂנְאוּ). The direct object marker (אֶת־הַעִוְרִים) makes the Ketib implausible. See Anderson, *2 Samuel*, 136; Olyan, "Anyone Blind or Lame Shall Not Enter the House, 218-19.

[249] Olyan, "Anyone Blind or Lame Shall Not Enter the House," 225. Olyan suggests that the epigrammatic reference to the blind and lame in verse 8 is a synecdoche for all persons with some physical blemish.

[250] Hentrich, "The 'Lame' in Lev 21, 17-23 and 2 Sam 5, 6-8," 27f.

[251] Stoebe, *Das zweite Buch Samuelis*, 166.

[252] Fokkelman, *Narrative Art and Poetry in the Books of Samuel: Throne and City*, 162.

[253] Fokkelman, *Narrative Art and Poetry in the Books of Samuel: Throne and City*, 164-65.

[254] Fokkelman, *Narrative Art and Poetry in the Books of Samuel: Throne and City*, 165.

Disabled Mephibosheth in the Judahite Court: 2 Samuel 4:4 & 9:5-13

2 Samuel 4:1-3, 5-10 narrates Isbosheth's assassination which serves to explain what became of the "heroes" who assassinated him (4:1-3, 5-10).[255] At verse 4 a statement concerning Jonathan's crippled son, Meribbaal,[256] and the cause of his disability interrupts this narrative. 2 Samuel 4:4 reads,

וְלִיהוֹנָתָן֙ בֶּן־שָׁא֔וּל בֵּן נְכֵה רַגְלָיִם בֶּן־חָמֵשׁ שָׁנִים הָיָה בְּבֹא שְׁמֻעַת שָׁאוּל וִיהוֹנָתָן
מִיִּזְרְעֶאל וַתִּשָּׂאֵהוּ אֹמַנְתּוֹ֙ וַתָּנֹס וַיְהִי בְּחָפְזָהּ לָנוּס וַיִּפֹּל וַיִּפָּסֵחַ וּשְׁמוֹ מְפִיבֹשֶׁת׃

> Now Jonathan, Saul's son, had a son with crippled feet. He was five years old when the report of Saul and Jonathan came from Jezreel, and his nurse lifted him up and fled. But it happened in her haste to escape, he fell and became lame. His name is Mephibosheth.

This digression, coming at this point, does not distract from the subject matter but contributes to the thematic progression of the pericope which involved the adversity distressing the house of Saul.[257]

The parenthetical statement of Jonathan's son as a cripple and the cause of his disability brings forward an emphasis on kindness connected to 1 Sam 20:14-15 and the oath David makes to Jonathan. Here, the reference to Meribbaal's disability in such a perfunctory manner serves as a traumatic etiology for the narrative which comes in chapters 9, 16 and 19 where the Meribbaal story line continues.[258] This statement may function as a prolepsis for what would come in 2 Samuel 15 when David would loose half his fortune and nearly his life.[259]

Some assert that this verse is an interpolation, intended to demonstrate just how reduced the house of Saul was at this time.[260] How ironic it is that it was Saul's physicality which garnered popular support for his kingship but now Meribbaal, the remaining Saulide contender for the throne, lacks even the strength to stand on his own. The unnamed nurse in verse 4 is remembered by

---

[255] Fokkelman, *Narrative Art and Poetry in the Books of Samuel: Throne and City*, 121.

[256] Mephibosheth's name, מְפִיבֹשֶׁת, (from the mouth of shame) is probably a euphemistic substitution for Meribbaal ("Baal strives"). There is some dispute regarding the reason for the name change. See Youngblood, *1 & 2 Samuel*, 484; Anderson, *2 Samuel*, 69-70; McCarter, *II Samuel*, 124-25, 128. It is possible that the original form of Meribbaal's name was Mippibaal (from the mouth of Baal).

[257] Fokkelman, *Narrative Art and Poetry in the Books of Samuel: Throne and City*, 128.

[258] Anderson, *2 Samuel*, 67. Anderson asserts that the insertion of the information concerning Meribbaal's physical condition is tantamount to asserting his unfitness for the throne.

[259] Meir Sternberg, *The Poetics of Biblical Narrative: Ideological Literature and the Drama of Reading* (Bloomington: Indiana University Press, 1985), 339.

[260] Smith, *The Books of Samuel*, 283; Hertzberg, *I and II Samuel*, 264.

her unintentionally contributing to the decline of the house of Saul by causing the crippling of Meribbaal.[261] The *niphal* verb (יִפָּסֵחַ) certifies that Meribbaal's lameness was not the result of a birth defect but a permanent disability acquired in childhood. Meribbaal, like Saul and Jonathan, fell (יִפֹּל).

After David establishes Jerusalem as his capitol, he again encounters Meribbaal. Again, his handicap is mentioned in 2 Samuel 9:3:

וַיֹּאמֶר הַמֶּלֶךְ הַאֶפֶס עוֹד אִישׁ לְבֵית שָׁאוּל וְאֶעֱשֶׂה עִמּוֹ חֶסֶד אֱלֹהִים וַיֹּאמֶר צִיבָא אֶל־הַמֶּלֶךְ עוֹד בֵּן לִיהוֹנָתָן נְכֵה רַגְלָיִם׃

> The king said, "Is there no man yet from the house of Saul that I could show the kindness of God?" The Ziba said to the king, "There is still the son of Jonathan who has crippled feet."

Interestingly, it is clear that Meribbaal is being referred to, but he is not called by name but by his handicap. This suggests to some that something more is taking place than an altruistic act on David's part.

The text that begins at 2 Samuel 9:1 and continues to 1 Kings 2 is commonly called the Succession Narrative by some scholars.[262] Here the disability motif intersects the royal motif. While some scholars are at a loss to reconcile this text with 2 Samuel 5 and the maxim that David loathed the lame and blind together,[263] others contend that there is something more than merely an example of David's kind heart here.

While it has been suggested that the attention drawn to Meribbaal's lameness is less a transparent description and more an encoded representation of royal political machination, it is more likely to have been inserted in anticipation of the חֶסֶד David shows toward Meribbaal in keeping the covenant between David and Jonathan (1 Sam 20).[264] Three times, the narrator puts forth the king's desire to keep his covenant with Jonathan by showing kindness to one of Jonathan's sons (9:1, 3, 7) and by so doing he honors Jonathan's memory and their mutual love.[265] Yahweh himself is the protector of their covenant and the standard of their relationship (חֶסֶד אֱלֹהִים).[266] With the phrase "faithfulness of God" (חֶסֶד אֱלֹהִים) the narrative reaches a level of moral and

---

[261] Fokkelman, *Narrative Art and Poetry in the Books of Samuel: Throne and City*, 127.

[262] Peter R. Ackroyd, "The Succession Narrative (so-called)," *Interpretation* 35 (1981): 383. It is called the Succession Narrative because beginning with 2 Samuel 9 the unifying literary theme appears to be David's successor.

[263] Sternberg, *The Poetics of Biblical Narrative*, 255.

[264] Birch, *The Book of 2 Samuel*, 2:1230.

[265] J.P. Fokkelman, *Narrative Art and Poetry in the Books of Samuel: King David*, vol. 1 (Assen, Netherlands: Van Gorcum, 1981), 26.

[266] Fokkelman, *Narrative Art and Poetry in the Books of Samuel*, 1:26.

religious values.[267] A narratival chiasm forms in this passage, showing the extent to which this stratum drives the action.[268]

a) Narrator→US	: חסד	v.1
b) David→Ziba	: חסד	v.3
c) David→Meribbaal	: חסד	v.7c
c') David→Meribbaal	: I give you all Saul's land	v.7d
b') David→Ziba	: all that is Saul's is for Meribbaal	v. 9c
a') Narrator→US	: the whole house of Ziba	v. 12b

This is supported by a literary chiasm:

A. David seeks to be kind to a descendant of Saul (9:1)
B. David speaks to Ziba, Saul's servant (9:2-5)
C. David shows kindness to Meribbaal (9:6-8)
B'. David speaks to Ziba, Saul's servant (9:9-11a)
A'. David set in motion kindness to a descendant of Saul (9:11b-13)

The disability motif in this passage reaches back to the capture of Jerusalem, referred to earlier (2 Sam 5).[269] David is said to have detested the blind and lame and banned them from his house. Some reason, then, that it is out of character for David to give Meribbaal a place at the royal table considering his proverbial hatred for the lame.[270] But it is David's character which is at issue. Rather than seeing this as an internal victory for David in overcoming his hatred for a specific people,[271] it is more prudent to suggest that there was no hatred toward the disabled to begin with. This pericope supports the interpretation of the lame referred to in 2 Samuel 5:6-8 as being the Jebusites rather than those who were physically disabled.

The section begins with David making inquiries as to whether there were any living descendants of Saul (9:1, 3). He is informed that Meribbaal, who was being cared for by Saul's servant Ziba,[272] was the only remaining

[267] Fokkelman, *Narrative Art and Poetry in the Books of Samuel*, 1:26.

[268] Fokkelman, *Narrative Art and Poetry in the Books of Samuel*, 1:27.

[269] Youngblood, *1 & 2 Samuel*, 856; Sternberg, *The Poetics of Biblical Narrative*, 255; Vargon, "The Blind and the Lame," 511.

[270] Bar-Efrat, *Narrative Art in the Bible*, 78; Sternberg, *The Poetics of Biblical Narrative*, 255. Sternberg suggest that David may have been motivated by either his devotion to Jonathan or for his concern to keep tabs on the last living contender for the Saulide throne, or both.

[271] Vargon, "The Blind and the Lame," 505.

[272] Ziba is referred to as Saul's servant. The Syriac version and a few medieval manuscripts omit the phrase נַעַר שָׁאוּל. I cannot explain this omission except for the possibility that it is an unintentional haplographic error.

descendant.[273] In 9:4 David inquires as to Meribbaal's whereabouts and sends for him (9:5). When Meribbaal arrives he acknowledges David's sovereignty, doing obeisance and referring to himself self-deprecatingly as a "dead dog."[274] In many ancient Near Eastern cultures, especially in Israel, dogs were looked upon as contemptible creatures.[275] Presumably, a dead dog would be even more contemptible than a living dog. It is then that David restores the Saulide lands to Meribbaal (9:7) and arranges for their care on his behalf (9:9-10).[276] In addition to this Meribbaal is granted royal patronage and a pension at the king's table in Jerusalem, effectively elevating him to the social status of a prince (9:12).[277]

Meribbaal was honored in a variety of ways. Ziba and his sons and servants were put to work farming Meribbaal's new estate.[278] David gives him a status which effectively promotes him to a status akin to the sons of the king

---

[273] Robert P. Gordon, "In Search of David," in *Faith, Tradition, and History: Old Testament Historiography in Its Near Eastern Context* (ed. R.A. Millard, James K. Hoffmeier, and David W. Baker; Winona Lake: Eisenbrauns, 1994), 293-94. For all intents and purposes, the Saulide dynasty died on Mount Gilboa (1 Sam 31:6). Even though this statement was not literally true since Ishbosheth was still alive, the author of Chronicles (1 Chron 10:6) still makes the case because, from a historical point of view, Ishbosheth was irrelevant.

[274] Birch, *The Book of 2 Samuel*, 2:1274.

[275] Birch, *The Book of 2 Samuel*, 2:1274. Akkadian (*kalbu*) and Ugaritic (*klb*) cognates are used in similarly pejorative senses.

[276] Concerning verse 10, the LXX^L replaces לְבֵן with לְבֵית. This addition in LXX^L suggests that the produce referred to here provided for Meribbaal's family in contrast with Meribbaal's personal provision at the king's table mentioned at the end of the verse. In addition, two medieval manuscripts, the Syriac version, and the LXX^{L,Mss} reads κὰι φάγονται (3rd pl.) as וְאָכְלוּ instead of וַאֲכָלוֹ (3rd sing.). This appears to be based on the interpretation that what is produced from the estate will be for the maintenance of Meribbaal's family rather than for him personally.

[277] Anson F. Rainy and R. Steven Notley, eds., *The Sacred Bridge: Carta's Atlas of the Biblical World* (Winona Lake: Eisenbrauns, 2006), 221. Rainey notes that Meribbaal may have eaten at the kings table, but this does not mean it was at the king's expense. Meribbaal's portion would have come from the land-grant he received from David.

[278] Variant readings of verse 11 involve two medieval manuscripts and the Syriac version contains the particle כל (all) alone without the inclusion of the preposition כְּכֹל (according to all) as the MT reads. This appears to be an attempt to place this part of the speech and all that follows this phrase in the mouth of Ziba rather than limiting the speech to 11a. However, the clause in question (שֻׁלְחָנִי כְּאַחַד מִבְּנֵי הַמֶּלֶךְ־ וּמְפִיבֹשֶׁת אֹכֵל עַל) should be considered part of the narrative rather than a part of Ziba's speech.

(9:11).[279] Through these actions, David again demonstrates that he is a man that is true to his word and worthy to be king.[280]

Some suggest that Meribbaal became a prisoner in David's house so as to keep an eye on a rival for the throne. Indeed, David had ordered the execution of seven Saulide heirs, leading to the interpretation that David was consolidating power and protecting his own dynastic future. However, other possibilities have been suggested. McCarter suggests that the execution of the Saulide heirs (2 Sam 21:8-9) was not personal but was in the best interests of Israel to satisfy the requirements of blood justice arising from Saul's treatment of the Gibeonites (21:1).[281] The suggestion that Meribbaal was there so that David could watch him also implies that David had an ulterior reason for his magnanimity. However, there are no clues available to us as to David's political ambitions. Considering that David is presented as a man without guile it is unlikely that the author of Samuel intended to present David as duplicitous here. It is more reasonable to conclude that David's covenant commitment to Jonathan is the primary (if not exclusive) reason for his treatment of Meribbaal.

Regarding the two primary characters, David and Meribbaal, some suggest the narrative has a comparative function. It is often asserted that an idealized concept of how a king in the ancient Near East should look and act is operating behinds the scenes in 2 Samuel 5:8f. It is asserted that the ancient Near Eastern concept of an ideal king consisted of one possessing a variety of physical attributes such as strength, good posture, height, vigor, and the ability to lead his army to victory in military campaigns.[282] These features were required in anyone who desired to be considered a candidate to the throne. Indeed, Egyptian and Assyrian iconography depicts rulers in military victory as larger in scale than their enemies.[283] In the Ugaritic *Epic of Kirta*, Kirta becomes ill and is forced to leave the throne (tablet III, col. 3, lines 22-25, 36-39).[284]

---

[279] A medieval manuscript, the LXX^BAMN, Syriac and Vulgate read עַל־שֻׁלְחָנְנוּ (at your table) rather than עַל־שֻׁלְחָנִי (at my table) as the MT reads. This is based on the same interpretation as 11a.

[280] Bergen, *1, 2 Samuel*, 354.

[281] McCarter, *II Samuel*, 265.

[282] Wilfried G. Lambert, "Kingship in Ancient Mesopotamia," in *King and Messiah in Israel and the Ancient Near East: Proceedings of the Oxford Old Testament Seminar* (ed. John Day; Sheffield: Sheffield Academic Press, 1998), 54-70; Mark W. Hamilton, *The Body Royal: The Social Poetics of Kingship in Ancient Israel* (Boston: Brill, 2005).

[283] Gay Robins, *The Art of Ancient Egypt* (Cambridge: Harvard University Press, 1997), 21; John Malcolm Russell, *Sennacherib's Palace without Rival at Nineveh* (Chicago: Chicago University Press, 1991), 193; Pauline Albenda, *Monumental Art of the Assyrian Empire: Dynamics of Composition Styles* (Malibu: Undena Publications, 1998), 23. Interestingly, in Israel Yahweh is likewise depicted as a great warrior with mighty limbs (Ps 98:14; Isa 62:8; Jer 21:5).

[284] See Edward Greenstein, "Kirta," in *Ugaritic Narrative Poetry* (ed. Simon b. Parker; Atlanta, Ga: Scholars Press, 1997), 34. Three words are used to describe Kirta's

However, there is iconographic and literary material suggesting that a disabled ruler was not as great a social stigma as some would suggest. Duppi-Tešub of Amurru was handicapped in some unknown way yet he was installed as king over Amurru by Muršili II.[285] The fact that it is mentioned in the preamble to their treaty suggests that the disability may normally have disqualified Duppi-Tešub from the throne. Egyptian mummies have been found with evidence of disabilities as well. For example, Thutmose IV (18th dynasty c. 1401-1391 B.C.) had a pelvic tilt, possibly the result of a fracture.[286] Siptah (c. 1204-1198 B.C.) had a withered left leg caused by polio.[287] Reliefs of Thutmose and Siptah do not show their true physical appearance. Some rationalize that their altered representations in relief was due to the social stigma attached to being handicapped.[288] However, it may simply be due to the idealized artistic conventions common in Egypt to show the power of the pharaoh.

Some suggest that Israel maintained a royal ideology also. Saul's physique was noted by the people as a basis for his selection as king (1 Sam 9:2; 10:23-24; 1 Kgs 1:6) and his first assignment after being anointed was to take a Philistine garrison at Gibeah (1 Sam 10:5). In 1 Samuel 9 there is an extensive description of Saul as "a choice and handsome man, and there was not a more handsome person than he among the sons of Israel; from his shoulders and up he was taller than any of the people" (v. 2); ". . . a man of God in this city, and the man is held in honor; all that he says surely comes true" (v. 6), suggests that an ideal royal concept is being employed. David's description likewise appears to suggest an idealized royal appearance and comportment (1 Sam 16:1-13, 18; 17:24). The physical appearance of Absalom (2 Sam 14:25) and Adonijah (1 Kgs 1:5-6) is also noted in connection with their bid for the throne of Israel. Some scholars suggest that physical disability was seen as a disqualifying trait for a king.[289] Although no biblical law can be cited that prohibits a disabled person from being king, some look to the priestly prohibitions in Lev 21:16-23 as the basis for this assertion.[290]

---

illness. All three words are ambiguous for illness; *mrs* (tablet III, col. 3, line 23), *zbl* (tablet III, col. 3, line 51), and *dwy* (tablet III, col. 3, line 23).

[285] Itamar Singer, "Treaties Between Hatti and Amurru," in *The Context of Scripture* (ed. William W. Hallo and K. Lawson Younger; New York: E.J. Brill, 1997), II:96, A i. 11'-18'.

[286] Walter M. Whitehouse, "Radiologic Findings in the Royal Mummies," in *An X-Ray Atlas of the Royal Mummies* (ed. James Harris and Edward Wente; Chicago: Chicago University Press, 1980), 289.

[287] Whitehouse, "Radiologic Findings in the Royal Mummies," 289, 8.25.

[288] Schipper, *Disability Studies and the Hebrew Bible: Figuring Mephibosheth in the David Story*, 86-87.

[289] Anderson, *2 Samuel*, 143; McCarter, *II Samuel*, 407. Both Anderson and McCarter point to Meribbaal's disability as a disqualifying physical feature but their support for this view is rather limited.

[290] Miller, *The Religion of Ancient Israel*, 194-95.

Yet, there is other biblical material which counters the concept of a royal ideology. Saul was "troubled by an evil spirit from God" (1 Sam 16:14-16, 23; 18:10; 19:9). David's description as the youngest[291] of his brothers (1 Sam 16:11; 17:14, 38-39) also does not fit a royal ideal.[292] David's description at times was clearly not complimentary (1 Sam 17:42).[293] It is possible that David's description (Yahweh's ideal king) is meant to contrast Saul (the people's ideal king) and by so doing, further the message that David is Israel's legitimate king.[294] Schipper points to the comment in 2 Samuel 3:1 summarizing the conflict between David's and Saul's houses using imagery of "strength" and "weakness" in support of this.[295] Furthermore, several claimants to the throne of Israel whose physical features fit an ideal, do not ultimately become kings.[296] In addition, several kings in Israel are noted as being sick at some point during their reign.[297] There is no biblical data that suggests that social stigma forced a monarch to leave the throne because he did not continue to meet the ideal royal concept rather than abdicating the throne because he could no longer fulfill his duties. Although a royal ideology based on the king's character was employed in Israel the assertion that a royal ideology based on a king's physicality is questionable. It appears from the evidence that many kings did not fit an ideal concept of a king, and a handicapped ruler was not a social pariah as royal theology proponents would have us believe.

A narratival shift begins with chapter 9 that moves the account from foreign to domestic affairs. The placement of this text at this point is most likely to be

---

291 קָטָן refers to his youth rather than stature.

292 The rejection of Saul as king and the choice of David in his stead (1 Sam 16, esp. v. 7) appears to serve as a polemic against a royal ideology by contesting the focus on a candidate's physical features. The ideal is centered in Yahweh's focus on the heart of a man. See Mark George, "Yhwh's Own Heart," *Catholic Biblical Quarterly* 64 (2002): 442-459. The Bible goes out of its way to describe potential kings as usurpers or rejected by God (Saul in 15:23, 26; 16:1; Eliab in 1 Sam 16:7; Absalom in 2 Sam 15:10-18:15; Adonijah in 1 Kgs 1:5-49).

293 עִם־יְפֵה is used with reference to David's inexperience. In 1 Samuel 16:12 this may or may not be complementary but in 1 Samuel 17:42 the Philistines clearly ridicule David's youth and inexperience in contrast with their mighty warrior, Goliath.

294 Jeremy Schipper, "Reconsidering the Imagery of Disability in 2 Samuel 5:8b," *Catholic Biblical Quarterly* 67 (2005): 424.

295 Schipper, "Reconsidering the Imagery of Disability in 2 Samuel 5:8b," 424. Schipper argues that דַּל normally refers to economic or social weakness (Exod 30:15; Lev 14:21; Ruth 3:10) but in 2 Samuel 3:1 (and 2 Sam 13:4) it connotes physical weakness. However, דַּל in 2 Samuel 13:4 refers to Amnon's emotional state rather than his physical state. חָלָה, the typical word for physical weakness, is used in 2 Samuel 13:5 and 6 to describe Amnon's feigned illness.

296 Absalom (2 Sam 14:25) and Adonijah (1 Kgs 1:6) to name two.

297 Asa (1 Kgs 15:23; 2 Chr 16:12), Ahaziah (2 Kgs 1:2), Joram (2 Kgs 8:28), Ben-Hadad (2 Kgs 8:7), Hezekiah (2 Kgs 20:2, 12; Isa 38:1-22), and Jehoram (2 Chron 21:15, 18-19) were all known to have been ill while on the throne.

in keeping with the structure of the book, building on the theme of loyalty rather than a chronological record of events.[298] Now that David had completed his campaigns against his enemies it was time to fulfill his promise to Jonathan.

The disability imagery continues. With domestic issues resolved, at least for now, David is able to concentrate on consolidating his royal power. Meribbaal, who was introduced earlier (4:4), immediately becomes the focus of David's attention. The disability motif suggests to some Meribbaal's disqualification from the throne in contrast to David's fitness.[299] Both are presented in coordinated, albeit antithetical, descriptions designed to provide cultural ideals rather than accurate depictions.[300] Meribbaal's arrival here marks the climax of the Saul narrative. He is the last and most disabled of Saul's descendants.[301]

The suggestion that a contrast between Saul's and David's physical appearance creates an antagonistic rhetorical thread through the books of Samuel suggests that physical appearance as attributive of greatness is perpetuated. However, the Bible continually points to the fact that it is a right heart which receives Yahweh's attention (1 Sam 2:1; 2:35; 7:3; 12:20, 24; 13:14; 16:7). It is David's heart that is being set in contrast and marks him as the legitimate king of Israel (1 Sam 16:7f), not his body. Interpretive models that reduce *any* disabled biblical character to a simple representation of disability fail to account for the complex and often overlapping nature of these characters.[302]

David was not an enemy to the house of Saul, but an agent of God's kindness (חֶסֶד).[303] What the gracious David intentionally does here distinguishes him from the brutal mercenary.[304] Stoebe writes,

---

[298] David had obligated himself to Jonathan's family to protect them when the Lord would give David rest from his enemies (1 Sam 20:15).

[299] 2 Samuel 3:1 provides the backdrop to this contrast with Meribbaal epitomizing this motif because his disability is mentioned every time he is mentioned. Thomas Hentrich asserts that Meribbaal was not disabled at all but his disabled persona in contrast with David's physique was inserted as a literary ploy (Hentrich, "Masculinity and Disability in the Bible," 85. See Schipper, "Reconsidering the Imagery of Disability in 2 Samuel 5:8b," 424; Brueggemann, *First and Second Samuel*, 268; Ceresko, "The Identity of 'the Blind and the Lame,'" 28; R.A. Carlson, *David the Chosen King: A Traditio-Historical Approach to the Second Book of Samuel* (Stockholm: Almqvist and Wiksell, 1964), 57. Carlson sees a rhetorical climax to the story.

[300] Schipper, "Reconsidering the Imagery of Disability in 2 Samuel 5:8b," 433-34.

[301] Many of Saul's family are identified in terms of weakness or disability. Ishbosheth (2 Sam 4:1); Michal is barren, a disability in the ancient Near East (See Avalos, *Illness and Healthcare in the Ancient Near East,* 331-34; Philip J. King and Lawrence Stager, *Life in Biblical Israel* [Louisville: Westminster/John Knox Press, 1971], 75.).

[302] Schipper, "Reconsidering the Imagery of Disability in 2 Samuel 5:8b," 433-34.

[303] Bergen, *1, 2 Samuel*, 354. It should be noted that the word "kindness" does not adequately bring out the covenantal obligations which the word חֶסֶד connotes. David and Jonathan entered into a covenant whereby they swore mutual faithfulness (1 Sam

> Es solle gezeigt werden, daß die Täter von einem Krüppel keine Blutrache mehr zu fürchten hatten oder daß nach dem Tode Isbaals nun tatsächlich kein Thronprätendent mehr da war . . .[305]

In other words, Meribbaal was not a threat to David nor was David a threat to Meribbaal and neither had anything to fear. The kindness shown to Meribbaal here is genuine. Meribbaal's treatment stems from David's promise to deal with Jonathan's house with loyalty after Jonathan helped David escape from Saul's court (1 Sam 20:14-16; 2 Sam 9:7). Therefore David returned Saul's lands to Meribbaal (1 Sam 9:9-10) and treated him as an honored guest rather than a prisoner (2 Sam 9:1). Certainly, Meribbaal does not appear to complain about the arrangement (2 Sam 9:25, 29). Bergen suggests that David actually put his own dynasty at some risk by having Meribbaal around.[306] The only way David could be presented as the rightful ruler of Israel was if he were presented as Yahweh's right choice. David's heart, unlike that of his predecessor, was right before the Lord.

David's kindness is concretely demonstrated both in the fact that Saul's properties, absorbed by the crown, are given to Meribbaal and in Meribbaal's being awarded a place of honor at the king's table.[307] Interestingly, חסד was the difference between life and death (1 Sam 20:3) that resulted in David making a covenant with Jonathan when Saul sought David's life (1 Sam 20:8, 14-16), and now Meribbaal acknowledges himself as part of the doomed Saulide dynasty in 2 Sam 29:28 (אַנְשֵׁי־מָוֶת) making David's gesture a life giving act to one who is dead. The circumstances with Meribbaal mirrors and inverts David's previous situation.[308]

It can be concluded, therefore, that the entire Meribbaal narrative, and the character of Meribbaal itself, is intended to demonstrate that the rule of the Saulide dynasty has ended. At the same time it legitimates David as Saul's rightful successor by showing that David was God's anointed ruler, protected and blessed from above while acting obediently toward Yahweh and impeccably toward men. This narrative functions polemically against those who want a king from the house of Saul to remain on the throne. The

---

18, 20, 23). David's treatment of Meribbaal here is not merely an act of benevolence but an act that is obligatory as well. The term חֶסֶד (kindness) appears three times in this pericope.

304 Stoebe, *Das zweite Buch Samuelis*, 151.

305 Stoebe, *Das zweite Buch Samuelis*, 151.

306 Bergen, *1, 2 Samuel*, 354.

307 Fokkelman, *Narrative Art and Poetry in the Books of Samuel: King David*, 27-28. Fokkelman notes that Meribbaal not only possesses the rights to the land but also what the land produces. He also points out that David confers acceptance and security to Meribbaal by giving Meribbaal a place of honor at his table (לֶחֶם עַל־שֻׁלְחָנִי בֶן־אֲדֹנֶיךָ יֹאכַל תָּמִיד).

308 Fokkelman, *Narrative Art and Poetry in the Books of Samuel: King David*, 30.

Meribbaal comment conveniently provides an example of David's willingness to show חֶסֶד, and even better, it shows this to one who is from the house of his friend Jonathan, making it possible for David to keep his promise to Jonathan. David is shown as one who keeps his promises, loves friendship, and shows mercy. There is no credible evidence to suggest that social stigmatization provides a sub-reading for the encounter between Meribbaal and David.

Ahijah the Blind Prophet: 1 Kings 14:4-5

In 1 Kings 14 the narrative thrusts forward the prophetic character of Ahijah and his relationship with King Jeroboam. Ahijah was a prophet of Yahweh dwelling in Shiloh. 1 Kings 14:4 describes him as being advanced in years and unable to see (אֲחִיָּהוּ לֹא־יָכֹל לִרְאוֹת כִּי קָמוּ עֵינָיו מִשֵּׂיבוֹ).[309] Yet, even though he was physically blind he retained his perceptive prophetic powers. Jeroboam's son had become ill and the king wanted to know if his son would recover (v. 1). He sent his wife to Shiloh to inquire of the prophet about this (v. 2).[310] It is reasonable that Jeroboam would utilize Ahijah's prophetic skills since it was Ahijah that had informed Jeroboam that he would be king over the Northern kingdom (1 Kgs 11:29-30). Although Ahijah had prophesied Jeroboam's kingship over the 10 tribes, it was a judgment on the nation rather than a blessing (1 Kgs 11:31-32). Rather than going himself and risking being captured, Jeroboam sent his wife in disguise to inquire of the prophet (1 Kgs 14:2).

This narrative validates the view that blindness is not a moral judgment from God, while at the same time presenting the predicted death of Abijah (Jeroboam's son) as divine interference in the natural course of life (14:12).[311] The basis for Ahijah's judgment on Jeroboam was the immorality associated with Jeroboam's religious heterodoxy. Ahijah, seeing through the disguise

---

[309] Mordechai Cogan, *I Kings* (Anchor Bible 10; New York: Doubleday, 2000), 378. עֵינָיו קָמוּ literally means "his eyes were fixed." Cogan notes that קָמוּ עֵינָי is idiomatic for "his eyes dimmed" (Gen 27:1; Deut 34:7); "X's eyes were heavy" (Gen 48:10); "the eyes failed" (Jer 14:6). It is also known that Eli, a priest of Yahweh, who served the tabernacle at Shiloh (1 Sam 1:3, 9), also became blind with age (1 Sam 3:2). The Bible also mentions that he continued to serve even after his vision began to fail (1 Sam 3:2; 4:15), ending his career when the ark was captured by the Philistines at the battle of Aphek (1 Sam 4:18).

[310] To disguise; from הִשְׁתַּנִּית a *hiphil* form of the root שָׁנָה meaning "to alter oneself." Apparently, Jeroboam's wife also took with her gifts that suggest she was of lowly status (compare 1 Samuel 9:8). See Richard D. Patterson and Hermann J. Austel, "*1, 2 Kings*," Expositor's Bible Commentary 3 (ed. Frank E. Gaebelein; Grand Rapids: Zondervan, 1991), 123, fn.3.

[311] The lack of deuteronomistic language in this narrative makes it unlikely that an older prophetic legend regarding consulting a prophet in case of illness was being utilized but that this narrative was unique in its own right. See H.N. Wallace, "Oracles Against the Israelite Dynasties in 1 and 2 Kings," *Biblica* 67 (1986): 22-23; Simon J. DeVries, *1 Kings* (Word Biblical Commentary 12; Waco Tex.: Word, 1985), 177-78.

Jeroboam's wife was wearing (v. 6), rebukes Jeroboam's hypocrisy and portends God's judgment for Jeroboam's apostasy (14:14). Ahijah further predicts the fall of the whole northern kingdom due to the pervasiveness of Jeroboam's sin (14:15). All Ahijah predicted came to pass (14:17; 15:27-28) and Jeroboam's sin became the moral ebb by which future kings of the Northern kingdom were judged.

Certainly if a physical disability were considered a sign of divine requital due to sin, Ahijah would not be functioning as he still did prophetically. The fact that Ahijah's speech (14:7-16) contains judgment on Jeroboam who is contrasted with David (God's ideal ruler) and charged with disregarding Torah, further suggests that Ahijah was not alienated from Yahweh but rather enjoyed Yahweh's endorsement. The narrative explicitly portrays the integration of disability into Israel's society and cultus.

Elisha and Second Sight: 2 Kings 6:17

The events of this narrative take place during the reign of Jehoram.[312] They are introduced with a statement regarding the resumption of military activity between the two nations (vv. 8-22). In this particular narrative, the king of Aram informs his advisors of the location of his camp.[313] Elisha is made aware of the location of the camp and warns the king of Israel not to enter that area (v. 9),[314] frustrating the covert military objectives of the Arameans (v. 10).[315] Their movements in the land somehow mysteriously are discovered by Jehoram, King of Israel. Each time the Arameans set a trap for the Israelite king, he escapes. Elisha seemed to know what would happen and was able to warn the king in advance (vv. 8-9). The Aramean king begins to suspect that there is a traitor in his camp (vv. 10-12). He finds out, however, that it is Elisha who is warning the king and sends his army to Dothan to capture him (vv. 13-14). That night they surround the town and in the morning Elisha's servant awakes to find them ready to attack (vv. 14-15). Beginning in verse 16, an amazing

---

[312] Miller and Haynes, *History of Israel*, 259-64.

[313] The MT (v. 8) reads תַּחֲנֹתִי at this point, but the LXX^{L} reads παρεμβαλῶ. The Vulgate reads *ponamus insidias* suggesting an ambush, in contrast to the LXX^{L}, the Syriac version, and Targum which suggest concealment. The emendations of either תחבאו (from חבא meaning "to hide") or תנחתו (from נחת meaning "to descend" [to battle]) have also been proposed. The LXX may be paraphrasing the Hebrew.

[314] Alterative variants נֶחְבָּאִים or נֹחֲתִים have been proposed where the MT reads נְחִתִּים. This would bring verse 9 into conformity with the proposed variants already discussed in conjunction with verse 8.

[315] The ketib has וְהִזְהִירָה at this point, however it is absent in the LXX. A few mss and qere have וְהִזְהִירוֹ in this place. It is possible that this is a scribal attempt to clarify the king's actions or it may be that the LXX considered the comment of being on guard as superfluous and thus glossed over it. It is unclear which is more accurate, but either way the message of the text is not altered.

exchange takes place between Elisha's servant and Elisha that provides insight into prophetic second sight.

Verse 16 opens with the prophetic formulaic phrase אַל־תִּירָא (do not fear). This is generally seen at the opening of salvation prophecies (cf. Gen 15:1; 26:24; Isa 41:10; Jer 1:8; Lam 3:57).[316] Here, Elisha declares to his frightened protégé that the Lord's deliverance is already on the horizon (v. 17). The prophet Elisha has, until this point, demonstrated the ability to see that which is hidden. He knew in advance the ambush set by the Arameans (6:10-12). So it was with a high degree of certainty that one can take Elisha's encouragement to "fear not" (v. 16) as more than wishful thinking. It is grounded in reality,[317] for the great host of unconventional warriors with their unconventional weapons protecting this prophet were more numerous than the Aramean forces sent to capture him. Verse 17 reads,

> וַיִּתְפַּלֵּל אֱלִישָׁע וַיֹּאמַר יְהוָה פְּקַח־נָא אֶת־עֵינָיו וְיִרְאֶה וַיִּפְקַח יְהוָה אֶת־עֵינֵי הַנַּעַר וַיַּרְא וְהִנֵּה הָהָר מָלֵא סוּסִים וְרֶכֶב אֵשׁ סְבִיבֹת אֱלִישָׁע׃
>
> Then Elisha prayed and said, "O Lord, please open his eyes and he will see." And the Lord opened the servant's eyes, and behold, the mountain was full of horses and chariots of fire surrounding Elisha.

As a result of Elisha's prayer, the servant is able to see what is hidden to everyone else except Elisha: a mountain full of protectors, not surrounding the city, but surrounding Elisha (הָהָר מָלֵא סוּסִים וְרֶכֶב אֵשׁ סְבִיבֹת אֱלִישָׁע). The description implies that the array functioned as bodyguards for the prophet. The servant is temporarily granted the ability to see by second sight what cannot be apprehended via "conventional discernment" (6:17).[318] With second-sight gifted to Elisha's protégé, this narrative points out that "normal laws of perception are in force unless God chooses to tamper with them for better or worse (6:14-23)."[319] The power to temporarily take human sight and to temporarily give supernatural sight is within the purview and power of the Creator. In verse 17 Elisha prayed for the ability to be given to his servant (יְהוָה פְּקַח־נָא אֶת־עֵינָיו), and again he will prayed in verse 18 for the disabling of the enemy (הַךְ־נָא אֶת־הַגּוֹי־הַזֶּה בַּסַּנְוֵרִים). Only God can do and undo what he has done. In making the powerful soldiers blind he has made the powerful powerless and in granting second sight to Elisha's servant, he has comforted the powerless.

Lacking second sight, the Aramean soldiers are blind to the overwhelming odds arrayed against them. This blindness will soon be compounded further by

---

[316] Mordechai Cogan and Hayim Tadmor, *II Kings* (Anchor Bible 11; New York: Doubleday, 1988), 73-4.

[317] Walter Brueggemann, *1 and 2 Kings* (Smyth and Helwys Bible Commentary; Macon, Ga: Smyth and Helwys, 2000), 347.

[318] Brueggemann, *1 and 2 Kings*, 347.

[319] Sternberg, *The Poetics of Biblical Narrative*, 175.

blindness to their surroundings.[320] The prophet prays for the soldiers to be blinded and the prayer is answered in the affirmative (6:18). The word סַנְוֵרִים (blinding light) is also found in Genesis 19:11 when the men of Sodom were temporarily blinded by the angels to facilitate the escape of Lot from the mob surrounding his house. סַנְוֵרִים is a loan word from Akkadian *šunwurum* (to make radiant). The use of this word indicates a distinction between ordinary blindness and a temporary disabling of one's sense of sight.[321] They were temporarily and suddenly blinded as if a flash-bulb had gone off in their eyes. The soldiers then follow into Samaria the one whom they have come to take captive only to find that it is they who have been taken into captivity.[322] This is a significant reversal of fortunes. The mighty are now at the mercy of the unarmed (yet certainly not defenseless).

The two issues which come to light here are the matter of second sight and that of the soldiers being smitten with blindness on the basis of Elisha's prayer then having their sight restored, also by prayer. The centerpiece of this narrative is the second sight granted to Elisha's servant.[323] Brueggemann notes that the demonstration indicates that there are forces "from Yahweh at work in the world that are not subject to the policies or maneuvers of ordinary politics."[324] Wealth, intelligence, scientific precision, and political concreteness do not always succeed.[325]

Brueggemann notes that in many other places in Scripture, the term sight is used to speak of "discernment informed by faith so that the world looks different."[326] This is particularly noted in Isaiah 6:9-10. Brueggemann suggests that the narrative "exhibits an alternative way in the world."[327] Ultimately, he argues, the issue is not one of sight in contrast to blindness, but in light of the feast being provided to the enemies of Israel, it is that of peace in contrast to violence.[328]

Elisha possessed second sight. This ability appears to be different from prophetic vision which is insight into actual events that occur at a distance of space and time. Elisha was able to see the unseen in real-time. Elisha also possessed tremendous confidence in the Lord and enjoyed a warm relationship with him. Elisha conferred the ability of second sight on his servant so that he was able to see the angelic chariots arrayed around them (v. 15). It is reasonable to suggest that it was Elisha's belief in God that facilitated his

---

[320] Iain W. Provan, *1 and 2 Kings* (New International Biblical Commentary; Peabody, Mass.: Hendrickson, 1995), 198.
[321] Cogan and Tadmor, *II Kings,* 74.
[322] T.R. Hobbs, *2 Kings* (Word Biblical Commentary; Waco, Tex.: Word, 1985), 74.
[323] Brueggemann *1 and 2 Kings*, 348.
[324] Brueggemann *1 and 2 Kings*, 348.
[325] Brueggemann *1 and 2 Kings*, 348-49.
[326] Brueggemann *1 and 2 Kings*, 349.
[327] Brueggemann *1 and 2 Kings*, 352.
[328] Brueggemann *1 and 2 Kings*, 352.

ability to see the unseen. One is left to wonder if it is second sight which Israel lacked (Deut 29:4) all along. Indeed, their lack of faith in Yahweh was a significant factor facilitating their faithlessness to the covenant, disobedience, and apostasy. If second sight was the norm or outgrowth of faith then this suggests that a confidence such as Elisha demonstrated can overcome human blindness of the "other side" which all humanity naturally possesses. The implication is that prophetic ability, in the classical biblical sense, was wrought by faith.

Conclusions

Legal protections for the disabled pivot on the Exodus event by which Israel's society was to be designated as distinctly the people of God (Exod 20:2; 22:21; 23:9, 15; 29:46; 34:18) and were motivated by the reality of the presence of Yahweh in Israel's midst (Lev 26:3-13; Deut 12:1-5). It was, therefore, a conscious concern that Israel's conduct reflect her Redeemer's, respecting for life, renounce moral and ritual impurity, and act beneficently.

Justice, being grounded on Israel's covenant association with Yahweh, affected all members of the community of faith. In Leviticus 19:13-14, consideration toward the disabled is based on a reverence for Yahweh's name and an understanding that this demands more than conformity and acquiescence. Leviticus 19 induces the people of God to practice holiness within the community. Verses 13-14 demand that the disabled were to have been treated with respect. Since Yahweh's nature is to treat his people in a way which does not exploit or abuse them so it was to be his people's nature as well.

Deuteronomy 27:16-26 calls for God's people to protect the disabled. Israel was to be just as covenantally oriented in private life as it was in public. Only in being so oriented publicly and privately could Israel truly correspond to a reverential estimation of Yahweh. The collection of socially-oriented laws in Deuteronomy 27 projects a sense of urgency regarding compliance and affirms that there was to be no hypocrisy in Israel. There was to be consistency between Israel's public bearing and its private bearing. Israel's world-view was to include the principle of concern and care for those classes of society that were traditionally left to fend for themselves. Their well-being was to be Israel's concern. Proper care of the disabled amounted to more than communal harmony or realizing an expected ethical decorum. Each act of custodial care effectuated authentic faith.

Priestly qualifications (Lev 21:16-24; Deut 23:2) show that a priest had to be free from physical defect in order to function at the altar. Yahweh is God of life, and his priests were to worship him as such. The priests represented life before the people in their intermediation and appearance. Consequently, having a defect permanently prohibit a priest from approaching the altar to officiate (Lev 21:16-23). However, verses 22-23 contain an epilogue explaining that although a Levite may not offer sacrifices, he is still fully vested as a priest and entitled to the same provisions as other priests.

The interpretation of Leviticus 21:17-23 as conflating immorality and disability is in dispute. Perfect physical condition is more likely a representation of Yahweh's wholeness and this provides a legitimate warrant for its proscription against those with disabilities from officiating as a priest. Fitness for the sacred precincts is at the heart of the prohibition regarding priests who come into contract with anything constituted as being unclean. It does not matter whether the degree of impurity is significant or minor (Lev 7:20-21). A priest who is in the state of uncleanness must not partake of an offering (Lev 22:3). A physical disability may disqualify a priest from officiating in the cult but he is still a priest in every respect and entitled to priestly emoluments.

Perfection in relation to sacrifices expressed reverence toward God. If the offering was to mean anything in terms of communicating worship it must be perfect, but priestly perfection was an extension of holiness. The concept of holiness is illustrated in separation, order, goodness and moral justice. The purity system arguably conveys in a symbolic way that Yahweh is the God of life (order) and is separated from that which has to do with death (disorder). Purification rituals symbolized movement away from death towards life (Lev 14:5, 50; 17:11; Num 19:2, 17).

Although purity laws distinguished that which was holy and appropriate for use in the worship of Yahweh from that which was common and relegated to the realm of everyday life, they do not demean those things which were common.[329] These laws simply identify that which is to be employed as a means of worshiping Yahweh and prevented that which is common from the same.

Robert Kugler has noted that Leviticus 17-26 envisions "a society in which holiness would be expanded and democratized with all its attendant consequences, namely higher standards of conduct . . ."[330] The observation of Yahweh's commandments generated holiness. When Israel placed her confidence in Yahweh and thus explicitly obeyed his commands, she was pure and he, in turn, was sanctified. When Israel lost confidence in Yahweh and his word and consequently turned to other gods she effected an intentional self-blinding. This validates the metaphorical use of disability language by the prophets to be discussed later in this study.

---

[329] Hartley, *Leviticus*, 144.

[330] Robert A. Kugler, "Holiness, Purity, the Body and Society: The Evidence for Theological Conflict in Leviticus," *Journal for the Study of the Old Testament* 76 (1997): 25.

What we find in Leviticus is the dissociation of uncleanness from sin. The effect of this is to defuse arbitrary accusations, calm prophetic attack and deflect sectarian denunciation.[331] As a result,

> It supports at a practical level the doctrine of the perfect unity and singleness of God by tendering into God's hands, through the work of his priests, all claims of magic spells to harm and to cure. Any claims not coming from an authenticated source are invalidated.[332]

There is no hint in biblical literature related to priestly qualifications that would associate a physical defect with moral impurity or to an arbitrary act of divine wrath.

The biblical historical narratives contain several examples of the social attitudes of the people of Israel in the early monarchal period toward the disabled. These historical narratives demonstrate that in Israel's early social history, the disabled were not segregated from society but were integrated into it. For example, the incident narrated in 2 Samuel 5 in which David attacks Jerusalem shows the Jebusite's mocking David's pretension (v. 6), David's response (v.8a), and David's statement regarding his disposition toward the blind and lame (v. 8b). The assumption is that David's abhorrence is directed toward those who are literally "blind and lame." However, no specific prohibition was known to have existed which excluded the physically disabled from the Temple. In fact, Eli served in the temple even though he was going blind (1 Sam 1:9; 3:2-3; cf. 3:15). In addition, Leviticus 21:18 specifically does not restrict disabled priests from entering the temple. It does not seem likely that David's banishment of the blind and lame from the house (2 Sam 5:8) can be taken as literally referring to disabled people. It is not on the physically blind and lame that David's derision falls but on the Jebusites themselves. The disability language here is more likely meant to be understood colloquially to express David's negative disposition toward either the Jebusites.

In conjunction with this, 2 Samuel 9:5-13 narrates David's relationship with Meribbaal. The disability motif in this passage reaches back to the capture of Jerusalem, referred to earlier (2 Sam 5). David is alleged to have detested the blind and lame and banned them from his house. This pericope, however, supports the interpretation of the lame referred to in 2 Samuel 5:6-8 as being the Jebusites rather than those who were physically disabled.

David's kindness shown to Meribbaal was genuine, stemming from David's promise to Jonathan (1 Sam 20:14-16; 2 Sam 9:7). The function of this narrative, along with others, is to demonstrate that David was a man after God's right choice and, therefore, the rightful ruler of Israel. David's heart, unlike that of his predecessor, was right before the Lord. The Meribbaal narrative is not only intended to demonstrate that the Saulide dynasty has ended

[331] Douglas, "Sacred Contagion," 98-99.
[332] Douglas, "Sacred Contagion," 99.

but also to legitimate David as Saul's rightful successor by showing that David was God's anointed ruler who acted obediently toward Yahweh and impeccably toward men. This narrative forms a polemic against those who want a king from the house of Saul to remain on the throne.

In 1 Kings 14:4-5, Ahijah is described as being advanced in years and unable to see. Yet, even though he was physically blind he retained his perceptive prophetic powers. This narrative validates the view that blindness is not a moral judgment from God. If a physical disability were considered a sign of divine requital due to sin, Ahijah would not be functioning as he still did prophetically. The narrative explicitly portrays the integration of disability into Israel's society and cultus.

In the Elisha and Second Sight pericope (2 Kgs 6:17) the prophet has, until this point, demonstrated the ability to see that which is hidden. The centerpiece of this narrative is the second sight granted to Elisha's servant at Elisha's request. Elisha also possessed great confidence in the Lord. It is reasonable to suggest that it was Elisha's belief in God that facilitated his ability to see the unseen. If second sight was the norm or outgrowth of faith then it is plausible to suggest that a confidence such as Elisha demonstrated could overcome human blindness of the "other side" which all humanity naturally possesses. The implication is that prophetic ability, in the classical biblical sense, was wrought by faith.

The Metaphorical use of Disability Language in the Old Testament

The Hebrew Bible makes substantial use of disability language metaphorically to express ideals related to Israel's social condition. While most metaphorical usage is found in the prophetic books, a few law texts provide insight into the idealized shape of life Israel was to experience as Yahweh's covenant people. This shape involves Yahweh's divine enablement and a summons to maintain justice toward all persons in or associated with the community.

A Theological Statement Concerning Human Disability and Divine Enablement: Exodus 4:10-12

Exodus 4:10-12 contains a theological statement regarding human agency within the activity of God. It is a resurgence of creation theology in which God's presence, transforming, restoring, and enabling is the predominant theme in connection with every engagement with man. It is a theology of shaping a people who would, by their own volition, choose and obey him and thereby achieve the potential and promise of God's purpose for them in creation. Exodus 4:10-12 reads,

10 וַיֹּאמֶר מֹשֶׁה אֶל־יְהוָה בִּי אֲדֹנָי לֹא אִישׁ דְּבָרִים אָנֹכִי גַּם מִתְּמוֹל גַּם מִשִּׁלְשֹׁם גַּם
מֵאָז דַּבֶּרְךָ אֶל־עַבְדֶּךָ כִּי כְבַד־פֶּה וּכְבַד לָשׁוֹן אָנֹכִי׃
11 וַיֹּאמֶר יְהוָה אֵלָיו מִי שָׂם פֶּה לָאָדָם אוֹ מִי־יָשׂוּם אִלֵּם אוֹ חֵרֵשׁ אוֹ פִקֵּחַ אוֹ עִוֵּר

הֲלֹא אָנֹכִי יְהוָה׃
12 וְעַתָּה לֵךְ וְאָנֹכִי אֶהְיֶה עִם־פִּיךָ וְהוֹרֵיתִיךָ אֲשֶׁר תְּדַבֵּר׃

> The Moses said to the Lord, "Please, Lord, I have never been eloquent, not recently, nor in recent times, nor from the time you began speaking to your servant; for I am heavy of mouth and heavy of tongue." Then the Lord said to Moses, "Who made man's mouth? Or who made the mute, the deaf, the sighted, or the blind? Is it not I, the Lord? Now go and I, even I, will be with you and teach you what you will say."

Moses has been shepherding at the back of the wilderness, at a place known both as the mountain of God (הַר הָאֱלֹהִים) and as Horeb (חֹרֵבָה). There he is commissioned by God to be the agent through whom the children of Israel would be delivered from their Egyptian bondage. Within this context is a dialogue between Moses and God in which Moses resists the offer to be Israel's deliverer.

Rhetorically there is an ascending order in Moses' reluctance and repetition of the promise of divine presence. The repeated promise appears designed to render the escalating misgivings irrelevant and at the same time provide a causal link between performative and performance, bridging the gap between God's power and human condition. Further, the paralleling of *qtl* and *yqtl* verbs in 4:11 מִי שָׂם פֶּה לָאָדָם אוֹ מִי־יָשׂוּם אִלֵּם (who made man's mouth or who makes him mute) stylistically[333] reinforces the notion of the ascendancy of divine power over and against the human condition.

In Moses' fourth and final resistance to Yahweh's commission is a flat-out rejection more than an objection (4:10). Moses' resistance to speaking for God centers on an unspecified vocalic deficiency. The language of verse 10 suggests that Moses considered the repair of his deficiency to be critical to being a credible messenger.[334] Was he expecting Yahweh to correct it? As far as Moses was concerned, he could not serve as Yahweh's messenger with such an impediment. Moses' carefully worded retort, "excuse me Lord but I am not an eloquent man, neither recently or in times past, nor since you spoke to your servant" (גַּם מִתְּמוֹל גַּם מִשִּׁלְשֹׁם גַּם מֵאָז דַּבֶּרְךָ אֶל־עַבְדֶּךָ) indicates this encounter with Yahweh has not corrected this circumstance, nor does Moses anticipate a change in the future.

---

333 Adele Berlin, "The Grammatical Aspect of Biblical Parallelism," in *Beyond Form Criticism: Essays in Old Testament Literary Criticism* (Sources for Biblical and Theological Study; Winona Lake: Eisenbrauns, 1992), 317. Berlin notes the shift from *qtl* to *yqtl* does not occur for semantic reasons (i.e., it does not indicate real temporal sequence) but represents a stylistic shift.

334 Dewey Beegle, *Moses, the Servant of Yahweh* (Grand Rapids: Eerdmans, 1972), 79. Noting Isaiah 45:7, Beegle argues that the normative point of view in Israel was to attribute everything that happened to Yahweh. In spite of the fact that Yahweh made Moses a stammerer, He would use him anyway.

To this objection Moses adds the causal phrase, stating, "I am heavy in mouth (speech) and heavy in tongue" (כְבַד־פֶּה וּכְבַד לָשׁוֹן אָנֹכִי). There is no doubt that this jargon is known to have existed as medical terminology in other ancient languages to designate speech defects.[335] It could very well be that Moses was playing, what Durham calls, "his trump card," suggesting that indeed Yahweh was all he claimed to be, but Moses was the same old heavy-lipped and thick-tongued Moses.[336] Another possibility is that Moses is concerned that his prolonged absence from Egypt may have caused his fluency in the language to deteriorate.[337] A third possibility is that Moses has a personal reservation regarding the art of public speaking and the lack of persuasive eloquence that he feels would be insufficient for the mission. The text is unclear as to what the exact dilemma is that lurks behind Moses' objection.[338]

The assertion, כְבַד־פֶּה וּכְבַד לָשׁוֹן אָנֹכִי, is likely intended to communicate that he is not a fluent or convincing speaker but has difficulty expressing himself and formulating his thoughts.[339] Although Moses focuses on his weakness in expressing himself, Yahweh introduces the idea of human disability bringing forth the reality that it is He who provides and determines the presence or absence of human capabilities of communication.[340] The inclusions of the phrase לֹא אִישׁ דְּבָרִים אָנֹכִי reinforces the fact that Moses is referring to a lack of eloquence.[341] Expressions involving eloquence are not common (Job 11:2; Ps 140:12; Prov 25:24) but not rare either. The phrase אִישׁ דְּבָרִים is idiomatic for

---

[335] Jeffry H. Tigay, "'Heavy of mouth' and 'Heavy of Tongue' On Moses' Speech Difficulty," *BASOR* 231 (1978): 58-60. Tigay argues that Moses indeed claims he is inarticulate, but adds כְבַד־פֶּה וּכְבַד לָשׁוֹן אָנֹכִי so as to give a reason for this state.

[336] John I. Durham, *Exodus* Word Bible Commentary 3; Dallas: Word, 1987), 49.

[337] Jacob, *Exodus,* 88. Jacob notes that Moses uses the word דָּבָר rather than אָמַר. The distinction between the words is one of form and style (דָּבָר) over that of content (אָמַר). He goes on to assert that אָמַר is never used for speech as a function of the physical organs. Further, he notes that while דָּבָר is mostly used for a direct address, אָמַר is used for an indicted address and does not demand a word-by-word repetition by the speaker. He sees the two words as ancillaries noting that "an important statement given through *a-mar* then need to be properly expressed through a vigorous *di-ber*." It is certain that the distinction exists between the word אָמַר and דָּבָר. אָמַר signifies the mere act of oral expression (see Jerome A. Lund, "אָמַר," in *NIDOTTTE* [ed. Willem A. VanGemeren; Grand Rapids: Zondervan, 1997], 1:443-49). דָּבָר, however, connotes more force, authority, and importance in and behind the utterance (see Frank Ritchel Ames, "דָּבָר," in *NIDOTTE* [ed. Willem A. VanGemeren; Grand Rapids: Zondervan, 1997], 1:912-15).

[338] Nahum M. Sarna, *Exploring Exodus: The Heritage of Biblical Israel* (New York: Schocken Books, 1986), 61.

[339] Cornelis Houtman, *Exodus,* (vol. 3; Historical Commentary on the Old Testament; trans. J. Rebel and Sierd Woudstra; Kampen: Kok, 1993), 408.

[340] Houtman, *Exodus*, 412.

[341] Cassuto, *Commentary on Exodus*, 48-49.

possessing the quality of an eloquent speaker.[342] This would suggest that perhaps either his fluency in the language of Egypt has diminished or his lack of persuasiveness as a speaker would not be effective in securing the release of Pharaoh's captives. The negative (לֹא) before the nominal predicate drives home Moses' concern regarding his oratorical limitations.[343]

Ultimately, any suggestion as to the reasons for Moses' reluctance amounts to mere conjecture since these reasons are not specified in the text. Such a gap as this gives credence to the suggestion that those reasons are irrelevant to the narrative.[344] After presenting his credentials to the elders of Israel, Moses raises the issue again (Exod 6:12, 30). This time God commands Moses to take his message to Pharaoh. Twice Moses declares his unfitness for speaking to Pharaoh saying, "I am unskilled at speech" (אֲנִי עֲרַל שְׂפָתָיִם).[345] This expression, Beegle notes, "is a priestly way of having Moses say 'My lips are inadequate.'"[346]

Moses' objection does not convince Yahweh of his unfitness for service. Yahweh does not deny whatever the basis is for Moses' objection. Instead, he responds with three questions. The first two questions are rhetorical, being initiated with the interrogative particle מִי and containing the verb שָׂם in the *qal* stem. Yahweh's opening challenge to the latest of Moses' objections פֶּה לָאָדָם מִי שָׂם (who made man's mouth?) is a rebuke to Moses for suggesting that his speech impediment would need correction in order to do the task God is calling him to. God's response draws attention to the issue of human design. The verb שִׂים implies responsibility and authority by virtue of creation. What God has created is man's mouth (פֶּה).[347] In essence, Yahweh declares that he is the designer of that member which makes human communication possible. Yahweh's response connects his Creatorship with his Lordship "over man and his faculties for perception and expression."[348]

God's second rhetorical question addresses the issue of functionality. The verb שִׂים is again utilized. Here, שִׂים implies the exercise of force. This second

---

342 Bruce K. Waltke, and M. O'Conner, *An Introduction to Biblical Hebrew Syntax* (Winona Lake, Ind.: Eisenbrauns, 1990), 149. Paul Joüon, *A Grammar of Biblical Hebrew* (trans. and rev. Takamitsu Muraoka; Subsidia Biblica, 14/I-II; Rome: Pontifical Biblical Institute, 1993), 2:468-69.

343 Waltke, and O'Conner, *An Introduction to Biblical Hebrew Syntax*, 2:603.

344 Sternberg, *The Poetics of Biblical Narrative*, 239-40.

345 Isaiah raises a similar objection at his own commissioning (אִישׁ טְמֵא־שְׂפָתַיִם). Isaiah's objection, however, raises the specter of impurity and directly addresses his unfitness to address God.

346 Beegle, *Moses, the Servant of Yahweh*, 79.

347 J.A. Thompson and Elmer A, Martens, "פֶּה," in *NIDOTTE* (ed. Willem A. VanGemeren; Grand Rapids: Zondervan, 1997), 3:583. The term simply refers to the oral cavity.

348 Martin Noth, *Exodus: A Commentary* (The Old Testament Library; trans. J.S. Bowden; Philadelphia: Westminster, 1962), 46.

use of the verb שִׂים in association with the four adjectives expresses a transformation of function. The syntactical value of the *qal* perfect plus *qal* imperfect verbal chain in verse 11 should not be taken as consequential but as sequential, conveying the idea of condition. By means of a coordinating conjunction (אוֹ) God claims all the adjectives in this verse as being equally within his purview.[349] What follows is a series of four adjectives. Together these four adjectives also communicate functionality. אִלֵּם means more than an impediment but a binding of the mouth; to be made mute. Consequently, it is unlikely that Yahweh's term parallels Moses' affliction. It refers to the total inability to articulate a human language.[350] The term is used again in Isaiah 35:6 for those who are mute having their ability to speak restored to them. חֵרֵשׁ used in parallel with אִלֵּם refers to the silence one is in due to auditory deficiency rather than to keeping oneself silent. The term is also used in Leviticus 19:14, giving protection to those who cannot hear. פִּקֵּחַ is used here to refer to the ability to see. Usually this term is used in connection with the mouth organ. The only instance when it is used with another organ is in Isaiah 42:20 where the Israelites are charged with having the ability to hear but nonetheless do not listen. Here, however, פִּקֵּחַ is contrasted with the following adjective (עִוֵּר) not to signify the organs of sight (the eyes) but to refer to the deficiency of sight. עִוֵּר refers to physical blindness (Lev 19:14; 21:18; Deut 15:21; 27:18; 2 Kgs 25:7; Isa 29:18; 35:5; 42:7, 16; Jer 31:8; 39:7; 52:11; Mal 1:8). The terms פִּקֵּחַ and עִוֵּר in tandem indicates that more than physical malfunction is in mind. It suggests that divine enablement is not in place of dysfunctional physical faculties but in place of all physical facilities. Not only does God not condemn abnormal function of human attributes but he does not require normal function of human attributes for his work to proceed.

Yahweh's last query, which opens with the negative particle הֲלֹא, draws Moses' attention (and that of the reader) to an obvious fact which anticipates an affirmative response.[351] These three questions are designed to demonstrate to Moses that the Maker of man's mouth does not depend on the mouth's functionality (whether it be an articulate, inarticulate, or a mute one). The phrase אָנֹכִי יְהוָה (I am the Lord) echoes the declarative revelatory statements already made to Moses of God's reality and character (3:6, 12, 14). Yahweh introduced himself to Moses with these words (3:6). He assures Moses of his continuous presence through his journey and completion of his mission (3:12). These words will be the credentials Moses will give to the children of Israel

---

[349] Christo H.J. van der Merwe, Jackie A. Naudé, and Jan H. Kroeze, *A Biblical Hebrew Reference Grammar* (Sheffield, England: Sheffield Academic Press, 1999), 238-39.

[350] *BDB*, 47.

[351] Allen Harman, "Particles," in *NIDOTTE* (ed. Willem A. VanGemeren; Grand Rapids: Zondervan, 1997), 4:1035.

when they ask who sent him (3:14). The phrase אָנֹכִי יְהוָה stressing God's power and authority.[352]

Verse 12 opens with the clause וְעַתָּה (now). This clause functions adverbially with the imperative לֵךְ, linking verses 11 and 12 together. The following *waw* introduces a sequential phrase וְאָנֹכִי אֶהְיֶה עִם־פִּיךָ (I will be your mouth). The pronoun אָנֹכִי is emphatic while the prepositional phrase עִם־פִּיךָ is specific. God is not merely promising divine presence when Moses goes to Egypt, God is promising oral enablement. The next phrase, introduced by a *waw* consecutive links the two phrases together. Not only is Moses's speech impediment brushed aside but he is assured that the very words he speaks will be coming from God himself. The other prophets were likewise assured that the words they spoke would be placed in their mouths by the Lord (Isa 49:2; 50:4; Jer 1:9; Ezek 3:27). Yahweh further responds to Moses' objection, "I will be your mouth and I will teach you what you will say." This promise expresses divine enablement within the circumstances. Without delay, Moses was to act. No intermediate correction of his speech impediment would be forthcoming. He was to go and God would use his mouth as is. Yahweh's attendance and instruction would come when needed, not before. The promise given here is the point of contact. To Moses' request that God find another instrument (v. 13) God sends Aaron "to supply any deficiency Moses might have felt."[353]

Theological themes running through the book of Exodus include those images of God as Lord (his control over nature in the plagues and the taking of life; the affirmation of his kingship in 15:18; the giving of the law in chapter 20 and following) and warrior (15:3).[354] These themes converge in Exodus 4:10-12 to compose, in part, a theology of physical disability and divine

---

[352] Some LXX texts simply have ὁ θεὸς while others contain the compound phrase, κύριος ὁ θεός at the close of this verse while the MT reads simply יְהוָה. By far, יְהוָה alone is the most common nomenclature for God used in Exodus. When אֱלֹהִים does appear in Exodus in conjunction with יְהוָה it is found in compound expressions such as יְהוָה אֱלֹהֵי אבֹתֵיכֶם "the Lord, the God of your fathers"(3:15, 16). The formulaic phrase, יְהוָה אֱלֹהֵי הָעִבְרִיִּים "the Lord, the God of the Hebrews" appears five times (3:18; 7:16; 9:1, 13; 10:3). יְהוָה אֱלֹהֵי אֲבֹתָ "the Lord, the God of their fathers" appears only once (4:5). יְהוָה אֱלֹהֵי יִשְׂרָאֵל "the Lord, the God of Israel" also appears three times (5:1; 32:27; 34:23). יְהוָה אֱלֹהֶיךָ/יְהוָה אֱלֹהֵיכֶם "the Lord, your God" is found twelve times (6:7; 10:8; 15:26; 16:12; 20:2, 5, 7, 12; 23:19, 25; 34:24, 26). The formulate יְהוָה אֱלֹהֵיהֶם "the Lord their God" appears twice (10:7; 29:46). אֱלֹהֵינוּ in יְהוָה "the Lord our God" is found once (10:26). יְהוָה אֱלֹהָיו "the Lord, his God" appears once (32:11). Only once when יְהוָה ends a verse in MT of Exodus does the phrase יְהוָה אֱלֹהִים "The Lord God" appear (9:30). The predominance of evidence suggests that the LXX may be looking to harmonize 4:11 with other texts and ought not be considered reliable.

[353] Kaiser, *Exodus,* 329. The word יָד is often uses to stress instrumentality or agency.

[354] Terence E. Fretheim, *Exodus* (Interpretation; Louisville: John Knox, 1991), 16.

enablement.[355] God is the provider of all human faculties.[356] He makes the disabled what they are and can cure them just as easily.[357] Sarna writes, "Whatever the circumstances, it is certain that the underlying idea is that prophetic eloquence is not a native talent but a divine endowment granted for special purpose, the message originating with God and not the prophet."[358] This fits with the play on Moses's human inability in contrast with Yahweh's supernatural ability. Moses' objections to being the instrument God would use to secure Israel's deliverance stem from his concern over his adequacy for the role God was calling him to.[359]

The theological statement of divine enablement regardless of the degree of human functionality dispels the myth that Hebrew literature disdains human disability. In addition, Exodus 4:10-12 does not teach that God takes responsibility for creating a disabled class. Rather, he created all men and all, regardless of their degree of human ability, need his empowerment for spiritual functionality. Knowing God is not just a matter of having eyes that see or ears that hear. Obedience and purity, born of faith, is required. Yahweh must equip with the power to obey and remain pure. Without divine endowment, man remains spiritually insensitive. Further, God's intention in the Book of Exodus is to dwell among his people (19:5-6; 25:8). For this to be possible, the people must reflect him. They must be a holy people and compliant to his will. As we shall see, the intention of the priestly regulations of Leviticus is to equip the people with personal purity, access to God and a means of maintaining fellowship with God so that his presence would remain uninterrupted.

The Preservation of Judicial Sight Purity: Exodus 23:8 and Deuteronomy 16:19

Exodus 23:8 and Deuteronomy 16:19 parallel and compliment one another. These texts demonstrate that disability terminology can be used as metaphor to condemn in the strongest possible way the negation of that aspect of Israel's spiritual identity as a just people through the subversion of justice. The metaphor provides a theological ground for the just use of the power to judge by those to whom that power is given. The first mandate is to make no injustice in judgment. Bribery is illegitimate because it makes power arbitrary, deposes God by advancing material good or personal gain over him, and nullifies God's sovereignty. It also projects distrust toward God through seeking to secure

---

355 Judith Z. Abrams, "Judaism and Disabilities," in *Encyclopedia of Medicine in the Bible and the Talmud* (Northvale, 1993), 1701.

356 Abrams, "Judaism and Disabilities," 1702.

357 Abrams, "Judaism and Disabilities," 1702.

358 Nahum M. Sarna, *Exodus* (JPS Torah Commentary; Philadelphia: Jewish Publication Society, 1991), 21.

359 Arie C. Leder, "Reading Exodus to Learn and Learning to Read Exodus," *Calvin Theological Journal* 34 (1999): 22-23.

favor apart from him. Exodus 23:8 is communal in nature, extending the practice of justice to ordinary citizens. It reads,

וְשֹׁחַד לֹא תִקָּח כִּי הַשֹּׁחַד יְעַוֵּר פִּקְחִים וִיסַלֵּף דִּבְרֵי צַדִּיקִים׃

> You shall not take a bribe, for a bribe blinds the clear-sighted and subverts the cause of the just.

The negative particle followed by the imperfect verb (לֹא תִקָּח) functions together in these apodictic laws to protect the poor and the alien against judgments biased in favor of the wealthy and powerful.[360] They provide for legal rights and a fair hearing for all. The *yiqtol* in verse 8 is the usual form communicating truths of experience and must be considered global in that, as Paul Joüon notes, "the gift blinds the clear sighted."[361] This *piel* denominative יְעַוֵּר (to blind), preceding an adjective פִּקְחִים (the sighted) describing the result of the judicial process rather than the process itself.[362] The *waw* conjunction connecting the two *piel* verbs וִיסַלֵּף . . . יְעַוֵּר (blind . . . pervert) reinforce a habitual usage. These habitual non-perfectives present an example of how self-inflicted blindness can take place and the result of these conditions is that justice no longer exists. סלף is used in only two other texts (Deut 16:19; Prov 22:12). It means to twist, subvert, or pervert.[363]

The word bribe (שֹׁחַד) is in the emphatic initial position.[364] The prohibition against bribes is found 23 times in the Old Testament. Those who take bribes are included in the list of those under divine curse (Deut 27:25).[365] God takes no bribe and shows no favor (Deut 10:17-18) and requires this of those who would represent him as administrators of justice among the people. This text serves as a harbinger of the concerns expressed by the prophets. Isaiah especially notes that only those who do not subvert justice through bribery will enter God's presence (Isa 33:15).

Like Exodus 23:8 and Leviticus 19:15, Deuteronomy 16:19 also applies to all in the community of faith (16:17), not just to those who adjudicate legal matters although it also applies to them (16:18).[366] Deuteronomy 16:19 reads,

לֹא־תַטֶּה מִשְׁפָּט לֹא תַכִּיר פָּנִים וְלֹא־תִקַּח שֹׁחַד כִּי הַשֹּׁחַד יְעַוֵּר עֵינֵי חֲכָמִים וִיסַלֵּף
דִּבְרֵי צַדִּיקִם׃

---

[360] Christiana Houten, *The Alien in Israelite Law* (Journal for the Study of the Old Testament Supplement Series 107; Sheffield: JSOT, 1991), 55.

[361] Joüon, *A Grammar of Biblical Hebrew*, 2:361, 366-67.

[362] Waltke and O'Conner, *An Introduction to Biblical Hebrew Syntax*, 413.

[363] *BDB*, 701.

[364] Sarna, *Exodus*, 143.

[365] Sarna, *Exodus*, 143.

[366] Patrick, *Old Testament Law*, 117.

> You shall not distort justice; you shall not be partial, and you shall not take a bribe, for a bribe blinds the eyes of the wise and perverts the words of the righteous.

Deuteronomy 16:19 contains three apodictic prohibitions: do not pervert justice; do not show partiality; do not accept a bribe. The *hiphil* verb תַּטֶּה in the phrase "you shall not distort justice," expresses intentionality of purpose and pre-conclusion as to outcome. The root נָטָה, in this context indicates a denial of justice through deviation from the norm. It implies a thrusting away of justice consequent of insensitivity to one's immoral behavior, aside from personal gain.[367] The warning in the phrase לֹא תַכִּיר פָּנִים "you shall not be partial," literally condemns the recognizing of the face. One was to discard the social status of both parties in a dispute. Again the *hiphil* verb (תַכִּיר) indicates deliberateness in obstructing justice through a pre-concluded decision.

The final clause of verse 19, כִּי הַשֹּׁחַד יְעַוֵּר, contains an idiom "for a bribe blinds the eyes." This idiom introduces a new clause, connecting personal gain via a bribe with partiality in the cause of justice. The effect is judicial ineffectiveness. Ironically, one's objectivity called for one to be blind to a person's position and reputation. Objectivity is a byproduct of integrity borne out of wisdom. For all intents and purposes, a bribe cancels the wisdom one needs to judge properly (הַשֹּׁחַד יְעַוֵּר עֵינֵי חֲכָמִים).

יְסַלֵּף is a *piel* form of the verb סלף meaning to twist or overturn.[368] Used in conjunction with the word נָטָה as it is here stresses the intensely adverse affect of taking a bribe. The words of righteousness (דִּבְרֵי צַדִּיקִם) are twisted. Bribery makes justice the property of the highest bidder. A bribe "makes even a just person give a crooked answer when in the role of a judge or witness."[369] דִּבְרֵי צַדִּיקִים deals with the legal adjudication of communal life.

Verse 20 witnesses to the seriousness of violating the righteous standard of judicial integrity. Taking bribes threatens the life and future of the people.[370] The pursuit of justice in the adjudication of communal life (צֶדֶק צֶדֶק תִּרְדֹּף) was critical (לְמַעַן) to remaining in the land (16:20). צֶדֶק צֶדֶק is emphatic, intensifying the motivation for judicial integrity as righteousness was the heart of covenantal loyalty. To pervert justice was to abandon Yahweh (Amos 5:7, 10).

The above texts use the word blind metaphorically to describe the effect that taking a bribe has on those responsible for maintaining justice in Israel. Justice was to be practiced by all members of the community toward every other member of the community and it was to be objective because God himself is

---

367 Victor P. Hamilton, "נטה," in *NIDOTTE* (ed., Willem A. VanGemeren; Grand Rapids: Zondervan, 1997), 3:92-93.

368 *BDB*, 701.

369 Richard D. Nelson, *Deuteronomy* (Louisville: Westminster John Knox, 2002), 212.

370 Michael A. Grisanti and J. Clinton McCann, "שחד," in *NIDOTTE* (ed., Willem A. VanGemeren; Grand Rapids: Zondervan, 1997), 4:75.

fair, not preferring any one person above another. Fairness, being the norm, would have been the right and expectation of every member of the community of Israel.

A Heart that sees the Hand of God at Work: Deuteronomy 29:4

Deuteronomy 29:4 reads,

וָאוֹלֵךְ אֶתְכֶם אַרְבָּעִים שָׁנָה בַּמִּדְבָּר לֹא־בָלוּ שַׂלְמֹתֵיכֶם מֵעֲלֵיכֶם וְנַעַלְךָ לֹא־בָלְתָה מֵעַל רַגְלֶךָ׃

But to this day the Lord has not given to you a heart to know, nor eyes to see, nor ears to hear.

As Moses reflects on the past forty years of wandering in the desert (29:2-8), he describes God's salvific acts from them from the Exodus to their present day, standing on the plains of Moab. He projects forward to what lay ahead of God's people after they cross the Jordan and begin the process of possessing the land. In this summary he attempts to describe what has engendered the dissociation between Yahweh and his people until this time. In verse 4, Moses summarizes the Hebrew demeanor typified during those years. He points to the fact that the experiences of their history have not led them to a better understanding of their God. Indeed God had been visible to them in the pillar of fire and cloud. They heard him speak to Moses and seen the great darkness on Mount Sinai. But they were still ignorant of his ways.

Verse 4 is critical to understanding why Moses takes this trip down memory lane (vv. 1-8). Israel lacked the needed heart to know (לֵב לָדַעַת), eyes to see (עֵינַיִם לִרְאוֹת), and ears to hear (אָזְנַיִם לִשְׁמֹעַ). These could only be acquired from the Lord (נָתַן). In this case, seeing is neither *real* seeing nor believing.

Structurally, the key words in Deut 29:1-4 are עֵינַיִם (eyes) and ראה (to see).[371] The pericope is a historical retrospective, recalling the various adversities as well as the divine assistance experienced during the wilderness wandering for the intended purpose of providing additional motivation for keeping the covenant (29:9). This nostalgic survey of divine intervention preludes Moses' appeal to Israel to remain faithful to her covenant with Yahweh.[372] McConville suggests that this verse raises the same moral issue raised in 9:4-6, "namely the people's disposition to unfaithfulness to Yahweh."[373] He suggests, too, that it was moral understanding that would produce right action.[374]

---

[371] Christensen, *Deuteronomy 21:10-34:12*, 709.
[372] Merrill, *Deuteronomy*, 376.
[373] McConville, *Deuteronomy*, 414.
[374] McConville, *Deuteronomy*, 415.

The structure suggests a contrast between the Israelites having seen what Yahweh had done yet at the same time they had no sense of understanding.[375] Kalland asserts that the issue is that God

> had not given the Israelites the realization of his intervention in the experiences of their history, he did not deny that they had knowledge of his part in the action; rather, he was asserting that the ultimate directive and operative power in all their national life–including immediate needs – was the Lord himself.[376]

The Israelites saw the mighty acts of Yahweh to deliver them but yet "they still were not able to grasp what this meant."[377] Verses 2 and 4 both correspond to and contrast with one another. Israel had witnessed the mighty hand of Yahweh in deliverance, his generous and sustaining hand via the manna and quail, observed his commanding presence leading them through the desert and on Sinai, but in spite of all this they had not come to grasp the implications of all these things. Perhaps none but Moses came nearest to Yahweh by means of his faith which could see beyond the miracles to the God of wonders who performed them. According to Kalland, the Apostle Paul (Rom 11:8) relates this to Isaiah 29:10 and Israel's inability to become believers.[378]

Tigay asserts that verse 4 suggests it is Yahweh who is to blame for Israel's ignorance. Tigay perceptively asks if it is God who gives "the perception necessary to understand the religious meaning of historical experiences," then how can he hold "the rebellious Exodus generation responsible for its faithlessness?"[379] However, Christensen points out that Deuteronomy 30:6 suggests that although it is indeed God who gives the heart the capacity for faith, he does so only "for those who seek it."[380]

The concept of covenant is an expression of the relationship between Yahweh and Israel. This relationship was collective in nature being ratified, maintained, and renewed communally. The collective nature of this relationship is evident constitutionally in the various law codes handed down at Sinai. It is also evident in the fact that Israel was either blessed or cursed collectively by the Lord. Clearly, the relationship does not appear to have been intended to remain collective but was meant to permeate the community through to the individual persons of the community and expressed in intentionally enacted faith rather than mechanical obedience to civil and cultic obligations. The people were to be holy, reflecting the nature and character of their God. They were also to be spiritual, interacting with the God whose intention it was to

---

375 Christensen, *Deuteronomy 21:10-34:12*, 709.
376 Kalland, *Deuteronomy*, 3:179.
377 Christensen, *Deuteronomy 21:10-34:12*, 711.
378 Kalland, *Deuteronomy*, 3:180, fn.4.
379 Tigay, *Deuteronomy*, 275-76.
380 Christensen, *Deuteronomy 21:10-34:12*, 712.

dwell in their midst. If, indeed, covenant serves to be the expression of relationship, what was the basis of Israel's identity?

It seems to me that the ultimate concern of Pentateuchal law was the honor of Yahweh and his holiness, the penultimate concern was the community. When these laws were not adhered to, all three constituents were negatively impacted. However, when these laws were maintained, Yahweh was honored, the covenant with his people was sustained, and mutual edification within the community was achieved. Maintaining the laws resulted in relationships between Yahweh and his people, and among members of the community being healthy and strong. This edification was not limited to members of the community as though they were the only ones to enjoy the benefits of covenant relationship with Yahweh. The morality, justice, mercy, and decency which Israel was to cultivate and enjoy was to be extended to aliens living among the members of the community as well (Lev 19:33-34). Functionality and heart (Isa 29:13) were connected in that the degree to which this society realized full compliance with their covenant was the measure of their passion for Yahweh.

Conclusions

Not all the metaphorical uses of disability language are found in prophetic literature. For example, Exodus 4:10-12 contains a theological statement regarding human agency within the activity of God. It is a resurgence of creation theology in which God's presence, transforming, restoring, and enabling is the predominant theme. Here, the idea that it is Yahweh who provides and determines the presence or absence of human capabilities of communication is introduced. In essence, Yahweh declares that he is the designer of that member which makes human communication possible and it is he alone who causes human organs to function as they do. The Maker of man's mouth does not depend on the mouth's functionality. He makes the disabled what they are and can cure them just as easily. Moses' human inability is placed in contrast with Yahweh's supernatural ability. However, God is not merely promising divine presence for Moses when he goes to Egypt, God is promising divine enablement. God is the provider of all human faculties. The theological statement of divine enablement regardless of the degree of human functionality dispels the myth that Hebrew literature disdains human disability.

Disability language is also used metaphorically in Exodus 23:8 and Deuteronomy 16:19, two texts which parallel and compliment one another. These texts demonstrate that disability terminology can be used as metaphor to condemn in the strongest possible way the negation of that aspect of Israel's spiritual identity as a just people through the subversion of justice via bribery. The metaphor provides a theological ground for the just use of the power to judge by those to whom that power is given. The first mandate is to make no injustice in judgment. Bribery is illegitimate because it makes power arbitrary, deposes God by advancing material good or personal gain over him, and nullifies God's sovereignty. It also projects distrust toward God through seeking to secure favor apart from him. Bribery makes justice the property of the highest bidder. Exodus 23:8 and Deuteronomy 16:19 use the word blind metaphorically to describe the effect that taking a bribe has on those responsible for maintaining justice in Israel.

Deuteronomy 29:4 contains a historical retrospective in which Moses laments the fact that even after forty years Yahweh's working for Israel the people had not yet acquired a heart that can see his hand. The pericope recalls the various adversities as well as the divine assistance experienced during the wilderness wandering. In this summary statement Moses describes what has engendered the dissociation between Yahweh and his people, pointing to the Hebrew demeanor typified during those years. The Israelites had seen what Yahweh had done yet at the same time they had no sense of understanding. The Israelites saw the mighty acts of Yahweh to deliver them but yet they could not grasp the implications of all these things. The concept of covenant is an expression of the relationship between Yahweh and Israel. The collective nature of Israel's covenant relationship with Yahweh is evident constitutionally in the various law codes handed down at Sinai. Obedience of the law was crucial. However, Israel's relationship with Yahweh was not intended to remain collective but was meant to permeate the community through to the individual persons of the community and expressed in intentionally enacted faith rather than mechanical obedience to civil and cultic obligations. As the prophets would later point out, functionality and heart (Isa 29:13) were connected in that the degree to which this society realized full compliance with their covenant was the measure of their passion for Yahweh.

Chapter 5

Prophetic Literature and the Metaphorical Use of Disability Language

Israel's Spiritual Disposition

Repeatedly, the prophets employ disability language to describe Israel's condition of self-inflicted spiritual obtuseness, divinely imposed imperceptibility, or to that anticipated event when Israel's faith and perception would be restored. In the background of each text citing the prophetic evaluation of Israel's condition is the hope that Israel would repentantly and responsively render to Yahweh his rightful place in their hearts.

Disability Language and the Soul of Israel: Isaiah

The use of disability language as metaphor in Isaiah primarily deals with Israel's lack of responsiveness to Yahweh. The dysfunction of the "physical" attributes of seeing, hearing, and walking in Isaianic literature expresses Israel's unwillingness to depend on, trust in, or obey the word of the Lord. The imagery of body reflects the soul of Israel. Israel was drafted to be a spiritual organism established by means of a new and vital relationship with Yahweh. Yahweh's presence was meant to be the impulse for holiness, obedience, and mobilization as Israel functioned in concert with Yahweh's purposes. Regardless of the physical faculty being referred to, the main issue is one of functionality. Whether the disability is self-inflicted or a result of divine judgment, the question is still one of functionality.

The theological themes presented in Isaiah are more fully orbed than any other book in Hebrew prophetic literature.[1] Through Isaiah we come to understand that judgment and salvation are not isolated from one another but instead should be viewed as cause and effect in the larger outworking of God's redemptive plans in which "salvation is made possible through judgment."[2] God is both Judge and Deliverer. Isaiah presents both aspects of Yahweh's divine nature for the purpose of showing his faithfulness and holiness. In the forefront of the book is Israel's syncretistic religious predilections and mechanistic compliance to some covenant obligations (with the exception of monotheism) rather than honoring the covenant with a heart of faith and love.

---

1 John N. Oswalt, "The Theology of Isaiah," in *NIDOTTE* (ed. Willem A. VanGemeren; Grand Rapids: Zondervan, 1997), 4:725.

2 Oswalt, "The Theology of Isaiah," 4:725.

For Isaiah, the covenant relationship Israel enjoyed with God did not privilege them above other nations. The covenant was not a birthright entitling Israel to behave in whatever manner they liked.[3] It did not protect them from divine judgment when they were morally corrupt. Judgment would indeed come, but neither this nor Israel's depravity could nullify the covenant.

Oswalt points out that "above everything else, sin is described as rebellion in Isaiah."[4] This rebellion is manifest in a variety of ways. The basis of judgment on their rebellion is either explicitly or implicitly the covenant.[5] Israel's disloyalty is flagrant and odious. Isaiah rails against a variety of rebellions behaviors, including idolatry (17:7-9), pride (2:12-17; 3:16-23; 65:1-5), and turning a blind eye and a deaf ear toward Yahweh. Oswalt notes, "This rebellion also manifests itself in the attempt to reduce religious behavior to ritual performance instead of a life in which the character of God is lived out in relation to others."[6] This theme is introduced early on in the book (1:10-15) and becomes full blown in the final chapters. Oswalt writes,

> God does not want religious behavior, he wants godly behavior. But godly behavior is a matter of every day and a matter of laying aside one's prerogatives for the good of others. Religious behavior is much more satisfying and much more uplifting to the proud. Isaiah 66:1-6 speaks in similar terms with ch.1 of the foolishness of self-exalting worship. Far from placating God, it infuriates him. Humility and contrition are essential signs of that covenantal obedience that alone ensures god's presence (57:15; 66:2).[7]

The message of Isaiah is that "sinful Israel would always be the object of divine terror; repentant Israel would receive his promises of forgiveness."[8]

Disability Language Describing Israel'sUnresponsiveness Toward Yahweh: Isaiah 6:9-10

Isaiah's first use of disability language comes in the commissioning pericope. In this passage Isaiah is commissioned to go to a people and communicate a message they will not hear or yield to. The language in this section introduces a theme that will be repeated through the book. That Israel, rather than being a viscerally spiritual people, is instead obtuse toward their God and outright contemptuous toward the covenant that defines them. It may be that the early portion of Isaiah reflects Exodus theology which sets up the redemption of Israel and Judah presented later in this book. There are corresponding motifs at work in both. The hardening of heart and fattening of ears is linked to

3 Oswalt, "The Theology of Isaiah," 4:725.
4 Oswalt, "The Theology of Isaiah," 4:731.
5 Oswalt, "The Theology of Isaiah," 4:731.
6 Oswalt, "The Theology of Isaiah," 4:731.
7 Oswalt, "The Theology of Isaiah," 4:731.
8 Childs, *Introduction to the Old Testament as Scripture*, 327.

Pharaoh's hardened heart so that he was unwilling or unable to yield to God's power and follow his will (Exod 8:11, 28; 9:7, 34). Another parallel with Exodus is Isaiah's comment regarding unclean lips (Isa 6:5) which corresponds to Moses' complaint of being slow of speech (Exod 4:10) and the uncircumcised lips (Exod 6:12, 30). In addition, Yahweh's response to Moses in Exodus 4:11 corresponds to Isaiah's commission in 6:10 which reads:

הַשְׁמֵן֙ לֵב־הָעָ֣ם הַזֶּ֔ה וְאָזְנָ֥יו הַכְבֵּ֖ד וְעֵינָ֣יו הָשַׁ֑ע פֶּן־יִרְאֶ֨ה בְעֵינָ֜יו וּבְאָזְנָ֤יו יִשְׁמָע֙ וּלְבָב֣וֹ יָבִ֔ין
וָשָׁ֖ב וְרָ֥פָא לֽוֹ׃

> Then I said, "Woe is me, for I am ruined. For I am a man of unclean lips and in the living midst of a people of unclean lips; for my eyes have seen the king, the Lord of hosts."

Isaiah 6:5 begins with the cry אוֹי. Although it is a different word than the one used in chapter 5 it has the same meaning.[9] It may serve as a climax to the woes delivered in chapter 5.[10] Isaiah senses the threat to himself due to his proximity with Yahweh's divine presence. The prophet has seen Yahweh and recognized his own ruin (כִּי־נִדְמֵית), and acquiesces to being אִישׁ טְמֵא־שְׂפָתַיִם (a man of unclean lips), a thing he holds in common with the people among whom he lives (בְתוֹךְ עַם־טְמֵא שְׂפָתַיִם אָנֹכִי יוֹשֵׁב). In a sense, Isaiah sees himself and his people as being no better, spiritually, than the people God would use later to take them into captivity. Isaiah's identification with his people is not mere ceremony but a recognition of the condition which characterizes him and his people. This confession is itself prompted by Yahweh's appearance. His own emotional confession prompts a seraphim (אֶחָד מִן־הַשְּׂרָפִים) to bring live coals from the altar to touch his lips and purge the uncleanness (6:6-7). Isaiah then accepts his commission to be Yahweh's messenger to a deaf and blind Israel (6:8). Israel's response to Isaiah's message stands in contrast with Isaiah's responsiveness to Yahweh in verses 5-8. At the appearance of Yahweh he saw, in one blazing epiphany, his condition and that of his people. Unlike Isaiah they will not see or repent. Isaiah 6:9-10 reads:

9 וַיֹּ֕אמֶר לֵ֖ךְ וְאָמַרְתָּ֣ לָעָ֣ם הַזֶּ֑ה שִׁמְע֤וּ שָׁמ֙וֹעַ֙ וְאַל־תָּבִ֔ינוּ וּרְא֥וּ רָא֖וֹ וְאַל־תֵּדָֽעוּ׃
10 הַשְׁמֵן֙ לֵב־הָעָ֣ם הַזֶּ֔ה וְאָזְנָ֥יו הַכְבֵּ֖ד וְעֵינָ֣יו הָשַׁ֑ע פֶּן־יִרְאֶ֨ה בְעֵינָ֜יו וּבְאָזְנָ֤יו יִשְׁמָ֙ע
וּלְבָב֣וֹ יָבִ֔ין וָשָׁ֖ב וְרָ֥פָא לֽוֹ׃

> Then He said, "Go and tell this people: 'Keep on listening, but do not perceive; keep on looking but do not understand.' Fatten the hearts of this people and their ears dull and their eyes dim lest they see with their eyes, and hear with their ears, and understand with their hearts, and return and be healed."

---

9 Geoffrey W. Grogan, *Isaiah* (Expositors Bible Commentary 6; Grand Rapids: Zondervan, 1998), 56.

10 Grogan, *Isaiah*, 56. Grogan notes that this possibility is strengthened by the concern for the people's sin.

The dialogue is acerbic. Isaiah is not assigned to engage in a mission designed to fail, but to one reflecting on the future reaction of the people to the divine message and at the same time seeing their reaction as being entirely within the divine purpose.[11] Noting the structure of this section Geoffrey Grogan writes,

> Once again we are impressed by the structure of the book; for this chapter immediately follows and precedes examples of wrong reaction to God's word. In 5:24 it is the people who reject it, and in chapter 7 Ahaz refuses it.[12]

It is clear that the people's reaction to Isaiah's preaching would have its opposite effect, generating within them an even more inflated sense of their own wisdom and implacable self-determination than before.[13] Following the pronouncement of judgment against Israel and Judah (5:1-30), this section provides explanation, cause, and outcome of the judgment pronounced upon Judah. Isaiah 6:1-13 specifically explains the cause for the impending judgment.

Verses 9-10 are part of Isaiah's commission, introduced by the standard speech formula (וַיֹּאמֶר). The paradoxical imperatives in verse 9 create a theological problem in that they are working toward contradictory purposes.[14] In effect they declare that the human faculties of hearing and sight are functional yet ineffectual. Isaiah's hearers see without seeing and hear without hearing.[15] The imperatives in verse 9 indicate that Isaiah's preaching will produce the effect that his hearers will neither understand, turn, nor be healed.[16] These imperatives point to the outcome of Isaiah's ministry rather than its purpose.[17] The infinitive in verse 9 functions adverbially, strengthening the main verb. The structure of the inner and outer faculties (heart, ears, eyes, eyes, ears, heart) clearly emphasizes the total inability to comprehend.[18]

Alexander asserts that this is a case of judicial blindness for national depravity (1:5).[19] The first use of disability language in Isaiah establishes the primary norm for understanding the use of this language through the rest of the

---

[11] Odil H. Steck, "Rettung und Verstockung: Exegetische Bemerkungen zu Jesaja 7:3-9," *Evangeliche Theologie* 33 (1973): 77-90.

[12] Grogan, *Isaiah*, 57.

[13] Otto Kaiser, *Isaiah 1-12: A Commentary* (The Old Testament Library; Philadelphia: Westminster, 1972), 83.

[14] The LXX seeks to soften the imperatives, making them indicatives. This attempt, however, is somewhat retrospective.

[15] Experience has shown us that humans are capable of seeing and hearing but at the same time failing to grasp that which is before them.

[16] Christopher R. Seitz, *Isaiah 1-39* (Interpretation; Louisville: John Knox, 1993), 56-57.

[17] J. Alec Motyer, *The Prophecy of Isaiah* (Downers Grove, Ill.: InterVarsity, 1993), 79.

[18] Motyer, *The Prophecy of Isaiah*, 79.

[19] Joseph Addison Alexander, *Commentary on the Prophecies of Isaiah* (Grand Rapids: Zondervan, 1977), 152.

book. The connection of dysfunctional human faculties with the fattened hearts (הַשְׁמֵן לֵב־הָעָם הַזֶּה) communicates a total inability to comprehend.[20] The language is reminiscent of chapter one and the dull-witted people of God contrasted with domesticated animals who know their master and the stall where they are fed and bedded. The combination of words and phrases describing Israel's condition in verse 4 formulates Israel's condition. God describes Israel as a sinful people (גּוֹי חֹטֵא), a people burdened with iniquity (עַם כֶּבֶד עָוֹן), they are offspring of evildoers (זֶרַע מְרֵעִים) and the descendents of those who effectuate corruption (בָּנִים מַשְׁחִיתִים). They have abandoned the Lord (עָזְבוּ אֶת־יְהוָה), they despise him (נִאֲצוּ אֶת־קְדוֹשׁ יִשְׂרָאֵל), and have reversed course away from him (נָזֹרוּ אָחוֹר). In chapter 5 the negative characterization continues. In 5:12 they are said to disregard the Lord's deeds (פֹּעַל יְהוָה לֹא יַבִּיטוּ), and in 5:13 their exile is attributed to their profound lack knowledge (מִבְּלִי־דָעַת). Yahweh's disdain at this point is palpable.

Even though Isaiah's message was articulated simply and clearly, the sophisticates of his day scorned him. Consequently, they could not understand, repent, and be healed. Oswalt suggests that the strange contradiction presented here indicates the depth of pride and rebellion that has so diseased the people that they "simply misperceive the truth of what they hear."[21] Although 6:10b suggests that blindness is already a state of being for the people and would not be removed by the prophet or his message, it seems more likely that the blindness would only be intensified by his message.[22] Dempster writes,

> He is told to speak in such a way that the people's hearts will harden, much like Pharaoh's when Moses spoke to him (6:9-10). This mission is the antithesis of the prophetic task, which is to bring conviction, restoration and repentance. He is to accelerate the hardening of sinful Israel through his prophesying, thus accomplishing God's mysterious purpose.[23]

Isaiah's preaching will not make it easier for the people to believe and repent, it will make it more difficult.[24] The message Isaiah proclaimed would contribute to the blindness of his generation.[25]

---

20 Motyer, *The Prophecy of Isaiah*, 78.

21 John N. Oswalt, *The Book of Isaiah: Chapters 1-39* (The New International Commentary on the Old Testament; Grand Rapids: Eerdmans, 1986), 189.

22 Kaiser, *Isaiah 1-12*, 131-32.

23 Stephen G. Dempster, *Dominion and Dynasty* (New Studies in Biblical Theology 15; Downers Grove, Ill.: InterVarsity, 2003), 175.

24 Oswalt, *The Book of Isaiah: Chapters 1-39*, 189.

25 Oswalt, *The Book of Isaiah: Chapters 1-39*, 189.

Disability Language Describing Israel's Inadequate Leadership: Isaiah 29:9-24

Isaiah not only uses disability language metaphorically to describe Israel's spiritual insensibility but also to describe the quality of leadership exhibited in Israel during the period of his ministry. Israel acts as though God is either ignorant or uncaring of their deeds. In judgment, Yahweh brings a finish to prophetic insight, a move that is to a large degree the equivalent to blinding his people. His presence and the message sent by his prophet is sealed making it inaccessible. A day is coming, however, in which the inaccessibility of the Lord's word will come to an end and he will again be known as he knows. Key to the issue of disability language is 29:9 which reads:

הִתְמַהְמְהוּ וּתְמָהוּ הִשְׁתַּעַשְׁעוּ וָשֹׁעוּ שָׁכְרוּ וְלֹא־יַיִן נָעוּ וְלֹא שֵׁכָר׃

> Be delayed and wait. Blind yourselves and be blind. They become drunk but not with wine. They stagger but not with strong drink.

The structure of chapters 28-33 suggest that Isa 29:9-24 falls within a section concerned with the significance and deliverance of Zion as the location of the deliverer's future throne and the place from which Yahweh will launch his final judgment on the earth.[26] The prominent theme is a lack of wisdom, binding 29:1-14 and 29:15-24 together.[27] Chapter 29 can, nevertheless, can be subdivided into three parts. Isaiah 29:1-8 portrays the desperate conditions Yahweh's judgment had brought; verses 9-14 illustrate the people's self-inflicted spiritual dullness expressed through the metaphor of blindness; verses 15-24 then projects into the envisioned age when the people's habitude is reversed. It will be a time when the wise will be humbled, the blind will see, the lame will walk, the poor will have joy, and evil ones will be cut off.

The imperatival statements in verse 9 introduce the second address to the audience, "be delayed and wait and blind yourselves and be blind" (הִתְמַהְמְהוּ וּתְמָהוּ הִשְׁתַּעַשְׁעוּ וָשֹׁעוּ) and builds on the previous subunit, identifying Yahweh as the one causing the assault against his own altar.[28] Sweeney writes,

> The command to blindness appears in vv. 9-10, identified by its imperative forms that call on the audience to be astonished and blind. The command proper appears in v. 9, including commands to be astonished and blind in v.9a and to stagger and reel in comprehension in v. 9b. The basis for the commands, introduced by a

---

26 The repeated use of הוֹי (28:1; 29:1; 30:1; 31:1) anchors and connects the section. Chapters 32-33 are linked by the material that is introduced by הֵן (32:1) forming a single climatic unit pointing to the outcome of Yahweh's retributive and salvific activities.

27 Marvin A. Sweeney, *Isaiah 1-39: With an Introduction to Prophetic Literature* (The Forms of Old Testament Literature 16; Grand Rapids: Eerdmans, 1996), 375.

28 Sweeney, *Isaiah 1-39*, 376.

> causative *kî* "because," appears in v. 10, which states YHWH has poured deep sleep on "you" (v. 10a) and that YHWH has blinded the prophets (v. 10b).[29]

The imperatives also parallel 6:9-10. Both 29:9 and 6:9-10 set forth the people's intentional, self-induced spiritual blindness, and this is the paradox. The incongruity of the dual antecedent cannot be overlooked. The warning imperative "be delayed and wait" in 9a (הִתְמַהְמְהוּ וּתְמָהוּ הִשְׁתַּעַשְׁעוּ) changes to a description in 9c: "they become drunk, but not with wine, they stagger about but not with beer," (שֹׁעוּ שָׁכְרוּ וְלֹא־יַיִן נָעוּ וְלֹא שֵׁכָר). The imperative in 9b (שֹׁעוּ) is an indirect imperative expressing the notion of purpose and consecution.[30] While there is no accessibility to the revelation now before them, at the same time, there is no perception among the people even if there was accessibility to it. The text emphasizes the inability of the people to comprehend the significance of this fact.[31] Young notes the reciprocal nature of the *hithpalpel* stem, asserting that the two *hithpalpel* verbs, followed immediately by two *qal* verbs (all of them imperative) suggests that the action was one the people chose for themselves and that Isaiah is merely enjoining Israel to continue in this condition as long as they wished.[32] Motyer likewise writes, "willfully to refuse to see induces blindness."[33]

The whole section is directed to the inhabitants of Jerusalem who are urged to continue in their self-delusion, yet at the same time their actions are attributed to Yahweh who's pouring out of a spirit of deep sleep "makes it impossible for them to act otherwise."[34] Their deliverance (29:1-8) was hidden from their understanding.[35] The implication is that spiritual blindness can be characterized as an insensitivity or callousness to God and to his word.

The prophets no longer clearly saw or understood divine actions as they once did. The question is, What would cause such a cessation of prophetic vision? Indeed, Yahweh takes credit for terminating it (v. 10), but why? They possess the information (v. 11) yet are unable to read or decipher it. It is as though it were a book that cannot be opened (v. 11). Again, the question is why Yahweh would bring about this turn of events. Oswalt suggests that

> The answer is the same in each case: those who should be gifted with discernment, who should be able to perceive the mysterious workings of God in history, are so stupid that they cannot understand God's ways even when they are

---

[29] Sweeney, *Isaiah 1-39*, 377.

[30] Joüon, *A Grammar of Biblical Hebrew*, 2:384.

[31] Sweeney, *Isaiah 1-39*, 377.

[32] Edward J. Young, *The Book of Isaiah: Chapters 19-39* (New International Commentary on the Old Testament, vol. 2; Grand Rapids: Eerdmans, 1969), 315.

[33] Motyer, *The Prophecy of Isaiah,* 239.

[34] J. Cheryl Exum, "Of Broken Pots, Fluttering Birds, and Visions in the Night: Extended Simile and Poetic Technique in Isaiah," *Catholic Biblical Quarterly* 43 (1981): 348.

[35] Exum, "Of Broken Pots, Fluttering Birds, and Visions in the Night," 351.

> presented to them in plain script. As a result, the ordinary people are led astray by spurious wisdom and the nation is sunk into degradation. The result is that God will once again, as in Egypt, have to do something shocking to show himself.[36]

Verse 10 informs us that it was not the priests who were chiefly to blame for the people's blindness (although they indeed have contributed to it). The real blame should fall on the prophets and seers who received and were changed to deliver corrective orations.[37] In spite of this declaration, Young places the blame directly at the feet of God himself because it was he who had decreed Israel's blindness.[38] Roberts, however, places the blame for Israel's situation on all of Israel's political and religious leaders as it was they who misled the people.[39] Isaiah, indeed, indicts the leaders for not looking at the Holy One of Israel (5:12; 22:11) and for not desiring to hear him (30:9-11) which ultimately led to the loss of their wisdom noted in this text.[40] J.J.M. Roberts notes,

> In the theology of the Old Testament there comes a point at which Yahweh's patience is overtaxed. When God's people refuse to see and hear, when "they say to the seers, 'do not see!' and to the prophets, 'Do not prophesy to us what is right; speak to us smooth things, prophesy illusions . . .'" (Isa 30:10), in God's poetic justice they eventually get what they ask for: "For Yahweh has poured out upon you a spirit of deep sleep, and has closed your eyes, the prophets; and covered your heads, the seers" (Isa 29:10).[41]

The theology parallels that of 1 Kings 22:22 where Ahab's choice to embrace falsehood brought on the very spirit he chose. Isaiah's metaphors (עֵינֵיכֶם for prophets; רָאשֵׁיכֶם for seers) serve to point out that a "determined spiritual insensitivity becomes judicial spiritual paralysis."[42]

Here, however, the Lord specifically addresses those who were supposed to be able to see beyond the circumstances to the will of Yahweh as expressed in Torah and set a course of action. In days of old, the prophets and seers would lead the people into the truth and to repentance resulting in compliance with the law, now they would be as lost as the people. As verses 11-12 note, the prophets "have the technical skills to understand God's word, but they lack the spiritual insight which would enable them to see plain meaning."[43] Although some commentators see verses 11-12 as later editorial commentary on verses 9-

---

36 Oswalt, *The Book of Isaiah: Chapters 1-39*, 530.

37 Oswalt, *The Book of Isaiah: Chapters 1-39*, 532.

38 Young, *Isaiah: Chapters 19-39*, 316.

39 J.J.M. Roberts, *The Bible and the Ancient Near East* (Winona Lake, Ind.: Eisenbrauns, 2002), 352.

40 Roberts, *The Bible and the Ancient Near East*, 352.

41 Roberts, *The Bible and the Ancient Near East*, 331.

42 Motyer, *The Prophecy of Isaiah*, 239.

43 Oswalt, *The Book of Isaiah: Chapters 1-39*, 532.

10,[44] a literary analysis supports their sustained unified thematic relationship of vision with the condemnation of idolatry within the whole structure of the section.[45]

What should be presented as a parallel between the lips and the heart appears in verse 13 as a contrast. The lips are supposed to reflect the heart but in this case they utter words that are not believed. Ritual intonation continues but it is in place of genuine belief rather than being an expression of it. Grogan notes that verses 13-16 partner with verses 9-12 in that bad teaching through a mishandling of the Scriptures has resulted in the cementing of traditions in Israel's religion. This further resulted in "a self-justifying complacency in the presence of the most holy God."[46] Under such conditions, tradition trumps law and acts as the religious control in men's minds.[47]

Verse 15 may refer to an attempt by the authorities to keep negotiations with Egypt a secret from Isaiah and by extension (from Isaiah's point of view) from Yahweh himself.[48] The verbs in verse 15 convey a sense of determined, settled, behavior. The leaders conspire to conceal their plan from the Lord (הַמַּעֲמִיקִים מֵיהוָה לַסְתִּר עֵצָה). Motyer suggests Isaiah is not exposing actions but attitudes.[49] This is reinforced by the rare use of הָיָה to express the perpetuation of actions occurring in darkness.[50] Their self-determination is expressed in the rhetorical interrogatives, מִי רֹאֵנוּ (who sees us?) and מִי יוֹדְעֵנוּ (who knows us?). Their mind-set is one of defiant, callousness of heart toward Yahweh like that shown in the wilderness rather than one of perception of, and tenderness toward, God's presence and sovereignty. They did not accord Yahweh his rightful place in their midst. Since the leaders could not see what God was doing they believed that they were invisible to the Almighty as well.

Verse 18 is linked to verses 9-10 by the disability motif. Isaiah 29:18 reads:

18 וְשָׁמְעוּ בַיּוֹם־הַהוּא הַחֵרְשִׁים דִּבְרֵי־סֵפֶר וּמֵאֹפֶל וּמֵחֹשֶׁךְ עֵינֵי עִוְרִים תִּרְאֶינָה׃

On that day the deaf will hear words of a book and from darkness the eyes of the blind will see.

Whereas in verses 9-10 the concern is the perpetuating of self-inflicted blindness and deafness, in verse 18 the barriers to clear sight and hearing are removed. Although Yahweh is not recognized as Lord, he is, nevertheless, sovereign (vv. 15-16). He will perform the transformation (v. 14) himself at some future time. Yahweh will put things in their proper order. The closed eyes and book (vv. 11-12) will be opened and the words of the book (דִּבְרֵי־סֵפֶר) that

44 Kaiser, *Isaiah 1-12*, 269-74.
45 Exum, "Of Broken Pots, Fluttering Birds, and Visions in the Night," 347.
46 Grogan, *Isaiah*, 188.
47 Grogan, *Isaiah*, 188.
48 Roberts, *The Bible and the Ancient Near East*, 289.
49 Motyer, *The Prophecy of Isaiah*, 241.
50 Joüon, *A Grammar of Biblical Hebrew*, 2:358.

could previously not be heard (vv. 9-12), because of their obdurate attitude, will then be heard. The blindness of the people is specific to דִּבְרֵי־סֵפֶר as previously mentioned in verse 11. This suggests that the blindness was not physical but spiritual. These forms of blindness and deafness are, however, more devastating to the person, and collectively to the people, than physical blindness or deafness.

The day will come when Isaiah's closed message will be opened to a generation not yet born and the words of promise will begin to bear fruit among them.[51] The healing of the blind and lame is a sign that the anticipated age is being ushered in on that day (בַּיּוֹם־הַהוּא). "The former spiritual insensitivity of the people will be a thing of the past."[52]

From this point on in Isaiah, disability language is used in eschatological tension with the work of the expected One. When he comes, disabilities will be no more. It becomes increasingly evident that the language expresses more than physical healing. Metaphor for spiritual ignorance is replaced by metaphor for spiritual acumen. The expected One will usher in an era where all people will possess insight into the Lord's person, will, and actions that until that time has been reserved for a select few prophets.

The New Society When Disability Disappears: Isaiah 32:3-4

With the advent of the expected One, a new era of insight and obedience to Yahweh begins. Verses 3-4 describe a transformation which takes place when he comes:

3 וְלֹא תִשְׁעֶינָה עֵינֵי רֹאִים וְאָזְנֵי שֹׁמְעִים תִּקְשַׁבְנָה׃
4 וּלְבַב נִמְהָרִים יָבִין לָדָעַת וּלְשׁוֹן עִלְּגִים תְּמַהֵר לְדַבֵּר צָחוֹת׃

> Then the eyes of those who see will not be blinded, and the ears of those who hear will listen. The mind of the hasty will discern truth, and the tongue of the stammerers will hasten to speak clearly.

As Isaiah's prophecy unfolds, there does not appear to be a suggestion of forced compliance to Yahweh's word but every act is volitional and in accord with Israel's new insight and perception of their God and their identity with him through covenant relationship. When the anticipated One comes, a new community will be formed in which the outward actions of the community toward all others within and without the community will be treated with full measures of holiness, grace, and love in conformity with her spiritual identity.

The structure of this section[53] describing the King's new society:

---

51 Oswalt, *The Book of Isaiah: Chapters 1-39*, 538.
52 Grogan, *Isaiah*, 189.
53 Motyer, *The Prophecy of Isaiah*, 257.

A The securing of true value: the king and his princes (v. 1)
B True rule–four comparisons (v. 2)
B[1] New people–four transformations (vv. 3-4)
A[1] The end of false values: the fool and the scoundrel (v.5)

This section is distinguished by the fact that it initiates an interruption in the midst of the woe oracles being delivered. Its purpose seems to be to offer hope in God and point to the ultimate triumph of his purposes in spite of these judgments against his people.[54]

The exclamatory particle הֵן (behold) in verse 1 introduces a subunit that focuses on the righteous rule of the ideal king. A shift from 3rd person verbal forms (vv. 1-8) to 2nd person feminine plural forms (vv. 9-14) suggests a structural shift between verses 8 and 9 from a discussion of the expected One which prepares the way for the introduction of another subunit concerning salvation from disaster following a period of trouble.[55] The image of wind and rain that provides relief from drought and heat (v. 2) describes the characteristics of the ideal king's rule and challenges the pessimistic view of the future held by Isaiah's listeners who "are later characterized as fools and misers who advocate apostasy and error, and bring hunger, thirst, and oppression of the poor (vv. 5-7)."[56] The rule of the righteous One is announced (vv. 1-2) followed by a disputation regarding those voices of rational leaders seeking a positive outcome to the situation which are quelled by irrational and pessimistic leaders (vv.3-4) whose perverted justice and evil counsel takes the ascendance for a season (vv.5-8).[57]

Grogan is uncertain whether this section is messianic or merely picturing the ideal government in the hands of a righteous man.[58] This ambiguity in itself shows the integrated nature of prophetic, wisdom, and law literature within it. Thematically, the reference to a king (v. 1) links it to the portrayal of the Messiah/King in chapter 11 and develops it further by emphasizing "the association of others with the king in his righteous reign."[59] This righteous king will establish his rule and subordinates will support him with their equally strong concern for righteousness and justice. The parallelism of verse 2 suggests it also refers to the king, expanding the role of the righteous king who will rule.[60]

Being of a self-determined mind and thinking that Yahweh cannot see them, Israel's leaders made every attempt to conceal their path from Yahweh (29:15-16; 30:1-2). This is entirely the opposite way of the king who would come and

[54] Grogan, *Isaiah*, 205.
[55] Sweeney, *Isaiah 1-39*, 410.
[56] Sweeney, *Isaiah 1-39*, 410.
[57] Sweeney, *Isaiah 1-39*, 411-14.
[58] Grogan, *Isaiah*, 205.
[59] Grogan, *Isaiah*, 205.
[60] Grogan, *Isaiah*, 205, 205-6.

rule righteously over his people (לְצֶדֶק יִמְלָךְ־מֶלֶךְ). Oswalt points out that in that day,

> Not only will the true leaders provide security for their people, they will also make possible that spiritual transformation in which the former blindness, deafness, and stammering are taken away. Given the larger context with its references to blindness and dullness of the leaders themselves (28:7-8; 29:9-10, 14; 30:1-2; 31:1), it seems logical to assume that the writer expects the first manifestations of this transformation to appear in the leaders, after which it will spread to the people (29:18-19, 24). As noted above, here there seems to be a clear reversal of the situation described in 6:10, where blindness, deafness, and dullness were the predicted results of the prophet's preaching.[61]

Spiritual clarity will be the result of submission by leaders which then will result in spiritual clarity for those who submit to these leaders.[62]

The first transformation that occur involves the restoration of the people's ability to perceive and receive (לֹא תִשְׁעֶינָה עֵינֵי רֹאִים וְאָזְנֵי שֹׁמְעִים תִּקְשַׁבְנָה) through restored sight and hearing. The antecedent for their condition עֵינֵי רֹאִים וְאָזְנֵי שֹׁמְעִים, found in verse 3, appears to be a reference to those whose sight and hearing have been restored. As Motyer points out, the verbal root for תִשְׁעֶינָה is שׁעע, also linking this passage with both 6:10 and 29:9-10.[63] The whole section is a reversal of the people's obdurate condition (6:9-10) to which Isaiah found himself called.[64] As if intoxicated, the people staggered in a self-induced darkness. Implied is a dynamic relationship between the king and the people. Here the situation is reversed upon the establishment of a just social order resulting in true discernment of knowledge rather than illusion.[65] That which has rendered the people's faculties useless will be removed and in compliant subordination with their king, the people will function according to their new understanding to induce righteousness within and for the entire community.

Social and legal justice is the primary means by which the cleanness required of holiness can be attained but even this was not to be viewed as a human accomplishment.[66] According to Gammie, "Isaiah's doctrine of justice and righteousness is intricately intertwined with his doctrines of place, the king, and holiness."[67] The place was to be Jerusalem (1:21, 26). The king's task is to

---

61 Oswalt, *The Book of Isaiah: Chapters 1-39*, 580.
62 Oswalt, *The Book of Isaiah: Chapters 1-39*, 581.
63 Motyer, *The Prophecy of Isaiah*, 257.
64 Joseph Blenkinsopp, *Isaiah 1-39* (Anchor Bible 19; New York: Doubleday, 2000), 430.
65 Blenkinsopp, *Isaiah 1-39*, 430.
66 John Gammie, *Holiness in Israel: Overtures in Biblical Theology* (Minneapolis: Fortress, 1989), 83.
67 Gammie, *Holiness in Israel*, 83.

establish justice and righteousness (9:7; 11:3-5; 32:5-7).[68] The exploitation of the defenseless and poor is the exact opposite of justice and righteousness and worthy of censure (1:17; 3:14-15; 10:1-4).[69] Justice and cleanness are linked in Isaiah 1:12-17, where the prophet affirms that justice is "the appointed means by which the cleanness required by the divine holiness can be achieved by human beings."[70] Only when the human faculties of sight and hearing result in vision and listening can human actions be conceived in genuine holiness and righteousness. "Trusting human resources leads to injustice, blindness, corruption, and destruction. But trust in God leads to justice, clarity, integrity, and life."[71]

Disability and the Satisfaction of Trust: Isaiah 35:5-6

Isaiah's comments in chapter 35 juxtapose the glorious power of God displayed in the restoration of the land with the equally glorious display of power in restoring the people. Here, the emotive response of the people to the awesome unfurling of God's purposes and power in restored Israel is in view. Disability language in this text functions in a song of elation concerning God's salvation of Zion and her restored people. Israel's faith in Yahweh will not languor but instead be sated with divine recompense as God's promises are crowned with consummation.

Chapter 35 follows the call to the nations to give attention to Yahweh's anger kindled against them in chapter 34. Although there is a shift of theme from Yahweh's power to one of rejoicing, the two chapters structurally function together to show Yahweh's power over all nations (ch. 34) which, in turn, provides the premise for the prophetic oracle regarding the return of those who have been redeemed from every corner of the earth to Zion (ch. 35).[72] Blenkinsopp argues that this pericope is metaphorical, referring to Cyrus's decree of allowing expatriate Judeans to return (42:7) while the reference to the blind and deaf is to those who cannot accept the message being told to them.[73]

Contra Blenkinsopp, Grogan suggests that this text refers to a literal healing of the people.[74] This is certainly possible, although it may be an idealized portrayal of the degree to which the restoration will take place when the righteous One comes or it may be a literal picture of a dry, barren land

---

[68] Hans Wildberger, *Jesaja 3 Teilband 28-39* (Biblischer Kommentar Altes Testament 10.3; Neukirchen: Neukirchener Verlag des Erziehungsvereins, 1982), 1255. As noted in the previous section, ancient Near Eastern kings believed themselves to have been charged with defending the weaker segments of the population by the god who sponsored his kingship.

[69] Gammie, *Holiness in Israel*, 83.

[70] Gammie, *Holiness in Israel*, 84.

[71] Oswalt, *The Book of Isaiah: Chapters 1-39*, 578.

[72] Sweeney, *Isaiah 1-39*, 434.

[73] Blenkinsopp, *Isaiah 1-39*, 457.

[74] Grogan, *Isaiah*, 222.

transformed into a place of refreshment and filled with the activity of pilgrims to that locale where the expected king will reign. It is reasonable to suggest, then, that this text should be understood as referring to both spiritually and physically blind, deaf, lame, and mute.[75]

The picture in chapter 35 contrasts the desolation of the desert in chapter 34. When restored, "God's purpose for his people will come to its consummation in a transfigured environment."[76] The land will become a haven for the holy in the shadow of the holy One. It is almost reminiscent of what happened during Solomon's reign when it was a magnate for all who sought to bask in the glory of his wisdom and wealth (1 Kgs 3:16-28; 2 Chron 9:1-12).

Isaiah 35:1-10 deals with Yahweh's coming (vv. 3-4) and the results of Yahweh's coming (vv. 5-10).[77] The entire twofold message of chapter 35 consists of consolation for feeble Israel along with the assurance of retribution against her enemies. The use of the masculine plural imperative verbs in verses 3-10 form a subunit of instructional material urging the weak to be strengthened in light of Yahweh's coming.[78] Verse 4 indicates that Yahweh will vindicate their trust in him through restoration and requital (נָקָם). "Then" in verse 5 (אָז) introduces the restorative results of Yahweh's coming:

5 אָז תִּפָּקַחְנָה עֵינֵי עִוְרִים וְאָזְנֵי חֵרְשִׁים תִּפָּתַחְנָה׃
6 אָז יְדַלֵּג כָּאַיָּל פִּסֵּחַ וְתָרֹן לְשׁוֹן אִלֵּם כִּי־נִבְקְעוּ בַמִּדְבָּר מַיִם וּנְחָלִים בָּעֲרָבָה׃

> Then the eyes of the blind will be opened and the ears of the deaf will be opened. Then the lame will leap like a fallow dear and the tongue of the mute will shout for joy.

The text utilizes disability language to communicate transformational activity by means of Yahweh's power. The reversal of spiritual and physical handicaps (6:10; 28:7; 29:9-10, 18; 30:20-21; 32:3-4) of blindness, deafness, and dullness communicates the reception of true guidance that comes from trusting in Yahweh rather than in human resources.[79] This section utilizes a hendiadys contrasting the faculties of reception (eyes and ears) and faculties of action (leaping and singing) expressing the wholeness of the person that is being redeemed.[80] The disability language employed here suggests that all is not right. The distortion implied by the use of this language will be corrected when all is made right and normal again, and this by Yahweh's hand.

The metamorphic aspect of this prophecy signifies a coming to terms between Yahweh and his people heretofore lacking. Israel's spiritual callousness gives way to affirmation. It is this renewed confidence (faith) in

---

75 Grogan, *Isaiah*, 222.
76 Grogan, *Isaiah*, 221.
77 Sweeney, *Isaiah 1-39*, 448.
78 Sweeney, *Isaiah 1-39*, 449.
79 Oswalt, *The Book of Isaiah: Chapters 1-39*, 624.
80 Motyer, *The Prophecy of Isaiah*, 274.

their God that changes and the power to undo the permanence of disability resulting from their previous callousness becomes operative. The connection of the metaphorical and the physical will be made when Israel's perfected spirituality and glorified bodies will both characterize God's future kingdom.[81]

Restored Sense Perception: Isaiah 42:6-7, 18-19

The servant of the Lord is identified as one who relies on divine empowerment to accomplish his task. The theme of divine empowerment reaches back to Exodus 3 and Moses' commission. The issue is one of functionality. Appropriating divine capacity for the work is the only means by which the servant would be successful in his mission and the people themselves restored. Isaiah 42:6-7 reads:

6 אֲנִי יְהוָה קְרָאתִיךָ בְצֶדֶק וְאַחְזֵק בְּיָדֶךָ וְאֶצָּרְךָ וְאֶתֶּנְךָ לִבְרִית עָם לְאוֹר גּוֹיִם׃
7 לִפְקֹחַ עֵינַיִם עִוְרוֹת לְהוֹצִיא מִמַּסְגֵּר אַסִּיר מִבֵּית כֶּלֶא יֹשְׁבֵי חֹשֶׁךְ׃

> I am the Lord, I have called you in righteousness, I will also hold you by the hand and watch over you, and I will appoint you as a covenant to the people as a light to the nations, to open blind eyes, to bring out prisoners from the dungeon, and those who dwell in darkness from the prison.

The section is a commissioning speech made by Yahweh about his Servant. Verses 6-7 mark a transition of focus from creation to providence.[82] Isaiah's repeated use of the phrase "(I have) called you in righteousness" (קְרָאתִיךָ בְצֶדֶק) links these verses to 41:2.[83] Yahweh's Servant is a commissioned conqueror (41:2) who functions in righteousness and is fitted to advance the purposes of his God toward establishing righteousness (42:4, 6).[84]

The pericope under examination is contained in the section encompassing 42:5 through 43:8, in which there is a significant degree of usage of the words עִוֵּר, קֹדֶר, לְאוֹר, שָׁמַע, and שִׁיר. Isaiah weaves the imagery of the sight (42:7, 16, 18, 19, 20; 43:8) with that of light (42:6, 16), darkness (42:7, 16), hearing (42:18, 19, 20, 23), and words related to the voice (42:10, 11, 12, 13) together with those of song and exclamation (42:10, 11, 12, 13). The disabled are no longer a prey (42:22, 24).

In these verses we find the purpose of the calling in 42:5. The emphatic identification of the one calling as the Lord (אֲנִי יְהוָה) in verse 6a combined with the work to which the servant is called (אֶתֶּנְךָ לִבְרִית עָם לְאוֹר גּוֹיִם) in 6b, "to be a light for the nations," and the promise of divine empowerment (אַחְזֵק בְּיָדֶךָ וְאֶצָּרְךָ) to accomplish the task in verse 5 results in the servant actually becoming

[81] Grogan, *Isaiah*, 222.
[82] Motyer, *The Prophecy of Isaiah*, 318.
[83] Motyer, *The Prophecy of Isaiah*, 318.
[84] Motyer, *The Prophecy of Isaiah*, 322.

the embodiment of the covenant.[85] Young argues that the blindness referred to in this section is the result of sin, not physical blindness.[86] Israel may have had the expectation that the relationship forged through the covenant had been hopelessly annulled, but instead Yahweh sends his servant to demonstrate his continuing loyalty to his people.[87]

The rhetorical questions of verse 5 are answered in verse 6.[88] He is like a covenant (לִבְרִית) and a light (לְאוֹר) to the people. The phrase בְּרִית עָם may not be a reference to the structure of the relationship between God and his servant but to functionality (not utilitarian) of the covenant and delight in the significance of it impact on life. The servant's plan is to become a covenant so as to procure sight and deliverance for the people. In other words, he will be "the means through whom people will come into a covenant relation with the Lord."[89] Motyer writes,

> Within the all-embracing concept of *covenant* there is the *light* of truth, the healing of personal disabilities (exemplified in opening blind *eyes*), the end of restrictions imposed by others (bringing out *captives*) and the transformation of circumstances (*darkness*).[90]

The success of the Servant's mission is contingent on the presence and power of the Spirit (42:1).[91] These descriptions form a composite of the person (42:6) and his work as the conqueror servant (42:7f). The revelation this servant brings will reverse the people's idolatrousness. The visible images will be replaced with an understanding of the invisible God. They will know him in covenant as he should be known and the bondage of their ignorance and isolation (42:7).

Scholarly debate continues as to the identity of this unnamed individual. Among the possible candidates: Idealized Israel, Israel represented by an ideal Israelite, the messianic King, Cyrus, a covenant, or an individual simply known as the servant have been suggested. Interestingly, the unnamed individual himself becomes a covenant (v. 6). This fact puts all three of the above identities in question. A comparison of the servant and Cyrus figures suggests that although their rolls show complimentary spiritual and temporal aspects of

---

[85] John N. Oswalt, *The Book of Isaiah: Chapters 40-66* (The New International Commentary on the Old Testament; Grand Rapids: Eerdmans, 1986), 117.

[86] Edward J. Young, *The Book of Isaiah: Chapters 40-66* (New International Commentary on the Old Testament, vol. 3; Grand Rapids: Eerdmans, 1972), 121.

[87] Oswalt, *The Book of Isaiah: Chapters 40-66*, 119.

[88] Motyer, *The Prophecy of Isaiah*, 322.

[89] Motyer, *The Prophecy of Isaiah*, 322.

[90] Motyer, *The Prophecy of Isaiah*, 322.

[91] Wilf Hildebrandt, *An Old Testament Theology of the Spirit of God* (Peabody, Mass.: Hendrickson 1995), 132.

the Lord's latter-day agent of redemption, they individually fall short of that ideal roll of the Lord's agent of deliverance.[92]

Isaiah ties Yahweh's righteousness and his keeping of his covenant together (vv. 6-7).[93] It is uncertain if the Lord's servant can be identified as Israel itself (or a faithful remnant), or an individual. Whatever the case, though, the servant is identified with Israel.[94] Dempster writes, "The servant has become the means of bringing covenant salvation to the world, which means the illumination of the nations."[95] It is not to Israel alone, but to the entire world that his servant will come.[96] Israel's world-wide ranking as a light to the nations and her mission to be the object by which the world would see and be reconciled to God is about to be realized.

The people walk in a prison of theological darkness and the appointed servant's task is to bring the people out from that darkness into light.[97] Blindness and freedom are metaphors communicating a restoration of that which is lacking current to the prophetic utterance. The release from bondage, insight and justice, which was lacking in Isaiah's Israel, will be apportioned by Yahweh's servant. The light comes by means of the covenant made with the people.[98] It is interesting that motivational clauses in the law relate to Israel's once being slaves in a foreign land (Deut 5:15; 15:15; 16:12; 24:18, 22). Astoundingly, this covenant announcement comes in response to the people's unfaithfulness to that covenant.

The motifs in this section work together exhibiting both the action of God to restore human sense faculties and the effect of these restored faculties. Together, the implications of these metaphors suggest that humans crave light and once they see it they leave darkness for it. Once they hear, silence is no longer tolerable. Once they walk, they cannot sit still. Once they can sing God's praises, his praises cannot go unvoiced. The euphoria of Israel's realized status is shared with the nations as they come to see what until that moment would only have been exposed (albeit misapprehended) to Israel by her God.[99]

Chapters 40-55 begin with the announcement of forgiveness, restoration, and return from exile. The entire section focuses on world redemption and the

---

92 Gileadi, *The Literary Message of Isaiah*, 122-23.

93 Walter C. Kaiser Jr., "Promise," in *The Flowering of Old Testament Theology* (Sources for Biblical and Theological Study, vol.1; ed. Ben C. Ollenburger, Elmer A. Martens, and Gerhard F. Hasel; Winona Lake: Eisenbrauns, 1992), 247.

94 Grogan, *Isaiah*, 255.

95 Dempster, *Dominion and Dynasty*, 177.

96 Motyer, *The Prophecy of Isaiah*, 318.

97 Oswalt, *The Book of Isaiah: Chapters 40-66*, 118.

98 Oswalt, *The Book of Isaiah: Chapters 40-66*, 119.

99 In verse 8 the servant's covenantal work is directed to Israel, but in verses 5 and 6 a parallelism is formed between the word עָם in verse 5 and גּוֹיִם in verse 6. See also Motyer, *The Prophecy of Isaiah*, 322.

inclusion of the Gentiles in God's plan.[100] From 41:1-42:17 the focus is on the means by which the world will experience consolation.[101] It is the incomparable God who will do this great work and extends an invitation to the whole Gentile world to partake of his salvation (41:1-7).[102] In 42:7 the deliverance of Israel by Yahweh's Servant is augured. After all, Yahweh is not only the God of Israel; he is the God of the whole world, having control of it and has concern for it. There are no other gods to reckon with who can make such a claim. Hence idolatry is abhorrent to him. The court scene of 41:21-29 affords an opportunity to idolaters to make their case. They fail, the so-called gods are exposed for what they are and the plight of the world as having no sure voice is made apparent, and it is only when the servant comes as an advocate for the Gentiles to bring justice to the nations that their future is made secure.[103]

An analysis of Isaiah's language and phraseology suggests that the provenance of the prophet's message is in Mesopotamian royal inscriptions.[104] Paul illustrates important theological dimensions of Isaiah's prophetic ministry. "That Israel was called to be a nation of prophets with a universal message and a role to play in history."[105] This whole section contains sharp gutturals and aspirants, orally suggesting the harshness of a woman in labor, picturing with words the image of anticipation at something new that was about to be born.[106]

The section also features a dispute regarding idols (v. 8). The fact that Israel has been defeated by Babylon does not suggest that Israel's national deity (Yahweh) was conquered by Babylon's national deity (Marduk) or that Yahweh abandoned Israel in her time of distress, but rather that Israel's destruction is a consequence of her sinfulness (Isa 42:25).[107] It was Yahweh himself who destroyed his own people. Yet, Isaiah's message of national destruction is replaced by one of national salvation and not only salvation, but the assurance of that salvation and it is Yahweh, not any other god, who will secure their salvation. This salvation will come from the hand of the same Deity who destroyed the nation on account of her sinfulness.

---

[100] Motyer, *The Prophecy of Isaiah*, 298.
[101] Motyer, *The Prophecy of Isaiah*, 298.
[102] Motyer, *The Prophecy of Isaiah*, 308.
[103] Motyer, *The Prophecy of Isaiah*, 315-18.
[104] Shalom M. Paul, "Deutero-Isaiah and Cuneiform Royal Inscriptions," *Journal of the American Oriental Society* 88 (1968): 180-82. Paul notes that the wording in this text is similar to that found in cuneiform inscriptions.
[105] John B. White, "Universalization of History in Deutero-Isaiah," in *Scripture in Context: Essays on the Comparative Method* (ed. Carl D. Evans, Williams W. Hallo, and John B. White; PTMS 34; Pittsburgh: Pickwick Press, 1980), 180.
[106] R. Norman Whybry, *Isaiah 40-66* (Grand Rapids: Eedrmans, 1975), 78f.
[107] Yehezkel Kaufmann, *The Babylonian Captivity and Deutero-Isaiah* (New York: Union of American Hebrew Congregations, 1970), 9.

18 הַחֵרְשִׁים שְׁמָעוּ וְהַעִוְרִים הַבִּיטוּ לִרְאוֹת׃
19 מִי עִוֵּר כִּי אִם־עַבְדִּי וְחֵרֵשׁ כְּמַלְאָכִי אֶשְׁלָח מִי עִוֵּר כִּמְשֻׁלָּם וְעִוֵּר כְּעֶבֶד יְהוָה׃

Hear you deaf! And look, you blind, that you may see. Who is blind by my servant, or so deaf as my messenger whom I send? Who is so blind as he that is at peace with me?

Regarding Isaiah 42:18-20 Abrams writes,

> Israel's deafness and blindness are not due to any lack of properly functioning organs, but the opposite is clearly stated: God's servants have eyes and ears that presumably operate, but they are too stubborn and willful to use them to see and understand the truth of God's message.[108]

Their disability became their prison (Isa 42:6-7). The blindness and deafness metaphors are symbolic of Israel's helplessness.[109] "The imagery of the blind and deaf illustrates the common redemptive purpose behind this Isaianic figure's mission."[110] The blind can do nothing being dependent on those who act on their behalf. In this case, Yahweh, like his servant (42:7) will function to deliver his blind people.[111] In the larger context (6:10; 29:18; 35:5; 42:7, 16, 18, 19; 43:8; 56:10; 59:10), Isaiah's use of the term עִוְרִים (blind) appears to be a self-induced spiritual blindness.[112] Oswalt writes,

> These are a people who cannot reveal God's light to the world because they cannot see it themselves. Nevertheless, God will work miracles both for them and in them that will indeed make them bearers of light for the nations.[113]

These imperceptive and misguided ones are censured for not comprehending the significance of events being interpreted by the prophets.

T.W. Mann suggests that in verses 15-16, Isaiah reinvigorates the Exodus typology of the divine vanguard with new life to convey the inauguration of a "new exodus" of Yahweh's eschatological rule over Israel that will lead them from their exile back to the Promised Land.[114] Motyer, on the other hand, asserts that the link commentators make between 41:17-20 and this section is superficial.[115] He claims that 42:10-17 (especially v. 16) is a call to world-wide praise in light of the work of the servant.[116] He points out that this procession

---

108 Abrams, *Judaism and Disability*, 76.
109 Alexander, *Commentary on the Prophecies of Isaiah*, 1:142-43.
110 Gileadi, *The Literary Message of Isaiah*, 128.
111 Oswalt, *The Book of Isaiah: Chapters 40-66*, 126-27.
112 Oswalt, *The Book of Isaiah: Chapters 40-66*, 127.
113 Oswalt, *The Book of Isaiah: Chapters 40-66*, 127.
114 T.W. Mann, *Divine Presence and Guidance in Israelite Traditions,* (Baltimore: Johns Hopkins University, 1977), 27, 51, 132-33.
115 Motyer, *The Prophecy of Isaiah*, 323.
116 Motyer, *The Prophecy of Isaiah*, 323.

consists of Gentiles, not Israel. Consequently, it is difficult to imply a second Exodus for Israel from Babylon.[117]

The blind mentioned in verse 16 are affiliated with the same group mentioned in verse 7.[118] These blind Gentiles will be ministered to directly by the servant/Lord.[119] They will be directed by the servant/Lord on a path known only to him. Yahweh leads those whom he favors (עִוְרִים בְּדֶרֶךְ לֹא יָדָעוּ בִּנְתִיבוֹת לֹא־יָדְעוּ אַדְרִיכֵם).[120] The Gentile blindness in 42:16 appears to be one of ignorance rather than a self-inflicted blindness as is the case with Israel to whom God's path was made known.[121] Yahweh "removes barriers so that there is no hindrance to going forward."[122]

Yahweh's declaration in verse 16 to "lead the blind by a way they do not know" is connected with the call to give attention in verse 18 and the series of interrogatives in verse 19. The idolaters are all (Gentile and Jewish) who trusted in idols (v. 17). It later becomes clear that the exile was precipitated by Israel's being a disobedient servant, "willfully deaf and blind (42:19-25)."[123] Israel is not only blinded to their sin, but blinded to the impact their sin has had on their relationship with Yahweh. In the image of the suffering servant there is a link between sin, disability, suffering, and atonement (Isa 52:13-53:5).[124] In 42:18-19 blind and deaf Israel are addressed. They are themselves just as spiritually needy as the Gentiles and cannot function to do the will of God or make him known to them.[125] The vocative in verse 18 is not to be taken as merely a nominative absolute (per Waltke and O'Conner), but it is to be understood as having the illocutionary force of attracting the addressee's attention.[126] The adjuration here, as in other places (1:2; 8:9; 28:14, 23; 29:9; 32:9; 33:13; 34:1; 41:1; 43:8-9; 48:1; 49:1; 51:1, 4, 7; 58:1; 60:4; 66:5) is for these blind ones to perceive what is directly in front of them.

The servant addressed here, who must have full use of auditory and visual faculties so as to serve the master well, actually sees nothing.[127] Israel is not simply ignorant like the Gentiles, she is faithless. Her faithlessness is portrayed in the disability imagery used in this text. In 42:18 Yahweh calls them "blind"

---

[117] Motyer, *The Prophecy of Isaiah*, 325.
[118] Motyer, *The Prophecy of Isaiah*, 323.
[119] Motyer, *The Prophecy of Isaiah*, 324. The servant interacted with the disabled in 42:7. Here it is the Lord himself. Motyer notes that the same identity merging with the servant and the Lord takes place here as with the Messianic king and Lord into one deity in chapters 1-37 (see especially 9:6-7).
[120] Motyer, *The Prophecy of Isaiah*, 323.
[121] Motyer, *The Prophecy of Isaiah*, 325.
[122] Motyer, *The Prophecy of Isaiah*, 325.
[123] Dempster, *Dominion and Dynasty*, 176.
[124] Abrams, *Judaism and Disability*, 76.
[125] Motyer, *The Prophecy of Isaiah*, 327.
[126] Michael Rosenbaum, *Word-Order Variation in Isaiah 40-55: A Functional Perspective* (Assen, Netherlands: Van Gorcum, 1997), 117.
[127] Oswalt, *The Book of Isaiah: Chapters 40-66*, 131.

(הַעִוְרִים) and "deaf" (הַחֵרְשִׁים). These two terms work in tandem to project their absolute culpability of failing to do his will and to hear his word.[128] Israel is called "my servant" (עַבְדִּי) and "my messenger" (מַלְאָכִי) in verse 19. As Israel served the Lord, she was to be a light to the Gentiles and a means by which the nations would be reconciled to God (Gen 12:3). Israel is reconciled (מְשֻׁלָּם)[129] with Yahweh and as such enjoyed a place of privilege yet they are blind to him and hence neglect their responsibility. They cannot function as servants as they are incapable of hearing or obeying their Master's voice.[130] Oswalt notes,

> Verse 20 makes it clear that this incommunicado condition is culpable. The faculties are in fact still present, but there is failure to attend. here is a blindness that is of the mind or heart rather than the eye.[131]

The blind cannot transcend their blindness; "they can only sink deeper."[132] Again, Oswalt notes,

> Thus everyone who trusts in the gods of this world must eventually be disgraced, when it is shown that what they trusted in is helpless. That will not be the case for those who believe in the true God.[133]

Yahweh's supremacy over all alleged gods impacts this text in that only he can intervene in this world.[134] The call for them to hear, see, and obey in verse 20 ties in to the reference to the Torah in verse 21. What the people had not yet seen was Yahweh's purpose for them in the world as well as what their experiences with Yahweh might have taught them.[135]

Yahweh's disputation with his wayward people continues until the end of the section. They are blind because they have failed to understand the lessons of the Exile: that their rebellion was the cause of it.[136] They cannot accept their condition as being a result of their own sin (v. 24), nor see Yahweh's hand in their current circumstances (v. 25). Consequently, they cannot to anything about it. Blindness is not the punishment for sin; exile is (v. 25). It was self-inflicted spiritual blindness that drove their disobedience.

Yahweh informs them that he has, in his grace, entered into a covenant with them but they have not honored their part through obedience (v. 25).[137] His arrested action, should it have come, would not have been the kind Israel would want but would have certainly been what was deserved.

---

128 Motyer, *The Prophecy of Isaiah*, 327.
129 The sense of this *pual* verb is that they are brought into peace, reconciled to God.
130 Grogan, *Isaiah*, 257.
131 Grogan, *Isaiah*, 257.
132 Oswalt, *The Book of Isaiah: Chapters 40-66*, 127.
133 Oswalt, *The Book of Isaiah: Chapters 40-66*, 127.
134 Oswalt, *The Book of Isaiah: Chapters 40-66*, 127.
135 Oswalt, *The Book of Isaiah: Chapters 40-66*, 132.
136 Grogan, *Isaiah*, 257.
137 Oswalt, *The Book of Isaiah: Chapters 40-66*, 130.

Disability as Ignorance of Past Events: Isaiah 43:7-8

Since Israel is precious in God's sight they can rest securely on the covenant God has entered into with them. Even more, their restoration will be vindication not only of their faith but of God himself. It was for their own good that Yahweh sent them into exile and for their own good he will bring them back in spite of their continuing transgressions. Oh that they would no longer be blind and deaf to the events of the past and learn from their own history that Yahweh is the one and only deity. Isaiah 43:7-8 reads:

7 כֹּל הַנִּקְרָא בִשְׁמִי וְלִכְבוֹדִי בְּרָאתִיו יְצַרְתִּיו אַף־עֲשִׂיתִיו׃
8 הוֹצִיא עַם־עִוֵּר וְעֵינַיִם יֵשׁ וְחֵרְשִׁים וְאָזְנַיִם לָמוֹ׃

> Everyone who is called by my name, and who I have created for my glory, whom I have formed, even whom I have made. Bring out the people who are blind, even though they have eyes, and the deaf, even though they have ears.

This section is thematically linked to chapter 42 and the consequences of Israel's refusal to obey (self-induced blindness).[138] Israel was Yahweh's creation (29:16; 43:1, 7, 21; 44:2, 21, 24; 45:9, 11; 64:7) for himself (27:11).[139] This confession dominates the section from 42:18-44:23.[140] The terminology recalls creation but extends to Yahweh's care for his creation as well (42:7).[141] The same voice which had once announced Israel's impending destruction now announces her ensuing restoration.[142] Immediately following the oracle pronouncing Israel's destruction as being the result of Yahweh's judgment comes an oracle declaring her future salvation (Isa 43:1-7). Yahweh declares that Israel was brought into existence "for my glory" (לִכְבוֹדִי) and consequently they cannot be left in bondage even if it is one of their own making because what happens to them is, according to Oswalt, "directly attributable to him."[143] Thus, Yahweh himself carries her (הָבִיאִי) back from her far country.[144] The formula גַּם־מִיּוֹם (from this day) in verse 13 functions to identify the effectuality

---

138 Grogan, *Isaiah*, 260.

139 H.W.M. van Grol, "Isaiah 27:10-11: God and His Own People," in *Studies in the Book of Isaiah: Festschrift Willem A. M. Beuken* (Leuven: Leuven University Press, 1997), 207.

140 H. Leene, "History and Eschatology in Deutero-Isaiah," in *Studies in the Book of Isaiah: Festschrift Willem A.M. Beuken* (Leuven: Leuven University Press, 1997), 228.

141 Motyer, *The Prophecy of Isaiah*, 333.

142 Albert K. Grayson, and Wilfried G. Lambert, "Akkadian Prophecies," *Journal of Cuneiform Studies* 18 (1964): 8f. There is a parallel in "The Prophetic Speech of Marduk," where Marduk causes the destruction of the people only to subsequently announce their salvation and restoration.

143 Oswalt, *The Book of Isaiah: Chapters 40-66*, 142.

144 J.T.A.G.M. van Ruiten, "'His Master's Voice'? The supposed Influence of the Book of Isaiah in the Book of Habakkuk," in *Studies in the Book of Isaiah: Festschrift Willem A. M. Beuken* (Leuven: Leuven University Press, 1997), 402.

of Yahweh's verdict. His legal decision, like that of any king, shall take effect immediately.

Motyer argues that the scene is once again the courtroom. Now, he writes, it is the idols themselves on trial. Yahweh's witnesses on his behalf are those who have eyes yet are blind. They have ears yet they are deaf. Their testimonies are, however, invalid because of their impaired senses. They fail in the most basic obligation of their covenant, which is to bear witness to Yahweh as their God. Consequently, Yahweh must bear witness of his ability to predict his actions and to fulfill that expectation (43:10-11).[145] It is Yahweh who enacted Israel's redemption in the past (43:11) and it is Yahweh who will deliver again (43:14f). He is Israel's only hope. Can any idol-god make that claim?

Raising up a New Generation unto Yahweh: Isaiah 56:10-11

Yahweh has such a nature as to be able to promise a heritage to the eunuch and foreigner within his house, a memorial and an everlasting name (56:5) although they were banned from worship (Deut 23:1-8). Physical limitations will no longer mean disqualification and exclusion from the sacred precincts. What is required is faithfulness, a characteristic Yahweh's elect failed to cultivate. In spite of their secure place in God's temple, they were blind and corrupt from their leaders and prophets down to the common man. Just as God could raise up rocks and rafters to sing his praise (Hab 2:11; Lk 19:40), he would also raise up a heritage for those incapable of producing one for themselves and these will supplant those elect who are blind, mute, and indolent toward their God. Isaiah 56:10-11 reads:

10 (צֹפָו) [צֹפָיו] עִוְרִים כֻּלָּם֙ לֹ֣א יָדָ֔עוּ כֻּלָּם֙ כְּלָבִ֣ים אִלְּמִ֔ים לֹ֥א יוּכְל֖וּ לִנְבֹּ֑חַ
הֹזִים֙ שֹֽׁכְבִ֔ים אֹהֲבֵ֖י לָנֽוּם׃
11 וְהַכְּלָבִ֣ים עַזֵּי־נֶ֗פֶשׁ לֹ֤א יָֽדְעוּ֙ שָׂבְעָ֔ה וְהֵ֣מָּה רֹעִ֔ים לֹ֥א יָדְע֖וּ הָבִ֑ין כֻּלָּם֙ לְדַרְכָּ֣ם
פָּנ֔וּ אִ֥ישׁ לְבִצְע֖וֹ מִקָּצֵֽהוּ׃

> His watchmen are blind, all of them know nothing, all of them are dumb dogs unable to bark, dreamers lying down, who love to slumber; and the dogs are greedy, they are not satisfied, and they are shepherds who have no understanding; they have all turned to their own way, each one his unjust gain, to the last one.

From 56:10 through 59:10 a great rebuke is delivered against Israel's prophets. Their denunciation is due to their lack of faith toward Yahweh. They would heed the call to repent (56:1-9; 57:17; 59:2-15). Consequently, the deliverance, although imminent, has been delayed (57:18f; 58:8-14) as a result. The conciliation is that the promise of deliverance has not been permanently invalidated by their conduct. Yahweh will keep his word (55:1-13; 59:1f).

---

[145] Motyer, *The Prophecy of Isaiah*, 333.

The theme of human inability to do righteousness begun in 56:1 continues and is expanded into verse 10.[146] In verses 10-11 Israel's leaders are described. They are blind watchmen (צֹפָו עִוְרִים) and mute dogs (כְּלָבִים אִלְּמִים) that do not bark at the sign of an intruder. Instead of protecting those they were charged to protect, they are asleep (הֹזִים), lying down (שֹׁכְבִים), loving slumber (אֹהֲבֵי לָנוּם). They are alternately described as greedy dogs (הַכְּלָבִים עַזֵּי־נֶפֶשׁ), as being unsatisfied (לֹא יָדְעוּ שָׂבְעָה), and as stupid shepherds who lack understanding (רֹעִים לֹא יָדְעוּ הָבִי). Verse 10 notes that, "they did not know" (כֻּלָּם לֹא יָדָעוּ). The terms of disability used in this section function by the same pattern previously seen in Isaiah. These leaders do not know God themselves and consequently have failed in their capacity as leaders of God's people. Rather than using their position to protect and lead God's people, they used it for self-aggrandizement and piracy.

Those complacent in their election will be brought to judgment.[147] The prophets were appointed as watchmen to see what was coming and to prepare the people for it.[148] They were supposed to guardedly evaluate the spiritual well-being of Yahweh's people. They were uniquely suited to do so because of their intimacy with Yahweh.[149] However, they did not perform their duties. They were blindly complacent toward their own sin and that of their people as well. They did not guard against the intrusion of sin and its consequent encroachment effected on their covenantal relationship with Yahweh. Their judgment is, to be specific, the result of their complacently. Their complacency made them culpable for the sin of the people. Their diligence would have prompted the people to make the right choice and avoid sin but the watchmen simply did not understand the critical nature of their task, the desperate nature of their times, or their own proclivity to fail.[150] Israel's leaders did not nurture the soul of Israel but allowed it to wither while they occupied themselves with their own self-interests.[151] It was not because of bad policy but because Israel's leaders were negligent, opportunistic, and wanton.[152]

---

[146] Oswalt, *The Book of Isaiah: Chapters 40-66,* 467. Oswalt notes that the causal construction in verse 1 (כִּי־קְרוֹבָה יְשׁוּעָתִי) not only indicates that obedience is lived out as a response to salvation, but also that these people are being asked to do what was previously impossible. He writes, "Because God will do what he alone can do, the people will be enabled to do what they in freedom must do." God will produce the righteousness that the people could not.

[147] Oswalt, *The Book of Isaiah: Chapters 40-66*, 467.

[148] Oswalt, *The Book of Isaiah: Chapters 40-66*, 468.

[149] Hildebrandt, *An Old Testament Theology of the Spirit of God*, 141-42.

[150] Oswalt, *The Book of Isaiah: Chapters 40-66*, 468.

[151] Motyer, *The Prophecy of Isaiah*, 468.

[152] Motyer, *The Prophecy of Isaiah*, 468.

The Servant of the Lord and the Repentant Remnant: Isaiah 59:10

An examination of Isaiah 59:9-10 reveals that in spite of the fact that there was mass rejection of Isaiah's message, a remnant did respond with repentance and confession (v. 9-13). Verse 10 describes that remnant using disability language:

10 נְגַשְׁשָׁה כַעִוְרִים קִיר וּכְאֵין עֵינַיִם נְגַשֵּׁשָׁה כָּשַׁלְנוּ בַצָּהֳרַיִם כַּנֶּשֶׁף בָּאַשְׁמַנִּים כַּמֵּתִים׃

> We grope along the wall like blind men, we grope like those who have no eyes; we stumble at midday as in twilight, among those who are vigorous we are like dead men.

Verses 9-11 are isolated from the rest of the passage by an inclusio. Verse 9 begins with the lament, רָחַק מִשְׁפָּט מִמֶּנּוּ (justice is far from us) and verse 11 completes the lament, ending with לִישׁוּעָה רָחֲקָה מִמֶּנּוּ (for salvation is distant from us). Verse 10 stands in dynamic parallel with verse 9. Alter suggests that the effect of the parallelism between verses 9 and 10 is emphatic, intensifying the initial assertion in verse nine,

> making the outer darkness an inner darkness, the total incapacity to see, and transforming the general image of walking in darkness of the preceding verses into a more concrete picture of a blind man groping his way along a wall.[153]

The plural form of the word "blind" (עִוְרִים) appears persistently in Isaiah (6:10; 29:9, 18; 35:5; 42:7, 16, 18, 19; 43:8; 56:10; 59:10). The use of the term in verse 10 is significant. Here it indicates the lack of sure footing on which to stand brought about as a result of darkness and results in stumbling about as though blind.[154] Isaiah seems to verbalize Israel's lament up to this point, acknowledging her condition without shifting blame.[155] All efforts to find relief through appeals to their own resources, their allies, or idols have failed. Once this acknowledgment becomes the people's assertion, their alienation from Yahweh will end and the hope of salvation (chs. 60-62) will become their reality.[156] This point brings the theme of divine enablement to the fore.

In 42:7 Isaiah predicts that the servant of God would open the eyes of the blind (לִפְקֹחַ עֵינַיִם עִוְרוֹת). This repentant remnant now knows what should be and seek it but what they seek cannot be found. Simply seeing, it seems, is not enough. The defective condition mentioned here should be understood as describing human nature rather than the ability of sight.[157] "Blindness is a misfortune which might be corrected, but to have no eyes is, humanly speaking, an irreversible condition, which can only be mended by an act of new

---

[153] Robert Alter, *The Art of Biblical Poetry* (New York: Basic Books, Inc., Publishers, 1985), 15.

[154] Joseph Blenkinsopp, *Isaiah 56-66* (Anchor Bible 19b; New York: Doubleday, 2002), 193.

[155] Oswalt, *The Book of Isaiah: Chapters 40-66*, 520.

[156] Oswalt, *The Book of Isaiah: Chapters 40-66*, 520.

[157] Motyer, *The Prophecy of Isaiah*, 487.

creation."[158] Hence, the groping and stumbling is not the result of circumstances, but a result of the internal defect of sin.[159]

The metaphorical use of light (אוֹר) and darkness (חֹשֶׁךְ) in contrast with one another suggests that these people look for God to establish justice and righteousness on the earth (נְקַוֶּה לָאוֹר וְהִנֵּה־חֹשֶׁךְ), but find no evidence of it.[160] These repentant individuals long for righteousness but cannot bring it forth themselves so they walk in gloom (בָּאֲפֵלוֹת נְהַלֵּךְ), groping like blind men (נְגַשְׁשָׁה כַעִוְרִים),[161] and stumbling about at noon (שַׁלְנוּ בַצָּהֳרַיִם). In effect, they are like the dead (כַּמֵּתִים). The issue is no longer a matter of circumstantial determinants but of internal renewal. Society or a man's conduct can be regulated but this does not mean that the heart of man is affected. Israel's soul is now in focus as repentance becomes the staging area for what Yahweh will affect (59:15b).

An Admonition to Return to the Old Ways: Jeremiah

The primary theme of Jeremiah appears to be a summons to Judah to turn from her idolatry and sin as a portent of the coming divine destruction and exile.[162] Jeremiah's forthright rebuking of Israel's infidelity to the covenant created much ill will between him and his fellow priests and relatives.[163] Like prophets before him, Jeremiah implores Israel to return to the old paths of righteousness.[164] Like Isaiah, Jeremiah uses disability language metaphorically to describe Israel's blatant disregard for the Sinai covenant entered into with Yahweh. While Isaiah uses disability language to depict Israel's indolence as well as the expected One's future ministry, Jeremiah uses this language to describe Israel in her idolatrous practices unfaithfulness, and unholiness. Nevertheless, Isaiah and Jeremiah share a common theme of the neglect of Yahweh's centrality in Israel's spiritual life.

Jeremiah portrays Yahweh as absolutely sovereign, holy, patient, compassionate, and awaiting the return of his obstinate and stiff-necked people.[165] Judah is portrayed as the Lord's first fruits, a choice vine, and Yahweh's beloved bride. She is God's flock, vineyard, and inheritance. At the

---

[158] Motyer, *The Prophecy of Isaiah*, 487.

[159] Motyer, *The Prophecy of Isaiah*, 487.

[160] Motyer, *The Prophecy of Isaiah*, 486-87. Motyer notes that Isaiah's use of light is specifically used of the Messiah (2:5; 10:17; 42:6; 49:6; 51:4; 58:8) while his use of darkness refers to the darkness of this world (29:18; 42:7; 45:3). They often are used in juxtaposition with one another (5:20; 30; 9:2; 42:16; 45:7; 49:9; 50:10; 58:10; 60:1-3).

[161] Waltke-O'Conner *Syntax*, 34.5.3b. This appears to be a "pseudo-cohortative indicating past time.

[162] Archer, *A Survey of Old Testament Introduction*, 399.

[163] Archer, *A Survey of Old Testament Introduction*, 400.

[164] Dillard and Longman, *An Introduction to the Old Testament*, 297.

[165] Dillard and Longman, *An Introduction to the Old Testament*, 297-98.

same time she is portrayed as a wayward son and a whore. His messages to wayward Judah include the call to return and obey the covenant so as to possess land, to not have false confidence in the Davidic covenant, and that the temple is no refuge for wicked people.[166] Jeremiah was a royal messenger of the heavenly king whose word is powerful, self-authenticating, overwhelming, and unstoppable.[167] As a type of Moses, Jeremiah is representing and interceding for the people before Yahweh.[168] Jeremiah entreaties to the nation to "ask for the ancient paths, ask where the good way is, and walk in it" (6:16).

Disability Language Describes Israel's Unfaithful Heart: Jeremiah 5:21-31

One senses that a comparison is being made between the senseless idols Israel has sworn by (v. 7) and Israel herself (v. 21). The only question is which is more devoid of sense, the idols or Israel? Chapter 5 sets forth the indictment against Israel and her impending doom. Her unfaithfulness is her undoing. Not only in the judgment to come but in the reality that in turning her back on Yahweh and the covenant, Israel has become a people without discernment, a society without justice. Verse 21 reads:

שִׁמְעוּ־נָא זֹאת עַם סָכָל וְאֵין לֵב עֵינַיִם לָהֶם וְלֹא יִרְאוּ אָזְנַיִם לָהֶם וְלֹא יִשְׁמָעוּ׃

> Hear this, O foolish and senseless people, who have eyes, but do not see; who have ears, but hear not.

Jeremiah 5:20ff contains a variety of poetic images following the general prophetic motifs of judgment and sentencing.[169] The people have failed and their perversity has resulted in their inability to make righteous judgments.[170] Verse 7 makes it plain that "the subject matter is idolatry and false forms of worship."[171] The accusation against the house of Judah (vv. 20-21) surfaces immediately and is identified with the imperatives to "declare" (הַגִּידוּ) in verse 20 and to "pay attention" (שִׁמְעוּ) in verse 21. This becomes the governing word through the remainder of this chapter. "Hear" is the foundational word for covenant responsiveness and through the use of this word this text invokes a summons to return to that.[172]

Serving alien gods is paramount to foolishness, that is, a lack of true understanding of Yahweh. Carroll suggests that this recalcitrant people "cannot

166 Dillard and Longman, *An Introduction to the Old Testament*, 298.

167 Dillard and Longman, *An Introduction to the Old Testament*, 298-99.

168 Dillard and Longman, *An Introduction to the Old Testament*, 299.

169 Walter Brueggemann, *A Commentary on Jeremiah: Exile & Homecoming* (Grand Rapids: Eerdmans, 1998), 67.

170 Peter Craigie, Page H. Kelley, and Joel F. Drinkard, Jr., *Jeremiah 1-25* (Word Biblical Commentary 26; Dallas: Word, 1991), 95.

171 Robert Carroll, *Jeremiah* (The Old Testament Library; Philadelphia: Westminster Press, 1986), 187.

172 Brueggemann, *A Commentary on Jeremiah*, 67.

see the obvious; they cannot understand nature.”[173] Yet it seems that the issue is not so much that the people are incapable of seeing or hearing, but that they are incapable of revering Yahweh. This is because they fail to perceive him at work or the implications of his working around them. They fail to see and hear, and not fearing Yahweh they are as fools.

As the chapter unfolds we see the reasons for the impending invasion from the North (4:11-18). Jerusalem is wicked (vv.1-9) yet the people deny their guilt (vv.10-17). The meter of the bicola in verse 20 and the tricolon in verse 21 makes it unlikely that these verses are an editorial addition to the text.[174] Verse 21a reads, “pay attention O foolish and heartless people” (שִׁמְעוּ־נָא זֹאת עַם סָכָל וְאֵין לֵב). This can be compared to Isaiah 48:1, “hear this O house of Jacob” (שִׁמְעוּ־זֹאת בֵּית־יַעֲקֹב). This may be a stock phrase being employed in both texts (עַם paralleling בֵּית־יַעֲקֹב).[175] In Jeremiah, the same sequence of all four words (eyes/ears- see/hear) constitutes two merisms.[176]

Verse 20 contains imperatives directed at the messengers. Verse 21 begins the actual speech. Yahweh’s repeated warnings to Judah and Jerusalem have been ignored. This text consists of a heavy use of wisdom language in the midst of the general accusations of unfaithfulness and a lack of reverence toward Yahweh.[177] The people are senseless and without heart (סָכָל וְאֵין לֵב). Brueggemann argues that the heart is “the organ of covenant” that here has “become alienated from Yahweh.”[178] The lack of heart, or will among the Judahites to remain in covenant with God is the issue. As evidence for this accusation, we read that they deliberately plan their evil actions, practicing iniquity by withholding from one another (v. 25), practicing wickedness by ensnaring hapless victims (v. 26), performing treachery by rapaciously consuming the resources of others (v. 27), and exploiting orphans and the needy (v. 28). Their theological disorientation is systemic, institutionally supported, and legitimated.[179] This rejection of Yahweh induces the blindness and deafness to which the people are prone. They are, in fact, as blind and deaf as the idols they turned to (5:19). “Where covenant with Yahweh is betrayed, covenant values in social relationships cannot be sustained.”[180]

The use of שָׁמַע at the beginning and end of verse 21 suggests an *inclusio*. The *waw* adversatives and the repetition of sound and words in the two cola

---

[173] Carroll, *Jeremiah*, 187.

[174] Robert Althann, *A philological Analysis of Jeremiah 4-6 in Light of Northwest Semitic* (Rome: E Pontificio Instituto Biblico, 1983), 171.

[175] Althann, *A philological Analysis of Jeremiah 4-6 in Light of Northwest Semitic*, 171.

[176] There is a parallel pair found in Ugaritic literature (*UT* 1008:16-21 [*KTU* 3.5:16-21]) and also in (*UT* 52:54 [*KTU* 1.23:54]).

[177] William Holladay, *A Commentary on the Book of the Prophet Jeremiah Chapters 1-25* (Hermeneia; Minneapolis: Fortress, 1986), 194.

[178] Brueggemann, *A Commentary on Jeremiah*, 68.

[179] Brueggemann, *A Commentary on Jeremiah*, 68.

[180] Brueggemann, *A Commentary on Jeremiah*, 69.

indicate alliteration and assonance.[181] אֹזֶן and שָׁמַע appear together in same sequence in Deut 29:3, Isa 6:10, 42:20, 43:8, Ezek 12:2, and 40:4 also suggesting the use of a stock idiomatic phrase.

Verses 26-28 cite what happens to a community with a disoriented heart.[182] Several specific sins of social injustice are identified that typifies the heart of one disoriented.[183] The courts are filled with iniquity as well. Rather than preserving integrity, the courts have subverted justice to satisfy their own ends, furthering the exploitation of the powerless who seek justice there.[184] While verses 26-28 focus on the community, verses 30-31 link the perversity and injustice of the people with their incompetent leaders.[185]

Disability Language Identifies Those Returning From Exile: Jeremiah 31:8-9

This text brings us to that portion of Jeremiah when the prophet no longer pleads with the people for repentance and with God for mercy. Judgment is inevitable and must be accepted as such. Now is the time to look beyond the impending exile to the restoration of the people. At this pivotal point Jeremiah again utilizes disability language to express the inclusiveness of the restored people when they return from exile. Jeremiah 31:8 reads:

הִנְנִי מֵבִיא אוֹתָם מֵאֶרֶץ צָפוֹן וְקִבַּצְתִּים מִיַּרְכְּתֵי־אָרֶץ בָּם עִוֵּר וּפִסֵּחַ הָרָה וְיֹלֶדֶת יַחְדָּו
קָהָל גָּדוֹל יָשׁוּבוּ הֵנָּה׃

> Behold, I am bringing them from the North country, and I well gather them from the remote pars of the earth, among them the blind and the lame, the woman with child and she who is in labor with child together; a great company, they shall return here.

The "north country" (אֶרֶץ צָפוֹן) represents the ends of the earth (see also 6:22).[186] Although they normally considered this territory the home of their enemy, in this text it is "the place from which the exiles return."[187] Holladay notes that the mention of the blind, the lame, the pregnant, and those in labor is a reversal of the list presented in 6:22. In 6:22 the handicapped would hinder migration, needing to be assisted and unable to fight. In this text, however, they seem to typify the קָהָל גָּדוֹל (great assembly) coming from the North which

[181] Althann, *A philological Analysis of Jeremiah 4-6 in Light of Northwest Semitic*, 171.
[182] Brueggemann, *A Commentary on Jeremiah*, 68.
[183] Holladay, *Jeremiah Chapters 1-25*, 194.
[184] Craigie, Kelley, and Drinkard, *Jeremiah 1-25*, 97.
[185] Craigie, Kelley, and Drinkard, *Jeremiah 1-25*, 95.
[186] William Holladay, *A Commentary on the Book of the Prophet Jeremiah Chapters 26-52* (Hermeneia; Minneapolis: Fortress, 1986), 184.
[187] Holladay, *A Commentary on the Book of the Prophet Jeremiah Chapters 26-52*, 184.

Yahweh will bring home to weep and supplicate Yahweh.[188] The weak, coming from exile, carry with them the promise of new life for the nation.[189] No one will be excluded. Keown, Scalise, and Smothers write,

> Blind and lame priests were excluded from service (Lev 21:18), and postpartum women were ceremonially unclean (Lev 12:1-8). They are unlikely pilgrims to Zion (v. 12). Mothers would be essential for repopulating the land, but the Lord's mercy and faithfulness are surely demonstrated by the inclusion of the blind and lame in the acts of redemption and guidance. If even these will be brought back, then certainly everyone can be included. Other passages promise healing for the blind and lame when they reach Zion (e.g., Isa 35:5-6), but this verse does not.[190]

"The return from exile is because of Yahweh's love for his firstborn son and his love for him (Jer 31:9)."[191] The remnant of Israel will be gathered under Yahweh's love and faithfulness (v. 3). This remnant includes the most vulnerable: the blind, lame, pregnant, and nursing mothers (v. 8). The use of the word "gathering" (קָבַץ) in verses 8 and 10 communicates a predominant anticipatory theme of restoration from exile.[192] This theme is a fixed aspect of Israel's expectation (Isa 11:12; 40:11; 43:5, 9; 54:7; 56:8; 60:4, 7; 66:18; Jer 23:3; 29:14; 32:37; Ezek 11:17; 20:34, 41: 28:25; 34:13; 36:24; 37:21; 38:8; 39:27). The metaphoric use of disability language here communicates inclusiveness. The exile was real enough and the return from exile was also real. God kept his eternal covenant, bringing Israel back from her exile.

Disability Language and Yahweh's Corrective Measures: Ezekiel

After the exile, the spiritual condition of the Jews appears to have worsened. According to Block, the exiles suffered from intense theological shock.[193] They simply could not understand why Yahweh had allowed their situation to become as it was in spite of their unshakable faith in him. Block writes,

> Even though the prophets justifiably denounced the people of Judah for their idolatrous and socially criminal ways, throughout the Babylonian crisis the people had maintained confidence in Yahweh's obligation to rescue them.[194]

---

[188] Holladay, *A Commentary on the Book of the Prophet Jeremiah Chapters 26-52*, 184-85. Holladay contends that "supplications" is not a correct reading and that it should be amended to read consolations.

[189] Carroll, *Jeremiah*, 591.

[190] Gerald L. Keown, Pamela J. Scalise, and Thomas G. Smothers, *Jeremiah 26-52* (Word Biblical Commentary 27; Dallas: Word, 1995), 113.

[191] Dempster, *Dominion and Dynasty*, 165.

[192] Brueggemann, *A Commentary on Jeremiah*, 284.

[193] Daniel I. Block, *The Book of Ezekiel: Chapters 1-24* (New International Commentary on the Old Testament; Grand Rapids: Eerdmans, 1997), 7.

[194] Block, *The Book of Ezekiel: Chapters 1-24*, 7.

What the Judahites did not take into account was their own rebellion against Yahweh and the consequences to that rebellion. Ezekiel (and other post-exilic writers) argues the case from God's perspective. It was not Yahweh who had abandoned them but they who had abandoned Yahweh (1 Kgs 9:6-9; 2 Kgs 17:19-23; 23:26-27; Ezek 5:5-17; 19:1-14; 23:35) resulting in their being spewed out of the land as he predicted would happen (Lev 18:24-30; 20:22; Deut 29:22-30:5).

Disability Language Used to Describe False Hope: Ezekiel 12:2

The theme of inevitable judgment in the form of exile continues in Ezekiel's oracles. For some time, through symbolic actions and pronouncements, Ezekiel has been warning his people of the imminence, severity and basis of their coming judgment (ch. 4-11).[195] His metaphorical use of disability language at the opening of this new section of speeches is a censure to Israel's false hope that their exile would be brief. Ezekiel 12:2 reads:

בֶּן־אָדָ֕ם בְּת֥וֹךְ בֵּית־הַמֶּ֖רִי אַתָּ֣ה יֹשֵׁ֑ב אֲשֶׁ֣ר עֵינַ֩יִם֩ לָהֶ֨ם לִרְא֜וֹת וְלֹ֣א רָא֗וּ אָזְנַ֨יִם לָהֶ֤ם
לִשְׁמֹ֙עַ֙ וְלֹ֣א שָׁמֵ֔עוּ כִּ֛י בֵּ֥ית מְרִ֖י הֵֽם׃

> Son of man, you live in the midst of the rebellions house, who have eyes to see but do not see; ears to hear but do not hear; for they are a rebellious house.

In their mind they had reason for hope and sound objections to Ezekiel's warnings. The people countered that judgment would not come in their lifetime (ch. 12), Ezekiel was the only prophet of doom among many prophets offering hope (ch. 13), Judah's leaders were more culpable than the exiles themselves so judgment should be against them rather than the exiles (ch. 14), God could not judge his own people so harshly for the sins of their forefathers (ch. 15-17), and Zedekiah could be trusted to throw off Nebuchadnezzar's yoke (ch. 19).[196] Their hope naively rested on the preservation of their eternal city, Jerusalem.[197] What they failed to see was their own rebellious nature which had to be quenched and this could only be accomplished through their current set of circumstances.

Chapters 12-24 constitute the third section of Ezekiel containing a judgment oracle against Israel.[198] Ezekiel 12:1-16 forms a subunit to the section being examined. The content of this subunit is a prophetic sign-act directed against the dynasty. The unit's boundaries are indicated by the word-event formula (12:1) and the recognition formula (12:15-16).[199] The section opens with an indictment regarding the spiritual condition of Ezekiel's audience (12:1-2).

---

[195] Ralph H. Alexander, *Ezekiel* (Expositors Bible Commentary 6; Grand Rapids: Zondervan, 1998), 795.
[196] Alexander, *Ezekiel*, 795.
[197] Alexander, *Ezekiel*, 795.
[198] Block, *The Book of Ezekiel: Chapters 1-24*, 360.
[199] *The Book of Ezekiel: Chapters 1-24*, 364.

Verse 2 introduces the divine assessment of Israel's intractable and hardhearted spiritual condition that is the dominant theme in this section. Verse 2 is more than a private oracle. It functions as the rationalization for the pantomime to come as explained at the end of verse 3.[200]

Seven times Ezekiel is commanded to perform this sign-act לְעֵינֵיהֶם (in their sight). The frequent use of words such as "by day" יוֹמָם (12:3, 4, 7), "evening" עֶרֶב (12:4, 7), and "darkness" עֲלָטָה (12:6, 7, 12) contribute to the central literary motif that is focused on the blindness to which Israel was prone. The reference to Zedekiah's expatriation to Babylon and eventual blinding (12:13) further advances this motif showing the divine perspective on a course of events which could have been adverted were it not for Israel's blind rebellion.

The text is reminiscent of Jeremiah 5:21 and Isaiah 6:9 which also lament Israel's blindness and deafness toward Yahweh. Here the complaint is unique in that the blindness and deafness is willful as the perfect form of the verb suggests.[201] They do not want to see or hear, lest they be compelled to accept the dismal reality in place of their futile hope. Renz suggests that "their rebelliousness consists in not being willing to hear or see what they should hear and see."[202] This, he says, provides the rationale for the sign acts (12:3b) in that the sign act were intended to make the exiles understand the message.[203] Those who are physically impaired from hearing or seeing may be forgiven for their oblivion to reality, but "the refusal to hear and to see not only results in the further dulling of the senses; sooner or later, the door of divine mercy will slam shut."[204] The Judge of all men's intentions will call to account all who have squandered his grace.

Disabilities and the Minor Prophets

As we have seen in the Major Prophets, the purpose of purity was, in part, so that the people would themselves be in a condition suitable for Yahweh's presence. In addition, purity was their state of being, their identity as that particular people who were identified by Yahweh as his own possession (Exod 19:5-6). This identity was defined for them by the covenant. The covenant and the identity by which Israel was to be known was cogent and cohesive only as long as Israel's faith was invested in the other party to the covenant, Yahweh. As long as this was so, justice, community coherence, and love prevailed. The disabled, disadvantaged, and aliens could all expect to be treated in a manner

---

[200] William H. Brownlee, *Ezekiel 1-19* (Word Biblical Commentary 28; Waco: Word, 1986), 171.

[201] Moshe Greenberg, *Ezekiel, 1-20* (Anchor Bible 22; New York: Doubleday, 1983), 208. Jeremiah employs the imperfect form suggesting he is denouncing the stupidity and mindless inconsideration of the people.

[202] Thomas Renz, *The Rhetorical Function of the Book of Ezekiel* (Supplements to Vetus Testamentum; Leiden: Brill, 1999), 70.

[203] Renz, *The Rhetorical Function of the Book of Ezekiel*, 70, 152.

[204] Block, *The Book of Ezekiel: Chapters 1-24*, 379.

consistent with covenant stipulations. When the community of faith disavowed Yahweh, these subclasses along with the community itself declined into physical and spiritual indolence and gradual atrophy. Like Isaiah, Jeremiah, and Ezekiel, the Minor Prophets consistently addressed Israel's willful blinding. They continually fixate on Israel's refusal to assume the spiritual identity meant for them by Yahweh.

Disability Language used to Describe Weakness and Dependence: Micah 4:6-7

Micah's prophecy looks forward to the destruction of Judah by the Babylonians (586 B.C.) and its eventual restoration.[205] In light of this, Micah delivers a message of judgment against Israel for cultic and social sins.[206] Like the other biblical prophets, Micah asserts that Israel's civil and religious leaders have forsaken Yahweh and that the people have broken their covenant with him.[207] Consequently, God comes as a warrior against them. Micah's concern is provoked by the apostate lifestyle of his listeners.[208] The people have perverted worship practices (1:7; 3:5-7, 11; 5:11-13) and justice (2:1-2, 8-9; 3:2-3, 9-11; 7:2-6). What God desires is the love of his people, justice among them, and so he calls them back to himself.[209] Micah's primary message is that practical holiness and social reform (both of which are lacking in the Northern and Southern kingdoms), based on the righteousness and sovereignty of Yahweh, are essential byproducts of faith.[210] Since there is no tangible evidence of Israel's faith, they would experience the wrath of Yahweh's judgment in the future and in the present (1:2-4, 6-7, 15; 2:3-5; 3:3-7, 9-12; 4:13; 5:1-15; 6:9-16). The numerous summons to hear (1:2; 3:1, 9; 6:1-2, 9) along with their attending features, function within the structure of Micah, on various levels, to call the listener to bear witness to the message, heralding a transition from judgment to salvation.[211] Micah 4:6-7 reads:

6 בַּיּוֹם הַהוּא נְאֻם־יְהוָה אֹסְפָה הַצֹּלֵעָה וְהַנִּדָּחָה אֲקַבֵּצָה וַאֲשֶׁר הֲרֵעֹתִי׃
7 וְשַׂמְתִּי אֶת־הַצֹּלֵעָה לִשְׁאֵרִית וְהַנַּהֲלָאָה לְגוֹי עָצוּם וּמָלַךְ יְהוָה עֲלֵיהֶם בְּהַר צִיּוֹן
מֵעַתָּה וְעַד־עוֹלָם׃

> "In that day," declares the Lord, "I will assemble the lame, and gather the outcasts, even those whom I have afflicted. I will make the lame a remnant, and the outcasts a strong nation, and the Lord will reign over them in Mount Zion."

---

205 Dillard and Longman, *An Introduction to the Old Testament*, 399.
206 Dillard and Longman, *An Introduction to the Old Testament*, 401.
207 Dillard and Longman, *An Introduction to the Old Testament*, 401.
208 Ralph L. Smith, *Micah-Malachi* (Word Biblical Commentary; Waco: Word, 1984), 5.
209 Dillard and Longman, *An Introduction to the Old Testament*, 401.
210 Archer, *A Survey of Old Testament Introduction*, 359.
211 David Gerald Hagstrom, *The Coherence of the Book of Micah: A Literary Analysis* (Society of Biblical Literature Dissertation Series 89; Atlanta: Scholars, 1988), 27.

Micah employs disability language in chapter 4 in the midst of his prophecy concerning the exaltation of Zion (a synonym for the city of Jerusalem in prophetic literature: Isa 4:3; 40:9; Jer 26:8; Amos 6:1) in the last days to describe the universal change of heart among all the peoples of the world and their emerging desire to walk in the name of the Lord (vv. 2, 5). Concerning the name of the Lord, Ross writes,

> If the power of the name is directly related to the power of the one named, then *šēm yhwy,* the name of the Lord, is understandably the predominant force in the OT. The name of the Lord is Yahweh, in all that fullness of divine power, holiness, wrath, and grace that he revealed as his nature. The name of the LORD does what the Lord does . . . Thus, the name of the Lord stands for God's essential nature revealed to people as an active force in their lives.[212]

According to McComiskey, walking in the name of the Lord

> means more than simply adhering to the religious requirements associated with the deity in question. It means to live in reliance on the strength of that deity. In the case of Yahweh, it involves reliance on the might of his power by which his attributes are manifested.[213]

In verses 6-7, the metaphor depicts the restored remnant's acknowledgment of their complete self-deficiency, misery, and helplessness. Only through God's intervention (v.7) can they become a mighty nation (v. 7).[214]

The genre of this pericope is an eschatological salvation oracle as seen in the בַּיּוֹם הַהוּא (in that day) formulaic introduction. Micah 4:1-7 is also bound together by a variety of grammatical and thematic features. The next temporal clause בַּיּוֹם הַהוּא (v. 6) starts a salvation section that is initiated with the phrase, "the former dominion will come, the kingdom of the daughter of Jerusalem" (לְבַת־יְרוּשָׁלִָם בָּאָה הַמֶּמְשָׁלָה הָרִאשֹׁנָה מַמְלֶכֶת) in verse 8.[215] Together, the temporal clause and the divine oracle formula נְאֻם־יְהוָה (declares the Lord) sets verse 6 out as the beginning of a new oracle. The text is also connected thematically by the terminology of mobility (walk: vv. 2, 5; lame: v.6). The primary theme of Yahweh's reign from Zion also indicates the continuity of chapter 4 with chapter 3. Another link to the previous oracle is the cataphoric demonstrative pronoun (הַהוּא) pointing back to the temporal stamp established in verse 1 "in the last days" (בְּאַחֲרִית הַיָּמִים).[216] The references to Zion (4:2, 7, 8) also link the motifs of the two oracles together. These factors maintain a continuity with

---

212 Allen P. Ross, "שֵׁם," in *NIDOTTE* (ed. Willem A. VanGemeren; Grand Rapids: Zondervan, 1997), 4:150.

213 Thomas Edward McComiskey, *Micah* (Expositors Bible Commentary 7; Grand Rapids: Zondervan, 1998), 422.

214 McComiskey, *Micah*, 423.

215 Smith, *Micah-Malachi*, 39. This view is not universally accepted.

216 Bruce Waltke, "Micah," in *The Minor Prophets: An Exegetical and Expository Commentary* (ed. Thomas E. McComiskey; Grand Rapids: Baker, 1993), 686.

what has already been declared, suggesting that verse 6 introduces a new prophecy that will be contemporaneous with the previous one (4:1-5).[217] The difference between chapters 3 and 4 is that Micah forsakes the gloom of Israel's immediate internal destruction for the ethereal future glory of the city.[218] In the book of Jeremiah the civil officials quote Micah 3:12 in their appeal to the priests to rescind Jeremiah's death sentence (Jer 26:16-19). They argue that when Micah preached about the destruction of the temple in Hezekiah's day but he was not put to death. According to Jeremiah's advocates, instead of Micah being threatened with death, Hezekiah and his people responded positively to Micah's message and repented (Jer 26:19).[219] This provides a possible explanation for the shift of sentiment between Micah chapters 3 and 4. The people responded to his message and God, always ready to forgive, responded to them. In the future, there will be a time of salvation when God will rule over the nations from Zion (4:1-5) which will become the center of the world to which all people will gather for worship, instruction, and judgment.

The remnant motif appears in verses 6-7 for the first time in Micah (see also 5:6-7). Although the word "the lame" (הַצֹּלֵעָה) is only used one other time in the Old Testament as a predicate for a person (Gen 32:32), it is not likely that the reference here is connected to that instance in that Jacob's name is not mentioned in the Micah text.[220] In spite of this fact, the description of the gathering of the remnant community here is reminiscent of other texts (Ezek 34; Mic 2:12; Zeph 3:19) where a gathering (קָבַץ) of the scattered (הנדחת) is described in first person Yahweh speech as well.[221]

A future time of restoration is in view.[222] The scene depicts the return of Israel's exiles from their diaspora.[223] Zion is the central topic of concern in the entire chapter (4:2, 7-8, 10-11, 13) emphasizing Yahweh's royal dominion and protection in and over all nations from Jerusalem by continuing the shepherd metaphor introduced in 2:12-13.[224] The Shepherd-King will restore his

---

[217] Waltke, "Micah," בַּיּוֹם הַהוּא is treated as an anacrusis.
[218] McComiskey, *Micah*, 421.
[219] H.L. Ellison, *Jeremiah* (Expositor's Bible Commentary 6; ed. Frank E. Gaebelein; Grand Rapids: Zondervan, 1991), 541. Ellison suggests Micah deserves credit for the reforms instituted by Hezekiah as recorded in 2 Kings 18:3-6.
[220] Hans Walter Wolff, *Micah: A Commentary* (trans. Gary Stansell; Minneapolis: Augsburg, 1990), 123.
[221] Wolff, *Micah: A Commentary*, 123-24. Wolff incorrectly asserts that Micah 2:12; 4:6; and Zephaniah 3:19 are variations on a single tradition summarizing the message of gathering the exiles predominant in Ezekiel 34. Since Micah is a preexilic prophet his dependence on Ezekiel is unlikely.
[222] בַּיּוֹם הַהוּא connects verse 4:6 with בְּאַחֲרִית הַיָּמִים in 4:1.
[223] William McKane, *The Book of Micah: Introduction and Commentary* (Edinburgh: T & T Clark, 1998), 128.
[224] Wolff, *Micah: A Commentary*, 125.

wounded (literally the limping one [הַצֹּלֵעָה]) and expatriated (הַנִּדָּחָה)[225] flock to himself at Zion where he will reign over them. Waltke suggests that הַצֹּלֵעָה, in tandem with the other two characteristics features; lame and outcasts (הַנִּדָּחָה and וַאֲשֶׁר הֲרֵעֹתִי), form a collective antimeria for sheep, an implied metaphor for Israel.[226] The people whom Yahweh has afflicted (הֲרֵעֹתִי) will come home.[227] Zion will be restored and will again be the dwelling place of the Lord to where many people from many nations shall stream. Some form of the word הלכ is used throughout the section as a theme suggesting the opportunity for a response to the going forth of the word of the Lord from Zion. This word is instruction which "calls for a response in a new way of living for those who hear it."[228]

Verse 7a reads,

וְשַׂמְתִּי אֶת־הַצֹּלֵעָה לִשְׁאֵרִית וְהַנַּהֲלָאָה לְגוֹי עָצוּם

And I will make the lame a remnant, and the Outcasts a strong nation.

This verse expressly identifies the purpose of the gathering, paralleling again the participles from verse 6. The Abrahamic promise will be fulfilled anew (cf. Isa 54:1ff; Jer 23:3; Deut 30:5) and God will begin a new community on Zion with the remnant (שְׁאֵרִית) in exile to make them a mighty nation.[229] שְׁאֵרִית becomes a title that ascribes salvation to Israel (cf. Isa 54:1).[230] The message of hope this piece brings seems more suited for a time of distress. Scholars are divided as to whether or not the text belongs to the attack of Sennacherib (701 B.C.) or to the time of the Babylonian exile. Given that the total destruction of the Zion is forecast (v. 8) and the reference to Babylon (v. 10); it seems safe to conclude that the Babylonian exile is in view.

The Language of Authentication: Micah 7:16

Micah 7:15 sets forth Exodus theology when it refers to the wonders seen at the Exodus suggesting that the future events about to be revealed will be a kind of second Exodus.[231] The text describes the effect of Yahweh's acts upon the nations. First there is shame (בּוֹשׁ) leading to a sense of being overwhelmed as suggested by the putting of their hands over their mouths (יָשִׂימוּ יָד עַל־פֶּה), then

---

[225] Both participles are feminine and ought to be understood collectively. The *niphal* adjectival participle corresponds to the Latin gerund suggesting judgment, by describing Israel as being banish-able. Together these participles describe Yahweh's activity (וַאֲשֶׁר הֲרֵעֹתִי) not only in Israel's future assembling but also in her present suffering and shame.

[226] Waltke, "Micah," 686.

[227] *BDB*, 949. הֲרֵעֹתִי means "to do injury or hurt."

[228] James Limburg, *Hosea-Micah* (Interpretation; Atlanta: John Knox, 1988), 181.

[229] Here, שְׁאֵרִית is not negative, but parallels and complements עָצוּם.

[230] Wolff, *Micah: A Commentary*, 124.

[231] Kenneth L. Barker, "Micah," in *Micah, Nahum, Habakkuk, Zephaniah* (New American Commentary 20; Nashville: Broadman & Holman, 1998), 131.

they are suddenly struck deaf (אָזְנֵיהֶם תֶּחֱרַשְׁנָה) when they see Yahweh. In spite of their apparent superiority they are humbled. This verse refers to people who are amazed at the powerful hand of Yahweh. Micah 7:16 reads:

יִרְא֤וּ גוֹיִם֙ וְיֵבֹ֔שׁוּ מִכֹּ֖ל גְּבוּרָתָ֑ם יָשִׂ֤ימוּ יָד֙ עַל־פֶּ֔ה אָזְנֵיהֶ֖ם תֶּחֱרַֽשְׁנָה׃

> Nations will see and be ashamed of al their might, they will put *their* hand on *their* mouth, their ears will be deaf.

The form of address changes to third person plural, suggesting the reader is being drawn into the audience which now responds to Yahweh's promise.[232] Verses 16-17 vividly picture how the nations will react when they see the wonders of Yahweh worked on behalf of his people.[233] God's intervention will humble those nations which took Yahweh's people into captivity.[234] They put a hand to their mouth (יָשִׂימוּ יָד עַל־פֶּה) indicating awe and reverence (Job 29:9-10; Isa 52:15), their ears are made deaf (אָזְנֵיהֶם תֶּחֱרַשְׁנָה) suggesting that they are witnessing a thunderous act.[235] The nations are depicted like serpents who lick the dust of the ground (יְלַחֲכוּ עָפָר כַּנָּחָשׁ) and tumble out of their burrows (יִרְגְּזוּ מִמִּסְגְּרֹתֵיהֶם). The result is that God and the faith of the remnant are vindicated before their enemies. This vindication is not the result of their hope, but that they claim their dependence on their God and all that he is.[236]

Disability Language used to Describe Divinely Induced Bewilderment: Zephaniah 1:17

Zephaniah's passion is for the social, moral, and religious condition of his people. The superscription (1:1) sets Zephaniah's ministry during the reign of Josiah, making him a contemporary of both Habakkuk and Jeremiah. The book, however, does not contain any clear allusions to the reform activities associated with the discovery of the law book (2 Kgs 22-23) suggesting that Zephaniah's ministry took place before 621 B.C.[237] Baalism is prevalent and the high places flourish at the time of his writing (1:4-5). As Zephaniah focuses on Judah (ch. 1), it is evident that his desire is to forewarn his people of the expected judgment and the wickedness prompting it. In verse 17 Zephaniah describes the coming judgment, utilizing disability language:

וַהֲצֵרֹ֣תִי לָאָדָ֗ם וְהָֽלְכוּ֙ כַּֽעִוְרִ֔ים כִּ֥י לַֽיהוָ֖ה חָטָ֑אוּ וְשֻׁפַּ֤ךְ דָּמָם֙ כֶּֽעָפָ֔ר וּלְחֻמָ֖ם כַּגְּלָלִֽים׃

---

232 Hagstrom, *The Coherence of the Book of Micah*, 102.
233 Hagstrom, *The Coherence of the Book of Micah*, 102.
234 McComiskey, *Micah*, 444.
235 McComiskey, *Micah*, 445.
236 McComiskey, *Micah*, 445.
237 Dillard and Longman, *An Introduction to the Old Testament*, 416. It is, however, not clear that Josiah's reforms did not begin until 621.

> And I will bring distress on men, so that they will walk like the blind, because they have sinned against the Lord, and their blood will be poured out like dust, and their flesh like dung.

His message oscillates between judgment and its cause (1:13, 17), noting that it is their sin against the Lord that brings this judgment (כִּי לַיהוָה חָטָאוּ). As he describes the day of the Lord, Zephaniah metaphorically employs disability language. They will stumble and stagger about like blind men (הָלְכוּ כַּעִוְרִים). This recalls the curse of Deuteronomy 28:29 which will become a reality in consequence to Israel's covenant perfidiousness.

The theme beginning in Zeph 1:12 is Israel's complacency toward Yahweh and the search to remove it. The phrase בָּעֵת הַהִיא points to the characteristics of the event, not to the date.[238] אֲחַפֵּשׂ (*piel*) is made more intensive by the instrument בַּנֵּרוֹת.[239] פָקַדְתִּי (repeated from v. 8) identifies an object of punishment distinct from that mentioned previously but exactly what it is that is visited on those Yahweh is looking for is not clear.[240] What is chear is that the object of this punishment are those who remain contented with their sin (הָאֲנָשִׁים הַקֹּפְאִים עַל־שִׁמְרֵיהֶם).[241] This phrase literally means "the men who are congealing on their lees."[242] It is descriptive of complacent men who, Motyer suggests, have changed their cognitive and emotive values.[243] Their insensitivity does not go unnoticed as the phrase referring to those who are "stagnant in spirit" (הַקֹּפְאִים עַל־שִׁמְרֵיהֶם) was a proverb for callousness.

In the process of fermentation, juice is put into jars. As the juice became fermented, sediment settles and coagulates on the bottom of the jar.[244] If the wine was not separated from the sediment it would become bitter. At some point, the people arrived at the mistaken belief that God either would not, or

---

[238] Alec J. Motyer, "Zephaniah," in *The Minor Prophets* (ed. Thomas E. McComiskey; Grand Rapids: Baker, 1992), 921. Motyer argues that this does not make the time arbitrary but more exact.

[239] Motyer, "Zephaniah," 921.

[240] Motyer, "Zephaniah," 921.

[241] Larry Lee Walker, *Zephaniah* (Expositor's Bible Commentary 7; ed. Frank E. Gaebelein; Grand Rapids: Zondervan, 1991), 549. Walker notes that this phrase does not communicate much.

[242] The term קפא is used in Exod 15:8 to describe the "piling up" of the Red Sea like a wall of water. In Job 10:10 where Job describes the wonder of his creation which was poured out like milk and "curdled up" like cheese and in Zechariah 14:6 it is used to describe the congealing of the stars so that they give forth no light. See Francis Foulkes "קפא," in *NIDOTTE* (ed. Willem A. VanGemeren; Grand Rapids: Zondervan, 1997), 3:952.

[243] Motyer, "Zephaniah," 921.

[244] Motyer, "Zephaniah," 921.

could not act (לֹא־יֵיטִיב יְהוָה וְלֹא יָרֵעַ) in one way or the other.[245] They embraced a self-indulgent and decadent lifestyle to such an extent that they became contemptuous even of the commandments.[246] They denied God's sovereignty and providence in the process. Zephaniah notes that when judgment comes upon them, it will be with such suddenness that they will be shocked and frantic (הָלְכוּ כַּעִוְרִים).

Verse 13 declares that in that day they will not even be able to enjoy their newly built houses and planted vineyards. This is not a reversal of the covenant promise (Deut 28:39) since built into the covenant is both blessing and curse (Deut 28-29). The day of judgment is near (קָרוֹב) and approaching quickly (קָרוֹב וּמַהֵר). Together these two terms indicate that the "great day of the Lord" (יוֹם־יְהוָה הַגָּדוֹל) is imminent.[247] גִּבּוֹר usually refers to an enemy but here it is Yahweh himself who is the assailant.[248]

This will be a day of wrath (יוֹם עֶבְרָה). The Lord has long contained his wrath, but it is now overflowing.[249] צָרָה conveys the idea of being hemmed in with no escape.[250] There will be צָרָה וּמְצוּקָה (from the same root word) a crash into ruin.[251] The rule of man has resulted in bringing back the primeval meaninglessness (חֹשֶׁךְ וַאֲפֵלָה) that was before creation.[252] Motyer suggests that עָנָן וַעֲרָפֶל is reminiscent of Sinai and points to God's holy presence.[253]

The שׁוֹפָר is not in this context a summons to worship but a "mustering of the Lord's host to battle (Jer 4:19; Amos 2:2)."[254] תְּרוּעָה reinforces the war motif that is typical of apocalyptic texts.[255] Those under attack will experience Yahweh's distress (הֲצֵרֹתִי).[256] The *hiphil* perfect makes clear that the Lord is the one causing their adversity.[257] It will become so distressful that men (lit.

---

[245] Adele Berlin, *Zephaniah* (Anchor Bible 25A; New York: Doubleday, 1994), 66. Berlin suggests that this is worse than those who always expect Yahweh to defend them (Jer 5:12).

[246] Berlin, *Zephaniah*, 88.

[247] Motyer, "Zephaniah," 922.

[248] Motyer, "Zephaniah," 922.

[249] Motyer, "Zephaniah," 923. עֶבְרָה etymologically means overflowing rage. See *BDB* 720.

[250] Motyer, "Zephaniah," 923.

[251] Motyer, "Zephaniah," 923.

[252] Motyer, "Zephaniah," 923.

[253] Motyer, "Zephaniah," 923.

[254] Motyer, "Zephaniah," 923.

[255] Motyer, "Zephaniah," 923.

[256] Motyer, "Zephaniah," 923. This verse is linked to 1:15 by הֲצֵרֹתִי.

[257] I. Swart and Robin Wakely, "צרר," in *NIDOTTE* (ed. Willem A. VanGemeren; Grand Rapids: Zondervan, 1997), 3:854. Nominal, verbal, and adjectival forms of the word צרר denote any kind of restricting, claustrophobic experience such as military defeat (Judg 2:15; 10:9), revolt (1 Sam 30:6), the frustration of unsatisfied lust (2 Sam 13:2), the foreboding of approaching danger (Gen 32:7[8]), the reversal of fortunes for an unscrupulously greedy person (Job 20:22), and the fear and cramped progress

mankind, אָדָם) will walk as though blind (הָלְכוּ כַּעִוְרִים).[258] כַּעִוְרִים conveys the idea of confusion, helplessness, and bewilderment, so that men stagger about (Deut 28:29; Lam 4:14; Isa 59:10).[259] The reason for their suffering can be summed up in the damning phrase "for they sinned against the Lord (חָטָאוּ כִּי לַיהוָה).[260] Man thinks lightly of his sin but Yahweh does not. The consequence of sin, long withheld because of his grace, will be unleashed in its full force. Yahweh's purging of man's uncleanness is unstoppable. He "pours out their blood like dust" (שֻׁפַּךְ דָּמָם כֶּעָפָר).[261] Man's corpses[262] are as sewage (כַּגְּלָלִים)[263] to be disposed of with prejudice.

Disability Language used to Describe Restored Israel's Pathetic Condition: Zephaniah 3:19

Zephaniah 3:19 uses the language of disability to create a picture of a flock of sheep, scattered (הַנִּדָּחָה) and pathetically weak (הַצֹּלֵעָה) that will characterize the remnant of Israel at the time Yahweh restores them. In contrast with Micah 4:6-7 which denotes utter dependence on Yahweh as a choice the remnant makes, Zephaniah's use of this terminology denotes the pathetic condition of the restored community.[264] Zephaniah 3:19 reads:

הִנְנִי עֹשֶׂה אֶת־כָּל־מְעַנַּיִךְ בָּעֵת הַהִיא וְהוֹשַׁעְתִּי אֶת־הַצֹּלֵעָה וְהַנִּדָּחָה אֲקַבֵּץ וְשַׂמְתִּים
לִתְהִלָּה וּלְשֵׁם בְּכָל־הָאָרֶץ בָּשְׁתָּם׃

> Behold, I am going to deal at that time with all your oppressors, I will save the lame and gather the outcast, and I will turn their shame into praise and renown in all the earth.

Zephaniah 3:19 opens with the declarative "at that time" (הִנְנִי), giving a sense of the immediacy of the event and the connection of the impending nature of their restoration with the destruction of those nations hostile to Yahweh's

---

of one who rejects the path of wisdom and righteousness in favor of folly and wickedness (Prov 4:12; Job 18:7).

258 Swart and Wakely, "צרר," 3:855-56. The idea is that of enfeeblement resulting from the circumstances.

259 Motyer, "Zephaniah," 924. Motyer notes that this is one of the curses of the covenant (Deut 28:29).

260 Motyer, "Zephaniah," 924. חָטָאוּ literally means to have missed the mark (Judg 20:16).

261 Motyer, "Zephaniah," 924. Motyer links the "pouring out" (שֻׁפַּךְ כֶּעָפָר) with Lev 20:16, the only other text where dust is poured out.

262 Robert B. Chisholm, "לחום," in *NIDOTTE* (ed. Willem A. VanGemeren; Grand Rapids: Zondervan, 1997), 2:783. לחום used in parallel with דמם as it is used here, refers to the human body in whole or in part.

263 Motyer, "Zephaniah," 924; Roy E. Hayden, "גלל," in *NIDOTTE* (ed. Willem A. VanGemeren; Grand Rapids: Zondervan, 1997), 1:868. Hayden points out that גלל literally refers to human excrement.

264 Walker, *Zephaniah* (Expositors Bible Commentary 7), 564.

purposes.[265] It also emphasizes Yahweh's coming distribution (עָשָׂה) of justice.[266] The temporal phrase "at that time" (בָּעֵת הַהִיא) establishes a context for the time of eschatological blessing when God will destroy Israel's enemies.[267]

Israel had undergone catastrophe as punishment for sin. The *piel* participle "those oppressing you" (מְעַנַּיִךְ) suggests humbling and afflicting and moves beyond the external oppressors mentioned in verse 18 (נוּגֵי).[268] Judgment is portrayed through the day of Lord; divine grace is portrayed through the motif of remnant and restoration.[269] Those who oppressed Israel (cf. Isa 60:14) and any nation that opposes the Lord (Isa 59:17-21; 66:15-16) will be dealt with. Their judgment is God's vindication of his own name.[270]

The surviving remnant becomes the nucleus for the continuation of the people of God.[271] בַּיּוֹם הַהוּא (3:11, 16) not only identifies the prophetic genre of this text, putting it within the messianic age when the people will be purified, but also expresses the decisiveness of this event.[272] בָּעֵת הַהִיא connects verse 19 with verse 16. Hopes for the future of the people of God now are focused in this purified, holy remnant who will inherit afresh the promises of God.[273] This remnant, as Zephaniah indicates, will be gathered from all nations and be restored to land and divine favor.[274] The lame (הַצֹּלֵעָה) and the refugee (הַנִּדָּחָה) are in syntactical equivalence. They are the objects of Yahweh's work. Likewise, the *hiphil* verb "save" (הוֹשַׁעְתִּי) and *piel* verb "gather" (אֲקַבֵּץ) function together. הַצֹּלֵעָה is used collectively.[275] This motif calls attention to the final pilgrimage to Jerusalem (Isa 35).[276] The fortunes of the disabled and outcast change from בּוֹשׁ (shame) to הָלַל (praise). They will transition from being subject to the hands of their oppressors to restoration from their exile.

Israel's shame (בָּשְׁתָּם) and disability (צָלַע) are mentioned in the same text. The question is whether the shame is due to their physical impairment or their punishment for sin. I would suggest that the mention of the removal of their judgment (הֵסִיר יְהוָה מִשְׁפָּטַיִךְ) in verse 15 provides the answer. Israel's shame is

---

265 Walker, *Zephaniah*, 564.
266 Motyer, "Zephaniah," 961.
267 Anthony Tomasino, "עת," in *NIDOTTE* (ed. Willem A. VanGemeren; Grand Rapids: Zondervan, 1997), 3:565.
268 Motyer, "Zephaniah," 961. Motyer notes this internal/external pattern through the three pieces of this oracle.
269 Dillard and Longman, *An Introduction to the Old Testament*, 419.
270 Dillard and Longman, *An Introduction to the Old Testament*, 419.
271 Dillard and Longman, *An Introduction to the Old Testament*, 419.
272 Motyer, "Zephaniah," 961. This circumstantial clause implies definitiveness.
273 Motyer, "Zephaniah," 961. Dillard and Longman, *An Introduction to the Old Testament*, 419.
274 Dillard and Longman, *An Introduction to the Old Testament,* 419. Motyer, "Zephaniah," 961.
275 Berlin, *Zephaniah,* 147.
276 Motyer, "Zephaniah," 961.

due to her rebellion which led to the disgracefulness of exile. The shame was suffered at the hands of their oppressors.[277] Verse 11 reinforces the connection between shame and Israel's rebellion. Shame is a recurring motif in Zephaniah (2:1; 3:5, 11, 19) usually referring to the insensitivity of the wicked who indulge themselves in sin (2:1; 3:5, 11). It refers not only to Israel who was once in rebellion (3:11, 19), but to any people who stand in rebellion against Yahweh (2:1; 3:5). The reference to disability in 3:19 is used metaphorically for Israel's weakened condition rather than a literal depiction of lameness. It seems right to conclude that the shame mentioned in v. 19 is not due to their disability. Further, the theme of this section of Zephaniah is of joyful song and praise, not humiliation.[278] There is no hint of shame among those present in this glad assembly. It is a complete reversal of the earlier parts of the oracle.[279] Shame is no longer an issue in the restored Israel.

Disability Language used to Describe Nullifying Judgment: Zechariah 11:17

Zechariah uses disability imagery in the context of describing the worthless shepherd (11:15-17) that replaces the rejected Shepherd-King (11:1-14). Zechariah acts out the role of the worthless shepherd, explicitly demonstrating his ineffectiveness and morally deficiency. He is a counterfeit shepherd who preys on the sheep, avariciously consuming them. He abandons them and for this reason judgment is passed on him. He is to suffer disabling wounds that nullify his power and intelligence.[280] Zechariah 11:17 reads:

> הֹוי רֹעִי הָֽאֱלִיל֙ עֹזְבִ֣י הַצֹּ֔אן חֶ֥רֶב עַל־זְרֹועֹ֖ו וְעַל־עֵ֣ין יְמִינֹ֑ו זְרֹעֹו֙ יָבֹ֣ושׁ תִּיבָ֔שׁ וְעֵ֥ין יְמִינֹ֖ו כָּהֹ֥ה תִכְהֶֽה׃
>
> Woe to you worthless shepherd who leaves the flock! A sword will be on his arm and on his right eye! His arm will be totally withered, and his right eye will be blind.

Verse 16 begins with the announcement formula "for behold" (כִּי הִנֵּה) plus the *hiphil* participle (מֵקִים) indicating something is about to happen.[281] So there

---

[277] Philip J. Nel "בּוֹשׁ," in *NIDOTTE* (ed. Willem A. VanGemeren; Grand Rapids: Zondervan, 1997), 1:626. Nel suggests that in Old Testament usage בּוֹשׁ most likely refers to the negative experience of the exile which brought disgrace and dishonor on the remnant. Nel also notes that the experience of shame, in a religious sense, is internalized and may be understood as a precondition for repentance (Jer 3:3; Zeph 3:5; 1 Cor 4:14; 6:5).

[278] Berlin, *Zephaniah*, 148.

[279] Berlin, *Zephaniah*, 148.

[280] Kenneth L. Barker, *Zechariah* (Expositors Bible Commentary 7; Grand Rapids: Zondervan, 1998), 680.

[281] Carol L. Meyers, and Eric M. Meyers, *Zechariah 9-14* (Anchor Bible 25C; New York: Doubleday, 1993), 283.

would not be any ambiguity, the Lord interprets his own command.[282] This parallels verse 6.[283] In verse 6, the Lord was active but took a "hands off" posture. Here in verse 16, however, the Lord authorized the worthless shepherd (אָנֹכִי מֵקִים רֹעֶה בָּאָרֶץ).[284] Petersen calls this a pernicious action.[285] Meyer and Meyer also note that

> The identity of this shepherd is linked with the shepherd imagery that dominates this chapter, expresses the bad leadership of the past, and reflects the tension between true and false prophets, which must surely derive from the prophets own experience.[286]

Meyers and Meyers also point to the shepherd imagery in this chapter (vv. 4, 5, 7, 8, 16, 17) and suggest that the shepherd is not a particular person but, "extends the prophet's own self-consciousness, his sense of being part of an ongoing prophetic tradition."[287]

Features such as the consistent rhythmic quality of the syllabic count, the parallelism in the sentence structure, the absence of either the object marker or preposition before the object shows an atypical prosaic stylization.[288] The use of the imperfect verbal sequence implies the same use of language as previous indictments against Israel have contained (Ezek 34:3-6, 16) which is, in fact, ongoing.[289] Each of these features work together to display the degree to which Israel's shepherds have been negligent.

Each phrase contains a negative particle (לֹא) drawing a picture of a shepherd who would not do the job shepherds normally do.[290] In each of the clauses, the object of the verb occurs in the emphatic position.[291] He does not tend them (הַנִּכְחָדוֹת לֹא־יִפְקֹד) or seek the lost (הַנַּעַר לֹא־יְבַקֵּשׁ). He does not feed the hungry (הַנִּשְׁבֶּרֶת לֹא יְרַפֵּא), or sustain those who are strong (הַנִּצָּבָה לֹא יְכַלְכֵּל). Instead, he devours them (יֹאכַל).[292] The reference to flesh (בְּשַׂר) and hooves (פַּרְסֵיהֶן) forms a merism expressing the totality of their consummation that would be down to

[282] David L. Petersen, *Zechariah 9-14 and Malachi* (The Old Testament Library; Philadelphia: Westminster, 1995), 98.

[283] Petersen, *Zechariah 9-14 and Malachi*, 98.

[284] Petersen, *Zechariah 9-14 and Malachi*, 98.

[285] Petersen, *Zechariah 9-14 and Malachi*, 98.

[286] Meyers and Meyers, *Zechariah 9-14*, 283.

[287] Meyers and Meyers, *Zechariah 9-14*, 284.

[288] Meyers and Meyers, *Zechariah 9-14*, 284-85.

[289] Meyers and Meyers, *Zechariah 9-14*, 285.

[290] Petersen, *Zechariah 9-14 and Malachi*, 99. The work of caring for the sheep is well attested in the Scriptures (Gen 45:11; 50:21; 2 Sam 19:33, 34; 20:3; Neh 9:21).

[291] Van der Merwe, Naudé, and Kroeze, *A Biblical Hebrew Reference Grammar*, 336.

[292] וּבְשַׂר הַבְּרִיאָה יֹאכַל וּפַרְסֵיהֶן יְפָרֵק are disjunctive clauses.

the bits of flesh in the sheep's hooves.[293] False prophets were taking advantage of the people they were sent to warn (see also ch. 13).[294]

Verse 17 begins with the a word of woe (הוֹי). This signals a lament for the impending punishment.[295] The interjection followed by a preposition and noun is the standard formula, warning the group or class alerted by the interjection.[296] Here it is a worthless (הָאֱלִיל) shepherd (רֹעִי), incapable of caring for the sheep.[297] The participial phrase עֹזְבִי הַצֹּאן is in apposition to the appellation "worthless shepherd" and means "the abandoner of the flock."[298] "The worthless shepherds are those false prophets who habitually, in their self-centered behavior, fail to serve the people."[299]

The expletive (הוֹי) does not express a wish but makes a pronouncement, and the phrase "sword on the shepherd's arm" (חֶרֶב עַל־זְרוֹעוֹ וְעַל־עֵין) identifies this as an imprecatory assertion. This is a punishment appropriately fitting the shepherd's dereliction of duty.[300] The ensuing clause "his right arm is withered and his right eye is totally darkened" (יְמִינוֹ זְרֹעוֹ יָבוֹשׁ תִּיבָשׁ וְעֵי יְמִינוֹ כָּהֹה תִכְהֶה) is an independent thought reasserting the reality of the threat against the shepherd.[301] The two infinitive absolutes יָבוֹשׁ (withered) and כָּהֹה (darkened) strengthen the verbs they precede.[302] Since the shepherd neglects his charge, it is the parts of the body not utilized in behalf of the sheep's care (arm and eye) that are affected.[303] "By dint of the intended blindness and paralysis the shepherd will no longer be able to plunder the flock."[304] Further, the metaphorical value of these two body parts represent the might (זְרוֹעוֹ) and mental or spiritual faculties (עֵין יְמִינוֹ).[305] Together they represent the physical and mental abilities of the shepherd and by their removal the shepherd is made a powerless and non-functioning individual.[306] Yahweh now intervenes to render ineffectual the false prophets who continually interfere with his true prophets.[307]

---

[293] Petersen, *Zechariah 9-14 and Malachi*, 99.

[294] Meyers and Meyers, *Zechariah 9-14*, 288.

[295] Thomas E. McComiskey, "Zechariah," in *The Minor Prophets* (ed. Thomas E. McComiskey; Grand Rapids: Baker, 1992), 1207.

[296] Meyers and Meyers, *Zechariah 9-14*, 289.

[297] Meyers and Meyers, *Zechariah 9-14*, 290. Meyers and Meyers suggests that the obsolete genitive renders the phrase רֹעִי הָאֱלִיל as shepherd of worthlessness.

[298] Meyers and Meyers, *Zechariah 9-14*, 291.

[299] Meyers and Meyers, *Zechariah 9-14*, 291.

[300] McComiskey, "Zechariah," 1207.

[301] McComiskey, "Zechariah," 1207.

[302] Meyers and Meyers, *Zechariah 9-14*, 292.

[303] McComiskey, "Zechariah," 1207.

[304] Petersen, *Zechariah 9-14 and Malachi*, 100.

[305] Meyers and Meyers, *Zechariah 9-14*, 291.

[306] Meyers and Meyers, *Zechariah 9-14*, 292.

[307] Meyers and Meyers, *Zechariah 9-14*, 292.

Conclusions

The use of disability language as metaphor in Isaiah primarily deals with Israel's lack of responsiveness to Yahweh. Yahweh's presence was meant to be the impulse for holiness, obedience, and mobilization as Israel functioned in concert with Yahweh's purposes. The main issue is one of functionality. In the forefront of the book is Israel's syncretistic religious predilections and mechanistic compliance to covenant obligations rather than honoring the covenant with a heart of faith and love.

Two texts (6:9-10; 29:9-24) address real-time issues in Israel's relationship with Yahweh. In Isaiah 6:9-10 disability language is used to describe Israel's unresponsiveness toward Yahweh. The disability language in this section introduces a theme that Israel, rather than being a viscerally spiritual people, is instead obtuse toward their God and outright contemptuous toward the covenant that defines them. Israel's faculties of hearing and sight were functional yet ineffectual. Consequently, they could not understand, repent, or be healed. In Isaiah 29:9-24 disability language is used to describe Israel's inadequate leadership. Israel acts as though God is either ignorant or uncaring of their deeds. In judgment, Yahweh brings a finish to prophetic insight, a move that is equivalent to blinding his people. Isaiah 29 portrays the desperate conditions Yahweh's judgment had brought, illustrating the people's self-inflicted spiritual dullness expressed through the metaphor of blindness and then the anticipation of the age when the people's habitude is reversed and the wise will be humbled, the blind will see, the lame will walk, the poor will have joy, and evil ones will be cut off.

From this point on in Isaiah, disability language is used in eschatological tension with the work of the expected One. Isaiah 32:3-4 discusses the new society created at the expected One's coming. When he comes, disabilities will be no more. The language used here expresses more than physical healing. Metaphor for spiritual ignorance is replaced by metaphor for spiritual acumen. The expected One will usher in an era where all people will possess insight into the Lord's person, will, and actions that until that time has been reserved for a select few prophets. This represents a reversal of the people's obdurate condition mentioned earlier in the book (6:9-10). That which has rendered the people's faculties useless will be removed and in compliant subordination with their king, the people will function according to their new understanding to induce righteousness within and for the entire community. Only when the human faculties of sight and hearing result in vision and listening will human actions be conceived in genuine holiness and righteousness.

Disability language in Isaiah 35:5-6 functions in a song of elation concerning God's salvation of Zion and her restored people. The text utilizes disability language to communicate transformational activity by means of Yahweh's power. The reversal of spiritual and physical handicaps (6:10; 28:7; 29:9-10, 18; 30:20-21; 32:3-4) of blindness, deafness, and dullness communicates the reception of true guidance that comes from trusting in Yahweh rather than in human resources. Isaiah 42:6-7, 18-19 continues this theme, describing Israel's restored sense perception. Yahweh's Servant is a commissioned conqueror (41:2) who functions in righteousness and is fitted to advance the purposes of his God toward establishing righteousness (42:4, 6). These descriptions form a composite of the person (42:6) and his work as the conqueror servant (42:7f) who will reverse the people's idolatrousness and replace the visible images with an understanding of the invisible God. The motifs in this section work together to exhibit both the action of God to restore human sensory faculties and the effect of these restored faculties.

In Isaiah 42:18-20, disability metaphors are symbolic of Israel's helplessness. In 42:18-19 blind and deaf Israel is described as being just as spiritually needy as the Gentiles. Israel is not simply ignorant like the Gentiles; she is faithless which is portrayed in the disability imagery used in this text. What the people had not yet seen was Yahweh's purpose for them in the world as well as what their experiences with Yahweh might have taught them (Isa 42:21).

In Isaiah 43: 7-8, disability language is used in reference to Israel's ignorance. Since Israel is precious in God's sight they can rest securely on the covenant God has entered into with them. Nevertheless, Israel turned to idols who are themselves blind and deaf. Israel fails in their most basic obligation of their covenant, which is to bear witness to Yahweh as their God. Consequently, Yahweh must bear witness of his ability to predict his actions and to fulfill that expectation (43:10-11).

Isaiah 56:10-11 speaks of raising up a new generation unto Yahweh when physical limitations will no longer mean disqualification and exclusion from the sacred precincts. What will be required is faithfulness, a characteristic Yahweh's elect failed to cultivate previously. Here, disability terms function the same way as previously seen in Isaiah. Israel's leaders do not know God and consequently have failed in their capacity as leaders of God's people. Rather than using their position to protect and lead God's people, they used it for self-aggrandizement and piracy. They were blindly complacent toward their own sin and that of their people and its consequent encroachment effected on their covenantal relationship with Yahweh.

An examination of Isaiah 59:9-10 reveals that in spite of the fact that there was mass rejection of Isaiah's message, a remnant did respond with repentance and confession of their blindness toward God. All efforts to find relief through appeals to their own resources, their allies, or idols have failed. Once this acknowledgment becomes the people's assertion, their alienation from Yahweh will end and the hope of salvation will become their reality. This point brings the theme of divine enablement to the fore once again.

The prophet Jeremiah summons Judah to turn from idolatry and sin. He forthrightly rebukes Israel's infidelity to the covenant and implores them to return to the old paths of righteousness. Like Isaiah, Jeremiah uses disability language metaphorically to describe Israel's blatant disregard for the Sinai covenant entered into with Yahweh. In Jeremiah 5:21-31 disability language is used to describe Israel's unfaithful heart. Jeremiah compares the senseless idols Israel has sworn by (v. 7) and Israel herself (v. 21). The only question is which is more devoid of sense, the idols or Israel? Serving alien gods is paramount to foolishness, that is, a lack of true understanding. Yet it is not so much that the people are incapable of seeing or hearing, but that they have failed to perceive Yahweh at work or the implications of his work around them. They fail to see and hear, and not fearing Yahweh they are as fools.

Jeremiah 31:8-9 uses disability language to identify those returning from exile. At this point the prophet no longer pleads with the people for repentance and with God for mercy. Judgment is inevitable and must be accepted. Now Jeremiah looks beyond the impending exile to the restoration of the people. Jeremiah utilizes disability language to express the inclusiveness of the restored people when they return from exile. In this text the disabled typify the great assembly coming from the North. The weak, coming from exile, carry with them the promise of new life for the nation. No one will be excluded. This remnant will be gathered under Yahweh's love and faithfulness (v. 3) and include the most vulnerable: the blind, lame, pregnant, and nursing mothers (v. 8). The metaphoric use of disability language here communicates inclusiveness.

In Ezekiel, disability language is used to describe the corrective measures Yahweh uses on his people. After they go into exile, the spiritual condition of the Judahites appears to have worsened because they could not understand why Yahweh allowed their defeat. What they did not take into account was their own rebellion against Yahweh and its consequences. Ezekiel argues that it was not Yahweh who had abandoned them but they who had abandoned Yahweh (1 Kgs 9:6-9; 2 Kgs 17:19-23; 23:26-27; Ezek 5:5-17; 19:1-14; 23:35). Note particularly, that in Ezekiel 12:2 disability language is used to describe Judah's false hope in a brief exile. The metaphorical use of disability language serves to censure this false hope. Their hope naively rested on the preservation of their eternal city, Jerusalem. Their choice not see was their rebellion against Yahweh. They did not want to see or hear, lest they be compelled to accept their dismal future.

In several passages in the Minor Prophets, the purpose of purity comes to the fore. This purpose was, in part, so that the people would themselves be in a condition suitable for Yahweh's presence. Purity was not only their state of being but their identity as that particular people who were Yahweh's own possession (Exod 19:5-6). This identity was defined for them by the covenant. The covenant and the identity by which Israel was to be known was cogent and cohesive only as long as Israel's faith was invested in the other party to the covenant, Yahweh. As long as this was so, justice, community coherence, and love prevailed. The disabled, disadvantaged, and aliens could expect to be treated in a manner consistent with covenant stipulations. When the community of faith disavowed Yahweh, these subclasses along with the community itself declined into physical and spiritual indolence and gradual atrophy. It was this uniform depreciation of all this that the Minor Prophets deplored.

Evidence of this is found in Micah 4:6-7 where disability language is used to describe weakness and dependence. Micah looks forward to Judah's exile and eventual restoration. In light of this, he delivers a message of judgment for Israel's cultic and social sins. Micah employs disability language to describe a future change of heart among all the peoples of the world and their emerging desire to walk in the name of the Lord (vv. 2, 5). The metaphor depicts the restored remnant's acknowledgment of their complete self-deficiency, misery, and helplessness. The imagery progresses in Micah 7:16 where disability terminology is used as a means of authenticating the effect of Yahweh's acts upon the nations in the future. This text vividly pictures the nations' reaction when they see Yahweh's wonders worked on behalf of his people.

Zephaniah 1:17 employs disability language to describe Judah's divinely induced bewilderment when the day of the Lord dawns. As he describes the day of the Lord, Zephaniah metaphorically employs disability language to depict Judah's stumbling and staggering about like blind men. At some point, the people embraced a self-indulgent and decadent lifestyle and became contemptuous of the commandments; in the process, denying God's sovereignty and providence. Zephaniah notes that when judgment comes it will be with such suddenness that they will be shocked and frantic. It will become so distressful that men will walk as though blind. Later, Zephaniah uses disability language to create a picture is of sheep, scattered and pathetically weak, to characterize the remnant of Israel at the time Yahweh restores them (3:19). Zephaniah uses this terminology to denote the pathetic condition of the restored community. This remnant will be gathered from all nations and be restored to land and divine favor.

Zechariah 11:17 uses disability imagery is used in the context of describing the worthless shepherd (11:15-17) who was not only ineffective and morally deficient. He is a counterfeit shepherd who abuses the sheep. For this reason judgment is passed on him and he suffers disabling wounds that nullify his power and intelligence. His punishment is appropriately fitting this derelict shepherd.

What is to be made of texts that appear so dissimilar to one another in content and yet so immense in application? Some attest to a divine imposition of judicial blinding on Israel, while others assert that Israel's blindness is self-induced. Still others indicate Yahweh's renewal and salvation of these physical functions. The prophets' metaphorical use of disability language brought Israel's spiritual disposition to the fore. Their analysis of Israel's faithless tendency toward idolatry showed them to be spiritually dysfunctional, not merely alienated from God. Idolatry itself rendered them spiritually disabled.

According to Dieter Schmalstieg, the concept of sight involves more than mere seeing.[308] Sight is not the act of seeing something, but creating the concept of it being there.[309] As the prophets speak of the restoration of sight *vis-à-vis* the anticipated One's mission (Isa 42:6), Hebraic visualization is presented in full circle from creation, to the fall, to eschatological restoration. When the anticipated One comes, those who believe will not stay blind,[310] but will have sight restored to them. This promise of restored sight through the anticipated One, though, appears to be a reference to a new and clear perception of God and all he is rather than a promise of restored vision.

Hebrew prophetic literature uses the terms of disability metaphorically. Human faculties of sight, hearing, and locomotion, function toward distinguishment and movement. The eye can distinguish light and darkness when functioning normally. Blindness arrests this ability. The ear can distinguish truth and error when functioning as it should. Deafness arrests this ability. The legs are designed for movement toward or away from. Lameness arrests this ability, placing a person in a state of dependence. The prophets look ahead to a time when the inability to distinguish light and darkness or truth and error is metaphorically restored and the ability to see, hear, and move in the direction of light and truth becomes the norm. In other words, the prophets may not have foreseen a literal ministry of healing at all but the action was that of making believers of those who do not believe. Although it is beyond the perimeter of this study, it is worth noting that New Testament authors attempted to portray Jesus' ministry as giving such sight and his advent as one in which God and the way to him was made known in a way not previously done so as to have their eyes opened (Matt 5:8; 11:4-5; 13:13-15; Mark 4:11-12; Luke 8:10; John 2:14, 18; 3:3; 8:56; 9:39; Acts 28:27; Rom 11:1, 10; 2 Cor 4:4; Heb 12:14; 1 John 1:1-3).

The healing and deliverance ministry of the anticipated One is largely metaphorical in nature. The literal features disability terminology takes on in association with the anticipated One's advent indicate they are shadows of a real yet invisible healing and deliverance they truly need and receive upon belief in him. The physical attested to the metaphorical. The metaphorical is the actual. The believer's physical return from exile and release from bondage are shadows of the intrinsic return from an exile from the Lord and release from the bondage of immorality. The absence of justice and righteousness in the covenant community had already resulted in isolating them from God and one

[308] Dieter Olaf Schmalstieg, "Das andere Sehen: Systematisches Interesse an hebräischer Tradition," in *Zur Aktualität des Alten Testaments: Festschrift für Georg Sauer zum 65 Geburtstag* (ed. Siegfried Kreuzer; Frankfurt: Peter Lang, 1992), 259.

[309] Schmalstieg, "Das andere Sehen: Systematisches Interesse an hebräischer Tradition," 266.

[310] Schmalstieg, "Das andere Sehen: Systematisches Interesse an hebräischer Tradition," 260.

another. The isolation of Israel's exile served as a literal demonstration of the metaphorical isolation caused by sin.

Chapter 6

Conclusions

This work examined the literal labels used to describe physical disability and analyzed the sociological implications pertaining to the physically disabled. This provided a foundation for analysis of the metaphorical use of disability labels. This, in turn, extended and broadened the usage of that language so as to determine the spiritual use of disability language found both in the sociological implications of literal labels and the metaphorical usage of these same labels in prophetic literature.

In the course of examining law collections throughout the ancient Near East concerning the disposition of the disabled it was found that no legislation could be found that explicitly relegated the disabled to an inferior class status or disenfranchised them from rights other members of society possessed. Instead, these texts suggest that they were integrated into society. The king was divinely charged to protect the oppressed and disadvantaged. This may be behind legal texts mandating that if a member of society was disabled he was to be compensated financially by the one who had done the disabling (*Code of Hammurabi*).

Likewise, biblical law indicates that Israel recognized that justice was a concept originating with God and endowed to men. The form of Israel's justice was generated by the divine covenant. Israel's justice toward all members of the community was to function as an expression of that spiritual orientation the covenant was designed to shape the people to be. The disabled were to be treated as equal members of the community of faith (Exod 20:2; 22:21; 23:9, 15; 29:46; 34:18; Lev 19:13-14; 21:16-23).

Social attitudes toward the disabled in the ancient world that could be discerned from the texts examined in this study indicate that there was little or no discrimination. Texts suggest that a moral imperative existed that supported descent treatment of the disabled (*Instruction of Amenemope*). The studied texts do not suggest that physical imperfection was socially stigmatizing (*Kirta*; *Hurrian Myth Cycle*). The biblical texts examined also do not suggest that a disability was stigmatizing in Hebrew society. Biblical historical narratives likewise demonstrate that the disabled were not segregated from society (Lev 21:18; 2 Sam 5:6-8; 9:5-13; 1 Kgs 14:4-5; 2 Kgs 6:17). Each of these narratives does not indicate that the disabled were discriminated against. Rather, disabled persons are found functioning in some way, even in religious ways, within Hebrew society.

While literature from ancient societies around Israel does not contain the use of disability language metaphorically, Hebrew literature does. The metaphorical use of disability language in the prophetic literature bears witness to the fact that the practice of Yahwism in Israel demanded more than mere mechanical compliance or vacant observance to prescribed rituals. The fact that the prophets lament and condemn Israel's superficial, syncretistic, and vacant cultic observances indicates that in Israel a positive relationship with God was not automatic. Yahwism required that Israel preserved their ritual observances with an impassioned and reverent devotion in the sober realization of Yahweh's elective grace. It required intentionality, purposefulness, and exclusivity as well. As evidenced during times of reform (i.e., Hezekiah in 2 Kings 18) Israel's blessings increased, but when these virtues were lacking the ultimate result was delinquence, isolation, and judgment.

The current trend in modern scholarship stereotyping the physically disabled persons as they appear in ancient literary motifs moves in two directions. Either the physically disabled are believed to have been a disenfranchised group on the fringes of all ancient societies or they were mere characters, inserted into ancient literature with a representational function. This analysis of ancient Near Eastern literature demonstrates the deficiencies of both stereotypes. The physically disabled were neither disenfranchised nor did they represent exclusion.

The representational meaning of disability language in ancient Near Eastern literature (as applied by Mitchell and Snyder and those following them) also, presumably, includes the Bible. In order to present disabilities as a normative social category they adopt an allegorical hermeneutic that permits physical disability to be viewed as a template for social grouping.[1] It is my contention that in doing so, they sacrifice hermeneutical integrity resulting in the formulation of illegitimate constructs that further minoritize the disabled.

The motivation and effort in modern scholarship to eliminate the barriers and categorizations endured by the physically disabled and to replace their exclusion with inclusion is laudable. However, juxtaposing different physiological phenomena in literary contexts, even though symbolic and broadened beyond physical features, only serves to further alienate disability and validates differentness as a basis for their stigmatization. The result is that it promotes exclusion and isolation along with the consequent partiality and rancor between classes with which humans identify. The issue is not simply a matter of juxtaposition, but of transcending the realities of differentness that no human can claim to be without, whether it is a social, physical, cognitive, moral, or emotional difference. Those who dare to surmount their limitations and differences inspire others rather than breed contempt. These are the heroes, but today, heroism is out of fashion. In our current climate, few dare distinguish themselves by rising above their limitations and risk potential

---

[1] Mitchell and Snyder, "Disability Studies and the Double Bind of Representation," 3.

depreciation for doing so. Is it any wonder why the derisiveness of difference perpetuates itself? It is safer to live within conformity and the median of mediocrity than to endure distinction and isolation.

The use of disability language in Hebrew literature ought not be understood as representational but structural and integral to the text. Hebrew law taught that the physically disabled were to be treated as equal members of the community. There is an unequivocal attitude of neutrality with respect to the meaning of physical disability. It is neither good nor bad, it simply is. Disabilities are a fact of life like aging and death. The community of faith is to attend to the physically flawed with respect. The language of disability, however, was also used for the condition of the community's soul, or spiritual condition, in relation to Yahweh.

In order to understand Israel's ethics, one must look to motivation clauses.

> The motivation of holiness in Leviticus is to accentuate the need for Israel to draw toward God and become holy, while the main idea in Deuteronomy was to remove the evil from among them, thereby keeping them holy. These motivations underscored the idea that in order to remain in the state of holiness Israel must actively seek God and remove the evil that is among them, both internal and external.[2]

Herein lies the character of God and the ethical foundation of his commandments.

> Such motivation as "I am the LORD your God who brought you out of Egypt" serve to remind Israel that the law that God has given them is not the means to salvation but a means to God's continued presence in sanctification.[3]

Jesus went beyond the laws themselves to their use and transformational purpose. The law did not merely reveal the character of Yahweh, nor was it intended to be viewed as a methodological way to live. The law was the vehicle by which a relationship with Yahweh was maintained, and more. It was the instrument by which human conduct would move beyond simple obedience to a required set of codes toward the internal transformation of a people and the holiness essential to, and connected with, God's purpose for Israel in the land.

Because Yahweh is the source of life, biblical law reflects an appreciation for the value of life. Biblical law prescribed a Yahwistic ideology and a spiritual identity in both covenantal and narratival formats, which are inseparably linked. Israel was devoted to life and to creation order. Anything outside of these two principles was unclean (Lev 15). The concern for ritual

---

[2] Gregory Chirichingo, "A Theological Investigation Of Motivation In Old Testament Law," *Journal of the Evangelical Theological Society* 24 (1981): 311.

[3] Chirichingo, "A Theological Investigation Of Motivation In Old Testament Law," 312.

purity, physical purity of both sacrifices and sacrificer, and dietary laws and moral propositions (Lev 18, 20) illustrated this.

While other nations acknowledged that life was important, Israel placed a high value on it which it incorporated in its legal code that distinguished her from the nations around her. The function of Israel's law code was to establish Israel's spiritual identity while narrative functioned to reinforce it. The locutionary force of Israel's legal code was, in essence, what defined Israel's spirituality. Yahwism was more than religious affectation, duty, or obligation. Yahwism is an immanent religion that is voiced in consummate and undeviating allegiance with the person of God and his statutes.

The law of *Talion* is a punitive reaction which occasionally resulted in disabling. Simply stated, *Talion* pronounced that a person who disables another would likewise be disabled. One thing is certain, *Talion* was retribution. Another thing that is certain is that a physical defect was not understood to be a sign of divine retribution.

This study has discovered that the disabled were not excluded from participation in the cult. Being among the disadvantaged, provisions were made for their food just as was for the poor. Likewise, they were entitled to and afforded justice in equal measure with the privileged of society and the alien (Exod 22:21f; Lev 19:15, 33-34; Deut 1:16; 10:17-19; 14:28-29; 16:11-14). Their treatment was the measure of a just and righteous society.

Disability language in biblical prophetic literature is used metaphorically to suggest that Israel's immorality, unfaithfulness, and rebellion against their covenant God has resulted in a condition which is out of order with God. The resulting disorder leads God to judge and punish. This is not so much as to totally reject his people but to bring them to the point of repentance which will in turn lead to restoration in a right and orderly covenant relationship with him. Prophetic literature clearly shows that Yahweh is cognizant, at all times, of positive response and movement toward him by his people.

The metaphorical usage of disability language in Hebrew prophetic literature suggests that the disability associated with Israel was internal and spiritual, not external and physical. It follows then, that the healing and restoration of Israel would also be internal and spiritual. At the advent of the One to come man's inner condition will be healed, affecting a renewal of relationship with Yahweh and a restoration of human relationships. He will open eyes and ears to see Yahweh and hear his word. Lameness would be removed to facilitate a whole-hearted pursuit of Yahweh and compliance with covenant stipulations.

As to John the Baptist's second thoughts regarding his identification of Jesus as the coming one (Matt 11:2; Luke 7:18), Jesus alludes to Isaiah 35:5-6 and 61:1, affirming that he was indeed the one was restoring the spiritual perceptibility of all who believe in him. The restoration of human physical faculties of sight, hearing, mobility, and speech were literal demonstrations of his divine identity and his power to restore the man's shattered relationship with God. The New Testament authors also portray Jesus' ministry as giving such sight and his advent as one in which God and the way to him was made known in a way not previously done so as to have their eyes opened (Matt 5:8; 11:4-5; 13:13-15; Mark 4:11-12; Luke 8:10; John 2:14, 18; 3:3; 8:56; 9:39; Acts 28:27; Rom 11:1, 10; 2 Cor 4:4; Heb 12:14; 1 John 1:1-3).

The body, eyes, and ears are referred to in metaphorical language as expressions of the attitude of the heart and movement of the person toward or away from God. In biblical literature, belief precedes behavior. By this I mean that faith was to prompt a code of conduct consistent to the precepts and quality of that faith. Yet faith and conduct were to merge as one. There is to be no belief without a behavior consistent with it. In Israel, faith without exemplary conduct was unfaithfulness to Israel's God. Elijah and other biblical prophets had faith. This translated into a sight beyond sight, a second sight which could see, through visions and dreams, the work of the Lord in their midst. Israel did not possess this second sight because they did not possess the faith to persevere in obedience to the covenant and its laws. Consequently, any covenant compliance became internally mechanistic and externally a religious and syncretistic facade.

Being a Yahwist in Israel involved more than the recognition of a divine name as a protective banner and offering sacrifices at God's temple, although such actions were significant. Equally significant was the willful and intentional expression of Israel's religion by every member of the covenant community toward every other member of the community. It involved one's whole being, every day, for the physically disabled, the indigent and those who were only resident aliens who were not excluded from the covenant but were also obligated to live according to its stipulations. The ethical, equitable, and moral standards embodied in covenant law were practical and at the same time ideal. In the practicing of them the nation's identity was made known. The implementation of these standards would preserve the essential holiness required by Israel's God for his persistent presence in their midst and project to Israel's neighbors that there is indeed one God that they were subject to. Ancient Israel failed to implement the statutes and decrees handed down to them through Moses and was consequently judged and exiled. All today who claim fidelity to the Old Testament and its God are obligated still to demonstrate these standards.

A physical disability precludes one's ability to identify points of reference, inability to know definitively where one is or where one is going. In such conditions, one is left to grope about and is vulnerable to dangerous external influences. One is dependent on the obligation of family or the compassion of strangers. Spiritually, one whose human faculties are diminished cannot know God by means of those courses in which he reveals himself and desires to be known. Impairment often results in distortion and misunderstanding. One is dependent on another to act as an agent.

Areas of further study would be to examine non-canonical literature of the Second Temple Period to determine if the legal, social and religious trajectories found in the Old Testament remained static or underwent change. If changes in theological or social attitudes occurred then the impact of these changes could very well be detected in the attitudes toward the physically disabled within later Judaic and early Christian literature. The New Testament appears to demonstrate that some enmity toward the physically disabled (John 9:2) had developed after the Old Testament canon closed and they appear to have become social pariahs (Matt 20:30; Mark 10:46; Luke 14:13, 21; 18:35; Acts 3:2). Further, the New Testament also associates demonic activity was associated with some physical impediments (Matt 9:32-33; 12:22; Mark 9:17, 25; Luke 11:14; Acts 8:7). This appears to be beyond the range of Old Testament revelation. It would be a worthy study to examine these issues.

Bibliography

Abrams, Judith Z. *Judaism and Disability: Portrayals in Ancient Texts from the Tanach through the Bavli.* Washington, D.C.: Gallaudet University Press, 1998.

—. "Judaism and Disabilities." In *Encyclopedia of Medicine in the Bible and the Talmud* (Northvale, 1993), 1696.

Ackerknect, E.H. *A Short History of Medicine.* Baltimore: John Hopkins, 1982.

Ackroyd, Peter R. "The Succession Narrative (so-called)." *Interpretation* 35 (1981): 383-96.

—. *The Second Book of Samuel: A Commentary.* The Cambridge Bible Commentary, New English Bible. Cambridge: University Press, 1979.

Albenda, Pauline. *Monumental Art of the Assyrian Empire: Dynamics of Composition Styles.* Malibu: Undena Publications, 1998.

Alexander, Joseph Addison. *Commentary on the Prophecies of Isaiah.* Grand Rapids: Zondervan, 1977.

Alexander, Ralph H. *Ezekiel.* Expositors Bible Commentary 6:735-996. Grand Rapids: Zondervan, 1998.

Alexander, T.D. *From Paradise to the Promised Land.* Grand Rapids: Baker, 2002.

Alter, Robert. *The Art of Biblical Poetry.* New York: Basic Books, Inc., Publishers, 1985.

Althann, Robert. *A philological Analysis of Jeremiah 4-6 in Light of Northwest Semitic.* Rome: E Pontificio Instituto Biblico, 1983.

Ames, Frank Ritchel. "דָּבָר." In *New International Dictionary of Old Testament Theology and Exegesis,* ed. Willem A. VanGemeren, 1:912-15. Grand Rapids: Zondervan, 1997.

Anderson, A.A. *2 Samuel.* Word Bible Commentary 11. Dallas: Word, 1989.

Archer, Gleason L., Jr. *A Survey of Old Testament Introduction.* Revised ed. Chicago: Moody Press, 1994.

Avalos, Hector. "Blindness." In *Eerdmans Dictionary of the Bible,* ed. David Noel Freedman, 193. Grand Rapids, Mich.: Eerdmans, 2000.

—. *Illness and Healthcare in the Ancient Near East: The Role of the Temple in Greece, Mesopotamia, and Israel*. Atlanta: Scholars Press, 1995.

—. "Ancient Medicine: In Case of Emergency, Contact Your Local Prophet." *Bible Review* (1995): 27-35, 48.

—. "Medicine." In *The Oxford Encyclopedia of Archaeology in the Ancient Near East*, ed. Eric M. Meyers, 3:450-59. New York: Oxford, 1996.

Averbeck, Richard E. "Clean and Unclean." In *New International Dictionary of Old Testament Theology and Exegesis*, ed. Willem A. VanGemeren, 4:477-86. Grand Rapids: Zondervan, 1997.

—. "Sumer, the Bible, and Comparative Methodology: Historiography and Temple Building." In *Mesopotamia and the Bible*, ed. Mark W. Chavalas and K. Lawson Younger, Jr., 88-125. Grand Rapids: Baker, 2002.

—. "The Theology of Leviticus." In *New International Dictionary of Old Testament Theology and Exegesis*, ed. Willem A. VanGemeren, 4:907-23. Grand Rapids: Zondervan, 1997.

Baker, David W. "עִוֵּל." In *New International Dictionary of Old Testament Theology and Exegesis*, ed. Willem A. VanGemeren, 3:342-44. Grand Rapids: Zondervan, 1997.

Bar-Efrat, Simon. *Narrative Art in the Bible.* Journal for the Study of the Old Testament Supplement Series, 70. Bible and Literature Series, 17. Sheffield: The Almond Press, 1989.

Barker, Kenneth L. "Micah." In *Micah, Nahum, Habakkuk, Zephaniah.* The New American Commentary 20. Nashville: Broadman & Holman, 1998.

—. *Zechariah.* Expositors Bible Commentary 7, ed. Frank E. Gaebelein, 593-697. Grand Rapids: Zondervan, 1998.

Baroody, Wilson G. and William F. Gentrup. "Exodus, Leviticus, Number, and Deuteronomy." In *A Complete Literary Guide to the Bible*, ed. Leland Ryken and Tremper Longman III, 121-136. Grand Rapids: Zondervan, 1993.

Beal, Richard H. "Assuring the Safety of the King During the Winter." In *The Context of Scripture: Canonical Compositions from the Biblical World*, ed. William W. Hallo and K. Lawson Younger, I:207-11. New York: E.J. Brill, 1997.

Beaulieu, Paul-Alain. "Nabopolassar's Restoration of Imgu-Enlil, the Inner Defensive Walls of Babylon." In *The Context of Scripture: Monumental Inscriptions from the Biblical World*, ed. William W. Hallo and K. Lawson Younger, II:307-08. New York: E.J. Brill, 1997.

Beckman, Gary. "Excerpts from an Oracle Report." In *The Context of Scripture: Canonical Compositions from the Biblical World*, ed. William W. Hallo and K. Lawson Younger, I:204-06. New York: E.J. Brill, 1997.

—. *Hittite Birth Rituals.* Studien zu den Boğazköy-Texten 29. Wiesbaden: Harrassowitz, 1983.

Beegle, Dewey. *Moses, the Servant of Yahweh.* Grand Rapids: Eerdmans, 1972.

Bergen, Robert D. *1, 2 Samuel.* New American Commentary 7. Nashville: Broadman and Holman, 1996.

Berger Peter L. *The Sacred Canopy: Elements of a Sociological Theory of Religion.* Garden City, N. J.: Anchor, 1967.

Berlin, Adele. "The Grammatical Aspect of Biblical Parallelism." In *Beyond Form Criticism: Essays in Old Testament Literary Criticism*, ed. Paul R. House, 311-48. Sources for Biblical and Theological Study. Winona Lake: Eisenbrauns, 1992.

—. *Zephaniah.* The Anchor Bible 25A. New York: Doubleday, 1994.

Biggs, Robert D. "Medicine in Ancient Mesopotamia." *History of Science* 8 (1969): 94-105.

Birch, Bruce C. *The Book of 2 Samuel.* The New Interpreter's Bible. Edited by Leander E Kect, et al., 2:1199-1383. Nahsville: Abingdon, 1994.

Blenkinsopp, Joseph. *Isaiah 1-39.* Anchor Bible 19. New York: Doubleday, 2000.

—. *Isaiah 56-66.* Anchor Bible 19b. New York: Doubleday, 2002.

Block, Daniel I. *The Book of Ezekiel: Chapters 1-24.* New International Commentary on the Old Testament. Grand Rapids: Eerdmans, 1997.

Boecker, Hans Jochen. *Law and the Administration of Justice in the Old Testament and Ancient Near East.* Minneapolis: Augsburg, 1980.

Borger, P. Rykle. "Die Weihe eines Enlil-Priesters." *Bibliotheca Orientalis* 30 (1973): 163-76.

Bottéro, Jean, and Marc Van de Mieroop. *Mesopotamia: Writing, Reasoning, and the Gods.* Chicago: University of Chicago Press, 1987.

Bottéro, Jean. "Magie A." In *Reallexikon Der Assyriologie und Vorderasiatischen Archäologie,* Band 7, ed. P. Calmeyer, J.N. Postgate, W. Röllig, E. von Schuler, W. von Soden, M. Stol and G. Wilhelm, 200-234. Berlin: Walter De Gruyter, 1990.

Braddock, David L. and Susan L. Parish. "An Institutional History of Disabilities." In *Handbook of Disability Studies*, ed. Gary L. Albrecht, Katherine D. Seelman and Michael Bury, 11-68. Thousand Oaks, Calif.: Sage, 2003.

Brown, Raymond. *The Message of Deuteronomy: Not by Bread Alone.* Downers Grove: InterVarsity, 1993.

Brownlee, William H. *Ezekiel 1-19*, Word Biblical Commentary 28. Waco: Word, 1986.

Brueggemann, Walter. *Deuteronomy.* Abingdon Old Testament Commentaries. Nashville: Abingdon, 2001.

—. *A Commentary on Jeremiah: Exile & Homecoming.* Grand Rapids: Eerdmans, 1998.

—. *1 and 2 Kings.* Smyth and Helwys Bible Commentary. Macon, Ga: Smyth and Helwys, 2000.

—. *First and Second Samuel.* Interpretation. Louisville: John Knox, 1990.

Brunet, Gilbert. "Les aveugles et boiteux jébusites." *Vetus Testamentum Supplements* 30 (1979): 65-72.

Byl, Simon. "Molière et la médecine antique." *Études Classiques* 63 (1995): 55-66.

Cairns, Ian. *Word and Presence: A Commentary on the Book of Deuteronomy.* Grand Rapids: Eerdmans, 1992.

Carlson, R.A., *David the Chosen King: A Traditio-Historical Approach to the Second Book of Samuel.* Stockholm: Almqvist and Wiksell, 1964.

Carpenter, Eugene. " כרת." In *New International Dictionary of Old Testament Theology and Exegesis*, ed. Willem A. VanGemeren, 2:729-31. Grand Rapids: Zondervan, 1997.

Carroll, Robert. *Jeremiah.* The Old Testament Library. Philadelphia: Westminster Press, 1986.

Cassuto, Umberto. *A Commentary on the Book of Exodus.* Translated by Israel Abrahams. Jerusalem: Magnes, 1967.

Castrén, Paavov, ed. *Ancient and Popular Healing.* Symposium on Ancient Medicine. Finnish Institute at Athens. Athens, 1986. Helsinki, 1989.

Catagnoti, Amalia. "Les nains à Ebla." In *Nouvelles Assyriologiques Brèves et Utilitaires* 31 (1989): 20-21.

Ceresko, Anthony. "The Identity of 'the Blind and the Lame' (*'iwwēr ūpissēah*) in 2 Samuel 5:8b." *Catholic Biblical Quarterly* 63 (2001): 23-30.
Chan, Alan Kam-Yua, and Thomas B. Song/Michael L. Brown. "רפא." In *New International Dictionary of Old Testament Theology and Exegesis,* ed. Willem A. VanGemeren, 3:1162-73. Grand Rapids: Zondervan, 1997.
Childs, Brevard S. *Introduction to the Old Testament as Scripture.* Philadelphia: Fortress, 1979.
Chirichingo, Gregory. "A Theological Investigation Of Motivation In Old Testament Law." *Journal of the Evangelical Theological Society* 24 (1981): 303-313.
Chisholm, Robert B. "לחום." In *New International Dictionary of Old Testament Theology and Exegesis,* ed. Willem A. VanGemeren, 2:783-84. Grand Rapids: Zondervan, 1997.
Christensen, Duane L. *Deuteronomy 21:10-34:12.* Word Biblical Commentary 6B. Dallas: Word, 2002.
Clay, A.T. "Documents from the Temple Archives of Nippur." In *The Babylonian Expedition of the University of Pennsylvania.* Vol. 15. Philadelphia: University of Pennsylvania Press, 1906.
Cogan, Mordechai and Hayim Tadmor. *II Kings.* The Anchor Bible 11. New York: Doubleday, 1988.
Cogan, Mordechai. *I Kings.* The Anchor Bible 10. New York: Doubleday, 2000.
Collins, Billie Jean. "The First Soldiers Oath." In *The Context of Scripture: Canonical Compositions from the Biblical World*, eds., William W. Hallo and K. Lawson Younger, I:165-76. New York: E.J. Brill, 1997.
Contenau, George. *La médicine en Assyrie et en Bablonie.* Paris: Maloine, 1938.
Coogan, Michael David. *Stories from Ancient Canaan.* Philadelphia: Westminster Press, 1978.
Craigie, Peter C., Page H. Kelley and Joel F. Drinkard, Jr. *Jeremiah 1-25.* Word Biblical Commentary 26. Dallas: Word, 1991.
Craigie, Peter C. *The Book of Deuteronomy.* The New International Commentary on the Old Testament. Grand Rapids: Eerdmans, 1976.
Currid, John. *Ancient Egypt and the Old Testament.* Grand Rapids: Baker, 1997.
Davis, Lennard J. "Constructing Normalcy." In *The Disability Studies Reader*, ed. Lennard J. Davis, 9-28. London: Routledge, 1997.
Dempster, Stephen G. *Dominion and Dynasty.* New Studies in Biblical Theology 15. Downers Grove, IL.: InterVarsity, 2003.
DeVries, Simon J. *1 Kings.* Word Biblical Commentary 12. Waco Tex.: Word, 1985.
Dick, Michael. *Born in Heaven, Made on Earth.* Winona Lake, Ind.: Eisenbrauns, 1999.
Dillard, Raymond B. and Tremper Longman III. *An Introduction to the Old Testament.* Grand Rapids: Zondervan, 1994.

Dorsey, David A. *The Literary Structure of the Old Testament.* Grand Rapids: Baker Books, 1999.

Douglas, Mary. "Atonement in Leviticus." *Jewish Studies Quarterly* 1, no. 2 (1993): 109-30.

—. "The Forbidden Animals of Leviticus." *Journal for the Study of the Old Testament* 59 (1993): 2-23.

—. *Leviticus as Literature.* London: Oxford University Press, 2001.

—. *Purity and Danger: An Analysis of Concepts of Pollution and Taboo.* London: Routledge, 1966/1969.

—. "Sacred Contagion." In *Reading Leviticus: Responses to Mary Douglas*, ed. John F. A. Sawyer, 86-106. Journal for the Study of the Old Testament Supplemental Series 227. Sheffield: Sheffield Academic Press, 1996.

Driver, G.R. and John C. Miles. *The Babylonian Laws.* Vol.1: *Legal Commentary.* Oxford: Clarendon, 1935.

Duguid, Iain M. *Ezekiel and the Leaders of Israel.* Supplements to Vetus Testamentum 56. New York: Brill, 1994.

Durham, John I. *Exodus.* Word Biblical Commentary 3. Dallas: Word, 1987.

Ebstein, Wilhelm. *Die Medizin im Alten Testament.* München: Werner Fritsch, 1965.

Edelstein, Ludwig. *Ancient Medicine.* Ed. Owsei and C. Lilian Temkin. Baltimore: Johns Hopkins University Press, 1987.

Eiesland, Nancy. *The Disabled God: Toward a Liberation Theology of Disability*. New York: Abingdon, 1994.

Ellis, Earl. "Foreword." In *Typos: The Typological Interpretation of the Old Testament in the New*. Ed. L. Goppelt. Grand Rapids: Eerdmans, 1982.

Ellison, H.L. *Jeremiah.* Expositor's Bible Commentary 6, ed. Frank E. Gaebelein, 357-691. Grand Rapids: Zondervan, 1991.

Ellison, R. "Some Thoughts on the Diet of Mesopotamia from c. 3000-600 B.C.E." *Iraq* 45 (1983): 146-150.

Els, P.J.J.S. "אָהֵב." In *New International Dictionary of Old Testament Theology and Exegesis*, ed. Willem A. VanGemeren, 1:277-99, Grand Rapids: Zondervan, 1997.

Erickson, Millard J. *How Shall They Be Saved? The Destiny of Those Who Do Not Hear of Jesus.* Grand Rapids: Baker, 1996.

Exum, J. Cheryl. "Of Broken Pots, Fluttering Birds, and Visions in the Night: Extended Simile and Poetic Technique in Isaiah." *Catholic Biblical Quarterly* 43 (1981): 331-52.

Finet, A. Les médecins ua royaume de Mari.: *Annuaire de l'Institut de Philologie et d'Histoire Orientales et Slaves* 14 (1954): 122-44.

Finkelstein, J.J. *The Ox That* Gored. Philadelphia: American Philosophical Society, 1981.

Floss, Johannes P. *David und Jerusalem: Ziele und Folgen des Stadteroberungsberichts 2 Sam 5:6-9 literaturwissenschaftlich betrachtet.* Arbeiten zu Text und Sprache im Alten Testament, Band 30. Erzabtei St. Ottilien: EOS Verlag, 1987.

Fokkelman, J.P. *Narrative Art and Poetry in the Books of Samuel: King David.* Vol 1. Assen, Netherlands: Van Gorcum, 1981.

—. *Narrative Art and Poetry in the Books of Samuel: Throne and City.* Vol 3. Assen, Netherlands: Van Gorcum, 1990.

Fontaine, Carole R. "Disabilities and Illness in the Bible: A Feminist Perspective." In *A Feminist Companion to the Hebrew Bible in the New Testament.* Feminist Companion to the Bible Series 10, ed. Athalya Brenner. Sheffield: Sheffield Academic Press, 1996.

—. "'Be Men, O Philistines!' Iconographic Representations and Reflections on Female Gender as Disability in the Ancient World." In *This Abled Body: Rethinking Disabilities in Biblical Studies*, ed. Hector Avalos, Sarah J. Melcher and Jeremy Schipper, 71. Atlanta: Society of Biblical Literature, 2007.

Foulkes, Francis. "דַּק." In *New International Dictionary of Old Testament Theology and Exegesis*, ed. Willem A. VanGemeren, 1:981. Grand Rapids: Zondervan, 1997.

—. "קפא." In *New International Dictionary of Old Testament Theology and Exegesis*, ed. Willem A. VanGemeren, 3:952-53. Grand Rapids: Zondervan, 1997.

Frazer, James G. *The Golden Bough.* 12 volumes. 3rd Edition. London: Macmillan, 1991-18.

Fretheim, Terence E. *Exodus.* Interpretation. Louisville: John Knox, 1991.

Freydank, Helmut. "Chirurgie im alten Mesopotamien?" *Das Altertum* 18 (1972): 133-137.

Friendenwald, Harry. *The Jews and Medicine.* Baltimore: Johns Hopkins University Press, 1994.

Frymer-Kensky, Tikva. "Pollution, Purification, and Purgation in Biblical Israel." In *The Word of the Lord Shall Go Forth: Essays in Honor of David Noel Freedman*, ed. C.L. Meyer and M O'Conner, Winona Lake, Ind.: Eisenbrauns, 1983.

Gammie John. *Holiness in Israel: Overtures in Biblical Theology.* Minneapolis: Fortress, 1989.

Garland, Robert. *The Eye of the Beholder: Deformity and Disability in the Graeco-Roman World.* Ithaca, N.Y.: Cornell University Press, 1995.

Gaventa, Bill and Christopher Newell. "Religion." *Encyclopedia of Disabilities*, ed. Gary L. Albrecht, 1374-75. Thousand Oaks, Calif.: Sage, 2005.

Gelb, Ignace J., Martha T. Roth, Benno Landsberger, Erica Reiner, A. Leo Oppenheim, John A. Brinkman, Robert D. Biggs, Miguel Civil and Donald Whitcomb. *The Assyrian Dictionary of the Oriental Institute of the University of Chicago.* Chicago: Oriental Institute, 1956.

George, Mark. "Yhwh's Own Heart." *Catholic Biblical Quarterly* 64 (2002): 442-459.

Gerstenberger, Erhard S. *Leviticus: A Commentary.* Louisville: John Knox, 1996.

Ghalioungui, Paul. *The House of Life, Per Ankh: Magic and Medical Science in Ancient Egypt*. Amsterdam: B.M. Israël, 1973.

Ghalioungui, Paul and Zeinab El-Dawakhly. *Health and Healing in Ancient Egypt*. Cairo: Dar Al-Maaref, 1965.

Gileardi, Avraham. *The Literary Message of Isaiah*. New York: Hebraeus Press, 1994.

Goetze, Albrecht. *Kleinasien: Kulturgeschichte des Alten Orients*. 2nd edition. Munich: C.H. Beck, 1957.

—. "Investigating the Anger of the Gods." In *Ancient Near Eastern Texts Relating to the Old Testament*, ed. James B. Pritchard, 497-98. Princeton N.J.: Princeton University Press, 1969.

—. "The Soldiers' Oath," In *Ancient Near Eastern Texts Related to the Old Testament*, ed. James Pritchard, 353-54. Princeton, N.J.: Princeton University Press, 1969.

Gordon, Robert P. *I and II Samuel: A Commentary*. Grand Rapids: Regency, 1986.

—. "In Search of David." In *Faith, Tradition, and History: Old Testament Historiography in Its Near Eastern Context*, ed. R.A. Millard, James K. Hoffmeier and David W. Baker, 285-98. Winona Lake: Eisenbrauns, 1994.

—. "קלל." In *New International Dictionary of Old Testament Theology and Exegesis*, ed. Willem A. VanGemeren, 3:926-27. Grand Rapids: Zondervan, 1997.

Grayson, Albert K. and W.G. Lambert. "Akkadian Prophecies." *Journal of Cunneiform Studies* 18 (1964): 7-30.

—. *Assyrian and Babylonian Chronicles*. Texts from Cuneiform Sources 5. Locust Valley, N.Y.: Augustin, 1975.

Greenberg, Moshe. *Ezekiel, 1-20*. The Anchor Bible 22. New York: Doubleday, 1983.

Greenstein, Edward. "Kirta." In *Ugaritic Narrative Poetry*, ed. Simon b. Parker, 9-48. Atlanta, Ga.: Scholars Press, 1997.

Grisanti, Michael A. and J. Clinton McCann. "שחד." In *New International Dictionary of Old Testament Theology and Exegesis*, ed. Willem A. VanGemeren, 4:75-76. Grand Rapids: Zondervan, 1997.

Grogan, Geoffrey W. *Isaiah*. Expositors Bible Commentary 6:1-354. Grand Rapids: Zondervan, 1998.

Grol, H.W.M. van. "Isaiah 27:10-11: God and His own People." In *Studies in the Book of Isaiah: Festschrift Willem A.M. Beuken*, ed. J. van Ruiten and M. Vervenne, 195-212. Leuven: Leuven University Press, 1997. 195-212.

Grünwaldt, Klaus. *Das Heiligkeitsgesetz Leviticus 17-26: Ursprüngliche Gestalt, Tradition und Theologie*. Beihefte der Zeitschrift für die alttestamentliche Wissenschaft 271. Berlin: De Gruyter, 1999.

Gurney, Oliver R. *The Hittites*. 2nd edition. Baltimore: Penguin Books, 1961.

Hagstrom, David Gerald. *The Coherence of the Book of Micah: A Literary Analysis*. Society of Biblical Literature Dissertation Series 89. Atlanta: Scholars, 1988.

Hallo, William W. "Biblical History in Its Near Eastern Setting: The Contextual Approach." In *Scripture in Context: Essays on the Comparative Method*, ed. Carl D. Evans, Williams W. Hallo and John B. White, 1-26. Pittsburgh Theological Monograph Series 34. Pittsburgh: Pickwick, 1980.

—. "Reforms of Uru-inimgina." In *The Context of Scripture: Monumental Inscriptions from the Biblical World*, ed. William W. Hallo and K. Lawson Younger, II:207-08. New York: E.J. Brill, 1997.

—. "Compare and Contrast: The Contextual Approach to Biblical Literature." In *The Bible in Light of Cuneiform Literature: Scripture in Context III.* Ancient Near Eastern Texts and Studies 8. Ed., William W. Hallo, Bruce W. Jones and Gerald L. Mattingly. Lewiston, N.Y.: Edwin Mellen, 1990.

Hamilton, Mark W. *The Body Royal: The Social Poetics of Kingship in Ancient Israel.* Boston: Brill, 2005.

Hamilton, Victor P. "חרם." In *New International Dictionary of Old Testament Theology and Exegesis*, ed. Willem A. VanGemeren, 2:277. Grand Rapids: Zondervan, 1997.

—. "נטה." In *New International Dictionary of Old Testament Theology and Exegesis*, ed. Willem A. VanGemeren, 3:91-93. Grand Rapids: Zondervan, 1997.

Harman, Allen M. "Particles." In *New International Dictionary of Old Testament Theology and Exegesis*, ed. Willem A. VanGemeren, 4:1028-42. Grand Rapids: Zondervan, 1997.

Harrison, R.K. "גרב." In *New International Dictionary of Old Testament Theology and Exegesis*, ed. Willem A. VanGemeren, 1:890. Grand Rapids: Zondervan, 1997.

—. "יַלֶּפֶת." In *New International Dictionary of Old Testament Theology and Exegesis*, ed. Willem A. VanGemeren, 2:461. Grand Rapids: Zondervan, 1997.

Harrison, R.K. and Eugene H. Merrill. "גִּבֵּן." In *New International Dictionary of Old Testament Theology and Exegesis*, ed. Willem A. VanGemeren, 1:804-05. Grand Rapids: Zondervan, 1997.

—. "פסח." In *New International Dictionary of Old Testament Theology and Exegesis*, ed. Willem A. VanGemeren, 3:641-42. Grand Rapids: Zondervan, 1997.

—. "שׂרע." In *New International Dictionary of Old Testament Theology and Exegesis,* ed. Willem A. VanGemeren, 3:1275. Grand Rapids: Zondervan, 1997.

—. "תְּבַלֻּל." In *New International Dictionary of Old Testament Theology and Exegesis*, ed. Willem A. VanGemeren, 4:273-74. Grand Rapids: Zondervan, 1997.

Hartley, John E. *Leviticus*. Word Bible Commentary 4. Waco, Tex.: Word, 1992.

Haas, Volkert. "Soziale Randgruppen und Außenseiter altorientalischer Gesellschaften in Alten Orient." In *Außenseiter und Randgruppen: Beiträge zu einer Sozialgeschichte des Alten Orients*, ed., Volkert Haas, 29-51. Xenia:

Konstanzer Althistorische Vorträge und Forschungen. Heft 32. Konstanz: Universitätsverlag, 1992.
Hawkins, J.D. "Azatiwata." In *The Context of Scripture: Monumental Inscriptions from the Biblical World*, ed. William W. Hallo and K. Lawson Younger, II:124-26. New York: E.J. Brill, 1997.
Hayden, Roy E. "גלל." In *New International Dictionary of Old Testament Theology and Exegesis*, ed. Willem A. VanGemeren, 1:868-69. Grand Rapids: Zondervan, 1997.
Helbling, Monika. *Der altägyptische Augenkranke, sein Arzt und seine Götter.* Zürcher Medizingeschichtliche Abhandlungen, Neue Reihe 141. Zurich: Juris, 1980.
Heller, Jan. "David und die Krüppel." *Communio Viatorum* 8 (1965): 251-258.
Hentrich, Thomas. "The 'Lame' in Lev 21, 17-23 and 2 Sam 5, 6-8," *Annual of the Japanese Biblical Institute* 29 (2003): 5-30.
—. "Masculinity and Disability in the Bible." In *This Abled Body: Rethinking Disabilities in Biblical Studies*, ed. Hector Avalos, Sarah J. Melcher and Jeremy Schipper. Atlanta: Society of Biblical Literature, 2007.
Herbert, Edward. "2 Samuel 5:6: An Interpretative Crux Reconsidered in Light of 4QSam[a]." *Vetus Testamentum* 44 (1994): 340-348.
Herion, Gary A. "The Impact of Modern and Social Science Assumptions on the Reconstructions of Israelite History." *Journal for the Study of the Old Testament* 34 (1986): 3-33.
Herodotus. *The History.* Translated by David Grene. Chicago: University of Chicago Press, 1988.
Hertzberg, Hans Wilhelm. *I and II Samuel.* The Old Testament Library. Philadelphia: Westminster, 1964.
Hobbs, T.R. *2 Kings.* Word Biblical Commentary. Waco: Word, 1985.
Hoffner, Jr., Harry A. "Ancient Views of Prophecy and Fulfillment: Mesopotamia and Asia Minor." *Journal of the Evangelical Theological Society* 30 (1987): 257-65.
—. "The Kumarbi Cycle: Song of Ullikimmi." In *Hittite Myths.* Atlanta, Scholars Press, 1990.
Holladay, William. *A Commentary on the Book of the Prophet Jeremiah Chapters 1-25.* Hermeneia. Minneapolis: Fortress, 1986.
—. *A Commentary on the Book of the Prophet Jeremiah Chapters 26-52.* Hermeneia. Minneapolis: Fortress, 1986.
Houten, Christiana. *The Alien in Israelite Law.* Journal for the Study of the Old Testament Supplement Series 107; Sheffield: JSOT, 1991.
Houtman, Cornelis. *Exodus.* Vol. 3. Historical Commentary on the Old Testament. Translated by J. Rebel and Sierd Woudstra. Kampen: Kok, 1993.
Huehnergaard, John. "Historic Phonology and the Hebrew Piel." In *Linguistics and Biblical Hebrew*, ed. Walter Bodine, 209-29. Winona Lake: Eisenbrauns, 1992.

Hull, John M. *In the Beginning There Was Darkness: A Blind Person's Conversations with the Bible.* Harrisburg, Pa.: Trinity Press International, 2002.
Hussey, I. Mary. "Sumerian Tablets in the Harvard Semitic Museum, Part II." In *Harvard Semitic Series.* Vol. 4. Cambridge: Harvard Press, 1915.
Jacob, Benno. *The Second Book of the Bible: Exodus.* Translated by Walter Jacob. Hoboken, N.J.: KTAV Publishing House, 1992.
Johnston, Gordon H. "סָרִיס." In *New International Dictionary of Old Testament Theology and Exegesis*, ed. Willem A. VanGemeren, 3:288-95. Grand Rapids: Zondervan, 1997.
Jones, Richard. "Lame, Lameness." In *Anchor Bible Dictionary,* ed. David Noel Freedman, 4:135-36. New York: Doubleday, 1992.
Josephus, Flavius. *Antiquities of the Jews.* Vol. 2. Translated by William Whiston. Grand Rapids: Baker, 1979.
Joüon, Paul. *A Grammar of Biblical Hebrew.* 2 Vols. Translated and revised by Takamitsu Muraoka. Subsidia Biblica, 14/I-II. Rome: Pontifical Biblical Institute, 1993.
Kaiser, Otto. *Isaiah 1-12: A Commentary.* The Old Testament Library. Philadelphia: Westminster, 1983.
Kaiser Jr., Walter C. *Exodus.* Expositor's Bible Commentary 2, ed. Frank E. Gaebelein, 297-497. Grand Rapids: Zondervan, 1991.
—. "Promise." In *The Flowering of Old Testament Theology,* eds. Ben C. Ollenburger, Elmer A. Martens, and Gerhard F. Hasel, 233-53. Sources for Biblical and Theological Study 1. Winona Lake: Eisenbrauns, 1992.
Kalland, Earl S. *Deuteronomy.* Expositor's Bible Commentary 3, ed. Frank E. Gaebelein, 3-235. Grand Rapids: Zondervan, 1991.
Kalluveettil, Paul. "The Marginalizing Dialectics of the Bible." *Bible Bhashyam* 11 (1985): 201-14.
Kaufmann, Yehezkel. *The Babylonian Captivity and Deutero-Isaiah.* New York: Union of American Hebrew Congregations, 1970.
—. *The Religion of Israel.* Chicago: The University of Chicago Press, 1960.
Keil, C.F. and Franz Delitzsch. *The Pentateuch.* Biblical Commentary on the Old Testament. Vol. 2. Grand Rapids: Eerdmans, n.d.
Keown, Gerald L., Pamela J. Scalise and Thomas G. Smothers. *Jeremiah 26-52.* Word Biblical Commentary 27. Dallas: Word, 1995.
King, Leonard W. *Bronze Reliefs from the Gates of Shalmaneser, King of Assyria B.C. 860-825.* London: The Trustees, 1915.
King, Philip J., and Lawrence Stager. *Life in Biblical Israel.* Louisville: Westminster/John Knox Press, 1971.
Klawans, Jonathan. *Impurity and Sin in Ancient Judaism.* Oxford, England: Oxford University Press, 2000.
Klein, Jacob. "Enki and Ninmah." In *The Context of Scripture: Canonical Compositions from the Biblical World,* ed. William W. Hallo and K. Lawson Younger, I:516-18. New York: E.J. Brill, 1997.
Kleinman, Arthur. *Patients and Healers in the Context of Culture.* Berkeley Calif.: University of California Press, 1980.

Klopfenstein, Christian. *La Bible et la Santé.* Paris: La Pensée Universelle, 1978.

Knight III, Henry H. "God's Faithfulness and God's Freedom: A Comparison of Contemporary Theologies of Healing." *Journal of Pentecostal Theology* 1 (1993): 65-89.

Koelbing, Huldrych M. *Arzt und Patient in der antiken Welt.* Zurich: Artemis, 1977.

Kornfeld, Walter. *Das Buch Leviticus.* Düsseldorf: Patmos Verlag, 1972.

Kraus, Hans-Joachim. *Theology of the Psalms.* Minneapolis: Augsburg, 1986.

Kugler, Robert A. "Holiness, Purity, the Body and Society: The Evidence for Theological Conflict in Leviticus." *Journal for the Study of the Old Testament* 76 (1997): 3-27.

Labat, René. "A propos de la chirurgie babylonienne." *Journal Asiatique* 242 (1954): 207-218.

—. *Traité Akkadien de Diagnostics et Pronostics Médicaux. I: Transcription et Traduction.* Collection de travaux de l'académie internationale d'histoire des sciences No.7. Paris: Académie internationale d'histoire de sciences, 1951.

Lambert, Wilfried G. "Enmeduranki and Related Matters." *Journal of Cuneiform Studies* 21 (1967): 126-38.

—. "Kingship in Ancient Mesopotamia." In *King and Messiah in Israel and the Ancient Near East: Proceedings of the Oxford Old Testament Seminar*, ed., John Day, 54-70. Sheffield: Sheffield Academic Press, 1998.

Landsberger, Benno. "Corrections to the Article 'An Old Babylonian Charm Against *Merhu*'." *Journal of Near Eastern Studies* 17 (1958): 56-58.

Leder, Arie C. "Reading Exodus to Learn and Learning to Read Exodus." *Calvin Theological Journal* 34 (1999): 11-35.

Leene, H. "History and Eschatology in Deutero-Isaiah." In *Studies in the Book of Isaiah: Festschrift Willem A.M. Beuken,* ed. J. van Ruiten and M. Vervenne, 223-50. Leuven: Leuven University Press, 1997.

Leichty, Erle. *The Omen Series Šumma izbu.* TCS 4. Locust Valley, N.Y.: Augustin, 1970.

Levine, Baruch. *Leviticus*. JPS Torah Commentary. Philadelphia: Jewish Publication Society, 1989.

Lichtheim, Miriam. *Ancient Egyptian Literature. Vol I: The Old And Middle Kingdoms.* Berkeley: University of California Press, 1973-80.

—. *Ancient Egyptian Literature, vol II: The New Kingdom.* Berkeley: University of California Press, 1976.

—. "The Instruction of Amenemope." In *The Context of Scripture: Canonical Compositions from the Biblical World*, ed. William W. Hallo and K. Lawson Younger, I:115-22. New York: E.J. Brill, 1997.

Limburg, James. *Hosea-Micah.* Interpretation. Atlanta: John Knox, 1988.

Longman, Tremper. "Literary Approaches to Old Testament Study." In *The Face of Old Testament Studies: A Survey of Contemporary Approaches*, ed. David W. Baker and Bill T. Arnold, 97-115. Grand Rapids: Baker, 1999.

Lund, Jerome A. "אָמַר." In *New International Dictionary of Old Testament Theology and Exegesis*, ed. Willem A. VanGemeren, 1:443-49. Grand Rapids: Zondervan, 1997.

Magonet, Jonathan. "The Structure and Meaning of Leviticus 19." *Hebrew Annual Review* 7 (1983): 151-67.

Malamat, Abraham. "'Love Your Neighbor as Yourself': What It Really Means." *Biblical Archaeology Review* 7 (1990): 50-51.

Martens, Elmer A. "קוּם." In *New International Dictionary of Old Testament Theology and Exegesis*, ed. Willem A. VanGemeren, 3:902-05. Grand Rapids: Zondervan, 1997.

Mathys, Hans-Peter. *Liebe deinen Nächsten wie dich selbst: Untersuchungen zum alttestamentlichen Gebot der Nächstenliebe (Lev 19, 18).* Orbis biblicus et orientalis 71. Göttingen: Vandenhoeck & Ruprecht, 1986.

Matthews, Victor H. and Don C. Benjamin. *Social World of Ancient Israel: 1250-587 BCE.* Peabody, Mass: Hendrickson, 1993.

Mazar, Benjamin. "Jerusalem in the Biblical Period." In *Jerusalem Revealed: Archaeology in the Holy City 1968-1974*, ed. Yigal Yadin. Jerusalem: Israel Exploration Society, 1975.

McCarter, P. Kyle. *II Samuel.* The Anchor Bible 9. New York: Doubleday, 1984.

McComiskey, Thomas Edward. *Micah.* Expositors Bible Commentary 7:393-445. Grand Rapids: Zondervan, 1998.

—. "Zechariah." In *The Minor Prophets*, ed. Thomas E. McComiskey, 3:1003-1244. Grand Rapids: Baker, 1992.

McConville, J.G. *Deuteronomy.* Apollos Old Testament Commentary 5. Downers Grove: InterVarsity, 2002.

McKane, William. *The Book of Micah: Introduction and Commentary.* Edinburgh: T & T Clark, 1998.

Meissner, Bruno. *Babylonien und Assyrien*. 2:283-323. Heidelberg: C. Winter, 1923.

Melcher, Sarah J. "Visualizing the Perfect Cult: The Priestly Rationale for Exclusion." In *Human Disability and the Service of God: Reassessing Religious Practice*, ed. Nancy Eiesland and Don Saliers, 55-71. New York: Abingdon, 1998.

Merrill, Eugene H. *Deuteronomy.* The New American Commentary 4. Nashville, Tenn.: Broadman Press, 1994.

—. "A Theology of the Pentateuch." In *A Biblical Theology of the Old Testament*, ed. Roy B. Zuck, Eugene H. Merrill and Darrell L. Bock. Chicago, Ill.: Moody Press, 1991.

Merwe, Christo H.J. van der, Jackie A Naudé and Jan H. Kroeze. *A Biblical Hebrew Reference Grammar.* Sheffield, England: Sheffield Academic Press, 1999.

Meyers, Carol L., and Eric M. Meyers. *Zechariah 9-14.* The Anchor Bible 25C. New York: Doubleday, 1993.

Milgrom, Jacob. *Leviticus 1-16*. The Anchor Bible 3. New York: Doubleday, 1991.

—. *Leviticus 17-22*. The Anchor Bible 3A. New York: Doubleday, 2000.

—. *Leviticus 23-27*. The Anchor Bible 3B. New York: Doubleday, 2001.

—. "The Changing Concept of Holiness in the Pentateuchal Codes with Emphasis on Leviticus 19." In *Reading Leviticus: Responses to Mary Douglas*, ed. John F.A. Sawyer, 65-75. Journal for the Study of the Old Testament Supplemental Series 227. Sheffield: Sheffield Academic Press, 1996.

—. *Studies in Levitical Terminology*. Berkeley: University of California, 1970.

Millar, J. Gary. *Now Choose Life: Theology and Ethics in Deuteronomy*. Grand Rapids: Eerdmans, 1998.

Miller, Patrick. *The Religion of Ancient Israel*. Louisville: Westminster/John Knox, 2000.

Mitchell, David T. and Sharon L. Snyder. "Disability Studies and the Double Bind of Representation." In *The Body and Physical Difference: Discourses of Disability*, ed. David T. Mitchell and Sharon L. Snyder, 1-31. Ann Arbor: University of Michigan Press, 1997.

Mitchell, David T. and Sharon L. Snyder. *Narrative Prosthesis: Disability and the Dependencies of Discourse*. Ann Arbor: University of Michigan Press, 2001.

Mitchell, David T. "Narrative Prosthesis and the Materiality of Metaphor." In *Disability Studies: Enabling the Humanities*, eds., Sharon Snyder, Brenda Jo Breuggemann and Rosemarie Garland Thomson, 15-30. New York: Modern Language Association, 2002.

Motyer, J. Alec. *The Prophecy of Isaiah*. Downers Grove: InterVarsity, 1993.

—. "Zephaniah." In *The Minor Prophets*, ed. Thomas E. McComiskey, 3:897-962. Grand Rapids: Baker, 1992.

Naudé, Jackie A. "Sexual Ordinances." In *New International Dictionary of Old Testament Theology and Exegesis*, ed. Willem A. VanGemeren, 4:1198-1211. Grand Rapids: Zondervan, 1997.

Nel, Philip J. "בוש." In *New International Dictionary of Old Testament Theology and Exegesis*, ed. Willem A. VanGemeren, 1:621-27. Grand Rapids: Zondervan, 1997.

Nelson, Richard D. *Deuteronomy*. Westminster John Knox: Louisville, 2002.

Nemet-Nejat, Karen Rhea. *Daily Life in Ancient Mesopotamia*. Westport, Conn.: Greenwood, 1998.

Neufeld, Edward. "Hygiene Conditions in Ancient Israel (Iron Age)." *Biblical Archaeologist* 34 (1971): 42-68.

Neusner, Jacob. *The Idea of Purity in Ancient Judaism*. Leiden: E.J. Brill, 1973.

Newman, Gene and Joni Eareckson Tada. *All God's Children: Ministry with Disabled Persons*. Rev. ed. Grand Rapids: Zondervan, 1993.

Nicolas, Maurice. *La Médecine dans la Bible*. Paris: Librairie le François, 1977.

Nissinen, Martti. *Prophets and Prophecy in the Ancient Near East.* Atlanta: Society of Biblical Literature, 2003.

Noth, Martin. *Exodus: A Commentary.* The Old Testament Library. Translated by J.S. Bowden. Philadelphia: Westminster, 1962.

O'Connell, Robert H. "רָכִיל." In *New International Dictionary of Old Testament Theology and Exegesis*, ed. Willem A. VanGemeren, 3:1114-15. Grand Rapids: Zondervan, 1997.

Olyan, Saul. "Anyone Blind or Lame Shall Not Enter the House: On the Interpretation of Second Samuel 5:8." *Catholic Biblical Quarterly* 60 (1998): 218-27.

Olivier, J.P.J. "תּמם." In *New International Dictionary of Old Testament Theology and Exegesis*, ed., Willem A. VanGemeren, 4:306-08. Grand Rapids: Zondervan, 1997.

Oswalt, John N. *The Book of Isaiah: Chapters 1-39.* The New International Commentary on the Old Testament. Grand Rapids: Eerdmans, 1986.

—. *The Book of Isaiah: Chapters 40-60.* The New International Commentary on the Old Testament. Grand Rapids: Eerdmans, 1986.

—. " The Theology of Isaiah." In *New International Dictionary of Old Testament Theology and Exegesis*, ed. Willem A. VanGemeren, 4:725-732. Grand Rapids: Zondervan, 1997.

Pardee, Dennis. "The Kirta Epic." In *The Context of Scripture: Canonical Compositions from the Biblical World*, ed. William W. Hallo and K. Lawson Younger, I:333-43. New York: E.J. Brill, 1997.

—. "Ugaritic Birth Omens." In *The Context of Scripture: Canonical Compositions from the Biblical World*, ed. William W. Hallo and K. Lawson Younger, I:287-89. New York: E.J. Brill, 1997.

Paschen, Wilfried. *Rein und Unrein; Untersuchung zur biblischen Wortgeschichte.* Studien zum Alten und Neuen Testament 12. München: Kösel-Verlag, 1970.

Patrich, Joseph. "Hideouts in the Judean Wilderness." *Biblical Archaeological Review* 5 (1989): 32-42.

Patrick, Dale. *Old Testament Law.* Atlanta: John Knox Press, 1985.

Patterson, Richard D. and Hermann J. Austel. "1, 2 Kings." Expositor's Bible Commentary 3, ed. Frank E. Gaebelein. Grand Rapids: Zondervan, 1991.

Paul, Shalom M. "Deutero-Isaiah and Cuneiform Royal Inscriptions." *Journal of the American Oriental Society* 88 (1968): 180-86.

—. *Studies in the Book of the Covenant in the Light of Cuneiform and Biblical Law.* Leiden: Brill, 1970.

Payne, J. Barton. *Leviticus.* The Biblical Expositor. Vol. 1. Edited by C.F.H. Henry. London: Pickering & Inglis, 1960.

Petersen, David L. "Defining Prophecy and Prophetic Literature." In *Prophecy in Its Ancient Near Eastern Context*, ed. Martti Nissinen, 33-44. Atlanta: Society of Biblical Literature, 2000.

—. *Zechariah 9-14 and Malachi.* The Old Testament Library. Philadelphia: Westminster, 1995.

Pleins, J. David. *The Social Visions of the Hebrew Bible: A Theological Introduction.* Louisville: Westminster John Knox, 2001.

Plumley, J.M. "The Teaching of Amenemope." In *Documents from Old Testament Times*, ed. D. Winton Thomas, 172-86. London: Nelson, 1958.

Preuss, Julius. *Biblical and Talmudic Medicine.* Translated by Fred Rosner. Brooklyn, N.Y.: Hebrew Publishing Co., 1977.

Provan, Iain W. *1 and 2 Kings.* New International Biblical Commentary. Peabody, Mass.: Hendrickson, 1995.

Rainy, Anson F. and R. Steven Notley. *The Sacred Bridge: Carta's Atlas of the Biblical World.* Winona Lake: Eisenbrauns, 2006.

Raphael, Rebecca, "Things Too Wonderful: A Disabled Reading of Job." In *Perspectives in Religious Studies* 38 (2004): 399-424.

Reiner, Erica. "Medicine in Ancient Mesopotamia." *Journal of the International College of Surgeons* 41 (1964): 544-550.

Renger, Johannes. "Kranke, Krüppel, Debile – eine Randgruppe im Alten Orient?" In *Außenseiter und Randgruppen: Beiträge zu einer Sozialgeschichte des Alten Orients*, ed., Volkert Haas, 113-36. Xenia: Konstanzer Althistorische Vorträge und Forschungen. Heft 32. Konstanz: Universitätsverlag, 1992.

Renz, Thomas. *The Rhetorical Function of the Book of Ezekiel.* Supplements to Vetus Testamentum 76. Leiden: Brill, 1999.

Ricoeur, Paul. *The Rule of Metaphor.* London: Routledge, 1978.

Roberts, J.J.M., *The Bible and the Ancient Near East.* Winona Lake, Ind.: Eisenbrauns, 2002.

Robins, Gay. *The Art of Ancient Egypt.* Cambridge: Harvard University Press, 1997.

Rosenbaum, Michael. *Word-Order Variation in Isaiah 40-55: A Functional Perspective.* Assen, Netherlands: Van Gorcum, 1997.

Ross, Allen P. *Holiness to the Lord: A Guide to the Exposition of the Book of Leviticus.* Grand Rapids: Baker, 2002.

—. "שֵׁם." In *New International Dictionary of Old Testament Theology and Exegesis*, ed. Willem A. VanGemeren, 4:147-51. Grand Rapids: Zondervan, 1997.

Roth, Martha. *Law Collections From Mesopotamia and Asia Minor.* SBL Writings From the Ancient World Series. Second Edition. Atlanta: Scholars Press, 1997.

—. "The Laws of Ur-Namma (Ur-Nammu)." In *The Context of Scripture: Monumental Inscriptions from the Biblical World*, ed. William W. Hallo and K. Lawson Younger, II:408-10. New York: E.J. Brill, 1997.

Rouault, Olivier. *Mukannišum: L'administration et l'économie palatiales à Mari.* In Archives royales de Mari, 18. Paris: Geuthner, 1977.

Ruiten, J.T.A.G.M. van. "'His Master's Voice'? The supposed Influence of the Book of Isaiah in the Book of Habakkuk." In *Studies in the Book of Isaiah: Festschrift Willem A. M. Beuken,* ed. J. van Ruiten and M. Vervenne, 397-412. Leuven: Leuven University Press, 1997.

Russell, John Malcolm. *Sennacherib's Palace without Rival at Nineveh.* Chicago: Chicago University Press, 1991.

Saggs, H.W.F. *The Greatness That Was Babylon: A Sketch of the Ancient Civilization of the Tigris-Euphrates Valley.* New York: New American Library, 1962.

Sarna, Nahum M. *Exodus.* JPS Torah Commentary. Philadelphia: Jewish Publication Society, 1991.

—. *Exploring Exodus: The Heritage of Biblical Israel.* New York: Schocken Books, 1986.

Sasson, Jack. "On Choosing Models for Recreating Israelite Pre-Monarchic History." *Journal for the Study of the Old Testament* 21 (1988): 3-24.

Schiffman, Lawrence H. "Exclusion from the Sanctuary and the City of the Sanctuary in the Temple Scroll." *Hebrew Annual Review* 9 (1985): 301-20.

Schipper, Jeremy. *Disabilities Studies and the Bible: Figuring Mephibosheth in the David Story.* Edinburgh: T & T Clark, 2006.

—. "Reconsidering the Imagery of Disability in 2 Samuel 5:8b." *Catholic Biblical Quarterly* 67 (2005): 422-34.

Schmalstieg, Dieter Olaf. "Das andere Sehen: Systematisches Interesse an hebräischer Tradition." In *Zur Aktualität des Alten Testaments: Festschrift für Georg Sauer zum 65 Geburtstag,* ed. Siegfried Kreuzer, 259-67. Frankfurt: Peter Lang, 1992.

Schoville, Keith N. "נטר." In *New International Dictionary of Old Testament Theology and Exegesis*, ed. Willem A. VanGemeren, 3:98-99. Grand Rapids: Zondervan, 1997.

Scurlock, JoAnn, and Burton R. Andersen. *Diagnosis in Assyrian and Babylonian Medicine.* Urbana: University of Illinois, 2005.

Seitz, Christopher R. *Isaiah 1-39.* Interpretation. Louisville: John Knox, 1993.

Seybold, Klaus and U.B. Mueller. *Sickness and Healing.* Translated by D.W. Stott. Nashville: Abingdon, 1978.

Sigerist, Henry E. *A History of Medicine Volume I: Primitive and Archaic Medicine.* Oxford: Oxford University Press, 1955.

Singer, Itamar. "Treaties Between Hatti and Amurru." In *The Context of Scripture: Monumental Inscriptions from the Biblical World*, ed. William W. Hallo and K. Lawson Younger, II:93-100. New York: E.J. Brill, 1997.

Singer, Peter. *Rethinking Life and Death: The Collapse of Our Traditional Ethics.* New York: St. Martin's Griffin, 1996.

Smith, Henry Preserved. *The Books of Samuel.* International Critical Commentary. Edinburgh: T & T Clark, 1977.

Smith, Ralph L. *Micah-Malachi.* Word Biblical Commentary. Waco: Word, 1984.

Snaith, Norman H. *The Distinctive Ideas of the Old Testament.* New York: Schocken, 1964.

—. *Leviticus and Numbers.* London: Oliphants, 1977.

Sneed, Mark. "Israelite Concern for the Alien, Orphan, and Widow: Altruism or Ideology?" *Zeitschrift für die Alttestamentliche Wissenschaft* 111 (1999): 498-507.

Snyder, Sharon, Brenda Jo Breuggeman and Rosemarie Garland Thomson, eds. *Disability Studies: Enabling the Humanities.* New York: Modern Language Association, 2002.

Sonsino, Rifat. *Motive Clauses in Hebrew Law.* Chico, Calif.: Scholars, 1980.

Soskice, Janet Martin. *Metaphor and Religious Language.* London: Oxford University Press, 1987.

Sparks, Kenton. *Ancient Texts for the Study of the Hebrew Bible: A Guide to the Background Literature.* Peabody, Mass.: Hedrickson, 2005.

Sprinkle, Joe M. "The Rationale of the Laws of Clean and Unclean in the Old Testament." *Journal of the Evangelical Theological Society* 43 (2000): 637-57.

Steck, Odil H. "Rettung und Verstockung: Exegetische Bemerkungen zu Jesaja 7:3-9." *Evangeliche Theologie* 33 (1973): 77-90.

Steinkeller, Piotr. "Comments on the Seal of Aman-Eshtar." In *Nouvelles Assyriologiques Brèves et Utilitaires.* No. 9: 7-8. Paris: F. Joannès, 1993.

Sternberg, Meir. *The Poetics of Biblical Narrative: Ideological Literature and the Drama of Reading.* Bloomington: Indiana University Press, 1985.

Stiker, Henri-Jocques. *A History of Disability.* Translated by William Sayers. Ann Arbor, Mich.: University of Michigan Press, 1999.

Stoebe, Hans Joachim. *Das zweite Buch Samuelis.* Kommentar zum Alten Testament 8/2. Gütersloh: Gütersloher Verlagshaus, 1994.

Stol, Marten. *Birth in Babylonia and the Bible: Its Mediterranean Setting.* Leiden: Brill, 2000.

—. "Old Babylonian Ophthalmology." In *Reflets des Deux Fleuves: Volume de Mélanges offerts à André Finet.* Akkadic Supplementum 6, ed. Marc Lebeau and Philippe Talon, 163-66. Leuven: Peeters, 1989.

Stuhlmueller, Carroll. "Sickness and Disease: An Old Testament Perspective." *Bible Today* 27 (1989): 5-9.

Swart, I. and Robin Wakely. "צרר." In *New International Dictionary of Old Testament Theology and Exegesis*, ed. Willem A. VanGemeren, 3:853-59. Grand Rapids: Zondervan, 1997.

Sweeney, Marvin A. *Isaiah 1-39: With an Introduction to Prophetic Literature.* The Forms of Old Testament Literature 16. Grand Rapids: Eerdmans, 1996.

Szlechter, Emile. *Tablettes juridiques et administratives de la IIIe Dynastie d'Ur et de la Ire Dynastie de Babylone.* Conservées au Musée de l'Université de Manchester et à Cambridge, au Musée Fitzwilliam, à l'Institut d'Etudes Orientales et à l'Institut d'Egyptologie. Paris: Publications de l'Institut de droit romain de l'Université de Paris, 1963.

Talmon, Shemaryahu. "The 'Comparative Method' in Biblical Interpretation– Principles and Problems." In *Congress Volume: Göttingen, 1977*, ed. J.A. Emerton. Vetus Testamentum Supplements 29. Leiden: Brill, 1978.

Theron, Jacques P.J. "Toward a Practical Theological Theory for the Healing Ministry in Pentecostal Churches." *Journal of Pentecostal Theology* 7 (1999):49-64.

Thompson, J.A. and Elmer A. Martens. "פֶּה." In *New International Dictionary of Old Testament Theology and Exegesis*, ed. Willem A. VanGemeren, 3:583-84. Grand Rapids: Zondervan, 1997).

Thompson, Reginald Campbell. *Assyrian Medical Texts from the Originals in the British Museum.* London: Milford, 1923.

Thomson, Rosemarie Garland. *Extraordinary Bodies.* New York: Columbia University Press, 1996.

Tigay, Jeffry H. *Deuteronomy.* JPS Torah Commentary. Philadelphia: Jewish Publication Society, 1996.

—. "'Heavy of Mouth' and 'Heavy of Tongue' On Moses' Speech Difficulty." *Bulletin of the American Schools of Oriental Research* 231 (1978): 57-67.

Tomasino, Anthony. "עת." In *New International Dictionary of Old Testament Theology and Exegesis*, ed. Willem A. VanGemeren, 3:563-67. Grand Rapids: Zondervan, 1997.

Toorn, Karel van der. *Sin and Sanction in Israel and Mesopotamia: A Comparative Study.* Assen/Maastricht, The Netherlands: Van Gorcum, 1986.

Trapnell, D.H. "Health, Disease and Healing." In *New Bible Dictionary.* 2nd edition, ed. I. Howard Marshall, A.R. Millard, J.I. Packer and D.J. Wiseman, 448-57. Downers Grove, Ill.: InterVarsity Press, 1996.

Trusen, Johann Gottlieb Peter *Die Sitten, Gebräuche und Krankheiten der alten Hebräer: Nach der heiligen Schrift historisch und Kritisch dargestellt.* Breslau: Verlag von Wilh. Gottl. Korn., 1853.

Tubb, Jonathan. "Two Examples of Disability in the Levant." In *Madness, Disability and Social Exclusion: The Archaeology and Anthropology of "Difference,"* ed. Jane Hubert, 81-86. London: Routledge, 2000.

Tylor, Edward. *Primitive Culture: Researches into the Development of Mythology, Philosophy, Religion, Language, Art and Custom*. 2 volumes. New York: Putman, 1920.

Uffernheimer, Benjamin. "From Prophetic to Apocalyptic Eschatology." In *Eschatology in the Bible and in Jewish and Christian Tradition*. Ed., Henning Graf Reventlow. Journal for the Study of the Old Testament Supplement Series 243. Sheffield: Sheffield Academic Press, 1997.

Vanhoozer, Kevin. "Language, Literature, Hermeneutics and Biblical Theology: What's Theological About a Theological Dictionary?" In *A Guide to Old Testament Theology and Exegesis: The Introductory Articles from the New International Dictionary of Old Testament Theology and Exegesis*, ed. Willem A. VanGemeren, 12-47. Grand Rapids: Zondervan, 1999.

Vargon, Shmuel. "The Blind and the Lame." *Vetus Testamentum* 46 (1996): 498-514.

Vellanickal, Matthew. "Just Society: Biblical Perspective." *Bible Bhashyam* 8 (1982): 81-93.

Vriezen, Theodorus C. "The Nature of the Knowledge of God." In *The Flowering of Old Testament Theology*, ed. Ben C. Ollenburger, Elmer A. Martens and Gerhard F. Hasel, 79-99. Sources for Biblical and Theological Study, 1. Winona Lake: Eisenbrauns, 1992.

Waetzoldt, Hartmut. "Der Umgang mit Behinderten in Mesopotamien." In *Behinderung als Pädagogische und politische Herousforderung: Historische und Systematische Aspekte.* Schriftenrihe zum Bayerischen Schulmuseum Ishenhousen 14, ed. Max Liedtke, 77-91. Bad Heilbrunn: Verlag Julius Klinkhardt, 1996.

Walker, Larry Lee. *Zephaniah.* Expositors Bible Commentary 7, ed. Frank E. Gaebelein, 535-65. Grand Rapids: Zondervan, 1998.

Wallace, H.N. "Oracles Against the Israelite Dynasties in 1 and 2 Kings." *Biblica* 67 (1986): 21-40.

Waltke, Bruce K. and M. O'Conner. *An Introduction to Biblical Hebrew Syntax.* Winona Lake, Ind.: Eisenbrauns, 1990.

Waltke, Bruce. "Micah." In *The Minor Prophets: An Exegetical and Expository Commentary*, ed. Thomas E. McComiskey, 3:591-764. Grand Rapids: Baker, 1993.

Walton, John H. *Ancient Israelite Literature in Its Cultural Context: A Survey of Parallels between Biblical and Ancient Near Eastern Texts.* Grand Rapids: Zondervan, 1989.

Walton, John H., Victor H. Matthews and Mark W. Chavalas. *The IVP Bible Background Commentary: Old Testament.* Downers Grove: InterVarsity, 2000.

Weinfeld, Moshe. "The Decalogue: Its Significance, Uniqueness, and Place in Israel's Tradition." In *Religion and Law: Biblical, Jewish, and Islamic Perspectives*, ed. E. Firmage, J. Welch and B. Weiss, 3-47. Winona Lake, Ind.: Eisenbrauns, 1990.

—. *Social Justice in Ancient Israel and in the Ancient Near East.* Minneapolis: Fortress, 1995.

Welch, Adam C. *The Code of Deuteronomy: A New Theory of Its Origin.* London: James Clark, 1925.

Wenham, Gordon J. *The Book of Leviticus.* New International Commentary on the Old Testament. Grand Rapids: Eerdmans, 1992.

Westbrook, Raymond. *Studies in Biblical and Cuneiform Law.* Cahied de la Revue Biblique 26. Paris: J. Gabalda et Cie, Éditeurs, 1988.

Whitehouse, Walter M. "Radiologic Findings in the Royal Mummies." In *An X-Ray Atlas of the Royal Mummies*, ed. James Harris and Edward Wente. Chicago: Chicago University Press, 1980.

Whybray, R. Norman. *An Introduction to the Pentateuch.* Grand Rapids: Eerdmans, 1995.

—. *The Making of the Pentateuch: A Methodological Study.* Journal for the Study of the Old Testament: Supplement Series 53. Sheffield: Sheffield Academic Press, 1987.

Wildberger, Hans. *Jesaja 3 Teilband 28-39.* Biblischer Kommentar Altes Testament 10.3. Neukirchen: Neukirchener Verlag des Erziehungsvereins, 1978.

Wilkinson, John. *The Bible and Healing: A Medical and Theological Commentary.* Grand Rapids: Eerdmans, 1998.

Wilson, J.V. Kinnier. "Medicine in the Land and Times of the Old Testament." In *Studies in the Period of David and Solomon*, ed., T. Ishida, 337-375. Winona Lake: Eisenbrauns, 1982.

—. "Two Medical Texts from Nimrud." *Iraq* 18 (1956): 130-46.

Winton Thomas, D. *Documents from Old Testament Times.* London: Nelson, 1958.

Wiseman, Donald. "Medicine in the Old Testament Word." In *Medicine and the Bible*. Carlisle, I.K.: Paternoster, 1986.

Wolff, Hans Walter. *Micah: A Commentary.* Translated by Gary Stansell. Minneapolis: Augsburg, 1990.

Wright, David P. *The Disposal of Impurity: Elimination Rites in the Bible and in Hittite and Mesopotamian Literature.* Society of Biblical Literature Dissertation Series 101. Atlanta: Scholars Press, 1987.

—. "The Spectrum of Priestly Impurity." In *Priesthood and Cult in Ancient Israel*, ed. G.A. Anderson and S.M. Olyan, 150-82. Sheffield: Sheffield Academic Press, 1991.

Young, Edward. J. *The Book of Isaiah: Chapters 19-39.* New International Commentary on the Old Testament. Vol. 2. Grand Rapids: Eerdmans, 1969.

—. *The Book of Isaiah: Chapters 40-66.* New International Commentary on the Old Testament. Vol. 3. Grand Rapids: Eerdmans, 1972.

Youngblood, Ronald F. *1 & 2 Samuel.* Expositor's Bible Commentary 3, ed., Frank E. Gaebelein, 553-1104. Grand Rapids: Zondervan, 1991.

Younger, K. Lawson. "The Panamuwa Inscription." In *The Context of Scripture: Monumental Inscriptions from the Biblical World*, ed. William W. Hallo and K. Lawson Younger, 158-60. New York: E.J. Brill, 1997.

Index of Authors

K

L

M

N

O

U

V

W

Y

Index of Scripture References

Ancient Texts Index

ND - #0090 - 090625 - C0 - 229/152/13 - PB - 9781842278482 - Gloss Lamination